Survey of Organ Literature and Editions

MARILOU KRATZENSTEIN is associate professor of organ and music history at the University of Northern Iowa. She holds the B.A. degree from Calvin College, the M.A. from Ohio State University, and the D.M.A. from the University of Iowa. She has studied organ with André Marchal and Jean Langlais in Paris on a Fulbright grant. Active as a performer, she has made six concert tours in major European cities in addition to recitals in the United States and Canada.

SURVEY OF

RGAN ITERATURE

AND

DITIONS

Marilou Kratzenstein

THE IOWA STATE UNIVERSITY PRESS / *Ames*

MARILOU KRATZENSTEIN is associate professor of organ and music history at the University of Northern Iowa. She holds the B.A. degree from Calvin College, the M.A. from Ohio State University, and the D.M.A. from the University of Iowa. She has studied organ with André Marshal and Jean Langlais in Paris on a Fulbright grant. Active as a performer, she has made six concert tours in major European cities in addition to recitals in the United States and Canada.

Printed by The Iowa State University Press, Ames, Iowa 50010

First edition, 1980

Library of Congress Cataloging in Publication Data

Kratzenstein, Marilou, 1937–
    Survey of organ literature and editions.

    "This book . . . originally appeared as a series of articles in the Diapason (1971–1977)"
    Bibliography: p.
    Includes index.
    1. Organ music—History and criticism.   2. Organ music—Bibliography.   I. Title.
ML600.K73   786.8'09   79-28497

ISBN 0-8138-1050-7

Contents

Foreword

THE FOLLOWING STUDIES in organ literature were written in the hope of stimulating fellow organists to explore more deeply the vast treasure-house of organ literature which is broadening every day. One too easily becomes satisfied with repeating the major works in the German and French repertory, while neglecting the contributions of other countries. Many new, interesting works exist that have not yet received much attention outside their own countries. Moreover, even in the countries with a major organ tradition such as Germany and France, old works are being uncovered each year.

Since a list of names and works has little meaning by itself, I have provided a short historical outline of organ composition in each of the countries that has an organ-playing tradition. Also included are some remarks about the organs of each country since a knowledge of the instruments is important for an understanding of the literature.

The amount of material that can be presented in these historical sketches is obviously limited. However, it is my hope that these studies will provide a comprehensive overview of organ literature while also furnishing a point of departure for more specialized studies in the history and performance of the various national schools.

Preface

THIS BOOK, *Survey of Organ Literature and Editions,* originally appeared as a series of articles in *The Diapason* (1971-1977). The book is a reprint of that series, but with the list of editions substantially augmented. Some of the best editions available today had not yet been published at the time I wrote the articles for *The Diapason,* so these new listings have been incorporated in the Addenda, found at the back of the book. I have also taken the opportunity to make minor corrections in the text. I am grateful to *The Diapason* for its kindness in permitting the republication of the articles and to its staff members for their assistance. Robert Schuneman, who was editor when this series began, gave me much support and encouragement. Arthur Lawrence, present editor, and David McCain, business manager, have also been most helpful.

Nearly ten years have elapsed since I began writing this survey. I conceived the work then as a practical tool for the performing musician, and I still see it that way today. However, the passage of time has, in some cases, brought a slightly different perspective. Ten years ago it seemed unlikely that an organist would program any music written prior to 1500. Thus I included no editions of music before the Renaissance. Today our interest in early music has advanced to a point where not one, but multiple, recordings of keyboard music from the Middle Ages are available. Occasionally this music is heard in live concert as well. Moreover, it is now customary for organ literature classes to begin with an overview of the earliest keyboard music. These considerations have prompted me to begin the Addenda with a short list of performing editions for music prior to 1500.

I would like to thank the many friends and colleagues in the United States and Europe who helped with the selection of composers. Since I wished to avoid excessive intrusion of my own personal biases, I relied heavily on their recommendations. Their combined judgment made the selection less arduous than it would otherwise have been, especially in the case of contemporary composers. Still, it is inevitable that not everyone's favorite composers will have been included. I regret, in particular, the omission of a survey of Canadian organ music. It had always been my intention to write such a survey, but commitment to other work prevented me from carrying this out.

I would also like to thank the various people who sent me corrections or additions to the articles after they appeared in print. Thanks to them, I have had a chance to incorporate the improvements in this book.

Numerous music publishers here and abroad generously lent large quantities of music for extended periods of time, and I thank them for their kindness. Wadler-Kaplan music store, Houston, performed the same service.

I am also indebted to the many composers who sent lists of their works and to other musicians who furnished needed details. Without the cooperation of many people, this survey would have been far less complete.

MARILOU KRATZENSTEIN

Survey of Organ Literature and Editions

1

Organn Music before 1500

HERE is virtually no organ piece written before the 16th century that one would consider playing in a public recital or in a church service today. Organ music was in a very primitive state at that time, and one need not feel apologetic about admitting this. Instrumental music as a whole seldom reached an artistic level commensurate with that of vocal music until the Baroque era. Still, since it will help us to appreciate the great advances that were made in the 16th and 17th centuries, we will begin by reminding ourselves about the state of organ playing prior to 1500.

The oldest surviving source of organ music is the *Robertsbridge Codex* dating from c. 1325. The six organ pieces in this manuscript are not original compositions for organ, but transcriptions of previously existing compositions. Three of these were taken from the dance repertory and are estampies; the other three are motet transcriptions. We know that organ music during the Middle Ages did not exist as an independent form of expression. It lived only in connection with the older, more established forms of vocal and dance music. Thus the transcriptions in the *Robertsbridge Codex* can, in this sense, be taken as typical examples of early organ music.

An Italian manuscript, the *Codex Faenza,* is the next earliest known source. Although compiled between 1470 and 1475, it holds music believed to date from the 14th century.[1] It contains organ versets for liturgical use

and transcriptions of vocal compositions. The versets, which include a complete *Kyrie,* constitute the earliest liturgical organ pieces of which we have record. They were intended to be performed in alternation with sung parts of the mass. As such, they represent the earliest documented evidence of the *alternatim* practice which prevailed for centuries and which was responsible for a sizable body of organ composition.

Other organ pieces (liturgical music and transcriptions of vocal pieces) have been preserved in several fragments of German origin dating from the first half of the 15th century. Like the *Robertsbridge Codex* and the *Codex Faenza,* the music in the German sources was still bound to the forms of the vocal idiom. It had been altered and embellished to fit the keyboard instrument, but it was not yet independent keyboard music.

Five *preambulae* preserved in the *Ileborgh Tablature* (1448), from Stendal in middle Germany, are the earliest keyboard pieces not based on a previously existing model and not using a preexistent *cantus firmus.* These *preambulae* are free-composed. The manuscript contains, in addition, three song transcriptions. Also significant in this tablature is an indication specifying the use of the pedal. It s the earliest preserved notice of this kind. As far as is known, Germany was the only country in which the pedal was used at such an early date.

That Germany was a leader in the field of organ playing is further attested by the fact that the next two sources, the major organ tablatures of the century, both came from Germany. They are the *Fundamentum organisandi* (1452) of Conrad Paumann and the *Buxheimer Orgelbuch.* The *Fundamentum organisandi* was a manual of organ

Note: In the list of editions found in each chapter, and in the Addenda, capital or lowercase letters indicate major or minor key, respectively.

composition written by Paumann for his students. It provided musical examples for the art of "organisare" — composing a lively descant to a slowly moving tenor which could itself be occasionally embellished. In compositions of this type the tenor would be taken from a pre-existent melody, but the upper voice would be free-composed. A number of compositions followed the pedagogical examples, most of them composed by the author himself. Only one of these confines itself to the techniques set forth in the instructive examples. In the others, the strong opposition between sustained tenor and rapidly moving descant has been replaced by a more uniform movement throughout. Among the compositions included at the end of the *Fundamentum* are three *preambulae* (original compositions for organ or other keyboard instrument).

Opposing the art of "organisare" was the more common practice of "intabulare." This consisted of altering a pre-existent piece to meet the technical demands of the keyboard and then adding "coloration," a kind of elaboration or embellishment consisting of repeated, more or less stereotyped, figures. Keyboard pieces so composed were called "intabulations." They constituted the major portion of all music played on the organ during this early period. The *Buxheimer Orgelbuch* (c. 1470), the most comprehensive source of 15th-century German organ music, encompassing more than 250 compositions, contained far more intabulations than anything else. It did have, however, a number of *preambulae* which were completely free of vocal antecedents. A notice at the beginning of the *Buxheimer Orgelbuch* indicates the use of the pedal — another witness to pedal playing in Germany at a time when it was probably still unknown, or at least ignored, in other countries.

Although the largest number of manuscripts containing organ music written before 1500 came from Germany, by the 16th century organ tablatures began to appear with greater frequency throughout other parts of Europe as well. Spain and Italy, in particular, joined Germany in producing organ compositions which exhibited a high level of craftsmanship. Advances were also made in France, in England, in Poland, and in other countries. Before moving on to a discussion of organ playing in these countries, we should first define one term which appears again and again — "tablature." This word was used for any system of instrumental notation which indicated by numerals, letters, or other signs the string, fret, organ key, etc., which was to be touched. The system of notation differed according to the instrument for which it was intended. In addition, tablatures for a specific instrument varied from country to country. In Germany, organ tablatures of the 15th and most of the 16th centuries used mensural notation, usually on a staff of seven lines, to indicate the notes of the top voice, while letters indicated the notes of the lower voice or voices. In Spain, a finger-placement system was employed to indicate all the parts, not just the lower ones. In Italy and France, a mensural system was generally employed throughout.

EDITIONS

See Addenda, p. 204, for the list of editions.

NOTES

[1]See D. Plamenac, "Keyboard Music of the 14th Century in Codex Faenza 117," JAMS IV, 179.

2

Spain and Portugal

SPAIN

 respected tradition of organ playing existed in Spain from the Middle Ages, long before the first Spanish tablatures were written. Names of several 13th, 14th and 15th-century organists, famous in their day, have been found. Many Netherlands, German, Italian, and French organists were also active in Spain. In the 16th century, organists from the Netherlands were employed in particularly large numbers due to the presence of a Netherlandish chapel attached to the Castilian royal court. An exceptionally high standard of organ playing prevailed in the 16th century, and the "Golden Age" of Spain produced organ music of an eloquence and nobility that has not again been equalled in the history of that nation.

Instrumental music in Spain had already acceded to a state of dominance in the 16th century, a unique phenomenon for that time. In other countries instrumental music still occupied a secondary position, while choral polyphony reigned supreme. In Spain, the favorite performing media were the solo instruments: the *vihuela*, a guitar-like lute, and the *tecla*, or keyboard, instruments. The *vihuela* was especially popular in court circles, and the ability to play this instrument well was a necessary accoutrement of the well-educated person. The keyboard instruments, the *monachordio*, or clavichord, and the organ, were likewise much admired. Unfortunately, only a fraction of the organ music of the 16th century has been notated and, of that fraction, a good portion has been lost. According to the theorist Bermudo, the fact that so little organ music has been preserved was partly due to the desire of Spanish organists to keep their works for their own use, a practice which Bermudo deplored. No doubt the fact that organ playing was largely improvisatory would also explain the paucity of published collections. Most of the pieces that have come down to us have been preserved in pedagogical works. The first of such works to appear was the *Declaración de Instrumentos musicales,* 1555, (Treatise on Musical Instruments) of Juan Bermudo (c. 1510-1565?). It was followed in 1565 by the *Libro llamado Arte de tañer fantasia assi para tecla como para vihuela* . . . . (Book of the Art of Playing the Fantasia on the Keyboard as Well as on the Vihuela) of Tomás de Santa María (born c. 1510-20; died 1570). To illustrate the text, both treatises contain pieces for keyboard instruments and *vihuela* composed by the authors and their contemporaries.

Overshadowing both of these was the *Obras de Musica para tecla, arpa y vihuela* (Musical Works for Keyboard, Harp, and Vihuela) of Antonio de Cabezón (c. 1510-1566), a truly monumental work. Written between 1540 and 1550, although published posthumously, this work contains a large number of liturgical compositions (hymn settings, *Kyries,* psalm versets, *Magnificat* versets). It also has a number of *tientos* (contrapuntal, ricercar-like compositions), *diferencias* (variations), and *glosas* (keyboard elaborations of vocal motets). According to Hernando de Cabezón, Antonio's son and the one who published the *Obras,* the pieces presented in this illustrious work represent the assignments that the master gave to his students. Thus this was also a pedagogical work, as were the books of Bermudo and Tómas de Santa María.

The *Kyrie del 7° Tono* shows the tranquillity of movement and the masterful handling of counterpoint which is typical of Cabezón's writing.

Ex. 1. Cabezon, *Kyrie del 7° tono* (Fol. 48r), m. 1–11.

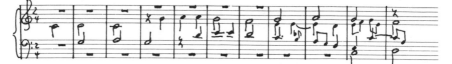

One other source of organ music has been preserved from this period: the *Libro de Cifra Nueva para tecla, harpa y vihuela,* 1557 (Book of New Notation for Keyboard, Harp, and Vihuela), compiled by Venegas de Henestrosa. Included in it are works by Francisco Perez Palero, Pedro Vila, Pedro de Soto, A. de Cabezón (40 pieces), Sister Gracia Baptista, and Julius de Modena (G. Segni).

To form an accurate picture of 16th-century organ music in Spain, it is important that one not confuse it with later developments in that country. There was nothing fiery or dramatic about Spanish organ playing in the 16th century. The core of Spanish organ literature in the Renaissance era was liturgical music. As illustrated in the preceding Cabezón example, these liturgical pieces were written in a clear, straight-forward polyphonic style without improvisational passagework or elaborate ornamentation of an individual line. These works were very reserved and serious, even austere. If one compares the liturgical music of Spain with liturgical music written by Italian organ masters of the same period (Girolamo Cavazzoni, etc.), the conservative nature of Spanish liturgical organ music becomes all the more apparent. Such sobriety is at least partly explained by the spirit of Spanish mysticism which pervaded all areas of Spanish culture.

Although liturgical pieces formed the single largest category within the realm of Spanish organ practice during the Renaissance, there were also pieces of secular inspiration. Some of these contained arpeggiated chords and figurations more suited to the other solo instruments than to the organ. Within this area, the most notable examples are the *diferencias,* or variations. These held considerable historical significance. The earliest known appearance of the variations form was in lute and keyboard tablatures compiled in Spain in the mid-16th century — in the lute tablature of Narvaez (1538) and in the *Libro de cifra nueva* . . . . (1557) of Venegas de Henestrosa. This form was handled with such a high degree of skill by the 16th-century Spaniards, especially by Cabezón, that we are safe in assuming that the variations form did not originate with these men. It must have gone through a previous period of development about which we know nothing. The *Diferencias Cavallero* of Cabezón is one of the most famous examples of this form.

(Example 2)

From the Spanish school, the variations form entered into the practice of the Sweelinck-North German school, and into other schools, and became one of the most important keyboard forms of the Baroque.

Another fact worthy of note in the old Spanish tablatures was the practice of including compositions for all solo instruments (*vihuela,* harp, and keyboard instruments) within the same collection. This indicates that a line had not yet been sharply drawn between literature for the various instruments. An interchange of performing media was presumably acceptable to some extent.

Before moving on to Spanish organ music of the early Baroque, we should consider briefly the organs which were used in the Renaissance. As a rule, Spanish Renaissance organs were quite small. Curiously, even in the large ca-

Ex. 2. Cabezon, *Diferencias Cavallero,* Var. 1, m. 1–4; Var. 2, m. 17–18.

thedrals. a number of small positives placed in various positions about the church was preferred over one large, fully-developed instrument. Principals and mixtures were mild and delicate, as was the character of the entire instrument. Reeds were rare, even though Netherlandish builders are believed to have introduced these stops into Spain in the middle or latter part of the 16th century. The pedal, on those few organs which had a pedalboard, was generally limited to a small number of keys, or toe studs, corresponding to some or all of the notes of the lowest octave. It would appear that the pedal generally had no sliders, but was attached to one rank of pipes, such as the 16' principal. In contrast to this, organs built by foreigners sometimes possessed a number of pedal stops and a much greater stop variety throughout the entire instrument. The main organ at El Escorial, constructed c. 1579-1584 by Gillis Brebos, from Antwerp, is one such example. Instruments of this type remained exceptions, however, and their more progressive features were largely ignored by the conservative native builders. Spanish organ builders, while choosing to work within the framework of a small instrument, did apparently feel the need for providing organists with greater variety in registration, since, near the end of the 16th century, they began halving stops into bass and descant, with the division at c' and c#'.

From the half century or more following the death of Cabezón (1566), only scant material has been found to indicate what path Spanish keyboard music took during the late Renaissance and the following transitional period. The couple of works which have survived (by Bernardo Clavijo de Castillo and Francisco Peraza) show that the conservative Renaissance counterpoint was giving way to a manner of writing in which suspensions and other dissonances played an important role. These dissonances were called *falsas*, the Spanish counterpart of the Italian *durezze e ligature*, a term more commonly known.

The first composer about whom we have more information and from whom more music has survived is Sebastian Aguilera de Heredia (born c. 1565). His preserved works consist of 13 *tientos* and some liturgical music. Four of his *tientos* were written to be performed on half stops, or divided stops. Such compositions were entitled *Medio registro* and featured a solo melody taken

by one hand, with the other hand providing a chordal accompaniment. Peraza is known to have written this type of composition, too, and one assumes that other composers of the transitional period did the same. Among Heredia's other *tientos* (those for full register), some are noteworthy for the expressiveness of their dissonances, especially the suspensions. In fact, the element of dissonance was considered to be so important that Heredia used the term *falsas* as the title for some of his *tientos*.

Ex. 3. Heredia, *Tiento de 4° tono de falsas*, m. 61-64.

Heredia's contemporary, Francisco Correa de Arauxo (born c. 1575; died 1663?), published in 1626 a work entitled *Libro de tientos y discursos de musica practica y theorica de organo intitulado Facultad Organica* (Book of Tientos and Practical and Theoretical Music Lectures for Organ, Entitled *Facultad Organica*). The majority of the works in this publication were *tientos*. This form now occupied the position which liturgical versets had taken during Cabezón day: the *tiento* was the leading form for composers of the transitional and Early Baroque periods. In it, composers took more freedom than they usually allowed themselves when working with the traditional liturgical verset. To avoid conveying a false impression, however, it must be added that *tientos* and liturgical versets were not necessarily two mutually exclusive realms. *Tientos* were sometimes used for liturgical purposes.

Of the 62 *tientos* in Correa's book, 36 were written for *registro medio,* while the remaining 26 were intended to be played on full-length stops. Correa's style of writing was basically Baroque (especially in his creative handling of dissonance), although some Renaissance elements were still in evidence.

Ex. 4. Correa, *Segundo Tiento de quarto tono*, m. 29-32.

In the half century after Correa (in the period between Correa and Cabanilles) organ music appeared to flourish in Spain, although many details of its development are not clear. A number of works have survived from this period, but they are from composers about whose life we know little or nothing. Josép Ximenes (d. 1672) and Pablo Bruna (birth and death dates unknown) appear to have been leading personalities during this time. Both composers wrote *tientos,* liturgical versets, and other works. An interesting feature of the *tientos,* particularly those written for *registro medio,* is the formalistic handling of figuration. In some cases the use of sequences and the modulating repetition of larger phrases seem to have supplanted counterpoint as the underlying principle of construction.

In the works of Juan José Cabanilles (1644-1712) sequences and formalistic figuration became even more prominent as compositional principles.

(Example 5)

Also typical of Cabanilles' style was the employment of lively, often obvious, rhythmic patterns. The following excerpt, taken from the first section of the *Batalla imperial,* illustrates the point. The rhythmic intensity of this work is heightened by virtuoso passages which occur later in the composition.

Ex. 6. Cabanilles, *Batalla imperial,* **m. 5-7.**

Cabanilles was the finest composer of Spanish organ music after Cabezón, as well as the most prolific. *Tientos,* toccatas, liturgical pieces, and variations on Spanish dances are among his preserved works. A number of other organists were active during Cabanilles' lifetime, but none seems to have been able to equal him in originality. Nor did any of his students attain to the same level.

The instruments which existed in Cabanilles' day were quite different from the Renaissance type discussed earlier. The Spanish organ of the latter 17th century and 18th century was much larger. Reeds, which previously had been quite rare, were now the most prominent feature of the instrument. Both horizontal and vertical reeds were employed, and often half of the stops on an entire organ would be members of the reed family. The imposing ranks of trumpets and regals "en chamade" which graced the facade must have been a particular source of pride for the organist of that day. One wonders what kind of music was played on these stops. It is most unfortunate that so little information is available concerning performance practices in Spain. The relatively small amount of organ literature which has been preserved doesn't provide enough answers. One can only assume that a great deal of improvisation went on during this period, and that such improvisation need not necessarily have fully corresponded with the literature which was printed or preserved in manuscript.

Alongside the reeds which gave the organ its most brilliant sonorities, the Spanish organ of the 17th and 18th centuries possessed principals and flutes which continued to have the traditionally delicate voicing. This sharp contrast between reedwork and fluework was apparently consciously cultivated. Spain has often been called a land of stark contrasts, and certainly this characteristic is apparent in 17th and 18th-century organs.

There is still some mystery concerning the characteristics and use of the pedal on the classic Spanish instrument, but we feel safe in saying that the pedal division had not advanced much beyond its Renaissance form. There were generally only a few pedal keys, or toe stubs (covering four to twelve notes), and these were often permanently connected with one or two ranks of pipes.

Two other features are worth noting.

Ex. 5. Cabanilles, *Pasacalles* (Mode 3), m. 21-23, 25, 26.

First, divided registers (bass and descant), introduced near the end of the 16th century, continued to be used on both small and large instruments. Second, a swell device was employed on some Spanish organs from the end of the 17th century. It became quite common during the 18th century. Often only one or two stops would be enclosed in the swell box, but by the latter part of the 18th century an entire division might be placed under expression.

Earlier, in connection with the music of Cabanilles, we noted that counterpoint no longer occupied as dominant a position as it had in the music of Cabezón. Now as we move further into the 18th century, we shall see that counterpoint virtually disappears. We don't know, of course, how organists improvised during liturgical services. Possibly they preserved some of the traditional, contrapuntal style. But in the published works dating from this period, it is obvious that Spanish keyboardists were welcoming with open arms the new, post-Baroque musical vocabulary, with its expressive melodies and lighter texture.

The dominant influence on Spanish organ music during the course of the 18th century was the Italian harpsichord school. More specifically, the most persuasive personality was the Italian harpsichordist, Domenico Scarlatti (1685-1757). A native of Naples, Scarlatti was employed at the Spanish court in Madrid from 1729 until his death in 1757. In other words, he spent half of his adult life in Spain. His style was thoroughly idiomatic to the harpsichord, although he did write a few pieces for organ—compositions calling for echo or dialogue effects between manuals. In addition to using all the keyboard techniques known to Italy, Scarlatti introduced the crossing of hands and other virtuoso elements which made him famous over much of the continent and in England. In some compositions he also adopted a mode of expression which was particularly Spanish in flavor. His harpsichord style, with its runs in 3rds and 6ths, its broken chords and other typical harpsichord figurations, was so wholeheartedly adopted in Spain that it eclipsed everything else in the realm of harpsichord and organ music.

The most famous of Scarlatti's students and followers was Padre Antonio Soler (1729-1783), who has left us six concerti for two keyboard instruments. Soler was basically a harpsichordist and only an organist in a very secondary way. This preference for the harpsichord was a phenomenon by no means limited to 18th-century Spain. In Italy, the country which exercised such a strong influence on Spanish keyboard music, the harpsichord had been preferred ever since Frescobaldi's day, and in the kingdom of Naples, even earlier than that. Also in 18th-century France, and in some other countries, the harpsichord was valued much above the organ. This was simply a characteristic of the age.

Soler's concerti are melodious and light-hearted. In Soler's day no one wanted to listen to learned counterpoint. One wanted to be amused, to be touched lightly, not to be moved deeply. Thus, considering the spirit of the time, Soler's concerti are quite successful. These works are generally well known in the United States, so no example will be quoted here.

In the 19th century, concurrent with the rising popularity of the piano, idiomatic organ music was increasingly neglected. Piano and harpsichord sonatas were played on the organ, along with dance movements and character pieces. Even versets and fugues, which earlier had been the exclusive property of the organist, were now so lacking in idiomatic features that they often carried the inscription, "for organ or piano."

In the present century, organ playing in Spain has remained at a generally low level. One sees a limited amount of new interest in organ building and hopefully, this will stimulate good organ composition. As yet, no contemporary Spanish organ composer has earned recognition outside of his own country.

As for organ building, the Romantic concept of organ construction entered Spain at a late date (close to 1900) and was then exaggerated out of all proportion. The Spanish instrument lost its national character and became a vague composite of elements taken from other countries, mainly from France and Germany. Later, after many organs had been destroyed during the years of the Civil War, a few organ builders began searching in the direction of a new organ type. This type was, essentially, a synthesis of traditional Spanish features with characteristics acquired from foreign countries. Unfortunately, other organ builders, and organists, too, have remained content with the old Romantic organ type. Their attitude toward organ building is typical of the general lack of interest in organs and organ playing which is prevalent in 20th-century Spain. One hates to end on a negative note, but to be accurate one has to report that there is very little interesting activity today in the field of Spanish organ literature and Spanish organ building.

EDITIONS

Bermudo: Facsimile edition of the *Declaración de Instrumentos musicales* by Kastner in *Documenta musicologica*, XI, Kassel, Baerenreiter, 1957. *Oeuvres d'orgues de Juan Bermudo*, ed. Froidebise (*Orgue et Liturgie*, Bk. 47), Paris, Schola Cantorum, 1960.

Cabanilles: *Musci organici Iohannis Cabanilles* (1644-1712) *opera omnia*, 4 vols., ed. H. Anglès, Barcelona, Publicaciones del Departamento de Música de la Biblioteca de Cataluña, 1927- 1958. *Opera Selecta pro Organo*, 3 vols., ed Peeters/Tournemire, Brussels, Schott Frères, 1948.

Cabezón: *Saemtliche Tientos und Fugen aus den 'Obras de Musica,'* ed. Kastner (*Alte Spanische und portugiesische Meister* series), Mainz, Schott S., 1958. *Orgelwerke*, 2 vols., ed. Gay, Kassel, Baerenreiter. Nearly all of the works of Cabezón can be found in volumes III, IV, VII, VIII of *Hispaniae schola musica sacra*, ed. F. Pedrell, Barcelona, Juan Bta. Pujol/Leipzig, Breitkopf und Haertel, 1904-08, but this edition is full of errors.

Correa de Arauxo: *Libro de Tientos . . . .,* 2 vols., ed. S. Kastner, Barcelona, Instituto Español de Musicolgía, 1948/1952.

Henestrosa: A complete edition of the *Libro de Cifra Nueva . . . .,* edited by H. Anglès, can be found in *La Musica en la Corte de Carlos V*, 1944, 2/1965 (*Monumentos de la Musica Española*, II), Barcelona, Instituto Español de Musicología.

Soler: 6 *Conciertos para dos Instrumentos de Tecla*, ed. S. Kastner, Barcelona, Instituto Español de Musicología. 2 x 2

Sonatas, ed. Kastner, Mainz, Schott S., 1956.

Tomás de Santa María: *Oeuvres transcrites de l'Arte de tañer Fantasia,* ed. Froidebise (*Orgue et Liturgie*, Bk. 49), Paris, Schola Cantorrum, 1961.

Collections

In addition to editions of works by single composers, there are several general collections. Among the newer ones are the following:

Alte Spanische Orgelmusik, ed. C. Riess, Copenhagen, W. Hansen (currently out of print).

Altspanische Orgelmeister, ed. Kaller (*Liber Organi,* III), Mainz, Schott S. (contains works of Cabezón and Santa María).

Les anciens maîtres espagnols, ed. Piédlièvre, Paris, Schola Cantorum (works by Cabezón, Jimenez, Palero, Cabanilles, Oxinagas, Soler, etc.).

Orgelmusik des spanischen Barock, ed. Wyly (*Liber Organi, XI*), Schott S. (works by Heredia, Elias, and anonymous composers).

Silva Ibérica, 2 vols., ed. M. S. Kastner, Schott S. (works by Spanish, Portuguese, and Italian composers, including among the Spanish: A Mudarra, Cabezón, Yepes, L. Puxol, Fr. Bartolomeo de Olague, Freixanet, J. Lidon, B. Clavijo del Castillo, S. Aguilera de Heredia).

Spanish Organ Masters, after Antonio de Cabezón, ed. Apel (*Corpus of Early Keyboard Music,* XIV), Dallas, American Institute of Musicology (works by Aguilera de Heredia, Clavijo, Francisco Peraza, etc.).

Spanish Organ Music, ed. E. White/ H. W. Hawke, Indianapolis, Ernest White Editions (works of Aguilera de Fuenllana, A. de Valderravano, C. Morales, Cabezón, Correa de Arauxo).

There are also several older anthologies. These usually contain many editing errors. The standard ones, among the older anthologies, are:

Antologia de organistas clásico españoles, 2 vols., ed. F. Pedrell, Barcelona, 1905/08 (reprinted and available through Associated Music Publishers).

Antología de organistas Clásico españoles, 2 vols., ed Villalba Muñoz, Madrid, Alier, 1914.

Catàlech de la Biblioteca musical de la Disputació de Barcelona, 2 vols., ed. Pedrell, 1909.

El Organista liturgical español, ed. Pedrell, Barcelona, 1905.

Hispaniae schola musica sacra, 8 vols., ed. Pedrell, Barcelona, Juan Bta. Pujol/Leipzig, Breitkopf & Haertel, 1894-1908.

PORTUGAL

Portuguese organ music can be treated, in this survey, only in the briefest of terms. At one time organ playing was certainly an important art in Portugal. Yet only a few manuscripts have survived from that country. Our knowledge of Portugese organ music is thus extremely limited. Much music is known to have been destroyed in the earthquake of 1775. Additional manuscripts have been lost at other times.

To characterize Portuguese organ literature in general, one can say that basically it moved parallel to Spanish organ music, an area which is certainly better known. Yet the organ music of the two countries is not identical. Just as the two languages, Spanish and Portuguese, are very closely related, yet distinct, so, too, the organ music of the two countries is related, but not absolutely identical.

According to Kastner, organ music was cultivated at least as early as the 15th century in Portugal, where the court, in particular, promoted organ playing.[1] In the Renaissance era, the first significant Portuguese organ master was Antonio Carreira (born between 1520 and 1530; died between 1587 and 1597). His works are contrapuntal, often imitative, and use dissonances which are very interesting for that period. Carreira was organist at the royal chapel in Lisbon.

Also organist at the royal chapel was Padre Manoel Rodriguez Coelho (c. 1555-1635), generally considered to be the greatest of the early Portuguese organ composers. His *Flores de Musica para o instrumento de Tecla e Harpa* (Musical Flowers for Keyboard Instrument and Harp) was published in 1620. It has the distinction of being the first book of instrumental music printed in Portugal. The title is interesting because it is a typically Baroque appellation and one which indicates that the pieces collected therein are selections from the best that the composer had to offer. Or, more precisely, they are "the very best of the best." In other countries, some famous counterparts to this title are the *Fiori musicali* of Frescobaldi and the *Musicalischer BlumenStrauss* of J. C. F. Fischer.

Tentos (the Portuguese equivalent of the Spanish *tiento*), intabulations, and liturgical pieces are included in Coelho's *Flores de Musica*. From the artistic standpoint, the *tentos* are Coelho's most important works. In them, Early Baroque style traits (dissonances, restless rhythmic figures, etc.) often occupy a prominent place.

Ex. 7. Coelho: *Tento No. 9*, m. 115, 116.

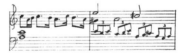

A number of other Portuguese composers are represented in three manuscripts dating from the latter part of the 17th century: *Livro de obras de orgão juntas pello curiosidade do P. P. Fr. Roque da Cöceicão*, 1695, (Oporto, Municipal Library, Ms. 1607); Ms. 964 of the Public Library in Braga; *Libro de cyfra adonde se contem varios Jogos de Versos ê Obras ê outras coriasidades de varios autores* (Oporto, Municipal Library, Ms. 1577). Since the contents of these manuscripts have not yet been published, the latter 17th century still forms a gap (one among many) in our knowledge of Portuguese organ music.

From the 18th century, one figure has become very famous—José Antonio Carlos de Seixas (1704-1742). A brilliant personality in his own day, he has continued to be best known of the Portuguese keyboardists. Like his Spanish contemporaries, he was strongly influenced by the Italian harpsichord school, and especially by Domenico Scarlatti, whom he knew personally. Besides being a member of the Spanish court, Scarlatti had been employed by

Ex. 8. Seixas, *Toccata in E minor*, m. 1-4.

the Portuguese court in Lisbon (c. 1720-1729). There he was musical tutor to the Princess Maria Barbara. When she married the heir to the Spanish throne, Scarlatti accompanied her to Madrid and took up residence there.

Seixas' compositions, under the influence of the Scarlatti style, are very lively pieces, often fiery and dramatic. Without a doubt, they were intended primarily for the harpsichord. Still, they may sometimes have been played on the organ since Iberian musicians seemed to have no qualms about using the organ for the performance of harpsichord pieces.

(Example 8)

Other Portuguese composers of the 18th century could perhaps be discussed, but their compositions seem to be even more obviously idiomatic to the harpsichord. In fact, some of the keyboardists had already made the transition to a pianoforte style (João de Sousa Carvalho, for example), so that one can't seriously consider them in a survey of organ literature.

In the 19th and 20th centuries, Portugal has had no organ composition worthy of note.

EDITIONS

Carreira: 3 *Fantasiën*, ed. Kastner, Hilversum, Harmonia-Uitgave, 1952.

Coelho: *Flores de musica*, 2 vols., ed. Kastner (*Portugaliae Musica*, I, III), Lisbon, 1959/ 61. 5 *Tentos, extraidos das "Flores de Musica,"* ed. Kastner, Mainz, Schott S., 1936. 4 *Susanas*, ed. Kastner, Mainz, Schott S., 1955.

Seixas: A complete edition is being prepared by Kastner as part of the *Portugaliae Musica* series. 12 sonatas are in the collection, *Cravistas portu-*

guezes, I, ed. Kastner, Mainz, Schott S., 1935. 13 other sonatas are in volume II of the same collection (1950).

Collections

There are not many general collections of Portuguese keyboard music available. The 2-volume *Cravistas portuguezes*, listed above, contains, besides the works of Seixas, pieces by Coelho, Jacinto de Sousa Carvalho, de Araujo, and anonymous.

A few other works by Portuguese composers can be found in: *Silva Ibérica*, 2 vols., ed. Kastner, Mainz, Schott S.

NOTES

[1] Kastner. "Foreword" to *Cravistas portuguezes.*

MUSICAL SOURCES

Ex. 1. *Antonio de Cabezon: Collected Works*, vol. IV/1, ed. Ch, Jacobs, p. 32.

Ex. 2. *Historical Anthology of Music*, I, ed. Davison/Apel, Cambridge, Harvard University Press, p. 145.

Ex. 3. Reproduced from *Spanish Organ Masters after Antonio da Cabezon;* ed. Apel (CEKM XIV). © Copyright 1971 by the American Institute of Musicology/Hänssler-Verlag, Neuhausen-Stuttgart, W. Germany. Used by permission.

Ex. 4. Correa de Arauxo: *Libro de Tientos*, vol. I, p. 98.

Ex. 5. *Johannis Cabanilles: Opera Selecta pro Organo*, ed. Peeters/Tournemire, p. 12.

Ex. 6. *Ibid.*, p. 17.

Ex. 7. W. Apel, *History of Keyboard Music to 1700.* Trans. & rev. by H. Tischler. Indiana Univ. Press, 1972, p. 522, Fig. 544.

Ex. 8. *Cravistas portuguezes*, I, ed. Kastner, p. 36.

3

Italy

N Italy, no organ music previous to the 16th century has been preserved other than the *Codex Faenza,* discussed in the first article of this series. One would imagine, however, that organ playing was a prominent art in Italy long before the major documents of organ literature began to appear. Francesco Landini (c. 1335-1397), Antonio Squarcialupi (1416-1480) and other famous musicians were skillful organists. The Italian organ, moreover, attained its definitive character at a very early age — in Tuscany in the 15th century, and elsewhere in Italy in the 16th.

The first book of keyboard tablatures printed in Italy was the *Frottole intabulate da sonar organi, libro primo,* published by Andrea Antico in 1517. It contained 26 *frottole* intabulations, in which one can see the evolving shape of a keyboard style.

More important was a collection which appeared in 1523, the *Recerchari motetti canzoni Libro I,* of Marco Antonio Cavazzoni (born before 1490; died after 1559). Two ricercars are present in this collection and represent the first known use of this term as the title of an organ piece. Predominantly homophonic, they contain relatively little imitative material. Among the motets of the collection, some were keyboard transcriptions, while others were newly-composed pieces based on motet melodies. The canzonas were probably transcriptions of French chansons. Historically significant, they constitute the first appearance of the term *canzone* in connection with instrumental music of any kind.[1]

Other organ music of the 16th century, particularly from c. 1530-1550, has been preserved in manuscripts in the Biblioteca Capitolare at Castell' Arquato.[2] Included are three masses for *alternatim* practice, and other liturgical pieces. There are also several ricercars by various composers, ricercars which reveal a wide variance in construction.

The ricercar first assumed a definitive form under the hands of Girolamo Cavazzoni (birth and death dates unknown), son of M. A. Cavazzoni. Imitative sections, few in number, but extensive in length, became characteristic. Each section had its own theme.

(Example 1)

In the area of canzona composition, Girolamo Cavazzoni was equally progressive since he wrote what are thought to be the earliest examples of the independent keyboard canzona. Earlier canzonas had been mere transcriptions of French chansons, but G. Cavazzoni's canzonas were actually new compositions which used chanson melodies only as thematic material. Short, concise themes, an opening theme which had

Ex. 1. G. Cavazzoni, *Ricercar,* m. 1-3, 10-13.

its initial tone repeated three times, and frequent repetition of sections were characteristic of Cavazzoni's canzonas.

This pioneering composer also wrote a large number of liturgical works in which he handled the Gregorian chant with remarkable freedom, subtracting and adding notes, and making rhythmic alterations. Contrary to usual 16th century practice, Cavazzoni did not feel bound to preserve the pure form of the chant, but used it as free thematic material. His complete works appeared in two publications: *Intavolatura cioe Recercari Canzoni Himni Magnificati . . . Libro primo,* 1543; *Intabulatura d'organo, cioe Misse Himni Magnificati . . . Libro secondo,* no date.

After the Cavazzoni's, the organists who successively occupied the posts at the church of San Marco in Venice became the foremost leaders of organ playing in northern Italy. Most notable among these were Buus, Padovano, Andrea and Giovanni Gabrieli, and Merulo. Jacques Buus (d. 1565), a Flemish composer, was chief organist at San Marco from 1541 to 1550. Four organ ricercars by him have been preserved in his *Intabolatura d'organo di Ricercari . . . Libro I,* Venice, 1549. One of these is a transcription for organ of an ensemble ricercar from a part-book collection of ricercars which the composer published in the same year. A comparison of the organ piece with the ensemble composition illustrates how 16th-century composers added coloration to an instrumental work when adapting it to the organ. (See Kinkeldey, *Orgel und Klavier in der Musik des 16. Jahrhunderts,* 245, where the organ composition and the beginning of the ensemble composition are reprinted).

Annibale Padovano (c. 1527-1575), chief organist at San Marco from 1552 to 1566, composed toccatas and ricercars preserved in a posthumous publication dating from 1604, *Toccate e Ricercari.* Noteworthy in one of the toccatas is a line of sustained notes which clearly calls for the use of the pedals. This is the earliest documented use of the pedal in Italy.

Andrea Gabrieli (c. 1520-1586), second organist of San Marco from 1564 or 1566 and first organist from 1584, contributed greatly to the development of two forms, the ricercar and the toccata. His ricercars are found in two posthumous publications, *Ricercari di Andrea Gabrieli . . . Libro secondo,* 1595, and *Il terzo libro de ricercari di Andrea Gabrieli,* 1596. Notable are the reduced number of themes. Some are even monothematic, representing the earliest known use of the monothematic ricercar in keyboard literature. His toccatas, published in the *Intonationi d'organo di Andrea Gabrieli et di Gio. suo nepote,* 1593 (Organ Intonations of Andrea Gabrieli and of His Nephew, Giovanni), are possibly the earliest examples of compositions bearing this title. Some (those which influenced the further development of the form) had three sections, with the first and third in a free, improvisational style and the middle section in strict counterpoint. Canzonas and liturgical works (organ masses and *intonazioni*) were among Gabrieli's other contributions.

Claudio Merulo (1533-1604), second organist at San Marco from 1557 to 1566 and first organist thereafter until 1584, wrote some of the finest organ music to be found anywhere in Europe at that time. The climax of the Venetian keyboard school was attained under his creative spirit. He wrote toccatas, ricercars, canzonas, various liturgical works and masses. In all of them, one senses the majesty and tranquillity of a true Renaissance master. Many works were published during his lifetime or shortly thereafter: *Ricercari d'intavolatura d'organo, libro Primo,* 1576 (1605); *Messe d'intavolatura d'organo, libro quarto,* 1568; *Canzoni d'intavolatura d'organo, libro primo,* 1592, *libro secondo,* 1606, *libro terzo,* 1611; *Toccate d'intavolatura d'organo, libro primo,* 1598, *libro secondo,* 1604.

Merulo was particularly skillful at interweaving chordal structure and florid passagework into one continuous fabric. As seen in his toccatas, canzonas, etc., this trait represents a technical and artistic advance over the toccata style of Gabrieli, who had separated the chords and the passagework from each other.

(Example 2)

Another aspect of Merulo's creativity which is important in his use of the 5-section toccata form in some, though not all, of his toccatas. These are believed to be the earliest examples of the 5-part form which would become a standard with many Baroque artists.

Giovanni Gabrieli (c. 1557-c. 1612), second organist at San Marco from 1584 and first organist from 1586, com-

Ex. 2. Merulo, *Canzon "La Rolanda,"* m. 12-14.

posed several organ pieces, but made no innovations other than the introduction of lively, playful elements into the sober ricercar style. In general, his keyboard works were not as effective as his ensemble and polychoral compositions.

While Venice was undoubtedly the most fascinating and influential center of organ culture in northern Italy, there were also well-known organists in other cities. One was Sperindio Bertoldo (c. 1530-1570), active in Padua. Another was Girolamo Diruta (born c. 1550), organist in Chioggia and later in Gubbio. Diruta wrote a treatise entitled *Il Transilvano* which has the distinction of being the first organ method book. In it, the author treats organ playing as a separate entity instead of handling all keyboard playing together.

In Brescia, the most famous name was Costanzo Antegnati (1549-1624), organ builder and composer. His treatise, *l'Arte Organica,* 1608, is extremely important for the history of organ building and for registration. Since the Antegnati family, active in organ building since the latter 15th century, were the foremost builders in northern Italy, a brief description of their instruments will be given here.

The usual Antegnati instrument had one manual, which was much shorter than present-day keyboards. There were generally a few pedal keys, but no independent pedal stops. The pedal could only be used for coupling down the lower notes of the manual. The fundamental stop of the organ was always a principal made of tin. On large organs this was a 16', on smaller instruments an 8'. Above this fundamental were successive ranks of octaves and fifths, up to the ½', ⅓', and even sometimes the ¼'. Although made of lead, the octaves and fifths were scaled like principals. Together with the fundamental principal they constituted the *Ripieno,* or full organ. The higher registers repeated one or more times at the distance of an octave. Other standard features of the Antegnati organ were the presence of

one or two flutes (normally at 8' and/or 4' pitch) and the *Fiffaro,* also known as *Voci umane.* This uniquely Italian stop, the *Fiffaro,* was a celeste-like principal. A favorite stop with Italian organists, it was used particularly for the *Elevazione* and at other mystical moments during the Mass.

With slight variations at the hands of each builder, the instrument just described was the standard type throughout much, perhaps one could even say most, of Italy. It remained standard during the Baroque era and in many cases continued until the advent of the Romantic movement. Foreign builders did introduce a few reeds and compound stops. But for the Italian craftsmen, such stops seldom became more than accessories to the main body of the organ, the principal chorus. Of course, on larger instruments a moderate number of flutes and reeds were found on the second and third manuals. But the first manual would still be constructed in the strict classic tradition, as a chorus of principals. In addition, some builders added to the pedal a single octave of *contrabassi* pipes, permanently connected with the pedalboard.

A standard characteristic of all Italian organs was delicate, transparent voicing. The division of the *Ripieno* into single ranks, moreover, provided many subtle variations of registration within the principal family — variations which were impossible on a north European organ having only compound ranks at the top of its principal chorus. The sweet, silvery tone of the Italian organs is the result, not only of the voicing, but of the fact that one could combine one or two of the highest principals with the 8' or the 8' and 4', without the necessity of drawing out all the principals in between.[3]

The transitional period from the High Renaissance to the Early Baroque was a time of intense creativity. In Italian keyboard practice this revealed itself somewhat in the works of north Italians, but was most strikingly present in the compositions of musicians centered around Naples. Among the northern composers, Adriano Banchieri (c. 1567-1634) stands out because of his treatises expounding new ideas. He did not compose very many organ works, but he merits attention because he helped prepare the way for Early Baroque organists. Ercole Pasquini (c. 1560-1620) was another progressive thinker. He composed in a transitional style. Of particular interest are two pieces entitled *Durezze* and *Durezze e ligature*. They are among the earliest examples of a type of composition which was to become a favorite with Baroque composers. Basically homophonic in texture, these pieces emphasized dissonant harmonies (*durezze*) and suspensions (*ligature*).

In Naples a remarkably adventuresome school of keyboard playing developed. It became extremely influential in the 17th century, but it began somewhat earlier. Antonio Valente (c. 1520-c. 1600) is the earliest known representative of the Neapolitan school. He published two books of keyboard music, one for the harpsichord, *Intavolatura de cimbalo*, 1567, the other for the organ, *Versi spirituali*, 1580, (Sacred Versets). The *versets* of the *Versi spirituali* were free-composed, i.e., they were not based on any pre-existent Gregorian chant. Considering the early date of these pieces, such freedom was quite daring. Also interesting is the difference in style between compositions of the first, or *cimbalo*, tablature and those of the second. A distinction in style between *cimbalo* music and organ music continued to be characteristic of the Neapolitan school. Also typical was an increasing preference for the stringed keyboard instrument over the organ.

The Neapolitan school drew inspiration from various sources. One of its leaders was a composer of Flemish origin, Giovanni Macque (Jean de Macque) (c. 1550-1614), who certainly brought with him his native heritage. Spanish keyboardists, lutenists, and harpists were also influential since the kingdom of Naples had been under the Spanish crown since 1504. There are a number of stylistic features, techniques, etc., which prove an unmistakeable Spanish influence.[4] In addition, the southern Italian's impulsive temperament probably found its natural expression in the daring chromaticism and the sudden harmonic and rhythmic sur-

prises of Early Baroque music. It is well worth noting that the traits associated with Frescobaldi and with Early Baroque music in general appeared consistently at an earlier date in the Neapolitan school than anywhere else in Europe. In some cases, these traits were already hinted at in the music of Rocco Rodio (born 1530-1540?; died between 1615 and 1626), but they became unmistakeably clear in the works of Giovanni Macque. His style can be most easily described by comparing it to the madrigals of Gesualdo and Monteverdi.

Ex. 3. Macque, *Consonanze stravaganti,* m. 26-30.

For the next generation of Neapolitans, the leaders were Ascanio Mayone (d. 1627) and Giovanni Maria Trabaci (c. 1575-1647), both Macque students. Mayone published two books of keyboard music (1603 and 1609) in which the Early Baroque mentality most definitely asserts itself, with constant tension, quivering motives, sudden, unexpected rhythmic movement, and audacious dissonances. The initial theme dominates in Mayone's ricercars (and sometimes in his canzonas). Such handling of thematic material is quite different from that of the north Italians who usually divided the ricercar into sections, each with its own theme.

Trabaci used basically the same principle in his ricercars as did Mayone. This compositional technique should be seen as a significant step in the preparation for the fugue form.

Trabaci wrote two keyboard books (1603 and 1615, respectively). In the preface to his *Libro primo,* he states that the pieces contained therein may be played on any instrument, but are most suited to the organ and harpsichord. In *il secondo Libro* he makes a similar statement, but mentions the harpsichord before, instead of after, the organ, and states that *il cimbalo* is Lord over all instruments in the world. This attitude explains the presence of so many idiomatic harpsichord features in keyboard music of the Neapolitans. Trabaci also wrote many liturgical versets, but they are extremely short and less interesting than his secular pieces.

The *durezze e ligature* technique, the chromaticism, the rhythmic innovations, and the forms which the Neapolitan composers cultivated — all of these were brought to a higher degree of refinement by the great Girolamo Frescobaldi (1583-1643), organist at St. Peter's in Rome.

Ex. 4. Frescobaldi. *Toccata cromaticha*, m. 1-3.

He used the ricercar technique of Mayone and Trabaci, but combined it with the sectionalization of the north Italians. After the entire thematic material was presented in the first section, he built the successive sections as new versions or modifications of the original material. The same principle became the basis for most of his canzonas, which is why they are called "variation canzonas." Like the Neapolitans, this prolific composer was inspired more by the stringed keyboard instruments than by the organ. The one book which has become the most famous down through the years happens to be the only volume which he expressly dedicated to liturgical organ music, the *Fiori musicali*, 1635. It contains compositions for three organ masses (*kyrie* versets, plus toccatas, canzonas and ricercars). Like the versets of Antonio Valente (the early Neapolitan composer), Frescobaldi's toccates, canzonas, and ricercars were completely free of any connection with liturgical melodies. Still, they were intended to fulfill a liturgical function, since they were given titles corresponding to parts of the Proper of the Mass.

In addition to the organ works in the *Fiori musicali*, Frescobaldi wrote a few other pieces which he specifically indicated for organ performance, either by giving them a liturgical title or by providing them with a pedal part. Aside from these, the vast majority of his compositions seem to be either harpsichord music or general keyboard pieces, i.e., playable on any keyboard instrument. Moreover, some of the pieces which we are accustomed to considering as keyboard music may even have been written for instrumental ensemble. There are many unanswered questions concerning the performance of Frescobaldi's music.

Although the classic Italian organ has already been described, it would be well to remind ourselves that the instrument which Frescobaldi had at his disposal was similar to the Renaissance instruments played by Merulo and other Venetians. Frescobaldi's organ was composed primarily of delicately-voiced principal stops, which implies that it was incapable of making brilliant tonal contrasts or sharp echo effects of the type practiced by Sweelinck and the North Germans during the same period. Frescobaldi, moreover, rarely used the pedals. Of his nearly 200 compositions, only six require pedal and in these cases, the pedal part consists only of long pedal points.

Ex. 5. Frescobaldi, *Toccata sopra i Pedali del Organo e senza*, m. 1-3.

In this respect, Frescobaldi is typically Italian. It was not until the late 19th and 20th centuries that pedal technique, as we think of it today, came to be cultivated in Italy.

In Frescobaldi's *Toccata e Partite, Primo Libro*, 1615, the composer provides a preface which is most helpful for interpreting Italian Baroque music. The preface can be found in the new editions of the *Toccate e Partite . . .* and has also been reproduced in Apel, *The History of Keyboard Music to 1700*, 456-457. According to Frescobaldi, one must execute his pieces with the kind of freedom which makes them sound thoroughly spontaneous. A freedom at cadences is required, a freedom in tempi, and in specific rhythmic patterns (slightly comparable to the French *notes inégales*).

Of Frescobaldi's many students, the most important were South Germans and Austrians who combined his ideas with their own tradition, thereby creating a distinctively South German school. In Italy, Frescobaldi's compatriots were generally limited to imitating his style. Michelangelo Rossi (c. 1600-c. 1670), the master's leading Italian pupil, did display some individuality, but his works still bear a strong resemblance to his teacher's.

A number of other organists and harpsichordists were active at this time. Among the north Italians, Tarquinio Merula (c. 1590; death date unknown), occupied a prominent place. Only a few of his keyboard works have survived, so we do not have an adequate picture of his compositional activity. Another north Italian organist was Giovan Fasolo (born in the first half of the 17th c.), who wrote a sizeable collection of organ music for liturgical use throughout the entire year.

In central Italy, more specifically in Rome, the leading keyboardist was Bernardo Pasquini (1637-1710). He wrote numerous organ versets, but the works which showed off his musical gifts to best advantage were his charming dance suites and secular variations. Together with the Neapolitans of the later 17th century, Pasquini is credited with being one of the creators of the keyboard sonata. In addition, he may well have been the earliest composer in Italy to write keyboard suites, although this form was already well known in France and southern Germany.

In Naples, the keyboard school which had furnished much of the stimulation for Frescobaldi's work continued to produce distinguished keyboardists. Giovanni Salvatore (born at the beginning of the 17th c.; died c. 1688) wrote liturgical music (mass versets) and a number of pieces in the usual secular forms. Noticeable in Salvatore's music is a tendency to modify the extremes of earlier Neapolitan music, a tendency typical for the mid-17th century.

In the latter part of the century there continued to be fine keyboardists in Naples (Bernardo Storace, Gregorio Strozzi, etc.), but they were primarily harpsichordists.

A major contribution of the Neapolitans during the later Baroque period was the evolution of the sonata form. While this was not immediately impor-

tant for organ playing, the sonata eventually became a chief form for organ composition throughout Europe, especially in the Romantic era.

The great opera and oratorio composer, Alessandro Scarlatti (1660-1725), wrote some keyboard works. They contain many harpsichord-like features. Only one, a sonata in four movements, bears the inscription *per cembalo e per organo*.

The most famous harpsichordist of the Neapolitan school, Domenico Scarlatti (1685-1757), also wrote a few sonatas which we know are for organ since he specified the registration. He may even have played some of his harpsichord sonatas on the organ, too. We know for a fact that many organists tried to imitate his brilliant harpsichord style on the organ. The creative period for Italian organ composition was clearly over. Organists had to rely on outside stimuli. Those who had connections with Bologna, a major center of violin playing, introduced violinistic figurations into their organ music. Others borrowed lyric features from Italian opera, together with obvious programmatic details and long lines of parallel thirds and sixths.

Domenico Zipoli (1688-1726) and Padre Martini (1706-1784) were among the few 18th century Italian organists who could employ current styles and techniques, while still exercising restraint and good taste. Zipoli is known for his expressive, song-like compositions.

(Example 6)

Padre Martini, a scholar of world-renown, is remembered for the skillfulness with which he united strict counterpoint to post-Baroque style traits. He wrote numerous sonatas for organ and harpsichord.

During the course of the 19th century, interest in organ music almost disappeared. Not until the introduction of Romantic organ building (near the end

Ex. 6. Zipoli, *Pastorale in Do*, m. 5-8.

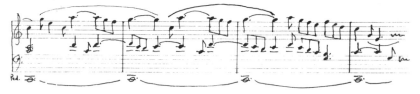

of the 19th century) did organ playing receive new incentive. Now, for the first time in Italy, a pedal division with independent stops was commonly considered a necessity. Multiple manuals and many flutes, reeds, and strings were other standard features, particularly on larger instruments. Naturally, most organ builders tried to imitate the sonorities of the Romantic orchestra. 8′ and 16′ stops dominated the instrument, and a thick, dark quality occupied the position formerly held by the crystal-clear Classic *ripieno*.

A chief crusader for this type of instrument was the concert organist, Marco Enrico Bossi (1861-1925). After having played large Romantic organs in other European countries, Bossi felt unduly limited by the Classic organ of his homeland. He began writing compositions suited to the new orchestral instruments and requiring techniques which must have been challenging for his Italian contemporaries. Alfredo Casella (1883-1947), prominent pianist and composer, contributed one concerto for organ and orchestra (1926).

Throughout the 20th century the Romantic approach to organ building has dominated. While the Classic instrument undoubtedly had its limitations, the Italian Romantic instrument had its own weak points. It was totally unsuited to contrapuntal music because it lacked the necessary clarity, and its stoplist was often no more than a conglomeration of orchestral sounds having no logical arrangement or organized function. Renato Lunelli, Luigi Tagliavini, and other scholars have done much research on historic Italian instruments and organ building in general. As a result, one would expect to see, by this time, a completely neo-classic trend in organ building, or perhaps a movement to combine the Classic instrument with the best features of the Romantic organ. Yet, unfortunately, no widespread organ revival has taken place in Italy. Even the old instruments are frequently left unrepaired and unplayable.

As for the technique of organ playing, there has been improvement. Some credit for this must be given to Fernando Germani, prominent teacher and author of a 4-volume organ method emphasizing pedalling, ornamentation, registration, and other matters which had long been weak points with Italian organists. More recently, Luigi Tagliavini

has become the foremost organist among the Italians. He has done much to give his countrymen (and others) an appreciation of the Italian heritage and to promote stylistically-accurate interpretations of old music.

One would hope, at the same time, to see some significant modern organ works being written, but aside from a few isolated exceptions there has been no interesting organ composition in Italy in the last few decades.

EDITIONS

Antegnati: *L'Antegnata Intavolatura de Ricercari d'Organo* (1608) (The Antegnati Tablature of Organ Ricercars), ed. Apel (*CEKM,IX*) *, 1965. The same is available in an edition published in Padua by Zanibon.

Banchieri A.: *Toccata I dell III tono* (per l'Elevazione), Padua, Zanibon. *Ricercare III e IV tono*, Padua, Zanibon.

Bertoldo: See the Padovano entry (*CEKM,XXXIV*).

Bossi: The following are representative works, but by no means do they constitute a complete listing. *Orgelwerke*, 2 vols, Frankfurt, Peters. Contents of Vol. I: *Allegretto, Ave Maria, Chant du soir, Elévation, Entrée pontificale, Idylle, Noël, Offertoire, Pièce héroïque, Rédemption, Résignation, Thème et Variations;* Vol. II: *Pièce de Concert, Hora mystica, Marche funèbre, Intermezzo lirico, Légende, 2 morceaux caractéristiques, Studie, Hora giocosa. Tre Brevi Pezzi*, Padua, Zanibon. Contents: *Studio, Piccolo corale, Ricercare, Six pièces*, Paris, Durand. Contents: *Prélude, Musette, Choral, Scherzo, Cantabile Alleluia final. Concerto in A Minor*, op. 100 (for organ, string orchestra, 4 horns, & tympani). Leipzig, Peters. *Etude symphonique*, op. 78, New York, G. Schirmer.

Buus: *Ricercari III e IV*, ed. Kastner, Hilversum, Harmonia-Uitgave, 1957.

Cavazzoni, G.: *Orgelwerke*, 2 vols., ed. Mischiati, Mainz, Schott S., 1958. Contents of Vol. I: ricercars, canzonas, hymns, magnificats; Vol. II: masses, hymns. The same works are in *I Classici della Musica Italiana*, VI, ed. Benvenuti, Milano, Società Anonima Notari

La Santa, 1919, but the editing is not as good.

Cavazzoni, M.A.: *M.A. Cavazzoni, J. Fogliano, J. Segni e anonimi: Composizioni per organo*, ed. Benvenuti (*I Classici musicali italiani*, I) , Milano, Fondazione Eugenio Bravi, 1941. Cavazzoni's works can also be found in Jeppesen, *Die italienische Orgelmusik am Anfang des Cinquecento*, II, Copenhagen, W. Hansen, 1943/2nd ed., Oslo, 1960.

Fasolo: *Annuale* (1645), ed. Walter, Heidelberg, W. Müller Verlag.

Frescobaldi: A nearly complete edition is the *Orgel- und Klavierwerke*, 5 vols., ed. Pidoux, Kassel, Bärenreiter, 1950 ff. Contents of Vol. I: fantasies and canzonas; Vol. II: capriccios, ricercars, canzonas; Vol. III: toccatas, partitas, etc.; Vol. IV: toccatas, canzonas, hymns, etc.; Vol. V: *Fiori musicali. Ausgewählte Orgelwerke* (Selected Organ Works) , 2 vols., ed. Keller, Leipzig, Peters, 1943. Contents of Vol. I: *Fiori musicali;* Vol. II: toccatas, canzonas, ricercars, capriccios, etc. *Ausgewählte Orgelsätze*, 2 vol., new edition, ed. Haberl/Richter, Wiesbaden, Breitkopf & Härtel. The *Orgue et Liturgie* series, Paris, Schola Cantorum, also has some of the Frescobaldi works. Bk. 26 of the series: *Toccatas;* Bk. 32: *Fantaisies;* Bk. 35: *Fantaisies;* Bk. 41: *Toccatas. Keyboard Compositions Preserved in Manuscripts*, ed. Shindle (*CEKM*,XXX) *, 1968. Contents: compositions which were not published during Frescobaldi's lifetime, plus some which were published but which are not now available in other modern editions . *Nove Toccate inedite per organo* (*Monumenti di musica italiana*, I/2) , Brescia, L'Organo.

Gabrieli, A.: The best edition is *Orgel- und Klavierwerke*, 5 vols., ed. Pidoux, Kassel. Bärenreiter, 1941 ff. Contents of Vol. I: intonations, toccatas; Vol. II: ricercars; Vol. III: ricercars; Vol. IV: canzonas and ricercari ariosi; Vol. V.: canzoni alla francese. *Three Organ Masses,* ed. Dalla Libera. Milano, Ricordi. *Toccate*, ed. Dalla Libera, Milano, Ricordi.

Gabrieli, G.: *Composizioni per organo*, 3 vols., ed. Dalla Libera, Milano,

Ricordi, 1956/57. (Note: Apel, *Geschichte* . . ., says that the authorship of some of the pieces in this edition is doubtful; moreover some may be pieces for instrumental ensemble rather than works for organ) .

Macque: Together with works by C. Guillet and C. Luython, Macque's preserved pieces are in *Monumenta musicae belgicae*, IV. ed. Watelet. Antwerp, "De Ring," 1938.

Martini: *Sonate d'intavolatura per l'Organo e il Cembalo* (1742), (facsimile), New York, Broude Bros. 12 *Sonate per Cembalo od Organo* (from the 1742 publication) , ed. Vitali, Milano, Ricordi. 6 *Sonaten* (from *Sonate per l'Organo e il Cembalo*, 1747), ed. Hoffmann/Erbrecht, Wiesbaden, Breitkopf & Härtel. 20 *Composizioni originali per Organo*, ed. Fuser, Padua, Zanibon, 1956.

Mayone: *Secondo Libro di diversi Capricci per Sonare* (1609), ed. Kastner (*Orgue et Liturgie*, books 63 and 65) , Paris, Schola Cantorum, 1964/65.

Merula, T.: *Composizioni per organo e cembalo*, ed. A. Curtis, Kassel, Bärenreiter, 1961.

Merulo: *Canzonen*, ed. Pidoux, Kassel, Bärenreiter, 1941. Contents: the 9 canzonas of the *Canzoni d'intavolatura d'Organo . . . Libro I*, 1592. *Composizioni per organo* (*Monumenti di musica italiana*, I/1) , Brescia, L'Organo. *Livre IV des Oeuvres d'Orgues de Claude Merulo*, ed. Labat, Paris, Richault, 1865. Contents: the masses from the *Messe d'intavolatura d'organo Libro 4.* Venice, 1586. *Toccate*, 3 vols., ed. Dalla Libera, Milano, Ricordi.

Padovano: *Annibale Padovano, Sperindio Bertoldo, d'Incerto* (anonymous): *Compositions for Keyboard*, ed. K. Speer (*CEKM*, XXXIV) *, 1969. *Composizioni per organo*, ed. Benetti, Padua, Zanibon. (Note: the 13 ricercari of the Pierront/Hennebains editions [Paris, L'Oiseau Lyre, 1934], although advertised as organ pieces, are transcriptions of ensemble music) .

Pasquini, B.: *Collected Works for Keyboard*, 7 vols., ed. Haynes (*CEKM*,V.

Bks. 1-7) *, 1968. Contents of Bk. 1: capriccios, fantasies, ricercars, canzonas, fugues, sonatas; Bk. 2: suites, arias; Bk. 3: variations; Bk. 4: variations; Bk. 5: toccatas; Bk. 6: toccatas; Bk. 7: figured bass pieces. 7 *Toccate di Pasquini*, ed. Esposito, Padua, Zanibon, 1956.

Pasquini,E.: *Collected Keyboard Works*, ed. Shindle (*CEKM*, XII) *, 1966.

Rodio: *Cinque Ricercate, Una Fantasia per organo, clavicembalo, clavicordo o arpa* (1575) (Five Ricercars, One Fantasy for Keyboard Instruments or Harp), ed. Kastner, Padua, Zanibon, 1958.

Rossi, M.A.: *Works for Keyboard*, ed. White (*CEKM*,XV) *, 1966. This is the best edition. The same pieces (his complete works) were published under the title *Composizioni per Organo e Cembalo*, ed. Toni, as vol. XXVI of *I Classici della Musica Italiana*, Milano, Società Anonima Notari La Santa, 1920.

Salvatore: *Collected Keyboard Works*, ed. Hudson (*CEKM*,III) *, 1964.

Scarlatti, A.: *Toccata No. 11 per cembalo e per organo*, ed. Vignanelli, Roma, Edition De Santis, 1941.

Scarlatti, D.: *Five Organ Sonatas*, ed. Greene, New York, G. Schirmer. *Sonaten und Fugen für Orgel*, ed. L. Hautus, Kassel, Bärenreiter.

Storace: *Selva di varie compositioni d'intavolatura per cembalo ed organo* (1644) (Anthology of Various Compositions in Tablature for Harpsichord and Organ), ed. Hudson (*CEKM*,VII) *, 1965.

Strozzi: *Capricci da sonare cembali et organi* (1687), ed. Hudson (*CEKM*, XI) *, 1967.

Tagliavini: *Passacaglia per organo su un tema di Hindemith*, Padua, Zanibon, 1954. *Cantabile* (in the collection, *Hora Mystica*, Padua, Zanibon, which contains works of 20th century Italian composers). *Corale pastorale: Puer natus est* (in the collection, *Pastoralia*, Zanibon, containing 28 pastorales by old and new composers).

Trabaci: *Composizioni per organo e cembalo*, I, ed. O. Mischiati (*Monumenti di musica italiana*, I/3), Brescia, L'Organo, 1964.

Valente: *Versi spirituali*, ed. Fuser, Padua, Zanibon, 1958.

Zipoli: *Orgel-und Cembalowerke*, 2 vols., ed. Tagliavini, Heidelberg, W. Müller Verlag. Contents of Vol. I: toccata, canzonas, short liturgical pieces, etc.; Vol. II: 4 keyboard suites. *Selected Works for Organ or Cembalo*, ed. Ruf, Basel, Symphonic Verlag. *Composizioni per Organo e Cembalo* (*I Classici della Musica Italiana*, XXXVI), gen'l ed., d'Annunzio, Milano, Società Anonima Notari La Santa, 1919.

Collections

There are also numerous general collections of Italian organ music. The following constitute a selected list.

Altitalienische Orgelmusik, ed. Gauzz, Tübingen, C.L. Schultheiss. Contents: 32 pieces by Frescobaldi, Gabrieli, Lotti, Palestrina, Zipoli, etc.

Altitalienische Orgelmeister, ed. Kaller (*Liber Organi*, IV), Mainz, Schott S. Contents: works of Banchieri, Fasolo, Frescobaldi, Zipoli.

Altitalienische Versetten in allen Kirchentonarten, ed. Kastner, Mainz, Schott S. Contents: liturgical versets from the 16th century.

Antologia organistica italiana, ed. Dalla Libera, Milano, Ricordi. Contents: works from the 16th and 17th centuries. (The editing is not always good).

L'Arte Musicale in Italia dal Secole XIV al XVIII, 7 vols., ed. Torchi, Milano, Ricordi, 1897-1908; new edition, 1959. Vol. III: *Composizioni per organo o cembalo, secoli XVI, XVII, e XVIII*. Contents: 169 compositions by a wide variety of composers.

Cantantibus Organis, ed. E. Kraus, Regensburg, Verlag Pustet. Bk. 2: *Orgelmusik an europäischen Kathedralen: Venedig, Augsburg, München*. Contents: pieces by A. & G. Gabrieli, Guami, Merulo, etc. Bk. 4: *Die Messe im Choralamt: IX Messe*. Contents: short pieces by Cavazzoni, Fasolo, etc. Bk. 6: *Orgelmusik an europäischen Kathedralen,* part II: *St. Peter in Rom.* Contents: pieces of Arcadelt, Frescobaldi, Palestrina, etc. Bk. 10: *Orgelmusik der Franziskaner.* Contents: 20 pieces by Belli and Fasolo. Bk. 11: *Orgelmusik an europäischen Kathedralen,* part III: *Bergamo, Passau.* Contents: works by Bassani, Brignoli, Cavaccio, Scandello, etc. (Note: not all of the compositions in these books are original organ works; some are probably ensemble compositions or motet transcriptions).

Classici Italiani dell' Organo, ed. Fuser, Padua, Zanibon, 1955. Contents: 66 composers from Antico through Martini.

Italienische und süddeutsche Orgelstücke des frühen 17. Jahrhunderts, ed. Schierning (*Die Orgel,* II/9), Lippstadt, Kistner & Siegel.

Liber Organi, vol. III (Pastorales of the Classical Era), ed. Dalla Libera, Vicenza, Editrice S.A.T. Contents: pieces by Lotti, Rossi, d'Aquin. *Liber Organi,* vol. VIII (*Raccolte di Musiche inedite per organo del Settecento Veneziano*), ed. Dalla Libera, Vicenza, Editrice S.A.T. Contents: works by Marcello, Galuppi, Pesceti, A. Hasse.

L'Organo Italiano (1567-1619), ed. Frotscher, Copenhagen, W. Hansen. Contents: 7 pieces.

10 *Sonaten* (from Aresti's *Sonate da organo di varii autori,* 1687), ed. A. Reichling, Berlin, Merseburger. Contents: pieces by Aresti, Pollaroli, Kerll, Giustiniani, Schiava, Colonna, anonymous.

Examples of early Italian music can also be found in *Die Italienische Orgelmusik am Anfang des Cinquecento,* vol. II, ed. Jeppesen, Copenhagen, W. Hansen, 1943/ 2nd ed., Oslo, 1960.

NOTES

[1]Reese, *Music in the Renaissance,* 520.

[2]Apel, *Geschichte der Orgel-und Klaviermusik bis* 1700, 162-165.

[3]An excellent discussion of Italian organs and authentic registration practices can be found in *The Diapason,* Feb., 1966. This article is a transcription of Luigi Tagliavini's lecture at the 1965 A.G.O. Mid-Winter Conclave.

[4]Apel, "Neapolitan Links between Cabezon and Frescobaldi," *Mus Q XXIV,* 4 (Oct., 1938), 419 ff.

MUSICAL SOURCES

Ex. 1. *Historical Anthology of Music,* I, ed. Davison/Apel, Cambridge, Harvard University Press, p. 121.

Ex. 2. *Claudio Merulo: Canzonen,* ed. Pidoux, p. 33.

Ex. 3. *Historical Anthology of Music,* I, p. 201.

Ex. 4. *Fiori musicali,* ed. Pidoux, p. 18.

Ex. 5. *Frescobaldi: Ausgewaehlte Orgelwerke,* II, ed. Keller, p. 2. Copyright C. F. Peters. Used by permission.

Ex. 6. *Anthology of Organ Music,* ed. Esposito, Bergamo, Edizioni Carrara, p. 132.

ABBREVIATIONS

*Corpus of Early Keyboard Music, Dallas, American Institute of Musicology, 1963-

4

Germany and Austria

SOUTH GERMANY

A rich organ culture existed in south Germany and Austria at an early date. In fact, the single most important organ composer previous to the 16th century was a south German—Conrad Paumann (c. 1410-1415—1473), discussed in the chapter "Organ Music Before 1500." Then, at the turn of the 16th century, the most significant figure was again a south German—Arnolt Schlick (born c. 1450-1460; died after 1520). The majority of the organists active in Germany in the century following him likewise came from the southern part of the country. Not until the 17th century did the north Germans take the lead.

Schlick's *Tabulaturen etlicher lobgesang und lidlein uff die orgeln und lauten* (Tablatures of Hymns of Praise and Songs for Organ and Lute), published in 1512, contains 14 organ pieces which reveal that rapid progress had been made in German organ music within the space of one century. At the beginning of the 15th century, German organ playing had been nothing more than an imitation of an antiquated vocal form—*organum*. Organ playing then passed rapidly through the same stages that vocal polyphony had formerly taken. The music of Paumann somewhat resembled the *conductus*. The pieces in the *Buxheimer Orgelbuch*[1] (*fauxbourdon* compositions and song transcriptions with coloration in the upper voice) called to mind the Burgundian school. The works of Schlick now emulated the Flemish masters, Ockeghem and, particularly, Obrecht. Schlick stressed equality of the voice parts, gave contrapuntal considerations preference over harmonic elements, and made considerable use of imitation. He also employed features distinctly idiomatic to the organ.

In addition to the tablature of 1512, other compositions by Schlick are preserved in a Trient manuscript. Notable is a 10-voice composition, *Ascendo ad Patrem meum*, requiring a pedal technique which would be phenomenal even today. According to Schlick, this work could be played with four voices in the pedal and six on the manual![2] Such virtuosity is really remarkable when one remembers that organists in most countries did not use the pedal at all during the Renaissance period.

Schlick's setting of the folk melody, *Maria zart*, (probably his most famous composition) is significant as a predecessor to the Lutheran *Choralbearbeitungen* which sprang up in profusion during the next centuries. Like many of the Lutheran tunes, this melody grew from native soil and thus shared traits with melodies later sung by Luther's followers. In addition, Schlick anticipated a technique which eventually became very common in chorale compositions. He took individual phrases of the *cantus firmus*, ornamented them, placed them in the soprano, and separated them from each other by brief interludes which sometimes imitated fragments of the soprano melody.

(Example 1)

A somewhat younger contemporary of Schlick was Paul Hofhaimer (1459-1537), a famous virtuoso who served at the courts of Innsbruck, Augsburg, and Salzburg. Less imaginative than Schlick, Hofhaimer confined himself to 3-part writing and generally handled the *can-*

Ex. 1. Schlick, *Maria zart von edler Art*, m. 48-52.

tus planus with absolute strictness. He used a certain amount of counterpoint, including imitation, but relied heavily on filigree-like "coloration." Most of his preserved works are song intabulations. Only four original organ pieces exist today.

The leading figure of the next generation was Hans Buchner (1483-c.1538), organist at the Cathedral of Constance. A student of Hofhaimer, he was spiritually as much a successor of Schlick as of his own teacher. Buchner wrote a *fundamentum* (c. 1520?) containing a number of liturgical pieces based on *cantus firmi* and some preambles. In the didactic part of the *fundamentum*, Buchner shows methodically how a *cantus firmus* can be treated contrapuntally, with special emphasis given to imitation. Despite his emphasis on counterpoint, he depended quite a bit on schemes and prescribed patterns, especially with respect to figuration.

Buchner's contemporaries, Hans Kotter (born c. 1480-85; d. 1541) and Leonhard Kleber (born c. 1490-95; d. 1556), followed Hofhaimer's path and used considerable coloration. Colored intabulations predominate in their tablatures (1513 and 1524 respectively), although some original preambles can be found. The Kotter collection is, in addition, the first German keyboard tablature to include dances. Stylistically and technically, the dances point more toward performance on the harpsichord than on the organ, thus indicating a gradually developing distinction in Germany between music for stringed keyboard instruments and music for organ.

The *Kärntner Tablature*, an Austrian manuscript of the mid-16th century (c. 1550), is another source of organ music. In addition to intabulated motets, it contains two true organ pieces, one by an anonymous composer, the other, a *Praeambulum 6 vocum*, by the famous choral composer, Ludwig Senfl (c. 1490-

1543). This is the only organ work by Senfl which has been preserved, but has high artistic merit. Apparently intended to be played with four parts on the manual and two on the pedal, it constitutes another witness to the unusually well-developed pedal technique of the German school.

A reliance on coloration, which was noted earlier, became generally more extreme as the century progressed. Decorative patterns were now rigid, mechanical, and unimaginative. Thus many later 16th century composers wrote in a manner which has subsequently caused them to be known as the "Colorists," a term which generally carries derogatory implications. Considerable confusion exists concerning the use of this word since some music historians have broadened the term to include Kotter and Kleber; others even designate Buchner as a "Colorist." In the present survey the term is being applied to German keyboardists of the later 16th century only, since in their works coloration became excessively dependent on schemes and patterns.

To view the "Colorists" in true perspective, one should consider them more as stringed keyboard players than as organists. They wrote lively keyboard dances which are extremely important for the later history of harpsichord music. It was in these dances, rather than in organ music, that the "Colorists" were best able to express themselves.

Several tablatures exist from the late 16th and early 17th centuries. Two of them, the tablatures of Bernhard Schmid the Younger (1584-1625?) and Johann Woltz (d. 1618), are of particular interest for organ music, while the others belong more properly within the realm of harpsichord music. Both the Schmid tablature (1607) and the Woltz tablature (1617) contain works by Merulo, the Gabrieli s and other leading composers. The Woltz tablature also has pieces by Steigleder and three composers of Flemish origin — Lohet, Luython, and Macque. Intabulations constitute the majority of the pieces, but there are enough original organ works in each tablature to show that an interest in original organ music was increasing. Woltz is generally considered to be the last of the "Colorists."

At approximately the same time that the Schmid and Woltz tablatures were being compiled, the fugue form made its appearance in Germany. A group of pieces entitled *Fuga* can be found in the Schmid tablature. These, Schmid explained, are identical with that which the Italians call *Canzona alla francese*. Of course, the fact that Schmid equated fugue with canzona should not be taken as indication that all musicians in Germany did so. In fact, there are several fugues by Simon Lohet (preserved in the Woltz tablature) which are concise monothematic compositions closely resembling the later Baroque concept of that term.

Foreign influences played a decisive role in the development of south German and Austrian music. In the 16th century all of the major cultural centers employed Netherlandish and Italian musicians, with Italians rising to positions of dominance near the end of the 16th century. The basic Italian keyboard forms — toccata, ricercar, canzona, etc — thus became standard for the south Germans. While the Venetian school was at its height, the south Germans followed the Venetians. Then, in the 17th century, when Frescobaldi was so widely venerated, his style was emulated. French and English keyboard schools also had an impact, but these developments will be discussed later. South German organs were likewise Italianized. Before proceeding to a discussion of the south German organ type, one should realize that "south German" is used here in a collective sense to encompass both south Germany and Austria. While this is bound to upset some Austrian colleagues, it is too cumbersome to keep repeating "south Germany and Austria," so this has been shortened to read simply "south Germany," or "south German," as the case might be. In fact, until more modern times this cultural unit encompassed Bohemia and the German-speaking part of Switzerland as well. Probably one should treat all of these countries together when discussing their musical production during the Renaissance, Baroque, and Classical eras. But, since Bohemia and German Switzerland have followed more independent paths in the modern era, it is more convenient to treat Bohemia (now a part of Czechoslovakia) and Switzerland under separate headings in later articles.

The south German organ had possessed a wide range of colors, multiple manuals, and independent pedal stops in the Renaissance era. Then, in the late 16th century, it was simplified and reduced in size, following the Italian example. It now consisted mainly of principal stops. Yet it did not completely forfeit its German heritage. Many south German organs, for example, continued to have a second manual — a rarity in Italy. Mixtures, too, could often be found in south Germany (again in opposition to the Italian practice of building separate principle stops even at the highest pitches), but they were milder and less plentiful than north German mixtures. A few flutes were present, while reeds were nearly nonexistent. On one-manual organs it was common to divide some of the ranks into descant and bass stops for solo use. Independent pedal stops continued to be used in south Germany but, as on Italian instruments, a short-length pedalboard was customary. This virtually eliminated the possibility of *cantus firmus* playing in the pedal, a favorite practice among the middle, and especially, among the north German organists. In southern Germany, most organs had but a few pedal stops, limited to the lower-pitched ranks. Throughout the entire Baroque era, then, the pedal was normally employed in south Germany only for a slowly-moving bass line. This type of organ (with allowance for certain variations between one organ builder and another) was the kind of instrument for which all south German organ music was written from the late Renaissance through the Baroque era.

The earliest south German composers whose organ works bear the clear markings of the Italian school, or more particularly, of the Venetian school, are Hans Leo Hassler (1564-1612) and Christian Erbach (c. 1570-1635), both transitional figures between the Renaissance and the Baroque. Hassler mixed the German tradition with the Venetian manner in his vocal works, but he appears to have preferred the Venetian style in his keyboard works. Since the majority of Hassler's compositions are not available in a modern edition, this generalization may have to be modified after we have access to more of his works.

(Example 2)

Christian Erbach likewise took Venetian keyboard forms and style traits, but combined them with elements of the German "coloristic" technique.

Hassler and Erbach were also involved in making music for mechanical instruments, especially mechanical clocks. Hassler built mechanical instruments and Erbach was one of the first persons to compose for the *Orgelwalze*. While such pieces are not true organ music, their performance on the organ has been generally accepted. For some unknown reason, south Germans were quite taken up with these mechanical devices, whereas, in other parts of Europe, musicians usually paid little attention to them. Even at a much later date, such illustrious figures as Haydn and Mozart continued the tradition of writing for mechanical clocks.

The first important south German organist-composer who wrote in an Early Baroque style was Johann Ulrich Steigleder (1593-1635). He was well acquainted with Italian techniques, as well as with the style of the English Virginalists, some of whom were employed with him at the Württemberg court in Stuttgart. His organ works were preserved in two publications, the *Ricercar Tabulatura*, 1624, and the Tabu-laturbuch darinnen das Vatter unser 40 *mal variiert wird.* . . , 1627. Both the ricercars of the first book and the 40 variations of the *Vater unser* of the second book reveal an amazing wealth of ideas and an avoidance of stereotyped patterns. Like Samuel Scheidt, his contemporary in middle Germany, Steigleder favored the type of chorale variation in which the chorale appeared as a *cantus firmus* in one of the voices. The other voices were then treated in a vareity of ways: as a polyphonic web; with virginalistic figuration; with pre-imitation of the chorale phrase, etc.

(Example 3)

Another Early Baroque musician was Johann Erasmus Kindermann (1616-1655), organist in Nürnberg, which is located in the northern part of that which is commonly called south Germany. Kindermann published a collection of organ pieces under the title *Harmonia organica*, 1645. Contained in this collection are *Preambulae*, fantasies, intonations, *Magnificat* versets, and a number of fugues. Particularly interesting are certain fugues which employ as theme the first line or two of a choral melody. They are early examples of the chorale fugue, or chorale fugato, which was soon to become a standard type of *Choralbearbeitung* among middle German composers. From the compositional standpoint, Kindermann is connected with the middle Germans as much as with the south Germans.

Around the middle of the century, one keyboardist rose to such prominence

Ex. 2. Hassler, *Canzona*, m. 104–109.

Ex. 3. Steigleder, *Vater unser im Himmelreich*, m. 25–30.

that he outshone all others in southern Germany: Johann Jakob Froberger (1616-1667). A student of Frescobaldi, he was court organist in Vienna and made guest appearances in Paris and other leading cities.. His compositons reflect his cosmopolitan life. He combined German and Italian elements, as was customary among south Germans, but also included certain specifically French features (ornaments, programmatic effects, etc.). He did not slavishly imitate either the Italians or the French, but combined foreign traits into a new style which can be recognized as distinctively south German. His style, moreover, was less exrteme than that of earlier Baroque musicians. Comparing him with Frescobaldi, one sees that the restless motives and sudden rhythmic changes of the earlier master have been modified into a Middle Baroque style.

(Example 4)

Many of Froberger's compositions are general keyboard pieces playable on either harpsichord or organ. At the mid-17th century, employment of a general keyboard style was common practice in south Germany, as well as in Italy and France, the two other countries which Froberger knew as well. Among Froberger's compositions in this category are a number of toccatas, capriccios, ricercars, canzonas, and fantasies. However, the works which earned him his greatest fame — his keyboard suites — are clearly idiomatic to the harpsichord. They mark the origin of that which has come to be known as the German keyboard suite.

In the period after Froberger, south German keyboardists, neglecting organ music, devoted themselves more and more to harpsichord music, just as Frescobaldi's successors in Italy were doing. A case in point is Alessandro de Poglietti (d. 1683), an Italian active at the Viennese court for many years. He was famous for his progressive harpsichord compositions with their lively, sometimes bizarre, programmatic effects. His organ compositions were reserved and traditional. The only innovation he made in organ playing was to stress the importance of appropriate registration. In his treatise *Compendium oder kurtzer Begriff und Einführung zur Musica,* 1676, (Compendium and Introduction to Music), he gave registration instructons. Since, in his harpsichord pieces, Poglietti was clearly influenced by French *clavecin* music, one wonders if, in the matter of registration, he might not also have been influenced by the Parisian practice of furnishing registration indications for specific types and forms or organ music.

Johann Kasper Kerll (1627-1693), like his colleague, Poglietti, was another South German who stated that the individuality of a piece should be underscored through meaningful registration. Gay and lively movements should have bright, clear colors, while solemn movements and pieces employing chromatic themes require dark colors.[3] In 1686 Kerll published a collection of 56 organ versets on the *Magnificat,* under the title *Modulatio organica.* Each of the verset cycles contains one piece based on a Gregorian melody (the first verset) and six others on newly invented material. These brief organ versets are generally less attractive than Kerll's harpsichord pieces. Still they constitute a minor historical landmark since they initiated in south Germany a tradition of liturgical verset composition based on independent material. Such cycles soon became one of the most common compositional types in use throughout south Germany.

(Example 5)

Vienna, where Froberger, Poglietti, and Kerll were active, was now a leading center of keyboard playing in Europe. Numerous keyboardists belonged to the Viennese school, but most of them were harpisichordists rather than organists. From their number, Johann Josef Fux (1660-1741), the famous theorist and pedagogue, must be men-

Ex. 4. Froberger, *Toccata II,* m. 1-3, 40-41.

Ex. 5. Kerll, *Magnificat Primi Toni*, Verset 3, m. 1-2; Verset 4, m. 1-2; Verset 7, m. 1-2.

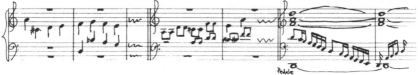

tioned because he exerted a powerful influence on many organists, although he himself composed little or nothing for the organ.

Elsewhere in south Germany and Austria, major organ positions were taken by Sebastian Anton Scherer, Georg Muffat, and Johann Speth. Scherer (1631-1712), organist at the Ulm cathedral, wrote a collection of free liturgical versets (following the Kerll model), plus a book of organ toccatas. Georg Muffat (1654-1704), a highly internaitonal figure, studied for six years in Paris, lived in Vienna, Prague, and Salzburg, then went to Rome for additional study, and later took a *Kapellmeister* position in Passau. His organ pieces were published in 1690 in the *Apparatus musico-organisticus* and represent a synthesis of French, German, and Italian style traits, with French elements predominating. An additional, unusual feature is the fact that Muffat did not restrict the pedal to occasional pedal points, as was customary in south Germany, but sometimes assigned it an independently moving line.

Ex. 6. Geo. Muffat, *Passacaglia*, m. 1-5.

Johann Speth (1664-?), organist at the cathedral of Augsberg, wrote a book of organ and harpsichord pieces including, among other things, 8 *Magnificat* cycles based on free material. Each cycle opens and closes with a piece in toccata style. The intermediate versets are, for the most part, short fugatos.

Farther to the north, three other south Germans occupied highly influential positions. They are Johann Pachelbel, Johann Philpp Krieger, and Johann Krieger. Pachelbel (1653-1706) was a native of Nürnberg. He studied in Vienna, was employed for many years in middle Germany, and then returned

to his hometown in south Germany. In many of his compositions he was a typical south German. He wrote, for example, toccatas featuring constantly moving figuration over sustained organ points in the pedal. He also composed numerous *Magnificat* fugues. Like the various liturgical cycles of other south German composers, Pachelbel's *Magnificat* fugues generally had no connection with liturgical melodies.

(Example 7)

In other respects, Pachelbel belongs more properly with the middle Germans. He wrote many *Choralbearbeitungen*, which constitute his greatest contribution. Moreover, as teacher and performer, he exerted a profound influence on Thüringian organists, including, indirectly, J.S. Bach. In south Germany he had fewer devoted followers. For these reasons, he will be discussed in more detail in the article on organ music in middle Germany.

The Krieger brothers, Johann Philipp (1649-1725) and Johann (1651-1735), are generally classified with the middle Germans since they spent most of their adult years in middle Germany. One mentions them in the south German survey only because they retained some traits of the south German style. In fact, together with Pachelbel, they brought the south German tradition (which included Italian and French elements) into the more provincial middle German culture.

Three additional keyboardists, active near the end of the Baroque era, merit attention: J.C.F. Fischer, F.X.A. Murschhauser, and Gottlieb Muffat. Johann Caspar Ferdinand Fischer (d. 1746) wrote two organ collections. One, entitled *Ariadne Musica*, is a collection of 20 preludes and fugues in 20 different keys. The purpose of the collection was to lead the performer through the maze of new major and minor keys made possible by the well-tempered system of tuning which was just coming into use.

Ex. 7. Pachelbel, *Fuga*, m. 1-4, 26-30.

This was a direct foreshadowing of Bach's *Wohltemperierte Klavier*, even to the extent of obvious thematic resemblance. Fischer's other organ collection is the *Musicalischer Blumen-Strauss*. It consisted of eight verset cycles for liturgical use. Fischer's organ works, however, were not his greatest contribution. As a typical south German, he was more interested in the harpsichord than in the organ. His German keyboard suites, which combine the French spirit with the German, are the most important works in this genre between Froberger and Bach.

Franz Xaver Anton Murschhauser (1663-1738) was a student of Kerll. Inspired by his teacher's *Modulatio organica*, Murschhauser wrote two books of cyclical versets: *Octo-Tonium novum Organicum* _and *Prototypon Longo-Breve Organicum*.

Gottlieb Muffat (1690-1770), son of Georg Muffat, is generally considered to be the last of the south German Baroque organ composers. He wrote liturgical versets, ricercars, canzonas, fugues, toccatas, preludes, and other organ works. Like his father, his approach to composition was definitely cosmopolitan. Next to Bach, he wrote some of the best fugues of the Late Baroque era.

EDITIONS

Buchner: *Das Fundamentbuch von Hans von Constanz*, ed. Paesler, with several pieces transcribed (*Vierteljahrsschrift für Musikwissenschaft, V*), Leipzig, 1889. *Sämtliche Orgelwerke*, 2 vols. (*Das Erbe deutscher Musik*, LIV/LV), Braunschweig. H. Litolff's Verlag, 1972.

Erbach: *Ausgewählte Werke*, ed. von Werra (*DTB*, IV/2)**, 1903. *Drei Introitus mit Versus* (*Die Orgel*, II/11), Lippstadt, Kistner & Siegel. *Acht Canzonen*, ed. Reichling, Berlin, Merseburger. Pieces for mechanical clock are in the musical supplement to Protz, *Mechanische Musikinstrumente*, Kassel, Bärenreiter 1939.

Fischer: *Sämtliche Werke für Klavier und Orgel*, ed. von Werra, Leipzig, Breitkopf & Härtel, 1901. Contents: *Pièces de Clavessin, Parnassus, Ariadne Musica*, and *Musikalischer Blumenstrauss*. The *Ariadne Musica* is included in *Deutsche Meister des XVI. und XVII. Jahrhunderts*, ed. Kaller (*Liber Organi*, VII), Mainz, Schott S. *Musikalischer Blumenstrauss: Praeludien, Fugen und Finali in den acht Kirchentonarten*, ed. Walter (*Süddeutsche Orgelmeister des Barock*, I), Altötting, Coppenrath.

Froberger: *Orgel- und Klavierwerke*, 3 vols., ed. Adler (*DTO*, IV/1,VI/2 and X/2)***, 1897-1903. *Ausgewählte Orgelwerke*, ed. Matthaei, Kassel, Bärenreiter, 1931, ³/1951. Contents: 4 fantasies; 8 ricercars. 10 *Orgelwerke*, ed. Seiffert (*Organum*, IV/11), Lippstadt, Kistner & Siegel. *Selected Keyboard Works*, Frankfurt/New York, Peters.

Hofhaimer: *Einundneunzig gesammelte Tonsätze Paul Hofhaimers*, ed. Moser, Stuttgart/Berlin, J.C. Cotta Nachfolger, 1929. Contents: mainly intabulations and pieces of dubious authorship.

Hassler: *Werke für Orgel und Klavier*, ed. von Werra (*DTB*) IV/2**, 1903. *Orgelwerke* (*Sämtliche Werke*, XII), Munich, Publication of the Gesellschaft für Bayerische Musikgeschichte.

Kerll: *Ausgewählte Werke,* ed. Sandberger *(DTB,* II/2) **, 1901. *Modulatio organica* (1686), ed. Walter *(Süddeutsche Orgelmeister des Barock,* II), Altötting, Coppenrath, 1956. *Passacaglia,* Vienna, Doblinger. *Ciacona,* Vienna, Doblinger.

Kindermann: *Ausgewählte Instrumental- und Vokalwerke,* ed. Schreiber/Wallner *(DTB,* XXI-XXIV) **, 1924. *Harmonia organica* (1645), ed. Walter *(Süddeutsche Orgelmeister des Barock,* IX), Altötting, Coppenrath.

J. P. Krieger and J. Krieger: Editions of their works will be listed together with the middle Germans.

Muffat, Georg: *Apparatus musico-organisticus,* New York, C. F. Peters. The same, ed. Walter *(Süddeutsche Orgelmeister des Barock,* III), Altötting, Coppenrath, 1957.

Muffat, Gottlieb: *Toccaten und Versetl für Orgel und Klavier,* ed. Adler *(DTOE* XXIX/2) ***, 1922. *72 Versetl und 12 Toccaten,* ed. Upmeyer, Kassel/Basel, Bärenreiter, 1952. *Toccata, Fuge und Capriccio,* ed. Riedel *(Die Orgel,* II/8), Lippstadt, Kistner & Siegel, 1958. *3 Toccaten und Capriccios (Die Orgel,* II/10), 1958. *3 Toccaten und Capriccios (Die Orgel,* II/13), 1960. *12 kleine Praeludien, (Die Orgel,* II/16), 1960. *6 Fugen (Die Orgel,* II/17).

Murschhauser: *Werke für Klavier und Orgel,* ed. Seiffert *(DTB,* XVIII) **, 1901. Contents: the *Octo-Tonium novum Organicum* and the *Prototypon Longo-Breve Organicum. Octo-Tonium novum organicum,* ed. Walter *(Süddeutsche Orgelmeister des Barock,* VI), Altötting, Coppenrath, 1961.

Pachelbel: *Orgelkompositionen,* ed. Seiffert *(DTB,* IV/1) **, 1903. Contents: preludes, toccatas, fantasies, fugues, choralbearbeitungen, etc. *94 Magnificat-Fugen,* ed. Botstiber/Seiffert *(DTO,* VIII/2***, 1901. *Klavierwerke,* ed. Seiffert *(DTB,* II/1) **, 1901. Contents: suites, chaconnes, chorale variations, etc. *Ausgewählte Orgelwerke,* 4 vols., ed. Matthaei, Kassel, Bärenreiter. Contents: Vol. 1: toccatas, fantasies, chaconnes, etc.; II: chorale preludes; III: chorale preludes; IV: chorale partitas. *Magnificat-Fugen,* ed. Hübsch, Heidelberg, W. Müller Verlag. The same, ed. Seiffert *(Organum,* IV/14), Lippstadt, Kistner & Siegel, 1929. *Praeludien, Fantasien und Toccaten,* ed. Seiffert *(Organum,* IV/12), 1929. *Ciaconen, Fugen und Ricercari,* ed. Seiffert *(Organum,* IV/13), 1929 *Ausgewählte Klavierwerke,* ed. Doflein, Mainz, Schott S. *Ausgewählte Klavierwerke,* ed. Schütz, Frankfurt, Peters. *Cent Nouveaux Versets de Magnificat,* 3 vols., ed. Pierront/Dufourcq, Paris, Bornemann. Contents: Vol. 1: 30 versets by Pachelbel; II: 40 versets by Pachelbel.

Paumann: *Locheimer Liederbuch und Fundamentum Organisandi* (facsimile), ed. Ameln, Berlin, Wölbing Verlag, 1925. The pieces are transcribed in *Das Locheimer Liederbuch,* ed. Arnold, Wiesbaden, Breitkopf & Härtel. They are also in *Music of the Fourteenth and Fifteenth Centuries,* ed. Apel *(CEKM, I)* *, 1963, nos. 41-57.

Poglietti: *12 Ricercare,* 2 vols., ed. Riedel *(Die Orgel,* II/5 & 6), Lippstadt, Kistner & Siegel, 1957.

Scherer: *Oeuvres d'Orgue de S.A. Scherer,* ed. Guilmant/Pirro *(Archives des Maîtres de l'orgue,* VIII), Paris, Durand.

Schlick: *Tabulaturen etlicher Lobgesang und Lidlein uff die Orgeln und Lauten* (1512), ed. G. Harms, Hamburg, 1924, 2/1937, Ugrino. *Hommage à l'Empereur Charles Quint, Dix Versets pour Orgue . . .,* ed. Kastner, Barcelona, Editorial de Música Boileau, 1954. Contents of the latter book: Schlick's works from a Trient manuscript, plus five pieces by T. de Santa Maria. *Orgelkompositionen,* ed. Walter, Mainz, Schott S., 1970.

Speth: *Magnificat* (1693), ed. Klaus, Heidelberg, W. Müller Verlag. Contents: preludes, versets, and finales in the 8 church modes. *Süddeutsche Orgelmeister: Johannes Speth,* ed. Klaus *(Liber Organi,* IX), Mainz, Schott S. Contents: 10 toccatas.

Steigleder: *Compositions for Keyboard,* 2 vols., ed. Apel *(CEKM,* XIII) *, 1968. Contents of Vol. I: *Tabulatur Buch Das Vatter Unser* (1627); Vol. II: *Ricercar Tabulatura* (1624). *Vier Ricercare für Orgel,* ed Emsheimer, Kassel, Bärenreiter, 1928.

Collections

From the general collections containing works by south Germans, the following is a selected list.

Deutsche Meister des XVI. und XVII. Jahrhunderts, ed. Kaller (*Liber Organi,* VI/VII), Mainz, Schott S. Contents: works by Buxtehude, Erbach, J. C. F. Fischer, G. Muffat, J. Pachelbel, Scheidt.

Early German Organ Music, ed. Marr, London, Hinrichsen. Contents: 6 pieces by Buchner, Finck, Ileborgh, Isaac.

Freie Orgelstücke alter Meister, I, ed. Graf, Kassel, Bärenreiter. Contents: J. C. F. Fischer, Kindermann, Krieger, Pachelbel, Zachow.

Fréie Orgelstücke alter Meister, ed. Stadtmüller, Tübingen, C. L. Schultheiss. Contents: Froberger, J. C. F. Fischer, Hassler, Kerll, Kindermann, J. Krieger, J. Ph. Krieger, Gottl. Muffat, Pachelbel, anonymous.

Frühmeister der deutschen Orgelkunst, I, ed. Moser-Heitmann, Wiesbaden, Breitkopf & Härtel. Contents: Brumann, Buchner, Hofhaimer, Isaac, Kleber, Kotter, Nachtigall, & Sicher.

Italienische und süddeutsche Orgelstücke des frühen 17. Jahrhunderts, ed. Lydia Schierning (Die Orgel 11/9), Lippstadt, Kistner & Siegel.

Orgelmeister des Barock, ed. H. A. Metzger, Tübingen, C. L. Schultheiss. Contents: 9 works by Buxtehude, Froberger, Hassler, Kerll, J. G. Walther, Zachow.

Orgelmusik an europäischen Kathedralen: Venedig, Augsburg, Müchen (Cantantibus Organis, Bk. II, gen'l ed., E. Kraus), Regensburg, Verlag Pustet. Contents: 12 pieces by A. & G. Gabrieli, Erbach, Guami, Hassler, Kerll, Lasso, Merulo, Murschhauser, Paix.

Orgelmusik an den Höfen der Habsburger; Wien zur Zeit Kaiser Leopolds I (Cantantibus Organis, Bk. XIII), Regensburg, Verlag Pustet. Contents: 23 pieces by Ebner, Froberger, Fux, Kerll, Poglietti, Reutter the Elder, Richter, Techelmann.

Orgelwerke alter Meister aus Süddeutschland, ed. H. A. Metzger, Tübingen, C. L. Schultheiss. Contents: 28 pieces by Erbach, Kerll, Kindermann, Lohet, Muffat, Murschhauser, Pachelbel, Scherer.

Ricercare, Canzonen und Fugen des 17. und 18. Jahrhunderts für Orgel oder Klavier, ed. Hillemann, Hannover, Nagels Verlag. Contents: Gabrieli, Cornet, Hassler, Erbach, Kerll, Murschhauser, Krieger, Pachelbel, Walther.

Süddeutsche Orgelmusik zum Weihnacht, ed. R. Walter, Altötting, Coppenrath. Contents: Christmas music by Pachelbel, Fischer, Poglietti, Murschhauser, Kindermann, etc.

Spielbuch für die Kleinorgel, I (Old Masters for the Small Organ), ed. Kaller, Frankfurt, C. F. Peters. Contents: 24 pieces by Cabezon, Frescobaldi, Froberger, Kerll, Maschera, Pachelbel, Paix, Scheidt, B. Schmid the Elder, B. Schmid the Younger, Steigleder, Sweelinck, Weckmann.

Toccaten des XVII. und XVIII. Jahrhunderts, ed. Kaller/Valentin (*Liber Organi,* V), Mainz, Schott S. Contents: Frescobaldi, Froberger, J. Pachelbel, W. H. Pachelbel, Geo. Muffat, Gottl. Muffat.

Zwei Orgelstücke aus einer Kärntner Orgeltabulatur des 16. Jahrhunderts, ed. Wilhelmer (*Musik alter Meister,* IX), Graz, Akademische Druck-und Verlagsanstalt, 1958. Contents: 1 piece by L. Senfl, 1 by an anonymous composer.

ABBREVIATIONS

Corpus of Early Keyboard Music, Dallas, American Institute of Musicology, 1963-   .

**Denkmaeler der Tonkunst in Bayern,* Braunschweig, H. Litolff's Verlag, 1900-1931.

***Denkmaeler der Tonkunst in Oesterreich, Vienna/Leipzig, Artaria/Breitkopf & Härtel (later, Vienna, Universal Edition) 1894-

MUSICAL SOURCES.

Ex. 1. *Alte Meister des Orgelspiels,* new edition, part II, ed. Straube, p. 64. Copyright C. F. Peters. Used by permission.

Ex. 2. *The First Four Centuries of Music for the Organ,* I, ed. Klein. Copyright 1948 by Associated Music Publishers, Inc. Used by permission.

Ex. 3. *Notre Pere* (*Orgue et Liturgie*, Bk. 24), Paris, Editions musicales de la Schola Cantorum, p. 3.

Ex. 4. *Historical Anthology of Music*, *II*, p. 64.

Ex. 5. *Geschichte des Orgelspiels und der Orgelkomposition*, Beispiel band, ed. Frotscher, pp. 63, 65. Copyright 1966 Merseburger, used by permission of C.F. Peters.

Ex. 6. *Historical Anthology of Music*, *II*, p. 113.

Ex. 7. *Muscia Sacra*, I, ed. F. Commer. Used by permission of Associated Music Publishers, Inc., Agents for Bote & Bock.

NOTES

[1] See "Organ Music Before 1500."

[2] See Apel, *Geschichte der Orgel-und Klaviermusik bis* 1700, p. 86, where a fragment of this piece has been reproduced.

[3] Frotscher, *Geschcihte des Orgelspiels*, I, 489.

NORTH AND MIDDLE GERMANY

Less is known about pre-Baroque organ music in north and middle Germany than in south Germany since most of the early manuscripts came from the southern part of the country. Still, the extremely progressive 17th-century north German school and the careful, orderly middle German school did not spring up full-blown without preparation. The *Ileborgh Tablature*[1] of 1448 was compiled in middle Germany, and several middle and north German manuscript fragments of the 15th century give evidence of early organ playing in this part of the country. From the *Ileborgh Tablature* it is clear that the pedal was used at least as early as the mid-15th century. Proof that pedal playing continued to be important in the 16th century is provided by north German Renaissance organs, which often had a variety of pedal stops. Thus, the virtuoso pedal technique which became a distinguishing feature of the north German Baroque school was based on an old tradition.

A few 16th-century manuscripts provide facts about compositional style in north and middle Germany. A Breslau manuscript, compiled c.1565, is believed to have contained a Lutheran chorale setting and liturgical versets written in imitative counterpoint in a style comparable to that of the south German, Hans Buchner. Although this manuscript disappeared after World War II, its contents are known through F. Dietrich's *Geschichte des deutschen Orgelchorals im* 17. *Jahrhundert* (1932), where they are listed and described.

From a Danzig manuscript of 1591

(Ms.300.R.Vv, 123, Archiwum Wojewódzkie), one sees that Italian keyboard music was influential in the north, since this manuscript was written in Italian, rather than German, keyboard notation. From style traits and forms employed by later German organists, it is clear that Italian keyboard music continued to be influential in north and middle Germany throughout the Baroque era. Yet it was not allowed to dominate as it did in south Germany and Austria.

A widespread use of Lutheran chorale melodies characterized organ playing in north and middle Germany. The organist often played a *Choralvorspiel* as the introduction to congregational singing. He also sometimes substituted *Choralbearbeitungen*[2] for congregational verses, since all of the stanzas of a chorale were supposed to be sung or played, regardless of their number. Given the liturgical importance of the chorale and its intensely personal meaning in the Reformation and post-Reformation eras, it is not surprising that chorale melodies were a chief source of inspiration for musicians in the Protestant areas of Germany. In middle Germany, *Choralbearbeitungen* actually outnumbered all other types of composition in the Baroque era. Among the early collections of chorale settings are two middle German tablatures: the *Orgel oder Instrument Tabulatur* (1571,[2]/1583) of Nicolaus Ammerbach and the *Tabulaturbuch auff dem Instrumente* (1598) of Augustus Nörmiger. While these books contained only simple, homophonic chorale settings, they formed part of the foundation for the middle German Baroque school of chorale composition. Other *Choralbearbeitungen,* most of them by anonymous composers, were collected in a north German manuscript, *Die Celler Orgeltabulatur* (1601). An interesting aspect of this tablature is the presence of style traits which point ahead to salient features of the north German Baroque school (fragmentation of a chorale melody, melismatic elaboration of the melody, echo effects, etc.).

The large, versatile instruments found in numerous churches in northern Germany, and to some extent, in middle Germany, must have had a formative influence on organ composition. The original impetus for these instruments had come from the Brabant builders of the Netherlands who were active in Germany (particularly northern Germany) in the 16th century. The north German instrument soon developed beyond its Brabant predecessor, with a greater variety of pedal stops being most noticeable. While the Brabant pedal was usually confined to *cantus firmus* stops, the German instrument had a full pedal chorus beginning at 16' or 32' pitch and going up to 2' or 1'. Nowhere in Europe did the full pedal chorus, with stops for both *cantus firmus* playing and for the bass line, appear with such regularity as in north Germany. Moreover, throughout the organ as a whole there existed a diversity of sonorities unequalled anywhere except in the Low Countries. An amazing variety of reed types was cultivated. The flutes, too, were distinctly different from each other. In addition, the *Werkprinzip,* on which the organ was based, created an independent character for each division. Each *Werk,* or division, of the organ was based upon a principal stop of a specific pitch, with the lowest located in the pedal, the next (an octave higher) in the *Hauptwerk,* the following in the *Positif,* and so on. The *Hauptwerk* had the fullest sound, the *Positif* was very penetrating, and the *Brustwerk* had high-pitched stops and a regal.

In middle Germany, the same general principles governed organ building in the early and middle Baroque periods, but middle German instruments seldom attained dimensions as imposing as those of prominent organs in the wealthy Hanseatic cities. Also, a smaller pedal division was typical in middle Germany. Otherwise, middle German organ building followed north German principles of construction until about 1700. At that time, a distinct middle German organ type evolved. It will be discussed later.

The leading center of organ playing in the north at the beginning of the 17th century was Hamburg. Lüneburg and Lübeck were also important, with Lübeck eventually superseding Hamburg. One of the earliest Hamburg organists of whom we have knowledge is Hieronymous Praetorius (1560-1629), who wrote a cycle of Magnificat versets. In some of the versets he took figuration and imitative motives drawn from fragments of the chorale phrase and interpolated these into the *cantus firmus.* This technique represents a preparatory step to the extremely free chorale treatment which eventually became characteristic of the north German school.

Another prominent figure among the north and middle Germans was the theorist and organ expert, Michael Praetorius (c. 1571-1621), whose immortality rests primarily on his *Syntagma musicum,* of which the second volume (*Organographia*) is a prime source of information on organs of that period. A transitional Renaissance-Baroque figure, Praetorius wrote only a few organ works. Three of his *Choralbearbeitungen* are extensive chorale motets employing Early Baroque style traits. They are precursors to the monumental chorale settings of the Baroque era.

Following these transitional figures, the leading organists of the Early Baroque period were men who studied with Sweelinck in Amsterdam: Samuel Scheidt, Jacob Praetorius, Melchior Schildt, and Heinrich Scheidemann. Small wonder that Sweelinck became known as the *Deutscher Organistenmacher!* Like Frescobaldi in Italy, Sweelinck's spiritual successors were his German students rather than his own countrymen. The Germans absorbed Sweelinck's technique (itself a union of English, Italian, Spanish, and Netherlandish traits), then combined it with their native tradition. A more extensive use of the pedal distinguishes Sweelinck's German students from Sweelinck himself.

Samuel Scheidt (1587-1654), one of Sweelinck's best students, stands somewhat apart from the others as the only middle German. His major organ works were published in 1624 under the title *Tabulatura nova.* This book contains fantasies, echo compositions, variations on secular songs and dances, and settings of German chorales, Latin hymns, Magnificats, and other liturgical pieces. The secular keyboard works and the fantasies and echos are closely modelled on Sweelinck's works. The other compositions are more individual. Nearly all of these remaining works, whether based on German chorales or on Latin chant, were written as variation cycles. Comparing his works with those of German composers a generation or two earlier (the "Colorists," for example), one sees that Scheidt's figuration is more varied and inventive — one result probably of his study with Sweelinck.

(Examples 8a, 8b)

At the end of the *Tabulatura nova* are registration indications, showing that Scheidt was not simply a general keyboardist, but an organist concerned with specific sonorities. In a typical Scheidt registration, the *cantus firmus* would be taken on the *Positif* or pedal with a sharp, biting sound, clearly differentiated from the other parts.

Strangely enough, Scheidt had no immediate followers of importance. The explanation for this may lie partly with the fact that the musician of prominence in middle Germany was the *Kantor,* or choir director, whose work overshadowed the organist's.

Scheidt, himself, was admired primarily for his choral music, much of it in the Venetian manner. Contrary to north German organists who sometimes became famous concert artists, middle German organists were provincial church musicians generally unknown outside their area.

As indicated by the relatively few surviving works of other early 17th century middle German organists (Christian Michael, Johann Klemm, etc.), Scheidt's contemporaries remained basically untouched by his organ style. More than anything else, they cultivated contrapuntal writing, especially fugal composition, and they showed a distinct preference for brevity — in opposition to the north Germans who were already writing very extended compositions. Fugal writing and brevity eventually became trademarks of the middle German school.

Since Scheidt had no real successors, it was Sweelinck's north German students who transmitted his art, together with their own important additions, to successive generations of organists in an unbroken line up to, and after, Bach. Among Sweelinck's disciples in the north, Jacob Praetorius (1586-1651) occupied a prominent place. That he was highly respected is underscored by the fact that Heinrich Schuetz, in Dresden, sent a student, Matthias Weckmann, to Hamburg to study with him. Included in Praetorius' preserved

Ex. 8a. Scheidt, *Cantio sacra: Warum betrübst du dich, mein Herz,* Verse 3, m. 1-5.

Ex. 8b. Scheidt, *Cantio sacra: Warum betrübst du dich, mein Herz,* Verse 7, m. 1-5.

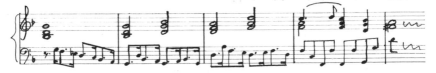

works are three pieces entitled *Preambula*. They are actually embryonic appearances of that combination "Prelude and Fugue" which later became important.

The Hannover organist, Melchior Schildt (c. 1592-1667) likewise attained fame, but, as in the case of J. Praetorius, only a few of his works have been preserved. Schildt's works do not show as much individuality as do those of Praetorius, nor as much as do the works of another Sweelinck pupil, Heinrich Scheidemann.

Scheidemann (c. 1596-1663) was a musician of broad scope. Unlike some composers who concentrated on only one or two forms of *Choralbearbeitungen*, Scheidemann cultivated all the major forms of chorale composition known in his day: chorale variations, chorale motets, the chorale with ornamented soprano melody line, compositions with the *cantus firmus* in the pedal, chorale fantasies, etc. Some of his chorale settings have an expressiveness which tends toward a subjective interpretation of the chorale. He also wrote free pieces, i.e., compositions not based on a chorale or *cantus firmus*. Among his works in the latter category are preludes, toccatas, fugues, a variation canzona, dances, and intabulations.

Contemporary with Praetorius, Scheidt, and Scheidemann were a number of lesser lights, some of whom are believed to have been Sweelinck students: David Abel, Paul Siefert (both active in northeastern Germany, now a part of Poland), Andreas Düben (employed in Stockholm), and Peter Hasse the Elder. There also exists a large body of anonymous literature from this period. Together with signed compositions, many anonymous works were preserved in the Lynar and the Lüneburg Tablatures, the two most comprehensive sources of Early Baroque north German organ music.

Delphin Strungk (1601-1694), organist in Wolfenbüttel and Braunschweig, is another organ composer worthy of note. Chief among his preserved works are a toccata and two variation cycles, one on the Magnificat, the other on a Lutheran chorale. In both of the variation cycles, the last variation resembles a chorale fantasy.

This form, the chorale fantasy, while prepared by numerous musicians, first crystallized into a firmly-outlined type under the hands of Franz Tunder (1614-1667). Tunder often presented each phrase of the *cantus firmus* both in the soprano (ornamented) and in the bass (unornamented). Taking fragments from the ornamented soprano *cantus firmus,* he made motives which he then treated in a variety of ways (with contrapuntal imitation, echo repetition, etc.). Fragmentation of the melody remained a basic principle of all subsequent chorale fantasy composition.

In addition to chorale fantasies, Tunder wrote other types of *Choralbearbeitungen*, a canzona, and preludes (which are actually 3-part toccatas). Characteristic of his style are virtuoso pedal lines, bold improvisational passagework, and melodic lines which are more flexible and flowing than the melodies of earlier north German composers. The grandeur and breath-taking qualities which would become the very soul of the north German school are first fully realized in the music of Tunder.

(Example 9)

Tunder organized a series of public organ recitals at St. Marien in Lübeck, where he was organist from 1641-1667. Some concerts took place during the day, when the merchants gathered to await the opening of the stock market, others during the evening. The eve-

Ex. 9. Tunder, *Christ Lag in Todtes Banden*, m. 10-12.

ning concerts, known as *Abendmusiken*, reached their greatest fame under the direction of Tunder's successor, Dietrich Buxtehude. During this era the north German organist was elevated to the role of concert artist.

Contemporary with Tunder was Matthias Weckmann (c. 1619-1674), whose works were totally different. Weckmann was born in middle Germany, but spent much of his adult life in the north. His chorale compositions consist exclusively of chorale variations written in a conservative manner. The following unusual type of composition frequently appeared in his variation cycles: the *cantus firmus* was placed in the bass and was overlaid with four or five contrapuntal voices. His free works — preludes, fugues, toccatas, suites, etc. — were influenced by Froberger, with whom Weckmann became acquainted during his (Weckmann's) years as court organist in Dresden.

Johann (Jan) Adam Reincken (1623-1722), like Tunder, was a true north German. His well-known toccata is composed of alternating free and fugal sections and displays that love of fantasy and brilliance which is synonymous with the north German school. Reincken's two preserved chorale compositions are extensive chorale fantasies employing the most progressive technical and compositional means of his day.

With Dietrich Buxtehude (c. 1637-1707), north German organ music reached its climax. A native of Denmark, although probably of German descent, Buxtehude was organist for many years at the Marienkirche, Lübeck, where he attracted numerous listeners and devout disciples. Chief among Buxtehude's works are the preludes and fugues, a passacaglia, and two ciacona. The preludes and fugues are actually toccatas in which free and fugal sections are set in opposition. Often the five-part toccata form was used. The free sections, with their audacious dissonances and forceful, driving passage work, are perhaps the most direct ex-

pression of his genius. Strongly-outlined fugue themes, some of them with tone-repetition (*Reperkussionsthema*), introductory pedal solos, and pedal trills are other noteworthy features. In all of his large works, one is impressed by the tension holding these monumental, highly-sectionalized works together. Thematic relationship between sections was certainly one of the techniques used to produce this tension. In the preludes and fugues, for example, a motivic relationship often unified the fugal sections: the subject of the first fugue would be altered melodically and rhythmically to become the subject, or subjects, of the next fugue(s).

(Example 10)

In addition to the free compositions mentioned, Buxtehude also wrote a number of canzoni and some pieces entitled *Toccata*.

Within the field of chorale composition, Buxtehude contributed a number of large works, plus 30 short chorale preludes. Among the more extensive *Choralbearbeitungen* are chorale variations, chorale motets, chorale fantasies, Magnificats, and a Te Deum. As in the free works, one marvels at his ability to combine bravura technique with a profound sensitivity to form and color. The chorale fantasies are lengthy, sectionalized works in the Tunder tradition.

The 30 short *Choralvorspiele* are among Buxtehude's most influential compositions. Nearly all of them belong to the type known as the ornamented melody chorale. With their emotional melody lines, they expressed perfectly the faith of that day, and they served as an inspiration to many composers, including J. S. Bach.

Approximately contemporary with Buxtehude were four distinguished organists — Vincent Lübeck, Nikolaus Bruhns, Johann Nikolaus Hanff, and Georg Böhm. Also active were Christian Ritter (c. 1645- after 1725), Andreas Kneller (1649-1724), Daniel Erich

Ex. 10. Buxtehude, *Praeludium und Fuge* (d), fugue subjects, m. 19-22, 64-68.

(c. 1660-1712), Georg Dietrich Leiding (c. 1664-1710), and Arnold Melchior Brunkhorst (c. 1670-1720).

Vincent Lübeck (1656-1740) was organist in Stade from 1675 to 1702 and thereafter in Hamburg. Among his preserved works are preludes and fugues and *Choralbearbeitungen*. Like Buxtehude's works of the same name, Lübeck's preludes and fugues are generally toccata-like compositions. Characteristic of Lübeck's work in this genre is a virtuoso display of manual and pedal technique, including occasional double pedalling.

(Example 11)

His preserved *Choralbearbeitungen,* doubtless only a fraction of that which he wrote, consist of a chorale fantasy, a set of chorale variations, and a chaconne based on a chorale theme.

Similar in style to Lübeck's preludes and fugues are the preludes and fugues of Nikolaus Bruhns (1665-1697). A fantastic, sensuous exuberance pervades them. Bruhns' large *Prelude and Fugue in E Minor* is particularly remarkable for its intense dramatic qualities. Bruhns also wrote a large chorale fantasy. He was organist at the church in Husum (North Friesland) until his early death at the age of 32.

A distinctly different contribution was made by Johann Nikolaus Hanff (1665-1711), middle German by birth, but one who spent most of his adult life in north Germany. All that have survived of his works are six *Choralvorspiele*. They follow basically the Buxtehude-type of ornamented melody chorale, and they have considerable imitative treatment in the lower voices during the interludes between chorale phrases. Noteworthy in Hanff's chorale preludes is the composer's conscious attempt to translate the meaning of the chorale text into musical language.

A versatile composer was Georg Böhm (1661-1733), who was educated in middle Germany, but spent his mature years in the north. He employed elements from all of the German schools (north, middle, and south), together with traits of the French manner. Some of his keyboard works are idiomatic to the organ, some were clearly written for a stringed keyboard instrument (the suites), and others fall into that intermediate category of general keyboard music. In some of his preludes and fugues he followed closely the north German model. In the *Prae ludium in F* and the *Praeludium, Fuge und Postludium,* however, he adopted a French approach. The overture style of Lully was the basis for the former work, while the various ornaments and mannerisms of the *clavecin* school gave the second work its particular flavor.

Ex. 11. Lübeck, *Praeludium und Fugue* (g), m. 49-52, 107-110.

Within the category of *Choralbear-beitungen,* he wrote chorale variations, chorale partitas, and *Choralvorspiele.* In the chorale variations, or chorale variation cycles as they are also called, Böhm followed the tradition of Scheidt, Scheidemann, Strungk, and others. This means that the melody might appear in any voice. Sometimes it was a strict *cantus firmus,* sometimes it was ornamented, other times it provided material for a chorale motet, etc. For the proper realization of cyclical chorale variations, the pedal was required and contrasting organ colors were needed. In Böhm's chorale partitas, on the other hand, the melody usually remained in the soprano voice. A general keyboard style predominated, so that the composition was as effective on harpsichord as on the organ. This type of composition — the chorale partita — first rose to prominence with Böhm, although earlier examples can be found in the works of other composers.

(Example 12)

Turning now to middle Germany, one recalls that Samuel Scheidt was the only organist of import during the first part of the 17th century. By the latter half of the century several significant organists were there. Heading the list of native-born Thüringians were members of the Bach family, who had been musical leaders in this province from the 16th century. Among organists of that family prior to J. S. Bach were two brothers, Johann Christoph (1642-1703) and Johann Michael Bach (1648-1694). Johann Christoph Bach (not to be confused with J. S. Bach's brother of the same name) wrote a collection of chorale preludes entitled

44 *Choräle zum Praembulieren.* Each composition was a chorale fugue, or chorale fugato, with the first phrase of the chorale serving as the fugue theme.

(Example 13)

Concentrated imitative treatment of some or all of the remaining chorale phrases sometimes followed. Because of its concise form and its appropriateness as an introduction to congregational singing, this form became increasingly popular with middle German organists. As indicated earlier, short, modest forms were typical of the middle German school, as opposed to the extensive virtuoso compositions of the north Germans.

Johann Michael Bach, is believed to have written a large number of chorale settings, although only eight have survived. From these few preserved works, it is apparent that he wrote *Choralbearbeitungen* of several different types. Like many middle Germans, he preferred contrapuntal writing.

Contemporary with Johann Christoph and Johann Michael Bach was Johann Pachelbel (1653-1706), a native of south Germany. His list of compositions includes free works and chorale settings. His *Choralbearbeitungen* made an immense impression in Thüringia. His free works (Magnificat fugues, toccatas, fantasies, suites, etc.), basically in the south German tradition, had less impact in Thüringia. Within the area of chorale composition, Pachelbel concentrated primarily on three types: the chorale fugue; the *cantus firmus* chorale, with pre-imitation of each phrase of the *cantus firmus* in the accompanying voices; the so-called "Combination-Form," which begins with a

Ex. 12. Böhm, *Ach wie nichtig, ach wie flüchtig,* Partita 4, m. 1–2; Partita 5, m. 1–2.

Ex. 13. J. C. Bach, *Wenn wir in höchsten Nöten sein,* m. 1–7.

chorale fugue on the opening phrase and continues with a 3- or 4-part setting of the entire melody. Pachelbel's development of the *cantus firmus* chorale was his most far-reaching contribution to middle German organ practice. This type of chorale setting soon joined the chorale fugato as a leading compositional form.[3]

Among the middle Germans influenced by Pachelbel were Johann Michael and Johann Bernard Bach (1676-1749). Both wrote *cantus firmus* chorales in the Pachelbel style. Another was Johann Christoph Bach (1671-1721), Johann Sebastian's oldest brother, who studied for three years with Pachelbel and may have transmitted the Pachelbel tradition to him (J. S. Bach). Zachow, Vetter, Armsdorff, and Buttstett are other middle Germans whose style was partially determined by Pachelbel's example.

Besides Pachelbel, the brothers Johann Philipp Krieger (1649-1725) and Johann Krieger (1651-1735) were two other south Germans active in middle Germany. While the older brother was the more famous of the two, the younger one, Johann Krieger, had the most to offer in the realm of keyboard music. He wrote preludes, ricercars, fugues, toccatas, *Choralbearbeitungen* (especially chorale fugatos), and suites. The Kriegers promoted south German and Italian forms and techniques among their middle German students and associates.

Another "foreigner" who settled in middle Germany was Johann Friedrich Alberti (1642-1710), a native of Schleswig in the north. His preserved works consist of four *Choralbearbeitungen*. Very few north German organists seemed drawn to middle Germany, although the reverse was certainly true. Among the middle Germans who took up residence in the north were Matthias Weckmann, Christian Ritter, Johann Nikolaus Hanff, and Georg Böhm. They could possibly be listed with the middle German school rather than with the northern one.

Andreas Werckmeister (1645-1706), organist in Quedlinburg and Halberstadt, merits attention by virtue of his *Orgel-Probe* and his *Musicalische Temperatur*. Together with other studies in temperament, the *Musicalische Temperatur* (1686/87; ²/1691) had a profound effect on Late Baroque keyboard literature. It made available

many new keys based on the circle of fifths. The most famous collections exploring the well-tempered system were J. C. F. Fischer's *Ariadne Musica* (c. 1702) and J. S. Bach's *Wohltemperierte Klavier* (1722). Johann Bernard Bach also wrote a number of fugues in the new keys, some of them with rather distant modulations.

In the generation following Pachelbel, the leading figures were Friedrich W. Zachow (1663-1712) and Johann Heinrich Buttstett (1666-1727). The chorale fugue was an important form for both of them. Zachow also favored the simple melody chorale (which is the type of composition that dominates in Bach's *Orgelbüchlein*). While both composers were strongly influenced by Pachelbel, Buttstett was drawn, in addition, to the north German school. He composed Buxtehude-type ornamented melody chorales and free works displaying north German features.

Active during the same period were Nicolaus Vetter (1666-1734) and Andreas Armsdorff (1670-1699). Both wrote chorale preludes in the usual middle German forms, plus ornamented melody chorales in the Buxtehude style. Also to be mentioned in passing is Johann Kuhnau (1660-1722), remembered primarily for his programmatic sonatas, *Musicalische Vorstellung einiger Biblischer Historien in 6 Sonaten*. Organist and *Kantor* at the Thomaskirche in Leipzig, Kuhnau left only a few organ works, including a toccata of north German inspiration.

The adoption of forms and style traits from the north Germans and the south Germans became more and more characteristic of the middle German school in the Late Baroque era. By virtue of its geographical location, or partly so, middle Germany gradually became a territory in which the more conservative south German manner could meet with the imaginative, adventuresome north German style. Perhaps the fact that middle Germany did not have as prestigious an organ tradition as did its southern and northern neighbors also helped to make this territory a fertile land for the mingling of outside influences.

In works of Johann Gottfried Walther (1684-1748), a union of diverse style traits is particularly obvious. Walther had an exceptionally broad knowledge of contemporary compositional practices. His *Choralbearbeitungen* encompass all the techniques known to the north and middle Germans. As a true middle German, he preferred contrapuntal writing and excelled in it by combining contrapuntal techniques in an unprecedented variety of ways. One of his specialties was canonic writing, ranging from simple, 2-part canon to subtle complicated types.

(Example 14)

In his free works, Walther aligned himself particularly with south German and Italian composition. Best known are his organ concerti — transcriptions for organ of instrumental concerti in the Italian style. His preludes and fugues were likewise inspired by instrumental concerto music, but in combination with the melodic figuration of the south German prelude. A limited adoption of the French overture style is also noticeable.

Next to J. S. Bach, Walther was the leading organ composer in middle Germany in the 18th century. Besides composing, he compiled the first music lexicon in the German language, the *Musicalisches Lexicon* (1732), which has considerable historical value.

Contemporary with Walther was the eminent Georg Philipp Telemann (1681-1767). A native of middle Germany, he was educated and employed there until 1721, when he moved to Hamburg to become general music director. Telemann was not primarily an organist, yet he did write a number of simple *Choralbearbeitungen* and other keyboard pieces.

Johann Sebastian Bach (1685-1750), like his cousin J. G. Walther, drew upon the techniques of several schools. Within his *Choralbearbeitungen* one finds chorale fugues, *cantus firmus* chorales in the Pachelbel style, simple melody chorales, ornamented melody chorales (Buxtehude-type), chorale partitas, chorale fantasies, and other traditional forms. In Bach's chorale compositions, the middle German preference for moderation was combined with the intense, emotional expression of the northern school. The intricate ornaments of the French keyboard style, promulgated in Germany by Böhm and other keyboardists, also appeared in Bach's *Choralbearbeitungen*. In addition, styles of writing idiomatic to opera and to cantata composition were sometimes transformed into an organ style (Schübler chorales, etc.). Bach obviously had mastered all of the styles and forms of the north and middle Germans, and could combine them with traits of the south German and French keyboard schools, as well as with the Italian operatic and instrumental styles. Yet, interestingly, in his late *Choralbearbeitungen,* the one element which usually dominates is a typically middle German one — well-balanced counterpoint.

In the realm of free composition, there are fantasies, toccatas, a passacaglia, preludes, fugues, trios, trio sonatas, concerti, and many other works. The spirit of the north German school presides over the preludes, toccatas, and fantasies written during Bach's early and middle periods. Dramatic passage-work, bold pedal solos, and other bravura techniques play a leading role in these works. Free compositions of his mature years are less easy to categorize, partly because a wider range of influences is present and partly because Bach often fused elements taken from other schools into new entities which had not existed before.

In Bach's organ fugues one notes that the subjects are particularly well-outlined and that a singing quality is

Ex. 14. Walther, *Mache dich, mein Geist bereit,* m. 1-4.

there, making these works more satisfying than earlier composition in this
genre. Often Bach combined the fugue
with a prelude, a toccata, or fantasie
to form the typical Late Baroque
"Prelude and Fugue."

The concerti, the trios, and trio sonatas are linked with contemporary
instrumental music. Bach's organ concerti, like Walther's, were transcriptions
of instrumental concerti in the Italian
manner. The trios and trio sonatas, although not transcribed from existing
pieces, were obviously inspired by Italian chamber music and by the Italian
violin concerto. This constant absorption of outer influences is astonishing
because it is never disruptive. The
highly divergent elements never conflict. They always submerge into something bigger than themselves, only to
reappear transformed into a new creation. Since the Bach works merit a
complete study by themselves, this survey will make no attempt to treat them
further.

Bach's historical position, as everyone
knows, was that of a finisher, not an
innovator. When one examines the
compositions of some of his contemporaries, it becomes apparent that other
organists were moving into a new
aesthetic. A case in point is
Georg Friedrich Kauffmann (1679-
1735). While his style of writing
was still basically Baroque, although
with added emphasis on harmonic
structure, his registration markings dis-
close a pre-Classic concept of sound.
There is no indication that he tried to
imitate the orchestra, as some later
Classical organ composers did, but he
favored mellow combinations with 8'
and 16' predominating.

Changes in middle German organ
building after 1700 denote an increasing preference for deeper, heavier
sonorities. The fundamental tone of
the *organo pleno* became more prominent than it had been in Early Baroque organs. More emphasis was laid
on blending of stops than on maintaining the independent character of each.
The snarling reeds of the north German
school were replaced by fuller, rounder
reeds. These were less successful as
cantus firmus voices, but could be combined more smoothly with other organ
stops. Mixtures and cymbals on the
middle German organ after 1700 were
characteristically mild. Fewer pedal
stops were present. In fact, the Gottfried Silbermann organs often had

only 16' and 8' pedal stops, indicating
that the pedal was usually confined to
playing the bass line.

Silbermann organs, which conformed
to Late Baroque sound ideals, became
the prototype for organ building in
the province of Saxony. They usually
had no *Rückpositif* and no independent
pedal towers — a visual reflection of
the new sonoral ideals. The specifications represent a synthesis of French
and middle German design.

In Thuringia, the foremost builder
of this period was Zacharias Hildebrandt, a Silbermann student. Although
Hildebrandt's instruments were definitely 18th century in concept, they
remained more in the German Baroque
tradition than did the instruments of
Silbermann. Most noticeable is the
greater variety of stop types in a Hildebrandt specification. Bach sometimes
served as consultant for Hildebrandt
organs.

There has been much speculation concerning the type of organ that Bach
may have preferred. From his student,
Agricola, we know that Bach was very
impressed with the large, 4-manual
organ in the Catharinenkirche in Hamburg, especially with its beautiful, north
German reeds.[4] The specification which
Bach designed for the re-building of
his organ in Mühlhausen (1708) was
basically in the north German tradition. A *Brustwerk* was added, plus new
stops on existing *Oberwerk*, *Rückpositif*, and pedal. Each of the manual
divisions had a *Sesquialtera*, and the
pedal was complete, from a 32' *Untersatz* up to a 1' *Rohrfeife*. The addition of a 32', Bach had said, would
add depth and solemnity to the tone.[5]

To what extent Bach's organ concept
may have been modified in later years
is not known. Some of Bach's later
works (the large *Prelude and Fugue in
E Minor*, for example) appear to call
for an organ in which the planes of
sound provide a continuity of concept,
rather than sudden contrast. Yet, from
the technical standpoint, this new,
milder, middle German organ type
could not have been the ideal vehicle
for all of the Bach works. First of
all, the limited number of pedal stops
could not do justice to the very active
pedal lines in many of the preludes
and fugues. Secondly, the smaller number of *cantus firmus* voices (especially
on the Silbermann instruments) would
not provide as much variety for the

42

Choralbearbeitungen as would the north German organs. Thus, the question of Bach's ideal organ type cannot be completely resolved.

EDITIONS

Bach, Joh. Christoph: 44 *Choräle zum Präambulieren,* ed. *Fischer, Kassel,* Bärenreiter.

Bach, J. S.: *Johann Sebastian Bachs Werke,* Leipzig, Bach-Gesellschaft, 1851-99/ suppl., 1932. Vols. III, XV, XXV, XXXVIII, XL contain the organ works. Dover Publications (New York, 1970) has republished the *Orgelwerke* of the Bach-Gesellschaft edition. *Neue Ausgabe Sämtlicher Werke,* Kassel, Bärenreiter (together with the Deutscher Verlag for Musik, Leipzig), 1954 — . The organ works are in Series Four, of which vols. II through VI have appeared to date. *Sämtliche Orgelwerke,* 9 vols., ed. Griepenkerl/Roitzsch, Leipzig, C. F. Peters, 1844 ff; republished, 1940. *Organ Works,* 8 vols., ed. Widor/Schweizer (vols. I-V) and Schweizer/Nies-Berger (vols. VI-VIII), New York, 1912-1967. *Oeuvres complètes pour orgue,* 12 vols., ed. Dupré, Paris, Bornemann. *Sämtliche Orgelwerke,* 9 vols., ed. Naumann, Leipzig/Wiesbaden, Breitkopf & Härtel. *Sämtliche Orgelwerke,* 10 vols., ed. Lohmann, Wiesbaden, Breitkopf & Härtel. Vols. VI-X have appeared; vols. I-V are in preparation. *Choralvorspiel-Sammlungen in der Folge des Autographs,* 3 vols., Frankfurt, C. F. Peters.

Böhm: *Klavier-und Orgelwerke,* 2 vols., ed. Wolgast *(Sämtliche Werke,* I), Leipzig, Breitkopf & Härtel, 1927. Contents: Vol. I — free compositions and keyboard suites; Vol. II — choralbearbeitungen. 5 *Praeludien und Fugen,* ed. Seiffert *(Organum,* IV/4), Leipzig, Kistner & Siegel.

Bruhns: *Orgelwerke,* ed. Stein *(Das Erbe Deutscher Musik,* Landschaftsdenkmäle, Schleswig-Holstein, Series II/2), Braunschweig, H. Litolff, 1937/39. Reprint of the *Orgelwerke* by C. F. Peters (Frankfurt). 3 *Präludien und Fugen,* ed. Seiffert *(Organum,* IV/8), Leipzig, Kistner & Siegel.

Buxtehude: *Sämtliche Orgelwerke,* 4 vols., ed. Spitta/Seiffert, Leipzig/Wiesbaden, Breitkopf & Härtel, 1875-1939, ²/1952. Contents: Vols. I/II — free works; Vols. III/IV — choralbearbeitungen, *Sämtliche Orgelwerke,* 2 vols., ed. Beckman, Wiesbaden, Breitkopf & Härtel. 1971-72. Vol I: free works, Vol. II: choralbearbeitungen. *Sämtliche Orgelwerke,* 4 vols., ed. Hedar, Copenhagen, Hansen, 1952. Vol. I: passacaglia, ciacona, canzone, etc.; Vol. II: preludes and fugues, toccatas; Vol. III: chorale fantasies and variations; Vol. IV: chorale preludes. *Neue Orgelwerke,* ed. Hedar, Copenhagen, Hansen, 1950. Contents: previously unknown organ works from the Wenster-Engelhardt collection. *Ausgewählte Orgelwerke* (Selected Organ Works), 3 vols., ed. Keller, Leipzig, C. F. Peters, 1938/39/66. Vol. I: free works; Vol. II: choralbearbeitungen; Vol. III: free works.

Hanff: 6 chorale preludes are in *Choralvorspiele alter Meister,* ed. Straube, Frankfurt, C. F. Peters, 1907. The same in *Masterpieces of Organ Music,* No. 61, ed. White, New York, The Liturgical Music Press, 1949.

Kauffmann: *Harmonische Seelenlust,* ed. Pidoux, Kassel, Bärenreiter, 1951. Contents: 63 choralbearbeitungen, of which 6 are for organ and oboe. *Six Chorales from the "Harmonischen Seelenlust,"* for organ and oboe, ed. Gore, St. Louis, Concordia.

Krieger, Joh.: *Gesammelte Werke für Klavier und Orgel,* ed. Seiffert *(DTB,* XVIII). See preceding entry. *Präludien und Fugen,* ed. Riedel *(Die Orgel,* II/3), Lippstadt, Kistner & Siegel, 1957. *Ausgewählte Orgelstücke,* ed. Seiffert *(Organum* IV/17), Leipzig, Kistner & Siegel, 1930.

Krieger, Joh.Ph.: *Gesammelte Werke für Klavier und Orgel,* ed. Seiffert *(Denkmäler der Tonkunst in Bayern,* XVIII), Leipzig, Breitkopf & Härtel, 1917. Contents: collected works of J.Ph. Krieger, J. Krieger, and Murschhauser.

Kuhnau: 2 *Praeludien mit Fugen und eine Toccata,* ed. Seiffert *(Organum,* IV/19) Lippstadt, Kistner & Siegel.

Lübeck: *Orgelwerke*, ed. Keller, Leipzig, C. F. Peters, 1941. Contents: complete preludes and fugues, choralbearbeitungen. 4 *Präludien und Fugen*, ed. Seiffert (*Organum*, IV/9), Leipzig, Kistner & Siegel. *Six Préludes et Fugues* (*Orgue et Liturgie*, Bk. 17), Paris, Schola Cantorum. *Praeludium og Fuga* (G), ed. Hedar, Copenhagen, Hansen, 1953. *Klavierübung*, ed. Trede, Frankfurt, C. F. Peters, 1941. Contents: *Prelude and Fugue* (a), *Suite* (g), *Chaconne on "Lobt Gott ihr Christen allzugleich."*

Pachelbel: See the survey of South German literature and editions.

Praetorius, Hieronymous: *Organ Magnificats*, ed. Rayner (*Corpus of Early Keyboard Music* IV), Dallas, American Institute of Musicology, 1963.

Praetorius, Michael: *Sämtliche Orgelwerke*, ed. Gurlitt (*Archiv für Musikwissenschaft*, III), Leipzig, C. F. W. Siegel, 1921. *Sämtliche Orgelwerke*, ed. Matthaei, Wolfenbüttel/Berlin, Kallmeyer Verlag; reprinted, Wolfenbüttel, Möseler Verlag, 1930. *Ein feste Burg*, ed. Fischer, Hannover, Nagel, 1929. *Fantasy on "A Mighty Fortress,"* ed. Fleischer, St. Louis, Concordia. *Fantasy on "We All Believe in One True God,"* ed. Fleischer, St. Louis, Concordia.

Reincken: *Collected Keyboard Works*, ed. Apel (*Corpus of Early Keyboard Music*, XVI), Dallas, American Institute of Musicology, 1967. Contents: chorale fantasies, toccata, suites, etc.

Scheidemann: 15 *Praeludien und Fugen*, ed. Seiffert (*Organum*, IV/1), Leipzig, Kistner & Siegel. *Choralbearbeitungen*, ed. Foch, Kassel, Bärenreiter, 1966.

Scheidt: *Tabulatura nova*, ed. Seiffert (*Denkmäler der Deutschen Tonkunst*, I), Leipzig, Breitkopf & Härtel, 1892. The same, ed. Mahrenholz (*Samuel Scheidts Werke*, VI/VII), Hamburg, Ugrino Verlag, 1934- . *Das Görlitzer Tabulaturbuch*, ed. Mahrenholz, Leipzig, Peters, 1941. The same, ed. Dietrich, Kassel, Bärenreiter, 1941. *Ausgewählte Orgelwerke*, ed. Keller, Frankfurt,

Peters. Contents: German and Latin hymns, fantasies, canons, lied variations, dance variations. *Liedvariationen für Klavier*, ed. Auler, Mainz, Schott S. *Magnificat quinti toni*, ed. Fleischer, St. Louis, Concordia. *Variations on "When Jesus on the Cross Was Bound,"* ed. Buszin, St. Louis, Concordia.

Schildt: *Choralbearbeitungen*, ed. Breig (*Organum*, IV/24), Lippstadt, Kistner & Siegel.

Siefert. P.: 13 *Fantasien à 3*, ed. Seiffert (*Organum*, IV/20), Lippstadt, Kistner & Siegel.

Strungk, D.: *Zwei Choralfantasien*, ed. Krumbach (*Die Orgel*, II/12), Leipzig, Kistner & Siegel.

Telemann: *Orgelwerke*, 2 vols., ed. Fedtke, Kassel, Bärenreiter. Vol. I: choralbearbeitungen; Vol. II: free works. *Forty-Eight Chorale Preludes*, ed. Thaler (*Recent Researches in the Music of the Baroque Era*, II), New Haven, A-R Editions, 1965. 20 *kleine Fugen*, ed. Uppmeyer, Hannover, Nagel. 12 *leichte Choralvorspiele*, ed. Keller, Frankfurt, C. F. Peters. 24 *Variirte Choräle*, 3 parts (*L'Organiste liturgique*, Bks. 28, 32, 36), Paris, Schola Cantorum.

Tunder: 4 *Praeludien*, ed. Seiffert (*Organum*, IV/6), Leipzig, Kistner & Siegel. *Sämtliche Choralbearbeitungen*, ed. Walter, Mainz, Schott S., 1959. Contents: 7 choralbearbeitungen of the Lüneburg tablatures.

Walther: *Gesammelte Werke für Orgel*, ed. Seiffert (*Denkmäler der Deutschen Tonkunst*, XXVI/XXVIII), Leipzig, Breitkopf & Härtel, 1906. *Ausgewählte Orgelwerke*, 3 vols., ed. Lohmann, Wiesbaden, Breitkopf & Härtel, 1966. Contents: Vol. I — choralbearbeitungen A-H; Vol. II — choralbearbeitungen A-Z; Vol. III — preludes, fugues, concerti, etc. *Orgelchoräle*, ed. Poppen, Kassel, Bärenreiter, 1930, 4/1956. Contents: 52 choralbearbeitungen. 3 *Orgelchoräle*, ed. Matthaei, Kassel, Bärenreiter. *Orgelkonzerte nach verschiedenen Meistern*, ed. Auler, Kassel, Bärenreiter, 1942. 5 *ausgewählte Orgelstücke*, ed. Seiffert (*Organum*, IV/5), Leipzig, Kistner & Siegel, 1930. *Orgelkonzert in c*, ed. Herford, Frankfurt, C. F. Peters. *A Collec-*

tion of Chorale Preludes, ed. Beck, St. Louis, Concordia. Memorial Collection of Organ Preludes and Variations by Johann Gottfried Walther, ed. Buszin (Anthology of Sacred Music, II), St. Louis, Concordia.

Weckmann: Gesammelte Werke, ed. Ilgner (Das Erbe Deutscher Musik, Landschaftsdenkmäle, Schleswig-Holstein und Hansestädte, Series II/4), Leipzig, H. Litolff, 1942. 14 Präeludien, Fugen und Toccaten, ed. Seiffert (Organum, IV/3), Leipzig, Kistner & Siegel.

Zachow: Gesammelte Werke, ed. Seiffert (Denkmäler der Deutschen Tonkunst, XXI/XXII), Leipzig, Breitkopf & Härtel, 1905. Gesammelte Werke für Tasteninstrumente (Collected Works for Keyboard Instruments), ed. Lohmann, Wiesbaden, Brietkopf & Härtel, 1967. 3 Fugen, ed. Seiffert (Organum, IV/16), Leipzig, Kistner & Siegel. Choralvorspiele für Orgel, ed. Adrio, Berlin/Darmstadt, Merseburger, 1953.

Collections

There are many general collections in which north and middle German works figure prominently. The following are some of the most important ones:

Allein Gott in der Höh sei Ehr, ed. Moser/Fedtke, Kassel, Bärenreiter. Contents: 20 settings of this chorale by members of the German Sweelinck school.

Alte deutsche Weihnachtsmusik, ed. Steglich, Hannover, Nagel. Contents: Christmas music by north, middle, & south German composers.

Alte Meister des Orgelspiels, new edition in 2 vols., ed. Straube, Frankfurt, C. F. Peters. Contents: 29 compositions by leading north and middle German composers, and by others.

Anonymi der Norddeutschen Schule, ed. Seiffert (Organum, IV/10), Leipzig, Kistner & Siegel. Six preludes and fugues by anonymous north German composers.

Choralbearbeitungen und freie Orgelstücke der deutschen Sweelinck-Schule, 3 parts, ed. Moser/Fedtke, Kassel, Bärenreiter. Contents: chorale settings and free works. Part 1 — Abel, Carges, Düben, Scheidemann, Sivert; Part 2 — Düben, Druckenmüller, Lorentz, Scheidemann, Scheidt, Sweelinck; Part 3 — Sweelinck.

46 Choräle von J. P. Sweelinck und seinen deutschen Schülern, ed. Gerdes, Akademie der Wissenschaften und der Literatur, Mainz, Schott S., 1957. Contents: choralbearbeitungen by Sweelinck, J. Praetorius, Schildt, etc.

Chorale Preludes by Masters of the XVII and XVIII Centuries, ed. Buszin (Anthology of Sacred Music, I), St. Louis, Concordia. Works by Armsdorff, J. C. Bach, Böhm, Buxtehude, Scheidemann, Walther, Weckmann, etc.

Choralvorspiele alter Meister, ed. Straube, Leipzig, C. F. Peters, 1907. Contains 45 chorale preludes.

80 Choralvorspiele des 17. und 18. Jahrhunderts, ed. Keller, Leipzig, C. F. Peters.

The Free Organ Compositions from the Lüneburg Tablatures, 2 vols., ed. Shannon, St. Louis, Concordia, 1958. Contents: mostly works by anonymous composers.

Freie Orgelvorspiele vorbachischer Meister, 2 vols., ed. Seiffert, Lippstadt, Kistner & Siegel. Contents: works by Praetorius, Pachelbel, Scheidemann, Tunder, Chr. Flor, D. Meyer, Zachow, Kuhnau, etc.

Keyboard Music from Polish Manuscripts, 2 bks., ed. Golos/Sutkowski (Corpus of Early Keyboard Music, X/1, 2), Dallas, American Institute of Musicology, 1967. Contents: Bk. 1 — choralbearbeitungen of N. Hasse and Ewaldt; Bk. 2 — choralbearbeitungen of Scheidemann and Tunder.

Laudamus Dominum, ed. Bangert/Rosel, St. Louis, Concordia. Chorale preludes by Walther, Vetter, Scheidt, Pachelbel, J. C. Bach, Krieger, etc.

Lüneburger Orgeltabulatur, KN 208[1], 208[2], ed. Reimann (*Das Erbe Deutscher Musik,* XXXVI/LXV), Frankfurt, H. Litolff.

Orgelchoräle des 17. und 18. Jahrhunderts, ed. Senn/Schmid/Aeschbacher, Kassel, Bärenreiter. Contents: works by Böhm, Buxtehude, Praetorius, Scheidt, Walther, Weckmann, and others.

Orgelchoräle um J. S. Bach, ed. Frotscher (*Das Erbe Deutscher Musik,* IX), Frankfurt, H. Litolff. Reprint of the same by C. F. Peters (Frankfurt). Contents: works by Bach's contemporaries.

Orgelmeister, 4 parts, ed. Seiffert (*Organum,* IV/2, 5, 7, & 21), Leipzig/Lippstadt; Kistner & Siegel. Part 1 — works of J. Praetorius, Schildt, J. Decker, D. Meyer, M. Olter, Chr. Flor; Part 2 — Reincken, Chr. Ritter; Part 3 — Brunckhorst, A. Kneller, Leyding; Part 4 — Scheidt, Düben, D. Abel, P. Hasse the Elder, W. Karges, P. Hasse the Younger.

Orgelmeister des 17. und 18. Jahrhunderts, ed. Matthaei, Kassel, Bärenreiter. Works by north and middle German masters, and others.

Orgelspiel im Kirchenjahr, 2 vols., ed. Rohr, Mainz, Schott S. Contents: 113 pieces for the liturgical year by a variety of composers, most of them middle and north Germans.

Orgelvorspiele alter Meister in allen Tonarten, ed. Keller, Kassel, Bärenreiter. Contents: compositions in all keys by German composers and others. Note: some works have been transposed.

Orgelwerke der Familie Bach, ed. Hellmann, Frankfurt, C. F. Peters. Contents: works by 10 members of the Bach family.

NOTES

[1] Discussed in the section "Organ Music Before 1500."

[2] The all-inclusive German term for organ compositions based on a chorale is *Choralbearbeitungen.* This has sometimes been translated as "chorale arrangements" or "chorale transcriptions." Both terms carry connotations not present in the original word. The term "chorale preludes" has also been equated with *Choralbearbeitungen,* but this is confusing since "chorale prelude" may also identify a specific type of *Choralbearbeitungen* — the *Choralvorspiel.* The term "organ chorale" has likewise been used, but this is misleading since its German equivalent (*Orgelchoral*) sometimes has a more limited meaning. To simplify matters, I shall leave the term untranslated.

[3] For further discussion of Pachelbel's works, See the section on South Germany.

[4] J. Adlung, *Musica mechanica organoedi,* I, p. 187.

[5] *Johann Sebastian Bach: Gesammelte Briefe,* ed. E. Müller von Asow, Regensburg, Bosse, 2/1950, p. 35ff.

MUSICAL SOURCES

Ex. 8a. *Scheidt: Ausgewaehlte Werke,* ed. Keller, p. 62. Copyright 1939 C. F. Peters. Used by permission.

Ex. 8b. *Scheidt: Ausgewaehlte Werke,* p. 66.

Ex. 9. Reproduced from Tunder, *Keyboard Music from Polish Manuscripts,* Vol. II (CEKM X/2). © Copyright 1967 by the American Institute of Musicology/Hänssler-Verlag, Neuhausen-Stuttgart, W. Germany. Used by permission.

Ex. 10. *Buxtehude: Ausgewaehlte Orgelwerke,* I, ed. Keller, pp. 12, 14. Copyright C. F. Peters. Used by permission.

Ex. 11. *Luebeck: Orgelwerke,* ed. Keller, pp. 19, 22. Copyright 1940 C. F. Peters. Used by permission.

Ex. 12. *Boehm: Klavier- und Orgelwerke,* I, ed. Wolgast, pp. 75, 76.

Ex. 13. *80 Choralvorspiele des 17 und 18 Jahrhunderts,* ed. Keller, p. 117. Copyright 1951. C. F. Peters. Used by permission.

Ex. 14. *Johann Gottfried Walther: Orgelchoraele,* ed. Poppen, p. 78.

After the Baroque era, the organ moved toward the periphery of musical development. Previously regarded as the instrument *par excellence* for the delineation of contrapuntal lines, it was now found lacking in the expressive and dynamic qualities needed for the realization of the *empfindsamer Stil*.

Looking first at south Germany and Austria, one notes that the organ was limited more and more to its *continuo* function. Orchestral instruments replaced the organ with increasing frequency at church services and festive occasions. South Germans who did compose for solo organ in this post-Baroque era were obviously torn between preserving the traditional contrapuntal style and venturing forth into the new style with its harmonic simplicity and melodic expressiveness. In the works of Johann Ernst Eberlin (1702-1762), organist in Salzburg, one sees a synthesis typical of this transitional period.

(Example 15)

Within the framework of a traditional form, Baroque counterpoint has been combined with new melodic and harmonic elements. Eberlin's toccatas and fugues are general keyboard pieces (not specifically organ music) and are clearly a continuation of the south German tradition initiated by Frescobaldi and Froberger.

The old style of writing and the new persisted side by side into the Classical Era (and beyond). Organ music for secular occasions was written in a preClassical or Classical style, like any other music. Liturgical organ music, on the other hand, was written in a more conservative style. Just as the *stile antico* remained the official ecclesiastical language for *a cappella* compositions, so Baroque counterpoint was still the norm for liturgical organ music. The works of Johann Georg Albrechtsberger (1736-1809), the Viennese court organist, illustrate this. His liturgical organ pieces

are simple, subdued, and contain both Baroque and Classical elements. His concerto for organ and orchestra, on the other hand, is a true Classical composition. The same disparity is seen in the works of Johann Michael Haydn (1737-1806), brother to the famous Haydn. His brief liturgical versets are very traditional and artistically unimportant (*Gebrauchsmusik*). His double concerto for viola and organ, however, is a concert work in the Classical idiom, with an expressive dialogue between the two solo instruments.

Franz Joseph Haydn (1732-1809) composed three organ concerti which exhibit typical Classical features. Their texture is light, the melodies are gracious. This is music for courtly entertainment. Haydn also wrote a number of lighthearted mechanical clock pieces (*Flötenuhrstücke*) which have been transcribed for keyboard. He composed no liturgical organ music, but used the organ as the *continuo* for his orchestral masses. In addition, he sometimes assigned it a solo role within the orchestra.

A Viennese contemporary of Haydn, Antonio Salieri (1750-1825), likewise wrote a concerto for organ and orchestra. Though technically brilliant, this work is less inspired than the concerti of F. J. Haydn.

Wolfgang Amadeus Mozart (1756-1791) was an accomplished organist, but the only liturgical organ music he wrote were the church sonatas for organ and chamber ensemble. These were played at the *Gradual* of the mass. In his orchestral masses he used the organ in the same manner that Haydn did, both as *continuo* instrument and as a solo voice of the orchestra. He wrote three works for mechanical clock, the most important contribution to this south German genre since its inception in the Renaissance.

Ludwig van Beethoven (1770-1827)

Ex. 15. Eberlin, *Toccata Quarta*, m. 5-6, 23-24.

wrote pieces for mechanical clock and two keyboard preludes (through all major keys) which can be played on the organ. A *Fugue in D* is the only work which he composed specifically for the organ.

Turning now to middle Germany and stepping back somewhat in time, one finds organ concerti by two members of the Berlin school, Carl Heinrich Graun (1704-1759) and Carl Philipp Emanuel Bach (1714-1788). Both musicians were employed at the court of Frederick the Great. Their concerti are light, graceful, typically *empfindsame* creations. They are undeserving of the neglect into which they have fallen. Other organ works by C. P. E. Bach include preludes, fugues, sonatas, and a suite for mechanical clock. A *Fantasie und Fuge* is one of his best organ works and illustrates the *empfindsamer Stil* applied to a keyboard instrument.

(Example 16)

Among C. P. E. Bach's other works, the organ sonatas are noteworthy as early examples of the classic sonata form. They are pure keyboard music. There is no separate line assigned to the pedal. Bach simply wrote "pedal" in the score and left the performer free to play whichever notes he wished on the pedal.

Wilhelm Friedemann Bach (1710-1784), unlike C. P. E. Bach, remained more aligned with the organ idiom of his father. In his fugues and chorale preludes, Baroque figuration and counterpoint still figure prominently. Wilhelm Friedemann is the only one of the Bach sons who actually had a reputation as an organist.

Most of the remaining men who merit attention for their organ compositions were either students of J. S.

Bach or persons who consciously attached themselves to the Bach tradition. Johann Ludwig Krebs (1713-1780) was reputedly Bach's favorite pupil. He wrote preludes, toccatas, fantasies, fugues, and chorale settings. He must have had a phenomenal pedal technique since the pedal solos in some of his works are quite intricate. The influence of the master is unmistakable in Krebs' compositional style, yet there are also features suggestive of the coming Classicism. His compositions are frequently too long, as he lacked adequate imagination for the development of his musical ideas.

Another Bach pupil, Gottfried August Homilius (1714-1785) attempted a synthesis of the Bach style with new compositional features. Johann Peter Kellner (1705-1772) and Friedrich Wilhelm Marpurg (1718-1795) did the same. Both were Bach admirers, although neither was a direct pupil.

(Example 17)

Johann Phillipp Kirnberger (1721-1783) and Johann Ernst Rembt (1749-1810), students of Kellner, continued writing in this synthetic style.

In the 19th century, organists who considered themselves carriers of the Bach tradition still combined late-Baroque counterpoint with current compositional elements. Good craftsmanship was characteristic of their work, but individuality and inspiration were often sorely lacking. Short simple pieces for the church service constituted the bulk of their contribution. The following excerpt from *Allein Gott in der Höh sei Ehr* by Johann Christian Rinck (1770-1846) is a typical product of this school.

(Example 18)

Ex. 16. C.P.E. Bach, *Fantasie und Fuge*, m. 1-5.

Ex. 17. Marpurg, *Wer nur den lieben Gott lässt walten*, m. 1-5.

Ex. 18. Rinck, *Allein Gott in der Höh sei Ehr'*, Var. 3, m. 1-4.

The piece is well-constructed, but not particularly imaginative. Michael Gotthard Fischer (1773-1829), Adolf Hesse (1809-1863), whose works are too sentimental for current taste, and Johann Schneider (1789-1864) also wrote large quantities of service music. Their works circulated in old anthologies, usually no longer available.

In north Germany there were no later 18th- or early 19th-century organists worth mentioning. Following such giants as Buxtehude, Luebeck, and Bruhns, there was suddenly a conspicuous void. The organist's social and artistic position had sharply declined in north Germany, as everywhere, and this may have been partly responsible for the dearth of competent organists. The local school teacher or a part-time church musician now carried out the duties previously performed by a professional. Related to this situation was the increasing prominence of the sermon in the Protestant churches. Organ playing was no longer liturgical in the old sense, but simply an embellishment to the "Service of the Word."

With this situation as background, one can better appreciate the full stature of the organ works of Felix Mendelssohn Bartholdy (1809-1847). His preludes and fugues and sonatas were the first major contribution to solo organ literature by a prominent German composer since the days of Bach. They are a convincing combination of traditional techniques (counterpoint, independent pedalling, etc.) with the melodic expressiveness of the early Romantic idiom. The thematic contour of his organ compositions is very strong. It is unfortunate that the true nature of his music is often obscured by performers who over-emphasize the lyric qualities at the expense of other elements.

As could be expected, Mendelssohn's works formed a primary model for organists throughout the remainder of the century. Large forms were now used with greater frequency. The most popular large form for organ composition was the sonata. The fantasy and the variations form were also widely used.

Another Mendelssohn contribution was the discovery and promotion of Bach's compositions. Paradoxically, the members of the so-called Bach school rarely performed the works of Bach. They simply studied Bach's compositional and performing techniques so as to incorporate these features into their own style. Thus Mendelssohn's research into the music of Bach constituted the first major impulse for the Bach revival which later ensued.

Mendelssohn's famous contemporary, Robert Schumann (1810-1856), wrote six fugues on the popular theme, BACH, for organ or *pedalklavier*. His sketches and studies, though now performed on the organ, were written for *pedalklavier*. His works had no formative impact on organ literature.

Franz Liszt (1811-1886), one of the chief proponents of contemporary music in his day, wrote three monumental organ works in a virtuoso style. They are actually symponies for organ. Two of them (*Weinen, klagen* and *Ad nos*) express that particular mystical religiosity which prevailed during much of the Romantic period. Often employing pianistic devices, these works (the two just mentioned plus the *Praeludium und Fuge über BACH*) demand considerable manual and pedal dexterity. In this respect, they contrast sharply with Liszt's easy church pieces (organ hymns, mass versets, etc.). In general, one can divide the bulk of 19th-century organ literature into virtuoso concert music requiring considerable technical proficiency and simple, often dull, service music for the more-or-less amateur organist. Although there are exceptions, service music of high artistic merit and demanding an advanced technique was not common at this time.

Julius Reubke (1834-1858), a student of Liszt, added one symphonic poem (*The* 94*th Psalm*) to the concert literature for the organ. His indebtedness to Liszt is obvious. Reubke died at the age of 24.

The great Johannes Brahms (1833-1897) devoted little attention to the organ, yet the few organ works he did write indicate that he understood the instrument very well. The eleven chorale preludes follow the north and middle German *Choralbearbeitung* tradition. Although appropriate as church music, these pieces are artistically on a totally different plane from the usual 19th-century service music. Brahms' text interpretation in these works is particularly fine. His other organ works (the two preludes and fugues, the A♭ minor fugue, and the *Choralvorspiel und Fuge über O Traurigkeit, O Herzeleid*) shows Brahms' mastery on a somewhat larger scale. The *Praeludium und Fuge in g* has some virtuoso passages. Still, all of the pieces are rather conservative if one compares them with contemporary writing by Liszt and Reubke.

Several other personalities contributed to German organ literature and to knowledge about organs and organ playing. Johann Gottlob Töpfer (1791-1870) wrote a considerable amount of organ music, but is remembered for his treatise on organ building, *Das Lehrbuch der Orgelbaukunst* (1855). August Gottfried Ritter 1811-1885) wrote an organ method, *Kunst des Orgelspiels*, and the first history of organ playing, *Zur Geschichte des Orgelspiels, vornehmlich des deutschen, im* 14. *bis zum Anfang des* 18. *Jahrhunderts* (1884). Gustav Adolf Merkel (1827-1885), trained in the Bach tradition, wrote sonatas and easy pieces for organ. Karl Piutti (1846-1902), organist of the Thomaskirche, Leipzig, wrote numerous *Choralbearbeitungen*, some sonatas, fugues, and other works. Heinrich von Herzogenberg (1843-1900), a lifelong friend of Brahms, wrote chorale fantasies, a type of chorale setting not very common at this time.

The men just mentioned lived in middle Germany, and most were connected with the Bach tradition. South Germans and Austrians active during the same period included Simon Sechter (1788-1867), the Viennese counterpoint teacher, and Johann Georg Herzog 1822-1909), teacher of Rheinberger and author of a widely-used *Orgelschule*. The symphonist Anton Bruckner (1824-1896) also wrote a small quantity of *Gebrauchsmusik* for the organ. Dating from his youth, these pieces display none of the brilliance for which he was known as an improviser. Like most other service music in Austria and south Germany, his organ works are rather old-fashioned, bound to the late-Baroque organ tradition.

The principal south German personality in the organ world at this time was Joseph Gabriel Rheinberger (1839-1901), the famous Munich composition teacher and organist. He composed 20 organ sonatas. Considered to be his best work, the sonatas are distinguished by lyrical qualities and a clear formal structure.

(Example 19)

Rheinberger also wrote trios, fughettas, and *Charakterstücke*.

At the close of the Romantic era, the various trends in organ composition merged in the work of one man: Max Reger (1873-1916). The music of Johann Sebastian Bach was Reger's greatest inspiration and model. This explains

Ex. 19. Rheinberger, *Sonata No.* 4, Movement 1, m. 1-5.

his preoccupation with polyphony and possibly his interest in chorale composition. At the same time, he was in sympathy with the symphonic style of organ writing and with the latest harmonic explorations of his contemporaries. Reger's writing is very linear, yet he makes extensive use of chromatic harmonies and distant modulations.

For Reger, unlike Brahms or Liszt, organ music was a chief compositional area. Not since Bach had a major German composer devoted so much of his energy to organ composition. Reger wrote seven enormous chorale fantasies, approximately 70 small chorale preludes, and numerous free works. Usually very extensive in length, the free works include two sonatas, many preludes and fugues, fantasies and fugues, suites, the *Variationen und Fuge fis-moll*, the *Introduktion, Passacaglia und Fuge e-moll*, and others. Pianistic techniques and a symphonic approach are seen in his *Phantasie und Fuge über den namen BACH*, as in his other large works.

Ex. 20. Reger, *Phantasie und Fuge über den Namen BACH*, m. 1-2.

In the chorale fantasies, Reger incorporated the symphonic style into the *Choralbearbeitung* tradition, thus narrowing the gap between the conservative middle German tradition of service playing and the more progressive concert style. From the standpoint of their historical impact, as well as from their artistic value, the chorale fantasies rank among Reger's most important contributions. Many of the small chorale preludes, such as *O Lamm Gottes, unschuldig* (opus 67), stand also on a high artistic level.

(Example 21)

Reger's sizeable contribution to *Choralbearbeitung* literature lent renewed stature to this type of composition, thus providing a major impetus for the renewal of church music and service playing in the 20th century. Already during his lifetime, Reger's works received enthusiastic recognition, due in part to the promotion given them by Karl Straube.

A contemporary of Max Reger was Sigfried Karg-Elert (1877-1933). Although influenced by the former, Karg-Elert also came under the spell of the French Impressionists. His chromaticism is often overdone, and the harmonies are cloying.

To describe all the developments in organ building during the 150-year period under discussion would go beyond the scope of this article, but a few traits of the German Romantic organ can be mentioned. The prevailing color of the instrument was dark, sombre, rather thick. There were stops imitative of the Romantic orchestra. However, and this is a fact sometimes not recognized, the German organ in the 19th century did not completely for-

feit its heritage in an attempt to imitate the orchestra. All of the better organs of this period (instruments by E. F. Walcker, Ladegast, J. F. Schulze, etc.) still had principal choruses in the various divisions. Naturally, the mixtures were not as high-pitched as Baroque mixtures had been. Mutations were also present, and 8′ stops were there in abundance. Several German builders were influenced, to a greater or lesser extent, by the work of Cavaillé-Coll. The disposition of the Ladegast organ in the Cathedral of Merseburg (1853) is illustrative. Liszt composed his *Praeludium und Fuge über BACH* for the inaugural concert of this instrument.[1]

HAUPTWERK
Bordun 32 ft. (from c)
Prinzipal 16 ft.
Bordun 16 ft.
Prinzipal 8 ft.
Doppelgedackt 8 ft.
Hohlflöte 8 ft.
Gemshorn 8 ft.
Gedacktquinte 5⅓ ft.
Gamba 8 ft.
Oktave 4 ft.
Gemshorn 4 ft.
Gedackt 4 ft.
Quinte 2⅔ ft.
Oktave 2 ft.
Doublette 4 + 2 ft.
Mixtur IV
Scharf IV
Cornett III-V
Fagott 16 ft.
Trompete 8 ft.

RUCKPOSITIF
Bordun 16 ft.
Prinzipal 8 ft.
Quintatön 8 ft.
Flauto traverso 8 ft.
Fugara 8 ft.
Oktave 4 ft.
Gedackt 4 ft.

Ex. 21. Reger, *O Lamm Gottes, unschuldig,* m. 1-4.

Oktave 2 ft.
Mixtur IV
Cornett II-V
Oboe 8 ft.

OBERWERK
Quintatön 16 ft.
Prinzipal 8 ft.
Rohrflöte 8 ft.
Gedackt 8 ft.
Flauto amabile 8 ft.
Gamba 8 ft.
Oktave 4 ft.
Rohrflöte 4 ft.
Spitzflöte 4 ft.
Quint 2⅔ ft.
Waldflöte 2 ft.
Terz 1⅗ ft.
Sifflöte 1 ft.
Mixtur IV
Schallmey 8 ft.
Stahlspiel 8 ft.

ECHOWERK (Swell)
Lieblich Gedackt 16 ft.
Geigenprinzipal 8 ft.
Lieblich Gedackt 8 ft.
Flauto dolce 8 ft.
Salizional 8 ft.
Unda maris 8 ft.
Oktave 4 ft.
Zartflöte 4 ft.
Salizional 4 ft.
Nasat 2⅔ ft.
Oktave 2 ft.
Progressivharmonika II-IV
Cymbel III
Acoline 16 ft. (Reed)

PEDAL
Untersatz 32 ft.
Prinzipal 16 ft.
Subbass 16 ft.
Violinbass 16 ft.
Grossnasat 10⅔ ft.
Prinzipal 8 ft.
Bassflöte 8 ft.
Violoncello 8 ft.
Terz 6⅖ ft.
Rohrquinte 5⅓ ft.
Oktave 4 ft.
Flöte 4 ft.
Scharfflöte 4 ft.
Mixtur IV
Cornett IV
Posaune 32 ft.
Posaune 16 ft.
Dulzian 16 ft.
Trompete 8 ft.

3 manual couplers, 3 pedal couplers, 4 ventils to manuals, 4 ventils to pedal, collective machine stop to pedal, "Pianissimo" machine stop to entire organ, Cymbelstern, Barker levers with slider chests and mechanical action.

EDITIONS

Albrechtsberger: *Instrumentalwerke,* ed. Kapp (*Denkmäler der Tonkunst in Oesterreich*, XVI/2) , Vienna, Universal Ed., 1909. *Concerto per l'organo,* ed. Vécsey (*Musica Rinata,* No. 1) , Budapest, Editio Musica Budapest, 1968. *Praeludium und Fuge,* Vienna, Universal Ed. *Twelve Trios,* ed. Marchant, New York, H.W. Gray.

Bach, C.P.E.: *Konzert in G,* ed. Winter, Hamburg, Musikverlag Sikorski. *Konzert in Eb,* ed. Winter, Hamburg, Musikverlag Sikorski. *Orgelwerke,* 2 vols., ed. Fedtke, Frankfurt, C.F. Peters. Vol. I: 6 sonatas; Vol. II: prelude, fantasia, fugues. *Praeludium und Sechs Sonaten,* ed. Brandts Buys, Hilversum, Harmonia-Uitgave. *Six Sonatas for Organ,* 2 vols., ed. Langlais, Chicago, H.T. Fitz-Simons Co. *A Suite for an Organ Clock,* ed. Altmann, Boston, McLaughlin & Reilly.

Bach, W.F.: *Orgelwerken,* 2 vols., ed. Fedtke, Frankfurt, C.F. Peters. Vol. I: fugues; Vol. II: chorale preludes, fugues. *Complete Organ Works,* 2 vols., ed. Brandts Buys, Hilversum, Harmonia-Uitgave. Vol. I: chorale preludes; Vol. II: fugues. *Les Oeuvres pour Orgue,* ed. deNys/Pierront (*Orgue et Liturgie, Bk.* 37) , Paris, Schola Cantorum. Contents: chorale preludes and 4 fugues. *8 Fugues sans pédale* (*Orgue et Liturgie,* Bk 45) , Paris, Schola Cantorum.

Beethoven: *Orgelwerke,* ed. Altman, London, Hinrichsen. Contents: suite for mechanical clock, 2 preludes, op. 39, and a fugue. *Zwei Praeludien,* op. 39, Vienna, Oesterreichischer Bundesverlag. The same, under title *Préludes circulaires,* ed. Dupré, Paris, Bornemann.

Brahms: *Sämtliche Werke,* ed. by the Vienna Gesellschaft der Musikfreunde, Wiesbaden, Breitkopf & Härtel, 1926-28. Vol. XVI has the organ works. *Sämtliche Orgelwerke* are available separately from Breitkopf & Härtel. *Complete Organ Works,* 2 vols., ed. Buszin/Bunjes, New York, C.F. Peters, 1964. *11 Choral-Vorspiele,* op. 122, Berlin Simrock. Other editions of the chorale preludes: ed. Biggs, New York Mercury Music, ed. West, New York, H.W. Gray;

Orgue et Liturgie, Bk. 21, Paris, Schola Cantorum.

Bruckner: Orgelwerke, ed. Haselböck, Vienna, Doblinger. Volledige Orgelwerken, Amsterdam, Annie Bank. Praeludium in C, Vienna, Universal Edition. Fugue in d, Vienna, Universal Ed.

Eberlin: Tokkaten und Fugen, ed. Walter (Süddeutsche Orgelmeister des Barock, IV), Altötting, Coppenrath. 9 Toccates et Fughes, Mainz, Zulehner. Fugen, Zürich, Nägeli. Toccata in g, ed. Johnstone (Early Organ Music, No. 7), London, Novello.

Graun, C.H.: Konzert für Orgel und Streichorchester, Heidelberg, W. Müller Verlag.

Haydn, F.J.: Concerto per l'Organo (C), No. 1 (with strings, oboes, French horns), ed. Schneider, Wiesbaden, Breitkopf & Härtel, 1953. Concerto per l'Organo (C), No. 2 (with strings, trumpets, timpani), ed. Landon (Diletto Musicale series), Vienna, Doblinger. Concerto per l'Organo (C), No. 3 (with strings), ed. Heussner (Nagels Musik Archiv), Hannover, Nagel. Flötenuhrstücke, ed. Schmid (Nagels Musik Archiv, No. 1), Hannover, Nagel, 1931. Content: 32 short pieces for mechanical clock. Musical Clocks, ed. Biggs, New York, H.W. Gray.

Haydn, M.: Konzert für Viola und Orgel (Diletto Musicale series), Vienna, Doblinger. Maitres anonymes et M. Haydn: Cent Vingt et un versets brefs, ed. Bonfils (L'Organiste liturgique, Bks. 23/24), Paris, Schola Cantorium. Brief Elaborations for the Organ, New York, Kalmus.

Herzog: 10 Tonstücke, op. 67, Leipzig, Leuckart. 8 Tonstücke, op. 78, Leipzig, Leuckart.

Hesse: Leichte Praeludien, ed. Hänlein, Frankfurt, C.F. Peters. Leichte Orgelvorspiele, op. 25, Leipzig, Leuckart. Hesse-Album, vol. III, Leipzig, Leuckart. Fantasie in d, op. 87 (for 4 hands), Leipzig, Leuckart.

Homilius: Fünf Choralbearbeitungen, ed. Feder (Die Orgel, II/I), Lippstadt,

Kistner & Siegel, 1957. Sechs Choralvorspiele, ed. Feder (Die Orgel, II/2), 1957.

Karg-Elert: Choral-Improvisationen, op. 65, 6 vols., Leipzig, Breitkopf & Härtel. The same, op. 65, 6 vols., ed. Bedell, New York, E. B. Marks. Selected works from op. 65 have also been published in 2 volumes by Breitkopf & Härtel. 3 Impressions, op. 72, London, Novello. 3 sinfonische Choräle, op. 87, Berlin, Simon. Passacaglia and Fugue on BACH, op. 150, London, Hinrichsen. Seven Pastels from the Lake of Constance, op. 96, London, Novello. 20 Praeludien und Postludien, op. 78, Berlin/Wiesbaden, C. Simon and Breitkopf & Härtel (now printed in London by British and Continental Music Agencies). 7 Idyls, op. 104, Frankfurt, C. F. Peters. Modal Interludes, London, Hinrichsen. Sketch Book, 2 vols., ed. Sceats, London, Hinrichsen. Leichte Pedalstudien, op. 83, Leipzig, C. F. Peters. Pax vobiscum, op. 86, no. 5, Leipzig, Leuckart. Cathedral Windows, op. 106, London, Elkin. Triptych, op. 141, London, Elkin. Plus other works.

Kellner: Ausgewählte Orgelwerke, ed. Feder (Die Orgel, II/7), Lippstadt, Kistner & Siegel.

Kirnberger: Orgelchoräle, ed. Riedel (Die Orgel, II/14), Lippstadt, Kistner & Siegel.

Krebs: Ausgewählte Orgelwerke, ed. Zöllner, Leipzig, C.F. Peters, 1938. Contains preludes and fugues, a toccata. Ausgewählte Orgelwerke, 3 vols., ed. Tittel (Die Orgel, II/18, 20, 21), Lippstadt, Kistner & Siegel. Vol. I: preludes, fugues, trios; II: Choralbearbeitungen; III: Choralbearbeitungen with obbligato wind instrument. Klavierübung, ed. Soldan, Frankfurt, C.F. Peters. Contains Choralbearbeitungen. Eight Chorale Preludes for organ with trumpet or oboe, ed. Biggs, Bryn Mawr, Theodore Presser, 1947. Fantasie in f for oboe and organ, ed. David, Leipzig, Breitkopf & Härtel, 1942.

Liszt: Sämtliche Orgelwerke, 2 vols., ed. Straube, Frankfurt, C.F. Peters. Osszes orgonaműve (Complete Organ Works), ed. Margittay, Budapest/New York, Editio Musica Budapest and Boosey & Hawkes, 1970. 3 Oeuvres pour Orgue, ed. Dupre, Paris, Bornemann, 1941. Contents: *Ad nos, Praeludium und Fuge über BACH*, and *Weinen, klagen*.

Marpurg: *Eight Chorale Preludes*, ed. Emery (*Early Organ Music*, No. 21), London, Novello. *Twenty-one Chorale Preludes*, ed. Thompson, Minneapolis, Augsburg.

Mendelssohn: *Sämtliche Orgelwerke*, Frankfurt, C.F. Peters. Contains 3 preludes and fugues, op. 37, and 6 sonatas, op. 65. Other editions of the same: ed. Dupré, Paris, Bornemann; ed. Widor, Paris, Durand; ed. Atkins, London, Novello; ed. Lemare, New York, G. Schirmer. *Three Unfamiliar Organ Compositions by Mendelssohn*, ed. Altman, Nashville, Abingdon.

Merkel: *Merkel Album*, Leipzig, C.F. Peters. *24 melodische Stücke*, Mainz, Schott S. *Orgelschule* (Organ Method), ed. Clausznitzer, Leipzig, C.F. Peters. *Organ Sonata* No. 6, op. 137, London, Hinrichsen.

Mozart: *Neue Ausgabe Sämtlicher Werke* (Publication of the Internationale Stiftung Mozarteum Salzburg), Kassel, Bärenreiter, ed. Dounias/Schleifer, which are also available separately from Bärenreiter. *Kirchensonaten*, Wiesbaden, Breitkopf & Härtel. *Organ Sonatas*, 5 vols., ed. Biggs, Bryn Mawr, Theodore Presser. *Drei Stücke für die Orgel-Walze*, KV 594, 608, 616, ed. Brinkman, Kassel, Bärenreiter. Other editions of the mechanical clock pieces have been published by C.F. Peters, Breitkopf & Härtel, Boosey & Hawkes, Bornemann, Novello, etc. *Mozart auf der Orgel*, 2 vols., ed. Proeger, Berlin, Merseburger. Contents: assorted keyboard pieces which the editor believes to be suited to the organ.

Piutti: *200 Choralvorspiele*, op. 34, Leipzig, Kahnt. *8 Praeludien*, op. 2, Leipzig, Leuckart. *Fest Hymnus*, op. 20, Leipzig, C.F. Peters.

Reger: *Sämtliche Werke*, ed. with the co-operation of the Max-Reger Institute (Bonn), Wiesbaden, Breitkopf & Härtel, 1954ff. Organ music is in vols. XV-XVII. *3 Orgelstücke*, op. 7, Mainz, Schott S.

Suite in e, op. 16, Mainz, Schott S. *Phantasie über "Ein feste Burg,"* op. 27, ed. Straube, Leipzig, C. F. Peters. *Phantasie und Fuge* (c), op. 29, Leipzig, C. F. Peters. *Phantasie über "Freu' dich sehr, o meine Seele,"* op. 30, Vienna, Universal Ed. *Sonata I* (f♯), op. 33, Vienna, Universal Ed. *Phantasie über "Wie schön leucht't uns der Morgenstern,* op. 40, no. 1, Vienna, Universal. *Phantasie über "Straf mich nicht in deinen Zorn,"* op. 40, no. 2, Vienna, Universal. *Phantasie und Fuge über BACH*, op. 46, Vienna, Universal. *6 Trios*, op. 47, Vienna, Universal. *Phantasien über "Alle Menschen müssen sterben," "Wachet auf, ruft uns die Stimme,"* und *"Halleluja! Gott zu loben,"* op. 52, nos. 1, 2, 3, Vienna, Universal. *5 leicht ausführbare Praeludien und Fugen*, op. 56, Vienna, Universal. *Symphonische Phantasie und Fuge*, op. 57, Vienna, Universal. *12 Stücke*, 2 vols., op. 59, Leipzig, C. F. Peters. *Sonata II* (d), op. 60, Leipzig, Leuckart. *Monologue*, op. 63, 3 vols., Leipzig, Leuckart. *12 Stücke*, op. 65, 2 vols., Leipzig, C. F. Peters. *25 leicht ausführbare Vorspiele*, op. 67, 3 vols., Berlin, Bote & Bock. *10 Stücke*, op. 69, 2 vols., Berlin, Bote & Bock. *Variationen und Fuge fis-moll über ein Originalthema*, op. 73, Berlin, Bote & Bock. *13 Choralvorspiele*, op. 79b, Langensalza, Beyer & Söhne, 1904. *12 Stücke*, op. 80, 2 vols., Leipzig, C. F. Peters. *4 Praeludien und Fugen*, op. 85, Leipzig, C. F. Peters. *Orgelsuite* (g), op. 92, Leipzig, Musikverlag Forberg. *Introduction, Passacaglia und Fuge* (e), op. 127, Berlin, Bote & Bock. *9 Stücke*, op. 129, Berlin, Bote & Bock. *30 kleine Choralvorspiele*, op. 135a, Leipzig, C. F. Peters. *Fantasie und Fuge* (d), op. 135b, Leipzig, C. F. Peters. *7 Orgelstücke*, op. 145, Wiesbaden, Breitkopf & Härtel. *Introduction und Passacaglia* (d), Wiesbaden, Breitkopf & Härtel. *Vorspiel: Komm süsser Tod,"* Mainz, Schott S. *Variationen und Fuge über "Heil, unserm König Heil"* (Variations and Fugue on the English National Anthem), Vienna, Universal Ed., 1901. *Praeludium und Fuge* (d), Dresden, E. Hoffmann, 1906. *Praeludium und Fuge* (f♯), Berlin, Bote & Bock, 1912. *O Haupt voll Blut und Wunden*, Leipzig, Breitkopf & Härtel, 1905.

Rembt: *50 vierstimmige Fughetten*, ed. Toppius, Frankfurt, C.F. Peters. The same, ed. Walter, Altötting, Coppenrath. 6 *Orgeltrios*, ed. Jeans, Mainz, Schott S.

Reubke: *Der 94. Psalm*, ed. Keller, Frankfurt, C.F. Peters, 1958. The same, ed. Ellingford, London, Oxford University Press, 1932. The same, ed. Koch, New York, G. Schirmer.

Rheinberger: *Sonatas*, Nos. 1-20, ed. Grace, London, Novello. *Sonatas*, Nos. 5, 10, 15, 16, & 17. ed. Weyer, Bad Godesberg, Musikverlag Forberg. *Sonata No. 20* (Zur Friedensfeier), London, Hinrichsen. *Ausgewählte Orgelwerke*, 2 vols., ed. Weyer, Bad Godesberg, Musikverlag Forberg. 24 *Fughettas*, op. 133, 4 vols., ed. Webber, London, Hinrichsen. 12 *Fughetten strengen Styls*, op. 123, Leipzig, Kahnt. 10 *Trios*, *op. 49*, Bad Godesberg, Musikverlag Forberg. 15 *Selected Trios*, op. 49,189, London, Novello. *Monologues*, op. 162, Nos. 1-12, London, Novello. 12 *Charakterstücke*, op. 156, 2 vols., Leipzig, Leuckart. *Miscellaneen*, op. 174, 2 vols., Leipzig, Leuckart. Plus other works.

Rinck: *Freie Vor- und Nachspiele*, ed. Hänlein, Frankfurt, C.F. Peters. *Sixteen Postludes*, ed. Nevin, Glen Rock, J. Fischer. *12 Chorals with Variations*, Goes (Netherlands), Edition Ars Nova. *59 pièces choisies* (*Les Cahiers de l'Organiste*, No. 5), Paris Schola Cantorum.

Ritter: *Kunst des Orgelspiels*, op. 15, new edition by Claus, Frankfurt, C.F. Peters, 1953.

Schumann:*Werke*, ed. C. Schumann/ Brahms, Leipzig, Breitkopf & Härtel, 1881-1893. The *Studies* and *Sketches* are in Series V (Piano Works) and the fugues on BACH in Series VIII. *Fugen über BACH*, Frankfurt, C.F. Peters. *Oeuvres complètes pour Orgue et Piano-pédalier*, ed. Dupré, Paris, Bornemann. *Six Etudes en forme de canon*, op. 56, Paris, Durand. *Studies*, op. 56, London, Galliard Ltd. *Quatre Esquisses*, op. 58, Paris, Durand. *Sketches*, op. 58, London, Galliard, Ltd. *Six Fugues*, op. 60, Paris Durand.

Collections

Most of the collections of German Classical and Romantic organ music are no longer in print. The few collections listed below are currently available.

Erstes Präludien Album, ed. Bungart, Rodenkirchen, Tonger Verlag. Contents: 286 short pieces and interludes, ranging from 3 measures to 2 pages in length. Intended for the beginning organist. Composers: Albrechtsberger, Eberlin, M. G. Fischer, M. Haydn, Rembt, Rinck, Sechter, Töpfer, etc.

Nineteenth Century Andantes, ed. Altman, London, Hinrichsen. Contains one piece each by Hummel and Mendelssohn.

Organ Book No. 1 and *Organ Book No. 2*, ed. Trevor, London, Oxford University Press. Krebs, J. C. F. Schneider, Merkel, Töpfer, Rembt, Herzogenberg, Albrechtsberger, M. G. Fischer, and Rinck are among the composers represented, although there are also works by earlier composers.

Orgelmusik im baierischen Raum (*Cantantibus Organis*, Bk III, ed. Kraus), Regensburg, Verlag Pustet. Contents: 12 pieces by Eberlin, Ett, Grätz, Hugl, Kolb, Muffat, Murschhauser, Vogler.

Orgelwerke der Familie Bach, ed. Hellmann, Frankfurt, C. F. Peters. Half of the works are by J. S. Bach's sons or younger relatives. The remaining pieces are by older members of the Bach dynasty.

NOTES

[1] Disposition from Metzler, *Romantischer Orgelbau in Deutschland*, Ludwigsburg, Verlag E. F. Walcker & Cie, pp. 49, 50.

MUSICAL SOURCES

Ex. 15. *Musica Sacra*, I, ed. Commer. Used by permission of Associated Music Publishers, Inc., Agents for Bote & Bock.
Ex. 16. *Orgelwerke der Familie Bach*, ed. Hellmann, p. 53. Copyright 1966 C. F. Peters. Used by permission.
Ex. 17. *F. W. Marpurg: Eight Chorale Preludes*, ed. Emery, p. 14.
Ex. 18. *Ch. H. Rinck: 12 Choraele mit Veraenderungen*, p. 14.
Ex. 19. Rheinberger: *Sonata No. 4*, ed. Phillips. Copyright 1965 Hinrichsen Edition. Used by permission of C. F. Peters.
Ex. 20. Reger: *Phantasie und Fuge über den Namen BACH*, p. 3. Universal Edition. Used by permission of European American Music.
Ex. 21. Reger: *Vorspiele fuer die Orgel*, op. 67, p. 27.

GERMANY AND AUSTRIA SINCE 1900

The leading figure in German organ literature at the beginning of the 20th century was Max Reger (1873-1916), a musical giant whose reputation and influence continued to mount in the years following his death. Reger's style was imitated, directly or with modifications, by numerous composers, especially during the first three decades of this century. Max Gulbins (1862-1932), Sigfrid Karg-Elert (1877-1933), Joseph Haas (1879-1960), and Karl Hoyer (1891-1936) are a few of the men who emulated the Reger style. Like Reger, they employed rich harmonies, but wrote contrapuntally. Their music has that particular brand of chromaticism which bears Reger's stamp. They also utilized the wide dynamic possibilities of the Romantic organ. Their works have sudden, dramatic drops from *fff* to *pppp,* as well as expansive *crescendi* and *decrescendi,* achieved through a skillful use of the *Rollschweller* (the German counterpart to our *crescendo* pedal).

In the period following the First World War, the Reger style continued to dominate, although it was frequently combined with new compositional methods to form a transitional style. Heinrich Kaminski (1886-1946) wrote in this manner, clearly indebted to Reger, yet experimenting with Neo-Baroque techniques. Kaminski is believed to have been the first 20th-century composer to employ terrace dynamics. In his *Toccata,* published in 1923, he gave the following instruction: "The author urgently requests that one limit oneself during the entire work to the indicated manual changes and that one completely forego the use of the crescendo and swell pedals, as well as all 'colorfulness,' since that would contradict the spirit of the work."[1] Hermann Grabner (1886-1969), prominent theorist, also employed elements of the Reger style, such as his chromaticism, in combination with techniques of the post-war era.

Franz Schmidt (1874-1939), Viennese composer and pedagogue, produced large quantities of Romantic organ music during the 1920's and '30's. Influenced by Bruckner and other late Romantics, Schmidt wrote organ compositions of symphonic scope, intended for an orchestral organ.

Schmidt's style of writing was not typical for this period. By the late 1920's and early '30's, most organ composers had adopted either a transitional or a true Neo-Baroque style. Several developments were responsible for this. Chief among these was the movement known as the *Orgelbewegung,* which began with the rediscovery of old instruments and their subsequent restoration. The essential characteristics of Baroque organ building, particularly of the north German type, then became the model for new organ construction. Albert Schweizer, Wilibald Gurlitt, Hans Henny Jann, and Oscar Walker, were leaders of this movement. Karl Straube, in addition, was one of the first musicians to prepare new, practical editions of Baroque organ works, thus acquainting the organ public with an enormous repertory of neglected music. As a result of intense research activity and publications, there arose an overwhelming interest in Baroque music.

As seen within a broader framework, the ideals of the *Orgelbewegung* coordinated beautifully with the search for clarity and objectivity which was sweeping over the European musical world in the 1920's. For producing clarity in all the parts and for delineating contrapuntal lines, the German Baroque organ was certainly unsurpassed.

In the Protestant church, and to a lesser extent in the Catholic church, a liturgical renewal was in progress during the same period. The movement gave added dignity to the organ profession and stimulated the creation of a large quantity of liturgical organ music.

Johann Nepomuk David (1895-1977) contributed an enormous body of organ music incorporating the ideals of the *Orgelbewegung* and the liturgical reform. His monumental series entitled *Das Choralwerk,* numbering 19 volumes, is the core of his organ production. The early volumes contain shorter chorale compositions of every conceivable type, a veritable encyclopedia of work in this genre. One finds plain and ornamented *cantus firmi* chorale preludes, the chorale fantasy, the chorale partita (in which canonic writing appears with great frequency), introduction and fugue, prelude and fugue, toccata, fantasy, passacaglia, and other forms, all of them based on chorale themes. David's early *Choralbearbeitungen* rank among the most important productions of the German organ school in the 1930's. His well-known preoccupation with canon and other contrapuntal techniques, stimulated by his study of Bach's *Kunst der Fuge,* is already apparent in these works, but the severity which is characteristic of his late compositions is lacking. The following example is taken from his *Partita: Ach, wie flüchtig, ach wie nichtig (Das Choralwerk,* vol. III).

(Example 22)

Another central figure in the church music renewal movement was Hugo Distler (1908-1942). Although his organ pieces are not as strong as his choral compositions, his organ style formed a point of departure for much subsequent organ composition, especially in Protestant circles. While organist at the Jakobikirche in Lübeck, he composed several *Choralbearbeitungen* for the side organ of this church, a particularly exquisite instrument dating in part from the 15th century and enlarged in 1636.

These pieces are believed to be the earliest examples of Neo-Baroque compositions specifying precise registration on a specific instrument. Inspired, on the one hand, by historic instruments, Distler was equally motivated by his study of pre-Bach music, especially Buxtehude. Distler's treatment of chorale melodies recalls Buxtehude's chorale preludes, with their octave figuration and tone repetition (*Reperkussionsmelodik*).

(Example 23)

Another pathfinder was Ernst Pepping (1901-   ). He, too, was most successful as a choral composer, yet held at the same time a prestigious position in the organ world. Inspired by the *Orgelbewegung,* the church music reform, and developments in the musical world at large, he wrote a great number of organ works employing Baroque forms and techniques in a modern context. As illustrated by his *Grosses Orgelbuch, Kleines Orgelbuch, Böhmisches Orgelbuch,* etc., Pepping devoted himself far more to *Choralbearbeitungen* than to free organ works. He especially preferred the *cantus firmus* chorale prelude and the chorale partita. Unlike Dist-

Ex. 22. David, *Partita: Ach, wie flüchtig, ach wie nichtig,* movt. 1, m. 1-4, and movt. 3, m. 1-2.

Ex. 23. Distler, *Vorspiel: "Christe, Du Lamm Gottes,"* m. 1-3.

ler, Pepping did not specify every detail of the registration. Still, he obviously had Baroque, or Neo-Baroque, sonorities in mind. Pepping's works have sometimes been criticized as being more idiomatic to the piano than the organ. In some cases (including some of his most famous pieces) this criticism is justified, but it does not hold true for all of his works.

(Example 24)

Several other composers made contributions to organ literature during the 1930's, among them, Wolfgang Fortner (1907-   ), Karl Höller (1907-   ), and Günther Raphael (1903-1960).

The 1930's also witnessed the birth of Hindemith's first two organ sonatas, with the third sonata appearing in 1940. These works were produced during the time that Hindemith was composing sonatas for nearly every existing instrument. The Hindemith sonatas, and the *Kammermusik Nr.* 7 for organ and chamber orchestra (1928), stand somewhat apart from other organ works of this period, since they have no connection with the *Orgelbewegung*, the Protestant chorale, or with any liturgy. A study of Hindemith's compositional style would exceed the scope of this article, but one would like to recall a single fact — often forgotten — that Hindemith, in his organ music, built upon certain elements of the Reger tradition. A close examination of the organ works of these men would reveal traits which they have in common. The reader is here referred to Hans-Ludwig Schilling's article, "Hindemiths Orgelsonaten" in *Musik and Kirche*, XXXIII/ 5, p. 202ff.

As for the performance of Hindemith's works, one should remember the composer's instruction: "Organists who have crescendo and swell pedals at their disposal are free to intensify the expression beyond the prescribed volume indications through the use of richer coloring and dynamic transitions."[2] The sonatas, seen from the standpoint of their form, call basically for terrace dynamics. Yet Hindemith, as the previous quotation indicates, was not a purist in this respect.

The sonatas of Hindemith immediately attained an authoritative position in the organ world. Nearly all German organ composers of the next two decades (and several Austrians) were influenced to a greater or lesser extent by these works. One sees this in the rhythmic and melodic patterns, in the form, the harmonies, the phrase divisions, etc.

Two other giants of modern music, Arnold Schönberg (1874-1951) and Ernst Krenek (1900-   ) contributed to organ literature, but only in a peripheral way. Schönberg's *Variations on a Recitative* is not idiomatic to the organ and, in this author's opinion, would attract little attention if it had been composed by someone less famous. Both the Schönberg work and the one-movement *Sonata* (1941) of Krenek were written after the composers had moved to the United States.

The bulk of German organ music of this period came, not from world-famous composers like Hindemith, but from organists and church musicians. Hans Friedrich Micheelsen (1902-1973), who wrote *Choralbearbeitungen* during the 1930's, began in the following decade a series of works which he entitled *Orgelkonzerte*. Usually based on chorale tunes, these extended compositions are for organ alone. Under Pepping's and, particularly, Distler's influence, Helmut Bornefeld (1906-   ) and Siegfried Reda (1916-1968) supplied considerable *Gebrauchsmusik* for the Protestant liturgy. Reda also wrote a number of

Ex. 24. Pepping, *Vorspiel*: *"Wir wollen alle fröhlich sein,"* m. 1-6.

larger works which he called organ *concerti*, although they are for organ alone. The model for Reda's *concerti* was obviously the Hindemith sonatas. Eberhard Wenzel (1896-   ) , Johannes Weyrauch (1897-   ) , Kurt Thomas (1904-   ) , Reinhard Schwarz-Schilling (1904-   ) , and Kurt Fiebig (1908-   ) also added to organ literature at this time.

The overwhelming majority of German organ composers were Protestant, but some musicians connected with the Catholic church are also worthy of note. Hermann Schroeder (1904-   ) and Joseph Ahrens (1904-   ) each furnished the Catholic liturgy with a considerable amount of new music. In addition to liturgical pieces, Schroeder has written several handsome concert works.

(Example 25)

Ahrens, besides his works for the Catholic church, wrote a 3-volume cycle of Protestant chorale settings for the liturgical year. J N. David, one would like to point out, was also a Catholic. His church affiliation did not hinder him from making the single most voluminous contribution to *Choralbearbeitung* literature in the 20th century (*Das Choralwerk*). Obviously, the chorale had become a general regenerative force for organ music. Its significance was not limited to Protestant circles.

In the 1950's and '60's, many of the composers who had been prominent in the previous two decades continued to make substantial contributions. Sometimes their late compositions were markedly different from those which they had written earlier. Ernst Pepping continued to write *Choralbearbeitungen*. J. N. David pursued his interest in chorale composition, as well as free composition. His late works are sometimes severely cerebral, exploring the most abstract types of polyphony. The polytonal excerpt from *Da Jesus an dem Kreuze stund* is a good example of his mature style before it became excessively abstract.

(Example 26)

Wolfgang Fortner, who had not written for organ since the mid-30's, made a noteworthy contribution with his three *Intermezzi* (1963) , serial compositions employing tone clusters, pedal glissandi, and complex rhythms. Paul Hindemith, whose most recent organ work had dated from 1940, made a welcome addition in 1962 with his *Concerto* for organ and orchestra. Weyrauch, Wenzel, Micheelsen, Ahrens, Schroeder, and

Ex. 25. Schroeder, No. VI of *Kleine Praeludien und Intermezzi*, m. 1-6.

Ex. 26. David, *Partita*: *"Da Jesus an dem Kreuze stund,"* movt. 8, m. 1-6.

Raphael continued to make frequent contributions to organ literature.

Several new names also rose to the foreground at, or after, mid-century. One of these was Harald Genzmer (1909-   ). Basing his style on the Hindemith tradition, he has written organ sonatas and other attractive works for organ alone or with instrumental combinations.

(Example 27)

Walter Kraft (1905-1977), whose early works were destroyed during the war, published in recent years four large organ compositions. His *Dies Irae,* rhythmically subtle and harmonically varied, recalls the north German *Choralfantasie* tradition.

(Example 28)

Max Baumann (1917-   ) has also provided some enjoyable pieces, such as his popular *Concerto* for organ and string orchestra with timpani and his *Sonatine* for organ alone.

(Example 29)

Johannes Driessler (1921-   ) has contributed 20 organ sonatas for use throughout the liturgical year. Heinz Werner Zimmerman (1930-   ), of the Spandau church music school in Berlin, wrote a set of *Orgelpsalmen,* attempting to translate into sound the psalm texts, word for word. Two other Berlin musicians, Helmut Barbe (1927-   ) and Frank Michael Beyer (1928-   ), have

Ex. 27. Genzmer, *Die Tageszeiten,* part I: *Der Abend,* m. 1-3 of the Coda.

Ex. 28. Kraft, *Fantasia*: *Dies Irae,* m. 1-3.

Ex. 29. Baumann, *Toccata,* m. 13-16.

also added to the literature, both for organ alone and with instrumental combinations. Also active were Helmut Walcha (1907-   ) and Kurt Hessenberg (1908-   ).

In Austria, Helmut Eder (1916-   ) and Josef Friedrich Doppelbauer (1918-   ), professors at the Salzburg Mozarteum, have written some successful organ works, including *concerti*. The rhythmic organization (sometimes serial organization) of Eder's works is perhaps the strongest single element of his style. The example which follows is taken from the delightful *Ostinato* movement of his *Partita über ein Thema von J.N. David.*

(Example 30)

Doppelbauer's works, some for concert, others for liturgical use, often show a marked influence of Hindemith and David.

In Vienna, **Anton Heiller** (1923-1979), active as a concert organist since 1940, began to acquire recognition as a composer in the 1950's. His spiritual kinship with Hindemith and David is particularly evident in his early works. Later compositions, such as the *Ecce*

lignum crucis and the *Tanz-Toccata*, were partially inspired by the French school, especially Messiaen and Alain.

(Example 31)

Franz Augustinus Kropfreiter (1936-   ), organist at the St. Florian monastery near Linz, has written a number of organ works which frequently appear on recital programs. For organists and listeners whose experience with modern music is limited, Kropfreiter's compositions are quite accessible. His manner of writing is often gentle, yet he usually manages to avoid clichés. One of his favorite forms is the partita.

(Example 32)

As other Austrians who have contributed to organ literature, one mentions Karl Schiske (1916-1969), Paul Angerer (1927-   ), Herbert Tachezi (1930-   ), and Peter Planyavsky (1948-   ).

In Germany, a country proud of its organ tradition, the number of composers who have written for organ in the last few decades is staggering. As is usual with the Germans, good crafts-

Ex. 30. Eder, *Partita über ein Thema von J. N. David*, movt. 2, m. 1-4, 6.

Ex. 31. Heiller, *Ecce lignum crucis*, m. 22-26.

Ex. 32. Kropfreiter, *Maria durch ein Dornwald ging*, movt. 5, m. 6-10, 16-18.

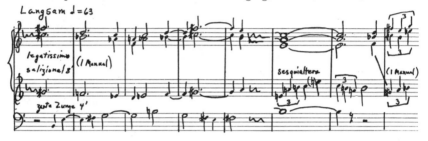

manship is virtually taken for granted. Thus, the list of names would be most impressive, if one were to mention all the German composers who have written well-constructed organ pieces. If all of their works — or even the majority of them — were inspired, one would rejoice at such a cache. This, unfortunately, is scarcely the case. For my own list of modern German organ composers, including those already mentioned and those about to be discussed, I have restricted myself to composers who, in my opinion, have something to offer beyond good craftsmanship. The choice is admittedly subjective, since I find it impossible to be otherwise when the subject matter is so close in time.

Among composers not yet discussed, Jürg Baur (1918-   ) and Hans-Ludwig Schilling (1927-   ) are worthy of note. Baur, whose works are concise and rhythmically alive, has composed in a dodecaphonic style from the 1950's until recently, when he appropriated certain *avant-garde* techniques in his *Choral-Triptychon*. The following excerpt is taken from the *Partita: Aus tiefer Not,* which dates from 1965.

(Example 33)

Schilling, who has integrated elements of the Hindemith tradition and of the modern French school into his style, likewise has a flair for rhythmic organization. Counterpoint plays an important role in his music, and he has a particularly fine understanding of organ color possibilities. The following excerpts illustrate certain aspects of his work, which deserves to be better known than it is.

(Examples 34a, 34b)

Wolfgang Stockmeier (1931-   ) has produced a large number of organ works of varying types (serial compositions, works graphically notated, and more conservative pieces). The following example, taken from the *Variationen für Orgel und Blechbläser,* shows one of his works based on the 12-tone technique.

(Example 35)

In addition to several concert works, Stockmeier has composed an impressive amount of organ music for the church service.

Serial composition has figured quite

Ex. 33. Baur, *Partita*: *"Aus tiefer Not,"* movt. 1, m. 4–8.

Ex. 34a. Schilling, *Fantasie 63 über Veni creator spiritus*, 1–10.

Ex. 34b. Schilling, *Chaconne nouvelle*, m. 31–34.

Ex. 35. Stockmeier, *Variationen für Orgel und Blechbläser*, m. 1-2, 8-12.

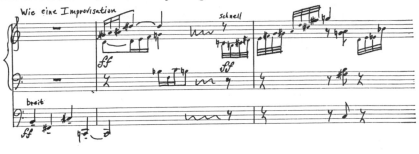

prominently in German organ literature, especially of the 1960's. In this regard, one thinks of the works of Konrad Lechner (1911-), Giselher Klebe (1925-), and several others. Complex rhythmic patterns and frequently changing registration have become trademarks of this type of organ composition.

Aleatory works for organ, partially or completely graphically notated, began to appear in the 1960's and have become fairly common in the present decade. Pesudo-electronic sounds are produced on the organ through manipulation of the motor, the stopknobs, and through other unconventional techniques. In this type of composition, many factors are left to the performer's discretion, so that the element of chance is an essential ingredient. Through these quasi-improvisational compositions, the sonoral possibilities of the organ have been greatly enlarged. It appears, however, that other musical values have been all too frequently neglected. One assumes that successful works in this genre will be forthcoming in the next few years, since several German composers have recently tried their hand at one or more compositions of this type.

The work which, more than any other, launched aleatory composition into the organ world was Ligeti's famous (or infamous, depending on one's point of view) *Volumina* (1961/62, revised 1966), which consists exclusively of tone clusters, both stationary and moving.

(Example 36)

György Ligeti (1923-), who took up residence in Austria in 1956 and later in Germany, has subsequently contributed two additional organ works, *Harmonies* and *Coulée*. The latter of the two tests the composer's theory that extremely rapid figurations will be heard as being almost static. While Ligeti is not a German, his impact on modern German organ music has been so remarkable that a survey of German-Austrian literature is not complete without reference to him. Another foreigner who has lived in Germany most of the time since 1957 and has made a name for himself there, is Mauricio Kagel (1931-). An *Improvisation ajoutée* (1961/62) and a *Phantasie für Orgel mit Obbligati* (1967), in which tape recorders provide the obbligato parts, are his contribution to organ literature.

Ex. 36. Ligeti, *Volumina*, rehearsal no. 34.

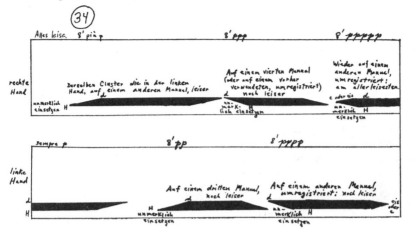

Isang Yun (1917-   ), who likewise is not German, but has been living in Berlin, has written a work entitled *Tuyaux sonores*. This appears to be one of the more successful organ works in the aleatory genre. An aleatory work more easily approachable than most is the *Myriaden II* of Dieter Acker (1940-   ), a Rumanian (from German-speaking Transylvania), who took up residence in West Germany in 1969. It is significant that Germany has offered more encouragement to composers of *avant-garde* music than has probably any other country.

Other composers who have made noteworthy contributions to modern organ literature are: Kurt Bossler, Dietrich von Bausznern, Harald Heilmann, Reinhold Finkbeiner, Werner Jacob, Rudolf Kelterborn, Manfred Kluge, Berthold Hummel, Aribert Reimann, Walter Schindler, Joachim Schweppe, and Wolfgang Wiemer. There is no particular connection between the various composers just mentioned. A wide variety of styles and techniques is represented in their works, the range extending from Hindemith-influenced compositions to extremely modern pieces.

The organ type which predominates today in Germany, and to some extent in Austria, is no longer the strict, north German Neo-Baroque organ favored by the *Orgelbewegung*. The current organ type, although based upon the same principles as the Neo-Baroque instrument, has been modified to accommo-

date a larger range of organ literature. Three-manual organs usually have one division under expression and furnished with a reed chorus appropriate, though not ideal, for Romantic music. Large instruments sometimes have variety stops, such as 1 1/7', 8/9', *Terznone* (1 3/5' + 8/9') or *Obertöne* (1 3/5' + 1 1/3' + 8/9' + 8/15'), prized for their usefulness in modern improvisation. The Neo-Baroque organ was an instrument perfect for the music of Buxtehude, Bach, and Distler, but it was ill-suited to Romantic music and to almost all foreign literature. The modern German organ, on the other hand, is designated for German music first of all (including Reger), but it accommodates fairly well much of the French *repertoire* and the literature of other countries as well. The following specification is of the "Marienorgel" built by the Rieger firm — one of four new organs in the Münster of Freiburg in Breisgau.

HAUPTWERK

Prinzipal 16'
Oktave 8'
Rohrflöte 8'
Spitzflöte 4'
Oktave 4'
Spitzquinte 2⅔'
Oktave 2'
Mixture VIII ranks, 2'
Cymbel III ranks, ⅔'
Kornett V ranks
Trompete 16'
Trompete 8'
Klarine 4'

POSITIV

Prinzipal 8′
Metallgedackt 8′
Prinzipal 4′
Rohrflöte 4′
Gemshorn 2′
Gemsquinte 1⅓′
Sesquialtera II ranks
Scharf IV-VI ranks, 1′
Dulzian 16′
Schalmey 8′
Tremolo

SCHWELLWERK

Gedacktpommer 16′
Bleiprinzipal 8′
Spillpfeife 8′
Unda maris 8′
Oktave 4′
Querflöte 4′
Nasat 2⅔′
Flautino 2′
Terz 1⅗′
Obertöne 1⅗′, 1⅓′, 8/9′, 8/15′
Mixtur V-VII ranks, 1⅓′
Terzzymbel III ranks, 1/6′
Fagott 16′
Trompete 8′
Französische Oboe 8′
Klarine 4′
Tremolo

BRUSTWERK

Holzgedackt 8′
Blockflöte 4′
Prinzipal 2′
Gedacktflöte 2′
Terzian 1⅗′ + 1⅓′
Oktave 1′
Glockenzymbel II ranks, ½′
Vox humana 8′
Cembalo-Regal 4′
Tremolo

PEDAL

Prinzipalbass 16′
Subbass 16′
Oktav 8′
Gedackt 8′
Koppelflöte 4′
Nachthorn 2′
Rauschpfeife III ranks, 5⅓′, 3⅕′, 2-2/7′
Mixtur VI ranks, 2⅔′
Contrafagott 32′
Trompete 16′
Trompete 8′
Zink 4′
Tremolo

EDITIONS

Acker: *Myriaden II* (1972), Cologne, Gerig Verlag. ORG. & INSTRUMENTS: *Myriaden I* (1971) for organ and percussion ad.lib., Cologne, Gerig.

Ahrens: Publishers are A. Böhm (Augsburg), B. Schott's Söhne (Mainz) and Willy Müller (Heidelberg). *Kleine Weihnachtspartita,* Böhm, 1929. *Canzone* (F), Böhm, 1930. *Praeludium, Arie und Toccata,* Böhm, 1931. *Toccata eroica,* Sch., 1932. *Passamezzo und Fuge,* Böhm, 1933. *Ricercare,* Böhm, 1934. *Partita: Christus ist erstanden,* Sch., 1935. *Hymnus: Pange Lingua,* Sch.. 1935. *5 kleine Stücke,* Böhm, 1936. *Regina coeli,* Böhm, 1937. *Dorische Toccata,* Böhm, 1938. *Fantasie, Grave und Toccata,* Böhm, 1940. *Kleine Musik in a-moll,* Böhm, 1940. *Konzert in e-moll,* Böhm, 1941. *Praeludium und Fugue,* Böhm, 1942. *Toccata und Fuge,* Böhm, 1942. *Partita: Jesu, meine Freude,* Böhm, 1942. *Fantasie* (b), Böhm, 1943. *Canzone* (c♯), Böhm, 1943. *Concertino* (G), Böhm, 1943. *Orgelmesse,* Sch., 1945. *Hymnus: Veni creator spiritus,* Sch., 1947. *Partita: Lobe den Herren,* Sch., 1947. *Partita: Verleih uns Frieden gnädliglich,* Sch., 1947. *Triptychon über B-A-C-H,* Sch., 1949. *Choralwerk, "Das heilige Jahr,"* 3 vols., W. M., 1948-50. *Concertino für Positif,* W. M., 1950. *Cantiones Gregorianae pro organo,* 3 vols., Sch., 1957. *Trilogia Sacra,* 3 parts, W.M. *Verwandlungen I* (1963), *II* (1964), *III* (1965), Sch. *Fantasie und Ricercare über ein Thema von J. Cabanilles,* W. M., 1967. ORG. & INSTRUMENTS: *Sonate* for viola and organ, W. M., 1953. *Konzert* for organ and brass, W. M., 1958.

Angerer: *Musica pro organo,* Vienna, Universal Edition. ORG. & INSTRUMENTS: *Sinfonia* for organ, strings, winds, and tympani.

Barbe: *Sonate,* Stuttgart, Hänssler Verlag, 1964. ORG. & INSTRUMENTS: *Hovs Hallar* (concerto for 12 solo strings, percussion & organ), Stuttgart, Hänssler, in preparation.

Baumann: Publishers are Sirius Verlag (Berlin) and Merseburger (Berlin). Sirius publications have been taken over by Heinrichshofen's Verlag (Wilhelmsthaven). *Postludium: Es ist ein Ros' entsprungen,* op. 66/2, Sir., 1961. *Orgel-Suite,* op. 67/1, Sir., 1962. *Postludium: Nun lobet Gott,* op. 67/4, Sir., 1962. *Invocation,* op. 67/5, Sir., 1962. *Sonatine,* Mer., 1963. *Drei Stücke,* Mer., 1965. *Fasciculus pro organo,* Mer., 1967. ORG. & INSTRUMENTS: *Psalmi,* op. 67/2 for org. & piano (also with baritone solo), Sir. *Konzert* for organ, strings, & timpani, Mer., 1964.

Baur: Publications by Breitkopf & Härtel (Wiesbaden). *Toccata,* 1956. *Trio und Passacaglia,* 1958. *Partita: Aus tiefer Not,* 1966. *Choral-Triptychon: Christ ist erstanden,* 1972.

Bausznern: *Nun danket all' und bringet Ehr* (Chorale Toccata), Berlin, Merseburger. *Meditatio super "Veni creator spiritus",* Berlin, Merseburger. ORG. & INSTRUMENTS: *Konzert* for organ and percussion, Berlin, Merseburger.

Beyer: *Toccata in Re* (1952), Berlin, Sirius Verlag (now Wilhelmshaven, Heinrichshofen's Verlag). *Lays* (1957), Kassel, Bärenreiter. *Toccaten sub communione,* Berlin, Bote & Bock, 1970. *Tiento II* (1972), Berlin, Bote & Bock. ORG. & INSTRUMENTS: *Sonate* for viola & org., Kassel, Bärenreiter, 1960. *Tiento* for flute & org. (or harpsichord) (1965), Kassel, Bärenreiter. *Konzert* for organ & 7 instruments (fl., oboe, trpt., viola, cello, contrabass, harp), photocopy available by Bote & Bock (Berlin).

Bornefeld: All publications by Bärenreiter (Kassel) unless otherwise indicated. *Begleitsätze (Das Choralwerk),* 6 vols. *Choralpartiten (Das Choralwerk),* 8 vols. Vol. I: *Wir glauben all;* II: *Der Herr ist mein getreuer Hirt;* III: *Nun komm, der Heiden Heiland;* IV: *Mit Fried und Freud;* V: *Gott der Vater wohn uns bei;* VI: *Komm, Gott Schöpfer;* VII: *Christus, der ist mein Leben;* VIII: *Herr Gott, dich loben wir.* *Choralvorspiele (Das Choralwerk),* 2 vols. *Orgelstücke (Intonationen),* 1949. *32 Choralvorspiele,* Frankfurt, C. F. Peters. ORG. & INSTRUMENTS: *Choralsonate I: Auf meinen lieben Gott,* for flute and org. (or positive organ, piano, or harpsichord).

Bossler: Publishers are Merseburger (Berlin), Kistner & Siegel (Lippstadt/Cologne), and Willy Müller (Heidelberg). *3 Orgelstücke,* Mer., 1956. *8 Choralvorspiele,* 2 bks., Mer. *Partita: Heut singt die liebe Christenheit (Die Orgel I/6),* K & S, 1961. *Freiburger Orgelbuch (Die Orgel, I/9),* K & S, 1965. *Heidelberger Orgelbuch (Die Orgel I/*

20), K & S, 1968. *Eschatologische Kontemplation* (1969/70), W. M., in preparation. ORG. & INSTRUMENTS: *Kontroverse* for organ and flute and piccolo, performed alternately by one flutist (2 recorders may be substituted), W. M., in preparation. TWO ORGANS: *Kaleidoskop* for one or two organs, W. M. Additional publications by Merseburger and W. Müller.

David: All publications by Breitkopf & Härtel (Leipzig/Wiesbaden), u n l e s s otherwise indicated. *Chaconne* (a), 1928. *2 Hymnen,* 1928. *Passamezzo und Fuge,* 1928. *Ricercare* (c), 1928. *Toccata und Fuge* (f), 1928. *F a n t a s i a super "L'Homme armé,"* 1930. *Das Choralwerk,* 19 vols., 1930-1969. Vols. I-V contain smaller *Choralbearbeitungen,* 1930-35; Vol. VI: *Christus, der ist mein Leben,* 1936; VII: *3 Stücke für Orgel-Positiv,* 1936; VIII: *Es sungen drei Engel,* 1941; IX: *Partita: Unüberwindlich starker Held,* 1944; X: *Partita: Es ist ein Schnitter,* 1946; XI: *Partita: Da Jesus an dem Kreuze stund,* 1953; XII: *Partita: Lobt Gott, ihr frommen Christen,* 1953; XIII: *Partiten über "Aus tiefer Not," "Ach Gott, vom Himmel sieh darein" und "Vater unser,"* 1960; XIV: *Phantasien über "Mitten wir im Leben sind," "Maria durch den Dornwald ging" und "Wenn mein Stündlein vorhanden ist,"* 1962; XV: *Christus, der ist mein Leben,* 1966; XVI: *O du armer Judas,* 1967; XVII: *Vater unser im Himmelreich,* 1970; XVIII: *Nun komm, der Heiden Heiland,* 1970; XIX: *Nun komm, der Heiden Heiland,* 1969. *Praeambel und Fuge* (d), 1931. *2 kleine Präludien und Fugen* (a), (G), 1933. *2 Fantasien und Fugen* (e), (C), 1935. *Ricercare* (a), 1937. *Partita über "Innsbruck, ich muss dich lassen,"* Vienna, Doblinger, 1955. *Toccata und Fuge,* 1962. *Chaconne und Fuge,* 1962. *Partita über B-A-C-H,* 1964. *12 Orgelfugen durch alle Tonarten,* 1968. *Partita,* 1970. *Hölderlin,* 1970. *Thomas von Aquin.* *Franz von Assisi.* ORG. & INSTRUMENTS: *Introitus, Choral und Fuge über ein Thema von Bruckner,* for org. & 9 brass instruments, 1940. *Concerto pro organo,* for org. & orch., 1965.

Distler: All publications by Bärenreiter (Kassel). *Orgelpartita: Nun komm, der Heiden Heiland,* op. 8/1, 1933. *Orgelpartita: Wachet auf, ruft uns die Stimme,* op. 8/2, 1935. *7 kleine Orgel-*

choralbearbeitungen, op. 8/3, 1938. 30 *Spielstücke für die Kleinorgel,* op. 18/1, 1938. *Orgelsonate* (Trio), op. 18/2, 1939.

Doppelbauer: Major publishers are Doblinger (Vienna) and Coppenrath (Altötting). *Toccata und Fuge* (in memoriam M. Ravel), Dob., 1951. *Toccatina,* Dob., 1954. *Partita,* Dob., 1955. "Capriccio" from the *Partita* is available separately. *Suite brève,* Dob., 1961. *Fünf Orgelchoräle,* Dob. *Partita: Vater unser,* Dob. *Partita: Ave maris stella,* Dob., 1963. 3 *kleine Praeludien und Fugen,* Dob., 1966. *Ornamente,* Dob. *Kleine Stücke,* Dob. *Sonatine,* Cop. 8 *kurze Stücke,* Cop. 4 *neue Stücke,* Cop. 7 *Choralvorspiele,* Cop. 10 *Pedaletüden,* Dob. ORG. & INSTRUMENTS: *Konzert* for organ and string orchestra, Dob., 1958.

Driessler: *Orgelsonaten durch das Kirchenjahr,* op. 30, 8 vols., Kassel, Bärenreiter, 1954/55. Vol. I: Advent; II: Christmas; III: New Year, Epiphany; IV: Passion; V: Easter; VI: Ascension and Whitsuntide; VII: Trinity & Saints' Days; VIII: End of the Church Year. *Toccata und Hymn über "Wach auf, wach auf, du deutsches Land,"* op. 46/1, Wiesbaden, Breitkopf & Härtel.

Eder: All publications by Doblinger (Vienna), except when otherwise indicated. 5 *Stücke,* op. 40. *Partita über ein Thema von J. N. David,* op. 42, Wiesbaden, Breitkopf & Härtel. *Partita: O Heiland, reiss die Himmel auf,* op. 47/1. *Partita: Ach wie flüchtig, op.* 47/2. *Partita: Es sungen drei Engel,* op. 47/3. *Partita: Gen Himmel aufgefahren ist,* op. 47/4. *Choral-Suite,* op. 48. *Vox media,* op. 53. ORG. & INSTRUMENTS: *Konzert, "L'homme armé,"* op. 50, for org. & orchestra. *Memento* for positive organ and 2 string groups.

Fiebig: *Präludium und Fuge,* Leipzig, C. F Peters, 1948. *Triosonate,* Leipzig, C. F. Peters, 1949. *Choralfantasie: In dich hab' ich gehoffet, Herr,* Berlin, Sirius Verlag (now Wilhelmshaven, Heinrichshofen's Verlag). *Orgelchoralbuch* (48 easy chorale preludes), Hamburg, Hüllenhagen & Griehl.

Finkbeiner: Publications by Breitkopf & Härtel (Wiesbaden). *Partita: In dich hab' ich gehoffet, Herr,* 1957. *Klangflächen,* 1963. *Toccata und Fuge,* 1965. *Choralfantasie: Wachet auf,* 1968.

Fortner: All publications by Schott S. (Mainz). *Toccata und Fuge,* 1930. *Praeambel und Fuge,* 1935. *Intermezzi,* 1964. ORG. & INSTRUMENTS: *Konzert* for org. & string orchestra, 1932.

Genzmer: Publishers are Schott S. (Mainz) and C. F. Peters (Frankfurt). *Tripartita* (1945), Sch. *Sonate I* (1953), Sch. *Sonate II* (1956), Pet. *Sonate III* (1963), Pet. *Adventskonzert* (1966), Pet. *Tageszeiten* (1968), Pet. ORG. & INSTRUMENTS: *Introduzione, Aria e Finale* for violin & org. (1968), Pet. *Sonate* for trumpet & org. (1971), Pet. *Konzert* for org. & orch., Pet.

Grabner: The major publisher is Kistner & Siegel (currently located in Porz am Rhein). *Media vita in morte sumus* (1926), Lindau, C. F. Kahnt/ now through Kistner & Siegel. *Partita sopra "Erhalt uns, Herr,"* op. 28, Leipzig, K & S. *Hymnus "Christ ist erstanden,"* op. 32, Leipzig, K & S. *Sonate,* op. 40 (1936), Leipzig, K & S. *Praeludium und Fuge,* op. 49 (1938), Leipzig, K &S. *Toccata,* op. 53, Leipzig, K & S. *Choralvorspiele über "Lobe den Herrn" und "Vater unser"* (1957), Kassel, Bärenreiter. *Choralfantasie: Wir glauben all,* Lippstadt, K & S. *Der 66.Psalm, "Jauchzt, alle Lande" (Die Orgel* I/5), Lippstadt, K & S. *Meditationen über ein geistliches Lied von J. S. Bach (Die Orgel* I/7), Lippstadt, K & S. *Zweite Orgelsonate (Musik aus der Steiermark* series, Bk. 35), Vienna, L. Krenn, 1962. *Orgeltrio,* Copenhagen, W. Hansen. ORG. & INSTRUMENTS: *Konzert,* op. 59, for org. & strings (1942), Kassel, Bärenreiter. Additional publications by C. F. Kahnt (Lindau), Merseburger (Berlin), etc.

Gulbins: *Sonate I* (c), op. 4, Leipzig, Leuckart (now located in Munich). *Sonate II* (f), op. 18, Leipzig, Leuckart. ORG. & INSTR: 4 *Stücke,* op. 14, for cello and organ, Leipzig, Leuckart. Plus numerous *Choralbearbeitungen* and other pieces by Leuckart (Leipzig/now Munich), Rieter-Biedermann (Leipzig), R. Forberg (Leipzig/now Bad Godesberg), Oppenheimer, etc.

Haas: *Sonate,* op. 12, Leipzig, Forberg (now located in Bad Godesberg), 1907. *Suite,* op. 20, Leipzig, Forberg, 1908. *Suite* (A), op. 25, Leipzig, Leuckart, 1909. ORG. & INSTRUMENTS: *Kirchensonate* in F, op. 62/1, for violin & org., Mainz, Schott S. *Kirchensonate* in d, op. 62/2, for violin & org., Mainz, Schott S. Additional publications by Forberg (Leipzig), Augener (London), Coppenrath (Regensburg), Edition Eres (Bremen), etc.

Heiller: *Sonate I*, Vienna, Universal Ed., 1946. 2 *Partiten für Orgel: "Freu dich sehr" und "Vater unser,"* Vienna, Ars nova Verlag Hermann Scherchen, 1951. *Sonate II* (1953), Vienna, Doblinger. *Fantasia super "Salve Regina,"* Vienna, Doblinger. *In Festo Corporis Christi,* Vienna, Doblinger. *Meditation on "Ecce Lignum Crucis"* (*Modern Organ Music,* Bk. 2), London, Oxford University Press, 1967. *Tanz-Toccata* (1970), Vienna, Doblinger. ORG. & INSTRUMENTS: *Konzert* for organ & orch., Vienna, Doblinger, 1964. *Konzert* for harpsichord, positive organ, and chamber orchestra (1972), Vienna, Doblinger (in preparation).

Heilmann: *Meditation über B-A-C-H,* Heidelberg, Willy Müller, 1959. *Diptychon,* Wiesbaden, Breitkopf & Härtel, 1960. *Partita über "Christ ist erstanden,"* Wiesbaden, Breitkopf & Härtel. 1961. *Pentasia,* Wilhelmshaven, Heinrichshofen's Verlag. TWO ORGANS: *Passacaglia,* Heidelberg, W. Müller. ORG. & INSTRUMENTS: *Fantasie für Violoncello und Orgel,* Berlin, Sirius Verlag. Sirius publications are now by Heinrichshofen's Verlag (Wilhelmshaven).

Hessenberg: 2 *Choralpartiten,* op. 43/1&2, Mainz, Schott. *Triosonate,* op. 56, Mainz, Schott, 1955. *Praeludium und Fuge,* op. 63/1 (1952), Frankfurt, C. F. Peters. *Toccata, Fuge und Ciacona,* op. 63/2 (1952), Frankfurt, C. F. Peters. *Fantasia über "Sonne der Gerechtigkeit,"* op. 66 (1956), Berlin, Merseburger. Plus other chorale settings.

Hindemith: *Sonate I* (1937), Mainz, Schott. *Sonate II* (1937), Mainz, Schott. *Sonate III* (1940), Mainz, Schott. ORG. & INSTRUMENTS: *Kammermusik Nr. 7* for org. & chamber orchestra (also known as *Konzert für Orgel und Kammerorchester*), Mainz, Schott, 1928. *Concerto* for org. & orch. (1962), Franckfurt, C. F. Peters.

Höller: *Partita: O wie selig,* op. 1 (1929), Leipzig, Leuckart (now located in Munich). 2 *Choralvariationen: "Helft mir Gottes Güte preisen" und "Jesu, meine Freude,"* op. 22/1&2 (1936), Leip-

zig, Leuckart. *Ciacona,* op. 54, Mainz, Schott. *Choral-Passacaglia über "Die Sonn hat sich mit ihrem Glanz gewendet,"* op. 61, Mainz, Schott. ORG. & INSTRUMENTS: *Konzert* for org. & orch., op. 15 (1932, revised 1966), Munich, Leuckart. *Phantasie* for violin and org., op. 49 (1949), Frankfurt, C. F. Peters. *Improvisation für Violoncello und Orgel über "Schönster Herr Jesu,"* op. 55 (1950), Frankfurt, C. F. Peters.

Hoyer: Publications by Leuckart (Leipzig), Breitkopf & Härtel (Wiesbaden), Portius (Stuttgart), Oppenheimer, etc.

Hummel: *Adagio,* Hamburg, Simrock, 1964. *Fantasie,* Hamburg, Simrock, 1967. *Marianische Fresken,* Hamburg, Simrock. *Tripartita,* Hamburg, Simrock.

Jacob: *Fantasie, Adagio und Epilog* (1963), Wiesbaden, Breitkopf & Härtel. *Improvisation sur E. B.* (Ernst Bloch zu Ehren), Wiesbaden, Breitkopf & Härtel, 1971.

Kagel: *Improvisation ajoutée* (1961/62); Vienna, Universal Ed. ORG. & TAPE: *Phantasie für Orgel mit Obbligati* (1967), Vienna, Universal Ed.

Kaminski: Publications by Universal Edition (Vienna) and Bärenreiter (Kassel). *Toccata über "Wie schön leuch't uns der Morgenstern,"* U. E., 1923. *Choralsonate,* U. E., 1926. 3 *Choralvorspiele,* U. E., 1928. *Toccata und Fuge,* Bär, 1939. *Andante,* Bär., 1939. *Choralvorspiel: Mein Seel' ist stille,* Bär., 1947. ORG. & INSTRUMENTS: *Canzona* for org. & violin, U. E., 1917. *Praeludium und Fuge* for org. & violin, U. E., 1929. *Canon,* for org. & violin, U. E., 1934.

Karg-Elert: See the section on German Romantic music.

Kelterborn: *Zwei Sonaten,* Kassel, Bärenreiter, 1969. *Monumentum,* Berlin, Bote & Bock, 1971.

Klebe: Publications by Bote & Bock (Berlin) and Bärenreiter (Kassel). *Introitus, Aria und Alleluja,* op. 47, B & B. *Passacaglia,* op. 56, Bär., 1968. *Surge, aquilo, et veni, Auster* (Paraphrase über ein Thema von Igor Stravinsky) (1970/71), Bär. *Fantasie und Lobpreisung,* op. 58 (1970), Bär. *Missa "Miserere nobis"* nach der gleichnamigen Bläsermesse, op.

63, B & B. ORG. & INSTRUMENTS: *Variationen über ein Thema von Hector Berlioz,* op. 59, for org. & percussion (1970), Bär.

Kluge: *Fantasie in drei Rhythmen,* Wiesbaden, Breitkopf & Härtel. *Vater unser* (1963), Wiesbaden, Breitkopf & Härtel. *9 Choralvorspiele,* Wiesbaden, Breitkopf & Härtel.

Kraft: *Partita über "Nun will sich scheiden Nacht und Tag,"* Kassel, Bärenreiter. *Fantasie: Dies Irae,* Mainz, Schott. *Toccata: Ite missa est,* Mainz, Schott.

Krenek: *Sonata,* op. 92 (1941) *(Contemporary Organ Series* No. 10), New York, H. W. Gray, 1942.

Kropfreiter: Publications, except when indicated otherwise, are by Doblinger (V i e n n a). *Dreifaltigkeits-Triptychon* (1959). *Partita: Maria durch ein Dornwald ging* (1959). *Introduktion und Passacaglia* (1961). *Partita: Wenn mein Stündlein vorhanden ist* (1961). *Partita: Ich wollt, dass ich daheime wär* (1961). *Der grimmig Tod mit seinem Pfeil* (1962). *Partita: Ach wie nichtig, ach wie flüchtig* (1964). *Ave Regina Coelorum* (1964). *Toccata francese,* London, Oxford University Press. *Sonate I. Sonate II. Variationen: Freu Dich Du Himmelskönigen,* Copenhagen, W. Hansen. *Triplum super "Veni Creator Spiritus,"* (1969). *Partita: Es kommt ein Schiff geladen.* ORG. & INSTRUMENTS: *Concerto responsoriale* for harpsichord and positive organ. *4 Stücke für Flöte und Orgel. Dialog für Violoncello und Orgel. 3 Stücke für Oboe und Orgel,* 1971. *Colloquia für Oboe und Orgel.*

Lechner: *Drei Orgelstücke,* Cologne, Edition Gerig, 1962/65. ORG. & INSTRUMENTS: *Requiem* for oboe, cello, & org. (1952), Frankfurt, C. F. Peters.

Ligeti: *Volumina,* Frankfurt, C. F. Peters, 1961/62, revised 1966. 2 *Etüden* (No. 1, *Harmonies;* No. 2, *Coulée),* Mainz, Schott.

Micheelsen: Major publications by Bärenreiter (Kassel) and W. Müller (Heidelberg). *Orgelkonzert in a-moll,* Bär. *Orgelkonzert über "Es sungen drei Engel,"* Bär. *Orgelkonzert III,* Bär. *Orgel-*konzert V über "Christe, der du bist Tag und Licht,"* Bär. *Orgelkonzert VI über "O dass ich tausend Zungen hätte,"* W. M., *Orgelkonzert VII: Der Morgenstern,* W. M. *Das Holsteinische Orgelbüchlein,* Bär. *Das Grenchener Orgelbuch,* 2 vols., W. M. Additional publications by Bärenreiter and by Hüllenhagen & Griehl (Hamburg).

Mohler: 2 *Canzonen,* op. 17 (1941), Heidelberg, W. Müller, 1964.

Pepping: Major publishers are Schott (Mainz) and Bärenreiter (Kassel). *Partita: Wer nur den lieben Gott lässt walten* (1932), Sch. *To Koralforspil,* Copenhagen, W. Hansen, 1932. *Partita: Wie schön leuchtet der Morgenstern* (1933), Sch. *Grosses Orgelbuch,* 3 vols., (1939-41), Sch. *Kleines Orgelbuch* (1940), Sch. *Toccata und Fuge: Mitten wir im Leben sind* (1941), Sch. *Concerto I* (1941), Sch. *Concerto II* (1942), Sch. *4 Fugen* (1942), Sch. *2 Fugen* (1943-46), Sch. *3 Fugen über B-A-C-H* (1943), Sch. *Partita: Ach wie flüchtig* (1953), Bär. *Partita: Wer weiss, wie nahe* (1953), Bär. *Partita: Mit Fried und Freud* (1953), Bär. *Böhmisches Orgelbuch,* 2 vols. (1953), Bär. *Partita: Hymnen* (1954), Bär. *Sonate* (1958), Bär. *12 Choralvorspiele* (1958), Bär. *25 Orgelchoräle nach Sätzen des Spandauer Chorbuches* (1960), Sch. *Praeludia-Postludia zu 18 Chorälen,* 2 vols., Sch.

Planyavsky: *Sonata pro organo,* Vienna, Doblinger. *Toccata alla Rumba,* Vienna, Doblinger.

Ramin: Publications by Breitkopf & Härtel (Wiesbaden).

Raphael: Publications by Breitkopf & Härtel (Wiesbaden), unless otherwise indicated. *5 Choralvorspiele,* op. 1 (1922). *Fantasie* (e), op. 4 (1924). *Partita: Ach Gott, vom Himmel,* op. 22/1. *Fantasie* (c), op. 22/2. *Praeludium und Fuge* (G), op. 22/3 (1930). *Introduktion und Chaconne* (c♯), op. 27/1 (1930). *Variationen über den Basso Continuo des Bachchorals "D u r c h Adams Fall,"* op. 27/2 (1931). *Toccata* (c), op. 27/3 (1934). *12 Orgelchoräle,* op. 37, 2 vols. *Fantasie und Fuge über einen finnischen Choral,* op. 41/1, 1939. *Partita über einen finnischen Choral,* op. 41/2, 1939. *Passacaglia über einen finnischen Choral,* op. 41/3, 1939. *7 Or-*

gelchoräle über finnischen Chorälen, op. 42, Helsinki, Westerlund. Toccata, Choral und Variationen, op. 53, Heidelberg, W. Müller. Sonate, op. 68, 1949. Kleine Partita: Herr Jesu Christ, Minneapolis, Augsburg, 1958. Fantasie und Fuge über "Christus, der ist mein Leben." ORG. & INSTRUMENTS: Sonate (C) for violin and org., op. 36. Sonate for cello and org., Stuttgart, Hänssler Verlag. Konzert: Ein feste Burg, for org., 3 trpts., strings, timpani, op. 57, Heidelberg, W. Müller.

Reda: All publications by Bärenreiter (Kassel). Choralsuite (1941). Choral-Spiel-Buch, for keyboard instrument, 1946. Choralkonzert: O Traurigkeit, o Herzeleid. Choralkonzert: O wie selig. Choralkonzert: Gottes Sohn ist kommen. Choralkonzert: Christ unser Herr zum Jordan kam. Triptychon über O Welt, ich muss Dich lassen (1951). Marienbilder. Adventspartita: Mit Ernst, o Menschenkinder (1952). 7 Monologe (1953). Präludium, Fuge und Quadruplem (1957). Vorspiele zu Psalmliedern des EKG (1956). Sonate (1960). Cantus-Firmus-Stücke zu den Wochenliedern des Fastenzeit. Choralvorspiele. Toccata novenaria modos vertens. Meditationen: Ein Lämmlein geht (1964). Choralphantasie: Herzlich lieb hab ich Dich, o Herr (1965). Choralkonzert: Ich weiss ein lieblich Engelspiel. Laudamus te. ORG. & INSTRUMENTS: Orgelkonzert I (1947). Orgelkonzert II (1947), for manuals alone. Orgelkonzert III 1948). Additional publications by Bärenreiter.

Reimann: Dialog I, Mainz, Schott.

Schilling: Publications by Breitkopf & Härtel (Wiesbaden), unless otherwise indicated. I. Partita in 4 Sätzen und 4 Ritornellen (1954/64). II. Partita: Canonische Variationen über "Singet, preiset Gott mit Freuden" (1958). III. Partita: Integration b-a-c-h (1961). Vom Himmel hoch (Kleine Suite) (1962). Fantasia e Ricercare 63 über "Veni creator spiritus" (1963). Chaconne nouvelle (1968). Versetten über "O Welt, ich muss dich lassen" (1968). Choralvorspiele (1969), Luzerne, Cron. Orgelmesse, Augsburg, A. Böhm u. Sohn, 1971. ORG. & INSTRUMENTS/VOICE: Psalm 150 in Form einer Ciacona for soprano/tenor and organ (1963). Canzona über "Christ ist erstanden," for trumpet and organ (1966). Drei Choral-

vorpsiele für Trompete und Orgel, Stuttgart, Hänssler, 1973.

Schindler: Publications by Kistner & Siegel and by Sirius Verlag (now Heinrichshofen's Verlag, Wilhelmshaven).

Schiske: Publications by Doblinger.

Schmidt: Fantaisie und Fuge (D), Vienna, L. Kern (now Universal Edition), 1924. Toccata (C), Vienna, L. Kern (now Universal Ed.) 1924. Praeludium und Fuge (Eb), Leipzig, Leuckart. Chaconne (c♯), Leipzig, Leuckart, 1926. 4 kleine Choralvorspiele, Leipzig, Leuckart, 1927. 4 kleine Praeludien und Fugen, Vienna, Oesterreichischer Bundesverlag, 1951. Praeludium und Fuge (C), Vienna, Weinberger, 1955. Toccata und Fuge (Ab), Vienna, Universal Ed., 1955. Fuge (F), Vienna, Weinberger Verlag, 1956. 2 Orgelzwischenspiele aus dem "Buch mit 7 Siegeln," Vienna, Universal. ORG. & INSTRUMENTS: Variationen und Fuge über ein eigenes Thema for org., 14 brass instruments and timpani, Leipzig, Leuckart. Fuga solemnis for org., 6 horns, 3 trpts., 3 trbns., tuba and percussion, Vienna, Doblinger, 1939. Choralvorspiel: Gott erhalt for organ with brass ad. lib., Vienna, Weinberger, 1959.

Schneidt: Publications by Leuckart and Bärenreiter.

Schönberg: Variations on a Recitative, op. 40 (1940) (Contemporary Organ Series, No. 13), New York, H. W. Gray.

Schroeder: Praeludium und Fuge: Christ lag in Todesbanden, Düsseldorf, Schwann, 1930. Toccata (c), Düsseldorf, Schwann, 1930. Fantasie (e), Mainz, Schott, 1931. 6 kleine Praeludien und Intermezzi, Mainz, Schott, 1932. 6 Orgelchoräle über altdeutsche geistliche Volkslieder, Mainz, Schott, 1934. Praeludia, Mainz, Schott, 1935. 4 Choralvorspiele, Freiburg, Christophorus Verlag, 1948. 2 Choralvorspiele, Munich, Leuckart, 1952. 4 Marianische Antiphone, Mainz, Schott, 1953. Fantasie: O heiligste Dreifaltigkeit, Düsseldorf, Schwann, 1955. Orgelsonate I, Mainz, Schott, 1956. Liturgische Vorspiele zur Messe "Puer natus est," Freiburg, Christophorus Verlag, 1957. Partita: Veni creator spiritus, Mainz, Schott, 1958. 7 kleine Intraden, Mainz, Schott, 1959. Liturgische Vorspiele zur

Messe XIII. Sonntag nach Pfingsten, Freiburg, Christophorus Verlag, 1959. *Pezzi piccolo,* Bergamo, Carrara, 1961. *Orgel-Mosaiken,* Düsseldorf, Schwann. *Praeludium in E,* Mechelen, Verlag Adagio, 1962. *Orgelordinarium IV,* Mainz, Schott, 1962. *Orgelbuch zu Uhlenbergs Psalmliedern,* Düsseldorf, Schwann, 1962. 8 *Orgelchoräle im Kirchenjahr,* Mainz, Schott, 1963. *Orgelsonate II,* Mainz, Schott, 1964. 2 *Choralvorspiele,* Cologne, Biehler, 1965. *Gregorianische Miniaturen,* Altötting, Coppenrath, 1965. *Praeambeln und Interludien,* Mainz, Schott. *Sonate III,* Mainz, Schott. *Orgelchoräle im Kirchenjahr,* Mainz, Schott. *Quadrinon,* Cologne, Gerig, 1971. 12 *Orgelchoräle für die Weihnachtszeit,* Düsseldorf, Schwann, ORG. & INSTRUMENTS: *Konzert* for org. & orch., op. 25, Mainz, Schott, 1938. 5 *Stücke* for violin and organ, Mainz, Schott. *Praeludium, Kanzone und Rondo* for violin and organ, Mainz, Schott. *Concertino* for violin, oboe and org., Mainz, Schott. 3 *Dialoge* for oboe and org., Mainz, Schott. *Sonate* for cello and org., Mainz, Schott. *Duplum* for organ and harpsichord (or for 2 positive organs), Mainz, Schott, 1970.

Schwarz-Schilling: Publications for organ alone by Bärenreiter (Kassel) and Merseburger (Berlin). ORG. & IN-MENTS: *Da Jesus an dem Kreuz stund* for flute, viola and organ (or for organ alone), Bärenreiter, 1949. *Concerto per Organo,* for organ and orch., Merseburger, 1959.

Schweppe: *Toccata und Fuge* (1963), Wiesbaden, Breitkopf & Härtel. 8 *Orgel-Choräle* (1965), Wiesbaden, Breitkopf & Härtel.

Stockmeier: Major publishers are Kistner & Siegel (Cologne/now located in Porz am Rhein) and Möseler Verlag (Wolfenbüttel). *Sonate I,* Mös., 1965. *Sonate II,* Mös. *Sonate III,* Mös. 10 *Orgelstüke,* Düsseldorf, Schwann. *Variationen über ein Thema von Johann Kuhnau (Die Orgel,* I/10), K & S, 1961. 3 *Inventionen (Die Orgel* I/II), K & S, 1965. *Tokkata I (Die Orgel,* I/12), K & S. 1963. *Variationen über "Herrscher über Tod und Leben," (Die Orgel,* I/13), K & S. 2 *Orgelstücke (Die Orgel,* I/14), K & S, 1966. *Pastoral-Suite für Orgel nach Klavier-stücken von Antonio Soler (Die Orgel,* I/17), K & S, 1965. *Choral-*

vorspiele und Begleitsätze (Die Orgel, I/19), K & S. *Tokkata II (Die Orgel,* I/23), K & S. *Choralvorspiele und Begleitsätze zu Advents- und Passionsliedern (Die Orgel,* I/24), K & S. ORG. & IN-STRUMENTS: *Konzert* for org. & string orch., Mös. *Partita: Jauchzet alle Lande, Gott zu Ehren* for org. and unison choir ad. lib. *(Die Orgel,* I/18), K & S. *Variationen* for org. & brass, Kassel, Bärenreiter.

Tachezi: *Partita: Veni Sancte Spiritus,* Vienna, Doblinger, 1966, *Ludus Organi Contemporarii,* part I, Vienna, Doblinger, 1973. (A pedagogical study consisting of compositions which explore technical and musical problems of contemporary organ music.)

Thomas: Publications by Breitkopf & Härtel.

Tiessen: *Werk 46, Passacaglia und Fuge,* Leipzig, Kistner & Siegel. *Musik für Viola mit Orgel,* op. 59, Berlin, Musikverlag Ries & Erler.

Walcha: *Choralvorspiele,* 4 vols., Frankfurt, C. F. Peters, 1945, 1963, 1966.

Wenzel: *Choralmesse,* Leipzig, Kistner & Siegel, 1939. *Toccata* (d), Wiesbaden, Breitkopf & Härtel. *Fuga variata,* Kassel, Bärenreiter. *Orgelmesse (Orgelbuch zum EKG,* ed. Brodde, vol. IX), Kassel, Bärenreiter. 3 *kanonische Partiten,* Tübingen, Schultheiss. *Sonate über ein Thema,* Berlin, Merseburger, 1963. *Fantasie und Fuge in d,* Tübingen, Schultheiss. Plus chorale preludes and other works.

Weyrauch: *Praeludium, Arie e Fuga* (1935), Leipzig, Breitkopf & Härtel, 1938, 2/1952. 7 *Partiten auf das Kirchenjahr,* Leipzig, Breitkopf & Härtel, 1938-40. *Sonate,* Leipzig, Peters, 1955. ORG. & INSTRUMENTS: *Passionssonate: Herzliebster Jesu* for viola and organ (1932), Stuttgart, Hänssler, 1963. Plus chorale preludes.

Wiemer: All publications by Breitkopf & Härtel (Wiesbaden). *Partita: Jesus Christus, unser Heiland* (1960). 6 *Choralvorspiele* (1961). *Choralfantasie: Erhalt uns, Herr* (1961). *Präludium, Trio und Fuge* (1963). *Evocation I,* 1965. *Evocation II,* 1969. *Evocation III,* 1971. *Pifferari,* 1969. *Choralvorspiele II,* 1969.

Yun: *Tuyaux sonores* (1967), Berlin, Bote & Bock.

Zimmerman: 4 *Orgelpsalmen*, Berlin, Merseburger.

Collections

There are many collections of modern German organ music. The following list is representative.

Choralvorspiele zu gebräuchlichen Melodien des Evangelischen Kirchengesangbuches, Berlin, Merseburger. Chorale preludes on common melodies of the Protestant hymnal. Published in connection with the church music division of the Protestant church in Hessen and Nassau.

Choralvorspiele Rheinland, Westfalen, Lippe, ed. Gottschick/Schwarz, Berlin, Merseburger. Introductions and chorale preludes for the Evangelische Kirchengesangbuch of Rheinland, Westfallen and Lippe. Composers: Acker, Kluge, Koch, Stockmeier, Wellmann, etc.

Choralvorspiele zum Kirchenlied, vols. IV, V, VI, VII, ed. Neuss, Freiburg, Christophorus-Verlag Herder. Chorale preludes on melodies sung in the Catholic church. Composers: Ahrens, Baur, Kickstat, Schwarz-Schilling, Schroeder, Quack, etc. Vols. 1-3 of this series have works by the old masters.

73 leichte Choralvorspiele, 2 vols., ed. Fiebig/Fleischer, Leipzig/Munich, Leuckart, 1941,2/1952. Chorale preludes by old and new masters, including David, Degen, Distler, Fiebig, Genzmer, Grabner, Hessenberg, Högner, Marx, Metzler, Micheelsen, Pepping, Reda, Rohwer, Wenzel, Werner, Weyrauch.

Musica Organi, vol. II, ed. Weman, Stockholm, Nordiska Musikförlaget, 1954. Works by Reger (op. 59), Schmidt, Raphael, Pepping, Micheelsen, and by modern composers from other countries.

Neue Choralvorspiele, vols. II, III, ed. Metzger, Tübingen, C. L. Schultheiss. *Choralbearbeitungen* based on the melodies of the EKG. Composers represented are generally unknown outside of Germany.

Neue Orgelvorspiele, 2 vols., ed. Haag/Hennig, Berlin, Merseburger. Chorale preludes for some of the less common melodies of the EKG.

Neue Weihnachtsmusik, ed. Baum, Kassel, Bärenreiter. Short Christmas pieces by Bornefeld, Rein, Marx, Kickstat, Reda, Schwarz, Distler, Walcha, etc.

Das Organistenamt, Part II, in 2 vols., ed. Ramin, Wiesbaden, Breitkopf & Härtel. A new edition by D. Hellmann is in preparation. Contents: chorale preludes by composers of the 17th-20th centuries. Among 20th c. composers are: Grabner, Hasse, Moser, S. W. Müller, Ramin, Reger, Thomas, Weyrauch, Distler, Hoyer, Karg-Elert, Raphael, F. Schmidt.

Organum in Missa Cantata, 3 vols., ed. Quack/Walter, Freiburg, Christophorus-Verlag Herder. Vol. I: Advent through Ascension; II: Pentecost through the end of the church year; III: Feast Days and postludes on the various "Ite missa est." The Germans/Austrians represented include: Doerr, Doppelbauer, Gindele, Heiller, Jaeggi, Roesling, Quack, Schroeder, H. Schubert, Trexler, etc. Works by composers of several other nationalities are also included (A. de Klerk, Fl. Peeters, J. Langlais, etc.)

Orgelbuch zum Evangelischen Kirchengesangbuch, 23 vols., ed. Brodde, Kassel, Bärenreiter. Each volume contains 2-7 chorale settings. Composers: Baur, Bornefeld, Barbe, Distler, Driessler, Fiebig, Grabner, Hessenberg, Micheelsen, Wenzel, etc.

Orgelvorspiele zum Evangelischen Kirchengesangbuch, ed. Poppen/Reich/Strube, Berlin, Merseburger. Chorale preludes by Barbe, Beyer, Bossler, Fiebig, Grabner, Hessenberg, Micheelsen, Raphael, Wenzel, Zipp, and many others.

The Parish Organist, 12 vols., ed. Fleischer/Goldschmidt/Gieschen, St. Louis, Concordia. A number of 20th century German composers are represented, although there are many composers from other countries and other periods, as well.

NOTES

[1] "Der Verfasser ersucht dringend, sich im ganzend Werk auf den jeweils angegebenen Manualwechsel beschränken und auf die Anwendung des Roll- oder Jalousieschwellers sowie auf jegliche 'Farbigkeit' überhaupt verzichten zu wollen, da solches dem Geist des Werkes durchaus widerspräche."

[2] "Spielern von Orgeln mit Walzen und Jalousieschwellern steht es frei, durch reichere Farbgebung und dynamische übergänge den Ausdruck über das in den Stärkegradvorschriften angegebene Mass zu verstärken." — Foreword to *Sonate I.*

MUSICAL SOURCES

Ex. 22. David: *Choralwerk III*, pp. 1, 4.

Ex. 23. Distler: *Kleine Orgelchoralbearbeitungen*, p. 18.

Ex. 24. Pepping: *Grosses Orgelbuch III*, p. 18.

Ex. 25. Schroeder: *Kleine Präludien und Intermezzi*, p. 14.

Ex. 26. David: *Choralwerk XI*, p. 14.

Ex. 27. Genzmer: *Die Tageszeiten*, p. 5. Copyright C. F. Peters. Used by permission.

Ex. 28. Kraft: *Fantasia: Dies Irae*, p. 5.

Ex. 29. Baumann: *Sonatina für Orgel*, p. 10. Copyright 1963 Merseburger. Used by permission of C. F. Peters.

Ex. 30. Eder: *Partita über ein Thema von J. N. David*, p. 5.

Ex. 31. *Modern Organ Music*, Bk. 2, London, Oxford University Press, p. 21.

Ex. 32. Kropfreiter: *Partita: Maria durch ein Dornwald ging*, p. 11.

Ex. 33. Baur: *Partita: "Aus tiefer Not,"* p. 2.

Ex. 34a. Schilling: *Fantasia 63 über Veni creator spiritus*, p. 1.

Ex. 34b. Schilling: *Chaconne nouvelle*, p. 3.

Ex. 35. Stockmeier: *Variationen für Orgel und Blechbläser*, p. 4.

Ex. 36. Ligeti: *Volumina*, p. 17. Copyright 1966 C. F. Peters. Used by permission.

5

France

THE documented history of French keyboard music begins in the 16th century with the keyboard tablatures of the Parisian music publisher, Pierre Attaingnant. Several books of anonymous keyboard compositions were published by Attaingnant in or around 1531. With a minor exception, these are the only 16th-century sources of keyboard music in France. By the publisher's indications, his books are for general keyboard use — organ, harpsichord, and clavichord. Four books contain intabulations of French chansons, written in organ tablature. One book has dance intabulations taken from the repertory of instrumental ensemble music. Another contains motet intabulations and a brief prelude, the latter free-composed: 13 *motetz musicaux avec ung Prelude le tout reduict en la tabulature des orgues.* . . . There are also two books of liturgical music: *Magnificat sur les huits tons avec Te Deum et deux Preludes, le tout mys en la tabulature des Orgues, Espinettes et Manicordions* . . . ; *Tabulature pour le jeu d'Orgues, Espinetes, et Manicordions sur le plain chant de Cunctipotens et Kyrie fons.* . .

The double repertory of the Renaissance keyboardist — sacred compositions for church, secular compositions for court and civic functions — is illustrated by the Attaingnant collections, with the secular repertory being the more important of the two. Since the French musical Renaissance manifested itself primarily in the secular genres, French keyboardists more consciously cultivated secular music, to the neglect of sacred music. While the words "Orgues, Espinettes, et Manicordions" appear in the titles of all the collections, the secular compositions would not have been played in church, but rather on small house organs or on stringed keyboard instruments.

The *Tabulature pour le jeu d'Orgues, Espinetes et Manicordions sur le plain chant* . . . contains versets for the *Ordinary* of two masses, *Cunctipotens Genitor Deus* and *Kyrie fons.* These are among the earliest known examples (anywhere in Europe) of organ masses encompassing the complete *Ordinary.* As was customary throughout Europe, the organ versets were used in alternation with sung parts of the mass. Free-voice writing and typical keyboard figuration are present in these works.

(Example 1)

From the remainder of the 16th century, only one keyboard composition has survived, a fragment of a *Fantaisie sus orgue ou espinette*[1] by Guillaume Costeley (c. 1531-1606). Other fantaisies by

Ex. 1. Attaingnant, *Magnificat du 8e ton,* 3rd verset, m. 1-4.

Claude le Jeune (c. 1530-1600) and Eustache du Caurroy (1549-1609), previously considered as organ music, are actually instrumental ensemble pieces. Some of Du Caurroy's 4-part *fantaisies* were copied into a 17th-century keyboard manuscript[2] and for this reason they were later thought to be organ music.

From the beginning of the 17th century, a manuscript containing short, anonymous liturgical organ pieces,[3] from either France or Belgium, has been found. Noteworthy are the registration indications in this manuscript. The practice of specifying registration later became a uniquely French feature, setting French organ music apart from all others in the 17th century.

In the 1620's, two monumental collections appeared — the *Hymnes pour toucher sur l'orgue* (1623) and the *Magnificat ou Cantique de la Vierge pour toucher sur l'orgue* (1626) of Jean Titelouze (1563-1633). Both books are for liturgical use. Written when Titelouze was about 60 years old, these works are the expression of a Renaissance mentality. Imitative counterpoint occurs in all of the pieces, and the motet style of the great Renaissance choral masters was frequently employed. Compared with Sweelinck or with the Neapolitan keyboardists of this period, Titelouze was very conservative. Chromaticism is minimal, and idiomatic keyboard figurations occur infrequently. A *cantus firmus* was often present.

(Example 2)

Although Titelouze's works were beautifully constructed, his style was already outdated when his publications came into print. Thus he left no followers, established no school. In fact, during the next four decades only scant music has survived to suggest how the transition may have been effected from the sober, liturgical style of Titelouze to the secularly-inspired compositions of Lebègue and his contemporaries. One *Fantaisie* by Charles Racquet (c. 1590-

1664) was preserved in Mersenne's *Harmonie universelle* (1636/37),[4] but this work has nothing in common with subsequent French composition. A lengthy sectional work in imitative counterpoint, the *Fantaisie* was clearly influenced by the Netherlandish school.

More indicative of 17th-century trends in keyboard writing are two organ preludes by Etienne Richard (active mid-17th century). The polyphonic web has been loosened, and the harmonic structure is more prominent than in the works of Titelouze. An anonymous collection, preserved in Paris at the Bibliotheque Ste. Geneviève,[5] has registration indications given for the individual pieces. Some of the combinations here employed are identical with ones which later became standard in the French Baroque school.

Henri Dumont (1610-1684) published four pieces bearing the inscription, "*Prelude en facon d'Allemande à 2 parties . . . serviront aussi pour les Dames Religieuses qui touchent l'Orgue en façon de Duo.*" These were ensemble pieces, but at the composer's suggestion, could also be performed on the organ.

Even Louis Couperin (c. 1626-1661), the oldest known member of the illustrious Couperin family, wrote very little for organ. He was primarily a harpsichordist, and nearly all of his keyboard compositions were dances for the stringed keyboard instruments. For organ he wrote a *Fantaisie* (which is actually a *Basse de trompette*), two psalms, and three *Carillons*. His *Chaconnes*, frequently played on the organ, are harpsichord pieces. They are not ostinato *chaconnes*, but rather *Rondeau chaconnes*, a form made popular by Couperin's teacher, the famous harpsichordist, Chambonnières. Consisting of several couplets alternating with a refrain, this form was cultivated almost exclusively by the French harpsichordists, and not by the organists.

A contemporary of Louis Couperin, François Roberday (1624-c. 1680), wrote

Ex. 2. Titelouze, *Pange lingua*, 1st verset, m. 1-6.

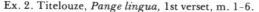

a book of *Fugues et Caprices* (1660) for the organ, but they stand totally apart from prevailing French currents. Totally under Italian influence (Frescobaldi, etc.), these pieces are in a general keyboard style, with no utilization of specific organ colors.

Other leading musicians played the organ (La Barre, Monnard, Chambonnières, etc.), but they either wrote nothing for organ, or their works were lost. For the *clavecin* (harpsichord), they wrote *Allemands, Courants, Sarabands,* and other dances. Their *clavecin* playing was based on the lute style of Denis Gaultier (c. 1603-1672), who had brought lute playing to an extraordinary level of refinement. Since the lute was the instrument most favored by the court, it is not surprising that it became the model for harpsichord playing during this period. Stylized dance suites, rich ornamentation, and the *style brisé* became standard features of *clavecin* music in the 17th century. That the lute style also influenced organ playing will soon become apparent.

The first major contribution to French organ literature in the period after Titelouze was the *Livre d'orgue contenant cent pièces de tous les tons de l'Eglise* (1665) of the Parisian organist, Guillaume-Gabriel Nivers (1632-1714). The 100 pieces in this publication were grouped according to mode, with 8 or 10 pieces in each group. The eight church modes were used, plus four transposed modes. The following compositional types were employed: *Prélude, Fugue, Récit du cromhorne, Basse de trompette, Plein jeu, Grand jeu, Duo, Récit du cornet.* In the preface, the composer provided registration indications and a table of ornaments. Nivers later published two other organ books: *Second Livre d'orgue contenant la Messe et les Hymnes de l'Eglise* (1667); *Troisième Livre d'orgue des huit tons de l'Eglise* (1675). The organ mass, presented in the second book, is based on the *Cunctipotens Genitor Deus* mass, but actually has fewer *cantus firmus* pieces than free ones. Artistically, the music of Nivers isn't on the same level as much that would come later. However, as one of the pioneers responsible for the crystallization of forms and registration which occurred during the 1660's and '70's, he is important.

From 1665 (the publication date of Nivers' first book) through the early 18th century, certain basic features characterize everything that was done in France in the field of organ composition. Before discussing specific traits of individual composers, the general characteristics of the entire period will be summarized. Among the first characteristics one notices is the declining interest in polyphony and in Gregorian melodies, accompanied by a more secular attitude toward organ conposition. The concept of alternating fast and slow movements, which was the basis of the lute and clavecin *suite*, became a governing principle in the arrangement of organ pieces into groups, or *suites*. Many organ pieces had a definite dance-like character, although they were not given dance titles. Others, particularly those entitled *Récit*, were clearly fashioned after the melodic style of the French opera. Lebègue states in the preface to his book that the *Récit* should be played "in imitation of the manner of singing."[6] The *ouverture* style of Lully, with its double-dotted rhythms and its division into slow-fast-slow sections, formed the basis for many organ *Dialogues* and *Offertoires*.

Another consistent feature was the prevalence of ornaments, adopted from lute and *clavecin* music. Still another was the use of *notes inégals*, a performance convention which required lengthening certain notes and shortening others, for a more graceful effect. A very limited use of the pedal was likewise characteristic. The pedal *Trompette* was used for *cantus firmus* melodies, and the 8' flute provided the bass line in certain trios, in *Quatours*, and in compositions with an ornamented melody in the tenor (*Récit en taille*). In addition, pedal stops were sometimes used to double the lowest part played on the manuals.

The practice of grouping pieces according to mode (called *ton* in French) was consistently applied to most organ music, with the exception of organ masses based on Gregorian chant. Often these groups were simply entitled *Premier ton* or *Messe du premier ton* or *Magnificat du deuxième ton*. In the latter part of the period under discussion, however, Du Mage, Marchand, Guilain, and others applied the term, *suite*, to such groups of pieces. The group, or *suite*, began usually with a piece entitled *Plein jeu*. This was frequently followed by a fugue. Then came any of a number of pieces, in varying order: *Duo, Trio, Récit du cornet, Basse de trompette, Récit de tierce* en taille, *Récit de cromhorne en taille,* etc. The group concluded with a composition entitled *Grands jeux* or *Dialogue.*

Another standard practice throughout this period was the composition of *alternatim* organ masses. In no other country were organ masses as numerous during the Baroque era as in France. The standard number of versets (called *couplet* in French) was as follows: five for the *Kyrie,* nine for the *Gloria,* two or three for the *Sanctus* and *Benedictus,* two for the *Agnus Dei.* To these could be added, optionally, a *Deo Gratias,* an *Offertoire, Elevation, Communion,* etc. Only one Gregorian mass was in use for French organ masses, the *Cunctipotens Genitor Deus* (Mass IV). Melodies from this mass normally appeared as *cantus firmi* in the first versets of each part of the *Ordinary.* The second *Kyrie* was traditionally a fugue based on the opening notes of the chant. The remaining pieces were generally free. They had thematically no connection with the chant, but remained in the same mode.

Registration followed certain stereotyped models, with little room for deviation. Registration types were, moreover, closely bound to compositional types, so that the registration combination often supplied the title for a composition. Briefly outlined, these were the most common compositional types:

Plein jeu, or *Prélude*: a type more sober than most, with block chords and suspension dissonances. It sometimes had a *cantus firmus* played on the *Trompette 8'* of the pedal. The registration consisted of the principals and mixtures of the *Grand Orgue* and *Positif,* plus 16' and 8' *Bourdons.* The *Plein jeu* chorus of the G. O. was called *Grand plein jeu,* that of the *Positif, Petit plein jeu.*

(Example 3)

Fugue: the French organ fugue was much less strict than the German fugue of the same period. The fugue subject was not treated with consistency, and often the texture was more homophonic than contrapuntal. Fugues were not played on the *Plein jeu,* as one might expect. The most common fugue registrations were the *Trompette* of the *Grand Orgue,* the *Cromorne* of the *Positif,* or the *Tierce.* In this connection it is necessary to note that nearly all registration indications refer to groups of stops, each group going under the name of its most prominent or characteristic member. French Baroque organists rarely used solo stops alone.

(Example 4)

Duo: a rapid, light-hearted piece for two voices of equal importance, in a somewhat imitative style. On a large or medium-size instrument, the lower part would be played on the *Grand tierce* of the *Grand Orgue (Bourdons 16', 8', flute 4', Grand tierce 3 1/5')* and the upper part on the *Petit tierce* of the *Positif (Bourdon 8', flutes 4', 2 2/3', 2', 1⅗')*. On small instruments not having a *Grand tierce* 3⅕', the *Duo* registration would have to be modified.

(Example 5)

Trio: a 3-part composition in which

Ex. 3. Boyvin, *Septiesme ton, Plein jeu,* m. 1-4.

Ex. 4. Clérambault, *Fugue* from the *Suite du premier ton,* m. 1-4.

Ex. 5. Fr. Couperin, *Duo sur les Tierces* from *Messe pour les paroisses*, m. 1-6.

the bass line is played on one manual and the two upper voices on another. A *Cromorne* combination was frequent-used for the upper voices, but other combinations were also possible.

(Example 6)

Only occasionally did French organists write a trio for two manuals and pedal. The 8' pedal flute would then supply the bass line, with solo combinations such as *Cromorne* and *Cornet,* or *Cornet* and *Tierce,* taking the two upper parts.

Récit: a melodic line in one voice with a simple accompaniment in the other parts. The solo might be above the accompaniment (*en dessus*), or in the tenor (*en taille*). The most common registrations for the melody were the *Cromorne,* the *Voix humaine,* the *Cornet,* or *Tierce.* The latter combination consisted of five independent flute ranks of the *Positif* (8', 4', 2 2/3', 2', and 1⅗'), as opposed to the *Cornet,* which was a compound stop playable only in the upper register (from mid-

dle "c" or from tenor "f"). The *Récit en taille* is a uniquely French phenomenon, apparently introduced by Lebègue. The following example, taken from Guilain's *Suite du quatrième ton,* shows the expressiveness of this type of composition.

(Example 7)

Basse de trompette, or *Basse et dessus de trompette*: a fiery solo line in bass, or as a dialogue between bass and soprano, with the other voices as accompaniment. The standard registration required the *Trompette 8'* of the *Grand Orgue,* fortified by *Bourdon 8', Prestant 4',* sometimes *Clairon 4'* and *Grand cornet 5* ranks. A smaller counterpart to this compositional type was the *Basse de cromorne.* The *Voix humaine* or the *Tierce* could also be used for compositions with a bass melody.

(Example 8)

Dialogue: a composition featuring alternation between contrasting keyboards. There were two types of *Dialogues*: dialogue between solo voices, and dia-

Ex. 6. Corrette, *Trio à deux dessus* from *Messe du 8e ton,* m. 1-9.

Ex. 7. Guilain, *Cromhorne en Taille* from *Suite du quatrième ton,* m. 4-9.

Ex. 8. Marchand, *Basse de Trompette,* m. 3–7.

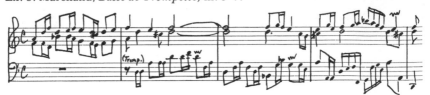

logue between full choruses. In the first category, the *Cromorne* of the *Positif* often replied to the *Cornet* of the *Récit,* or the *Tierce* to the *Cornet.* In the second category, the most frequent combination was the *Grands jeux* of the *Grand Orgue* pitted against the *Petit jeu* of the *Positif.* Thus, the brilliant sound of the *Trompette* and *Clairon* of the *Grand Orgue,* reinforced by principals, flutes and *Grand cornet* (but no mixtures), was answered by the *Cromorne* combination in the *Positif.* A *Dialogue sur les Grands jeux* frequently began and ended in the French *ouverture* style. Some *Dialogues* were written not only for two divisions, but for three or four. Short phrases would then be heard in rapid succession between *Grand Orgue, Positif, Récit,* and *Echo.*

(Example 9)

A few additional types of composition were employed by some composers, but the types listed are the standard ones utilized by everyone.

A fine example of the type of instrument for which French Baroque organ music was composed is furnished by the specification of the organ at Saint-Louis-des Invalides.[7] Commissioned by Louis XIV for his famous chapel in Paris, this instrument was built by Alexander Thierry in 1679. Capable of providing any registration desired by the French school, this organ was basically a 2-manual instrument. Only two divisions were complete (*Grand Orgue* and *Positif*), since the *Récit* and *Echo* sounded in the treble range only, and the *Pédale* had but two stops.

GRAND ORGUE

Montre 16 ft.
Bourdon 16 ft.
Montre 8 ft.
Bourdon 8 ft.
Prestant 4 ft.
Flute 4 ft.
Double tierce 3⅕ ft.
Nasard 2⅔ ft.
Doublette 2 ft.
Flute 2 ft.
Tierce 1⅗ ft.
Flajollet 1 ft.
Fourniture 5 ranks
Cymbale 4 ranks
Grand Cornet 5 ranks
Trompette 8 ft.
Voix humaine 8 ft.
Clairon 4 ft.

POSITIF

Bourdon 8 ft.
Montre 4 ft.
Flute 4 ft.
Nasard 2⅔ ft.
Doublette 2 ft.
Tierce 1⅗ ft.
Larigot 1⅓ ft.
Fourniture 3 ranks
Cymbale 2 ranks
Cromorne 8 ft.

RÉCIT

Cornet séparé 5 ranks
Trompette séparée

ECHO

*Bourdon 8 ft.
*Flute 4 ft.
*Quinte 2⅔ ft.
*Quarte á la quinte 2 ft.
*Tierce 1⅗ ft.
Cymbale 3 ranks
Cromorne
(*Cornet décomposé)

Ex. 9. De Grigny, *Dialogue sur les Grands Jeux* from *Veni creator,* m. 1–5.

PEDALE
Flute 8 ft.
Trompette

Two tremulants: Tremblant fort and tremblant doux

Not all church instruments were this large, of course. Moderate-size instruments would have fewer stops in the *Echo*, or no *Echo* division at all. The *Montre* 16' and the *Double tierce* 3⅕' of the *Grand Orgue* would be missing. Certain other flutes of the *Grand Orgue* and *Positif* might also be omitted, and the number of ranks in the *Fournitures* and *Cymbales* might be reduced.

In addition to Nivers, two other Parisian organists appear to have been particularly active in standardizing organ composition and registration in the 1660's and '70's; Nicolas Antoine Lebègue (1631-1678) and Nicolas Gigault (1624/25-1707). Lebègue published three *Livre d'orgue* (1676, 1678/79, and 1685). Like Nivers, he gave registration and other performance instructions in the preface to his first book. "My purpose in this work," he stated, "is to give the public some acquaintance of the manner in which the organ is played presently at Paris . . . They [these pieces] contain practically all the varieties that are practiced today on the organ in the principal churches of Paris . . . I wish very much that all those who will do me the honor of playing these pieces will choose to play them according to my intention, i.e., with the combination of stops and with the tempo proper to each piece. . . ."[8]

Lebègue aligned himself strongly with the secular idioms, much more than did Nivers or Gigault. In addition, Lebègue had a gift for writing attractive melodies of song-like or dance-like character. His melodic gift is particularly apparent in his first *Livre d'orgue*, which contains eight groups, with six to ten pieces per group.

Lebègue's second organ book features an organ mass (in the standard format),

plus nine groups of versets for the *Magnificat*. Book three has assorted pieces — noels, *Offertoires*, etc. Lebègue and Gigault were the first organists to write variations on noels and thus initiated a genre which was to bring fame and success to many organists for more than a century.

(Example 10)

The *Livre de musique pour l'orgue* of Nicolas Gigault appeared in 1685. Containing 180 pieces, the book opens with three organ masses, of the type previously described. These are followed by six groups of pieces, plus a 21-verse *Te Deum*, and a few noels, etc. In his preface, Gigault calls attention to certain 5-voice compositions, which he claims have never before been written for organ. Another book by Gigault, *Livre de musique dedié à la Très Ste. Vierge* (1683) contains pieces for organ, cembalo, and other instruments.

Among other organists active in Paris was André Raison (d. 1719), who wrote two *Livre d'orgue* (1688 and 1714). Book one contains music for five masses, although they are not connected with Gregorian chant in any way. All of the versets are completely free. Each mass is treated as though it were a lengthy organ *suite*. Thus, the first mode was used for all pieces of the first mass, the second mode for those of the second mass. The secular approach which has been noted in the music of Lebègue is even more apparent in the mass versets of Raison. The composer says that the character of the *Sarabande, Gigue, Gavotte, Bourreé*, etc., should be observed just as it would be on the harpsichord. However, one should play a little more slowly because of the sanctity of the church.[9] Raison's second book contains assorted pieces, including noels.

Jean-Henri d'Anglebert (1628-1691), the greatest French harpsichordist of the latter 17th century, included a few organ pieces (5 fugues and a *Quatour*)

Ex. 10. Lebègue, *A la venue de Noël*, m. 1-3, 23-25, 33-35.

in his *Pièces de clavecin,* which was published in 1689. Rich, diversified ornamentation, a chief feature of d'Anglebert's *clavecin* style, is as much evident in his organ fugues as in his harpsichord dances. Incredible as it may seem, in the table accompanying the *Pièces de clavecin,* d'Anglebert lists no fewer than 29 different ornaments.

The organ style cultivated in Paris was propagated in provincial centers by musicians who had studied in the capital. Jacques Boyvin (c. 1653-1706), organist at the Cathedral of Rouen, wrote two *Livre d'orgue* (1689 and 1700) containing groups (or suites) of pieces arranged according to mode. He prefaced his *Premier Livre d'orgue* with notes on registration, tempi, ornaments, and touch. According to the composer, these were provided because organists in distant parts of the country might not be familiar with standard practices.

Gilles Jullien (c. 1650-1703), who is believed to have studied with Gigault, advanced the Parisian style at Chartres, where he was organist at the cathedral. In the preface to his *Premier Livre d'orgue* (1690), Jullien stated that he would not discuss the ordinary combinations of stops since everyone who would use his book must surely know them by this time. He would give only a few performance instructions.

As far away as Huys, in Belgium, the compositional types, registration, and style of the Paris school were practiced by a Belgian organist, Lambert Chaumont (c. 1635-1712). A gifted musician, he published eight groups (or suites) of organ pieces under the title *Pièces d'orgue sur les huit tons* (1695). Like his French contemporaries, he furnished instructions for registration and ornamentation.

Manuscript collections of works by anonymous composers also exist. A manuscript belonging to a member of the Geoffroy family (Paris Conservatory, Res. 476) contains an organ mass, noels, and other pieces. The organ book of Marguerite Thiéry (Paris Conservatory Ms. 2094) has two organ masses, three *Magnificats,* and hymn versets, all anonymous. An organ book copied by the Père Pingré contains pieces which have been identified as Boyvin's, plus anonymous works of the later 17th century.

The French Baroque organ school reached its peak in the final decade of the 17th century with Francois Couperin le Grand and Nicolas de Grigny. Francois Couperin (1668-1733), at the age of 22, wrote two organ masses, one for large parish organs, such as his instrument at St. Gervais, the other for smaller instruments in convents. Both have the traditional verset arrangement (5 *Kyrie* versets, 9 *Gloria* versets, etc.) The first mass is a *Cantus firmus* mass, in which melodies from *Cunctipotens Genitor Deus* appear as *cantus firmi* in the first verset of each part of the *Ordinary,* and in the final verset of the *Kyrie.* The second *Kyrie* verset is a fugue based on a fragment of the chant. The remaining pieces are free. The second mass, *Messe pour les Convents,* consists exclusively of free compositions. No Gregorian chant was used whatsoever.

In Couperin's organ masses a perfect balance between secular and sacred elements appears to have been reached. The elegance and sophistication of secular keyboard music is present, yet the composer has not lost the sobriety of the traditional church style. In addition, there is a deeper level of expressiveness than one finds in the works of organists previously discussed. This is particularly evident in the compositions entitled *Récit.* Apel describes Couperin's *Récits* succinctly in the following words: "In the *Récits* the solo voices lose their former character of organ recitatives and become well-formulated, strictly rhythmical melodies: The arioso is replaced by the aria."[10]

Another serious young organist, Nicolas De Grigny (1672-1703), consistently maintained an aura of dignity throughout his *Premier Livre d'orgue* (1699). Organist at the Cathedral of Reims, De Grigny wrote one organ mass, five hymns (each with three to five versets) and a composition based on organ points. Both his style of writing and his choice of compositional types indicate that he was less influenced by the world of secular keyboard music than were his contemporaries. He wrote only a few *Duos* and *Trios,* and not any *Echos,* but instead a large number of 5-voice compositions, including fugues. He actually wrote more pieces in 5-parts than in four. The fact that he chose to write five sets of hymn versets, based on chant, indicates that he identified strongly with the liturgical organ playing tradition. In his organ mass he used *cantus firmi* from the *Cunctipotens Genitor Deus* mass.

De Grigny's organ works cannot be as easily appreciated as Couperin's. Couperin's music is much more direct, while De Grigny's is more intricate, also more modal. Still, an intelligent reading of De Grigny's music will reveal the power of his *Dialogues sur les Grands jeux* and the extraordinary lyricism of his contemplative pieces, such as this *Récit de tierce en taille*.

(Example 11)

J. S. Bach appears to have valued this music, since he copied De Grigny's organ book in its entirety. De Grigny is considered to be the supreme poet of the Old French school.

Expressiveness also characterizes the works of Jean-Adam Guillaume Guilain (dates unknown). A German (his name was originally Wilhelm Freinsberg), Guilain settled in Paris, where he published a collection of four *suites* entitled *Pièces d'orgue pour le Magnificat* (1706). With their direct, singable qualities, his compositions resemble Couperin's more than De Grigny's. Moreover, patterns indicating an influence of Italian instrumental music can be found in certain pieces by both Couperin and Guilain. These are not present in the works of De Grigny.

Some impressive compositions were contributed by the much-admired virtuoso, Louis Marchand (1669-1732). The expressive qualities of the great Couperin and De Grigny are less evident in Marchand's work, but there is still an undeniable grandeur in much of his music. True, some of his compositions tend toward the Rococo style, but others display all the eloquent splendor of the High Baroque. A selection of his best pieces was published in a posthumous collection, *Pièces choisies pour l'orgue*. Handwritten copies of other pieces (of generally inferior quality) were also preserved.

Pierre Du Mage (c. 1676-1751), a student of Marchand, wrote a *Suite du premier ton*, published in 1708 under the title *Premier Livre d'orgue*. The *Grand jeu* which concludes this suite of eight pieces is a majestic *ouverture* in the Lullian manner. It is one of the most effective examples of this genre.

(Example 12)

Nicolas Clérambault (1676-1749), Raison's student and successor, was best known for his *clavecin* music and his numerous cantatas. For organ, he wrote two *suites* contained in a *Premier Livre d'orgue* (1710?). Like Raison, Clérambault approached organ playing from a very secular point of view. Notable is his frequent use of arpeggiated chords and other idiomatic *clavecin* features. Certain pieces, especially the *Duos* and *Trios*, contain elements of

Ex. 11. De Grigny, *Récit de Tierce en taille*, m. 35-38.

Ex. 12. Du Mage, *Grand Jeu*, m. 1-5.

the Rococo style, but are not trivial. Although they have strayed far from an idiomatic organ style, Clérambault's organ *suites* are brilliant and clever.

Other French organists active in the early 18th century were small figures, by comparison. One of them, Gaspard Corrette (dates unknown), organist in Rouen, published what may well be the last organ mass from this school, the *Messe du 8e ton pour l'orgue* (1703). The pieces in it are attractive, but somewhat bland. Francois d'Agincourt (c. 1680-1758), cathedral organist in Rouen, composed six *suites* on the *Magnificat*. Pierre Dandrieu (c. 1660-1733) published in 1715 a collection of variations on noels and other songs. The frivolity and charming superficiality of the Rococo style is most evident here. His nephew, Jean-Francois Dandrieu (1682-1738), also wrote variations on noels and other songs. In them he, too, demonstrates a willingness to flatter the listener's ear through simple music, colorfully decorated in a manner easy to understand. Some of the effects he achieves are amusing, others are unfortunately trite.

J.-F. Dandrieu also composed six *suites*, published posthumously in his *Premier Livre de Pièces d'orgue* (1739). His *suites* illustrate well a trend which had been noted already in the works of Couperin and Guilain, namely the adoption of elements from the Italian instrumental style. Observable also in the music of Clérambault, G. Corrette, and other early 18th century organists, the Italian influence is now overwhelmingly present in the *suites* of Jean-Francois Dandrieu.

(Example 13)

Major and minor have now completely eclipsed the other modes, and circle-of-fifth progressions are common. The harmonic accompaniment and the concept of a tonal center determine to a large extent the melodies. The previously lengthy melodies of the French Baroque style have been shortened into more obvious tonal contours.

An almost total adoption of the *clavecin* style and an increasing preference for concert pieces over liturgical music are two other pervasive characteristics of French organ playing in the 18th century. Of all types of secular, or concert, literature, the most popular in France were the noel variations. They were brought to their peak by that grand organ virtuoso, Louis-Claude d'Aquin (1694-1772). A brilliant and nimble improviser, d'Aquin committed to paper only 12 sets of variations. His *Nouveau Livre de Noëls pour l'orgue et le clavecin* (c. 1745) can be played on either organ or stringed keyboard instrument.

Michel Corrette (1709-1795) wrote a number of noels and other concert pieces, often with glib, picturesque effects. He also composed *concerti* for organ or harpsichord, which are probably the earliest examples of this type of composition in France. Compared with the concerti of *Handel* or *Haydn*, Corrette's works are uninspired, although pleasant. A contemporary, Antoine Dornel (c. 1695-1765) wrote some pieces in the traditional French forms (*Duo, Trio, Récit*, etc.), but their musical content is slim.

Claude-Bénigne Balbastre (1727-1799) furnished a quantity of descriptive music. Thunder, bell-ringing and other programmatic effects figure prominently in his works. He also composed noels, which are degenerated versions of that most popular form, and keyboard *concerti*.

Other organists active near the end of the 18th century (and into the 19th) include Guillaume Lasceux (1740-c. 1831) and Nicolas Séjan (1745-1819). Some of their pieces were bombastic and tasteless, but others were more sober, such as the fugues that one can find in Raugel's collection, *Les Maîtres francais*. . . . In either case, no originality can be seen.

Ex. 13. J. F. Dandrieu, *Dialogue* from the *Magnificat in D*, m. 1-7.

The creative spirit of the Old French school had long been exhausted. Within the narrow framework of the *suite* and the organ mass, there was nothing more to be said. The attempts of 18th-century organists to write entertaining concert pieces had led only to a decline in artistic values. Now, near the end of the century, the French Revolution extinguished the sparse musicality that remained. Many organs were destroyed during the revolutionary period. Others were allowed to fall into ruin. Some organists succeeded in saving their instruments by co-operating with the new forces in power and agreeing to perform patriotic songs and variations on revolutionary hymns. Naturally, their music had to be performed in a manner that could be understood by the common man. The artistic effect was devastating. Previously the privilege of an elite society, music was now the tool of a people obsessed with the ideas of *liberté, égalité, fraternité.* Obvious rhythms and painfully simple melodies were obligatory. Canons, thunder, and other programmatic effects lavishly underscored pieces of an already overly enthusiastic nature. Organ playing in France remained at a deplorably low level until reforms were introduced in the mid- and latter-19th century.

EDITIONS

Attaingnant: Deux livres d'orgue parus chez Pierre Attaingnant en 1531, transcr. and ed. by Rokseth *(Psfm,* I/1) * ,Paris, Heugel, 1925. Contents: *Magnificat sur les huit tons avec Te Deum et deux Preludes . . .* and the *Tabulature pour le jeu d'Orgues. . . . Treize motets et un prélude pour orgue parus chez Pierre Attaingnant en* 1531, transcr. & ed. by Rokseth *(PSfm,* I/5) *, Paris Heugel, 1930. Contents: motet transcriptions and an organ prelude. *Pierre Attaingnant, Transcriptions of Chansons for Keyboard,* 3 vols., ed. A. Seay *(Corpus mensurabilis musici)* , Rome, American Institute of Musicology, 1961.

Balbastre: *Livre de Noëls,* 3 vols. *(L'Organiste liturgique,* Bks. 48,52, 55/56) , Paris, Schola Cantorum. *Noels,* 2 vols., Opa-Locka, Kalmus.

Boyvin: *Oeuvres complètes d'orgue (AMO,* VI) **, 1905. *Premier Livre d'orgue,* 2 vols., ed. Bonfils, Paris, Les Editions ouvrières, 1969/70.

Chaumont: *Livre d'orgue,* ed. Hens/ Bragard *(Monumenta Leodiensium musicorum)* , Liège, Editio Dynamo, 1939. *Pièces d'orgue sur les huit tons,* ed. Ferrard, Paris, Heugel.

Clérambault: *Premier Livre d'orgue (AMO,* III) **, 1901. *Premier Livre d'orgue (LGHO)* ****, 1954. The same, under the title, Organ Book, Opa-Locka, Kalmus. *Suites in the First and Second Tones (WTO)* *****.

Corrette, Gaspard: *Messe du 8e ton pour l'orgue (OL,* Bks.50/51) ***. The same, under the title, *Missa Octavi Toni,* Opa-Locka, Kalmus.

Corrette, Michel: *Concerto in d,* op. 26, no. 6, for harpischord or organ, flute, and strings, ed. Ruf, Hannover, Nagels Verlag, 1959. 6 *Orgelkonzerte,* 2 vols., arr. for organ alone by R. Ewerhart, Cologne, Verlag E. Bierler. *Nouveau Livre de Noëls,* 2 vols. *(OL,* Bks. 77, 78) ***.

Couperin, Francois: *Pièces d'orgue (AMO,* V) **, 1903. *Pièces d'orgue,* ed. Brunold, Monaco, Editions de l'Oiseau Lyre, 1949. *Messe à l'usage des paroisses (LGHO)* ***. *Messe à l'usage des couvents (LGHO)* ***. The same, under the titles, *Mass for the Parishes,* and *Mass of the Convents,* Opa-Locka (Fla.) , Kalmus. *Solemn Mass for Parishes (WTO)* *****. *Mass for Convents (WTO)* *****.

Couperin, Louis: *Oeuvres complètes,* ed. Brunold, Monaco, Editions de l'Oiseau Lyre. Contents: pieces for clavecin and organ. *L'oeuvres d'orgue (OL,* Bk. 6) ***.

D'Agincourt: *Pièces d'orgue des 1er, 2e, 3e, 4e, 5e, et 6e tons (OL,* Bk. 31) ***. *Pièces, d'orgue,* Paris, Hérelle, 1934.

Dandrieu, Jean-Francois: *Premier Livre de Pièces d'Orgue de J.F. Dandrieu (AMO,* VII) **, 1906. *Noëls,* 4 vols. *(L'Organiste liturgique,* Bks. 12, 16, 19/ 20, 22) , Paris, Schola Cantorum. *Noels,* Opa-Locka, Kalmus. *Offertoires and Magnificats (WTO)* *****. *10 Pieces and 3 Magnificats (WTO)* *****.

D'Anglebert: *Pièces de clavecin,* ed. Roesgen-Champion *(PSfm,* I/8), Paris, Heugel. The five organ fugues and the *Quatuor sur le Kyrie* constitute book 25 of Guilmant's *Ecole classique de l'orgue,* Paris, Durand, 1903.

D'Aquin: *Nouveau Livre de Noëls (AMO,* III) *, 1901. *Nouveau Livre de Noëls (OL,* Bks. 27/28) ***. *New Book of Noels,* 2 vols., ed. Biggs, New York, Mercury Music. *Noels,* Opa-Locka, Kalmus.

De Grigny: *Premier Livre d'orgue (AMO,* V) **, 1904. *Premier Livre d'orgue (LGHO)* ****, 1953. *Les plus belles Pages des "Archives des Maîtres de l'Orgue,"* fascicle 2, ed. Dufourcq/ Schmidt, Geneva, Edition Henn. Contents: selected works by De Grigny. *Mass in the First Tone (WTO)* *****. *Suites on Hymns (WTO)* *****.

Dornel: *Livre d'orgue,* in 3 parts *(OL,* Bks. 68,69, & 71/72) ***. *Organ Book,* 2 vols., Opa-Locka, Kalmus.

Du Mage: *Premier Livre d'orgue (AMO,* III) **, 1901. *Livre d'orgue,* ed. Raugel *(LGHO)* ****, 1952. *Suite in the First Tone (WTO)* *****. Included in this same volume *(WTO)* are *Preludes in the 8 Tones* by Scherer.

Dumont: *L'oeuvre pour clavier (L'Organiste liturgique,* bk. 13), Paris, Schola Cantorum. Contains *clavecin* pieces and the *préludes en facon d'Allemande.*

Gigault: *Livre de musique pour l'orgue (AMO,* IV) **, 1902.

Guilain: *Pièces d'orgue (AMO,* VII) **, 1906. *Suites in Tones* 1,2,3, *and* 4 *(WTO)* *****.

Jullien: *Livre d'orgue,* ed. Dufourcq *(PSfm,* I/13) *, Paris, Heugel, 1952.

Lanes: *Petites Pièces d'orgue de Mathieu Lanes,* ed. Dufourcq *(PSfm* I/18), Paris, Heugel.

Lebègue: *Oeuvres complètes d'orgue (AMO,* IX) **, 1909. *Les plus belles Pages des "Archives des Maîtres de l'Orgue,"* fascicle 3, ed. Dufourcq/ Schmidt, Geneva, Edition Henn. Contents: selected works of Lebègue. *Noëls variés (OL,* Bk. 16) ***. *Deux grands Messes (OL,* Bk. 29) ***. Contains a mass by Lebègue and one by Litaize.

Marchand: *Pièces choisies pour orgue, Livre* 1 *(AMO,* III) **, 1901. The pieces from manuscript collections are in *AMO,* V, 1904, *Oeuvres de Louis Marchand,* I, Paris, Les Editions ouvrières. *Pièces d'orgue de Louis Marchand (WTO)* *****.

Nivers: *Premier Livre d'orgue,* 2 vols., ed. Dufourcq, Paris, Bornemann. *Second Livre d'orgue,* ed. Dufourcq *(PSfm,* I/14), Paris, Heugel, 1958. *Suite du Ier ton,* ed. Bonfils, Paris, Schola Cantorum, 1954.

Raison: *Premier Livre d'orgue (AMO,* II) **, 1899. *Premier Livre d'orgue,* in 3 parts, ed. Dufourcq *(OL,* Bks. 55/56, 58/59, 61) ***, 1962. *Second Livre d'orgue,* in 2 parts, ed. Bonfils *(L'Organiste liturgique,* Bks. 39/40, 43/44), Paris, Schola Cantorum. *Masses* 1 *toni,* 2 *toni,* Opa-Locka (Fla.), Kalmus. *Masses* 5 *toni,* 8 *toni,* Opa-Locka, Kalmus. *Various Compositions,* Opa-Locka, Kalmus.

Richard: *Deux préludes,* ed. Raugel, Paris, Hérelle.

Roberday: *Fugues et Caprices (AMO,* III) **, 1901. 12 *Fugues and Caprices (WTO)* *****

Titelouze: *Oeuvres complètes d'orgue (AMO,* I) **, 1898. *Hymnes de l'Eglise pour toucher sur l'orgue,* ed. Dufourcq, Paris, Bornemann, 1965. *Les plus belles Pages des "Archives des Maîtres de l'Orgue,"* fascicle 1, ed. Dufourcq/ Schmidt, Geneva, Edition Henn. Contains selected works of Titelouze.

Collections

There are also various collections in which more than one composer is represented. The following is a selected list.

Altfranzösische Orgelmeister, 2 vols., ed. Kaller, Mainz, Schott S. D'Anglebert, d'Aquin, Clérambault, Couperin, Gigault, de Grigny, Guilain, Lebègue, Marchand, Roberday, & Titelouze are represented.

Cent nouveaux versets de Magnificat, vol. III: *Ecole francaise,* ed. Dufourcq/ Pierront, Paris, Bornemann.

Douze Noëls anciens, ed. Tournemire, Brussels, Schott Fr. Contents: noels by Dandrieu, d'Aquin, Lebègue.

Five French Baroque Organ Masses, ed. Howell, Louisville, University of Kentucky Press, 1961. Three masses by anonymous composers, plus one each by Nivers and G. Corrette.

Keyboard Dances from the Earlier Sixteenth Century, ed. Heartz (*Corpus of Early Keyboard Music,* VIII), Dallas, American Institute of Musicology, 1965. Contains the *Quatorze Gaillardes* . . . published by Attaingnant and a collection of Italian keyboard pieces (Gardane, Venice, 1533) .

Le Livre de Marguerite Thiéry, ed. Hardouin (*L'Organiste liturgique,* Bk. 25), Paris, Schola Cantorum. Contents: masses and other pieces by an unknown 17th century master(s) .

Le Livre d'orgue du Père Pingré (*L'Organiste liturgique,* Bks. 45/46), Paris, Schola Cantorum. Anonymous works, some of which have been identified as Boyvin's. The same, under the title, *Père Pingré: Organ Book by Anonymous French Composers,* Opa-Locka, Kalmus.

Les Maîtres francais de l'orgue aux XVIIe et XVIIIe siècles, 2 vols., ed. Raugel, Paris, Schola Cantorum. Contents: 100 compositions representing nearly all the composers of this period. Volume I is out of print.

Les pré-Classiques francais, 3 vols., ed. Bonfils (*L'Organiste liturgique,* Bks. 18, 31, & 58/59) , Paris, Schola Cantorum. Contains primarily *clavecin* music by Richard, La Barre, Thomelin, Monnard, etc.

L'Orgue Parisien sous le regne de Louis XIV (1650-1715) , ed. Dufourcq, Copenhagen, W. Hansen, 1956. 25 pieces by Richard, L. Couperin, Roberday, Nivers, Gigault, Lebègue, d'Anglebert, Fr. Couperin, de Grigny, Dandrieu.

Orgelstücke altfranzösischer Meister, ed. Lutz, Tübingen, C. L. Schultheiss. 39 pieces by Boyvin, Lebègue, Dandrieu, Gigault, Marchand, Raison, Titelouze.

NOTES

[1] Preserved in Paris, Bibliothèque nationale, ms.fr.9152.
[2] Paris, Bibliotheque Ste-Geneviève, ms. 29486.
[3] Preserved in the British museum, ms. 29486.
[4] The *Harmonie universelle* also contains 12 *Duos* of Racquet, but these are thought to be pedagogical examples rather than true organ compositions.
[5] Bibliotheque Ste-Geneviève, ms. 2348.
[6] From the preface to Lebègue's *Livre d'orgue* of 1676 (*Archives des Maitres de l'Orgue,* IX).
[7] Archives de l'Hotel des Invalides, Paris, Carton 34, piece no. 4, as quoted in Dufourcq. *Documents inedits relatifs a l'Orgue francais* II, pp. 250-253 (Paris, E. Droz, 1934/35).
[8] Translated from the preface to Lebègue's *Livre d'orgue,* 1676 (*Archives des Maitres de l'Orgue,* IX).
[9] From the preface to Raison's *Premier Livre d'orgue* (*Archives des Maitres de l'Orgue,* II).
[10] Apel, *The History of Keyboard Music to 1700,* translated & revised, H. Tischler, Bloomington, Indiana University Press, 1972, p. 737.

MUSICAL SOURCES

Ex. 1. *Deux livres d'orgue parus chez Pierre Attaingnant en* 1531, ed. Rokseth, p. 49. Copyright 1925 Heugel et Cie. Used by permission of the publisher. Theodore Presser Co., sole representative U.S.A.

Ex. 2. Titelouze: *Oeuvres completes d'Orgue,* ed. Guilmant/Pirro, p. 24.

Ex 3. Boyvin: *Premier Liuvre d'orgue,* vol. 2, ed. Bonfils, p. 84. Used by permission of Galaxy Music Corp., N.Y., sole U.S. agent.

Ex. 4. Clérambault: *Premier Livre d'orgue,* ed. Dufourcq (*LGHO*)***, p. 8.

Ex. 5. Francois Couperin: *Pieces d'orgue*, ed. Brunold, p. 22.
Ex. 6: *Five French Baroque Organ Masses*, ed. Howell, p. 55.
Ex. 7. Guilain: *Pieces d'orgue*, ed. Guilmant/ Pirro, p. 35.
Ex. 8. Marchand: *Pieces d'orgue (The Well Tempered Organist)*, p .6.
Ex. 9. De Grigny: *Premier Livre d'orgue*, ed. Dufourcq (*LGHO*)****, p. 63.
Ex. 10. Lebègue: *Noels varies*, pp. 8, 9.
Ex. 11. De Grigny: *Premier Livre d'orgue*, ed. Dufourcq (*LGHO*)****, p. 21.
Ex. 12. Du Mage: *Livre d'orgue*, ed. Raugel (*LGHO*)****, p. 18.

Ex. 13. *Jean Francois Dandrieu*, vol. I (*The Well Tempered Organist*), p. 22.

ABBREVIATIONS

* *Publications de la Societe francaise de musicologie.*
** *Archives des Maitres de l'Orgue*, ed. Guilmant/Pirro, Mainz, Schott S.
*** *Orgue et Liturgie* series, ed. Dufourcq/ Raugel/de Valois, Paris, Schola Cantorum.
**** *Les Grandes Heures de l'Orgue* series, gen'l ed., Dufourcq, Paris, Schola Cantorum.
***** *The Well Tempered Organist*, Bridgeport, Ernest White Editions.

FRANCE SINCE 1800

At the beginning of the 19th century, French organ playing was incredibly tasteless, far removed from the sophisticated art it had once been. Having become increasingly superficial during the 18th century, organ music reached absolute bottom during the French Revolutionary period when it was used as a political tool to touch the common man. Several decades had to pass before musical taste could recover from such a degeneration. Sentimentality and blatant obviousness attacked the listener from every side. Operas and program music occupied the entire stage, leaving little room for other musical endeavors.

Organ composition, as a serious art, was virtually non-existent in the first half of the 19th century, with the exception of Alexander Boëly (1785-1858), who lost his post at St-Germain l'Auxerrois for not playing in a sufficiently frivolous manner. The complaint was that he played too many fugues. In other churches organists entertained their congregations with popular opera excerpts, march tunes, and well-known piano and song transcriptions. Small wonder, then, that Boëly's contrapuntal organ versets with their Gregorian *cantus firmi* were rejected even by his musical contemporaries. He was really "a voice crying in the wilderness." Students sometimes came secretly to seek his advice.

Scattered attempts were made to raise the level of organ playing, but the first organized reform was provided by the Ecole Niedermeyer, founded in 1853. Established with the express goal of reforming organ and church music, this school taught Gregorian chant and the church modes.

In Malines, Belgium, a similar school was founded in 1878 by Nicolas-Jacques Lemmens (1823-1881) — the Ecole de musique religieuse. As teacher of two leading Parisian organists (Guilmant and Widor), Lemmens greatly influenced the course of French Romantic organ music. Lemmens' method book, which stressed equal fluency on pedals and manuals, was adopted by the Paris *Conservatoire* for use over many years. A good pedal technique is expected of every organist today, but in previous centuries French organists had seldom known how to play an independent pedal part. The brilliant pedal and manual technique which has become synonymous with the French school of the late 19th and 20th centuries was largely based on Lemmens' work. Lemmens, moreover, was a great admirer of Bach. From his teacher, Adolf Hesse in Breslau, he had acquired a veneration for the works of the Leipzig master. Passing this on to his own students, Lemmens prepared the way for the Bach revival and for the renewal of interest in other old masters.

Camille Saint-Saëns (1835-1921), a versatile composer, virtuoso, and author, was another key figure in the movement to raise standards of organ playing and to create new respect for the profession. In addition to being an avid church music reformer, Saint-Saëns was a concert organist whose sensational improvisations aroused great admiration. He wrote many organ pieces of widely varying quality. Some are loosely organized and wander aimlessly. Others, such as the preludes and fugues (op. 99 and 109) are remarkably compact and tasteful. The preludes sometimes have a French *toccata* character. The thematic material of the fugues is quite captivating, even capricious, as in the second fugue of opus 99.

(Example 14)

The organ builder, Aristide Cavaillé-Coll, likewise exercised a formative influence on French organ playing. His organs became the standard type throughout all of France, remaining uncontested even through much of the 20th century. Fully Romantic in concept, these organs were provided with a larger wind supply and a new action through the use of the Barker lever. A full keyboard was assigned to the *Récit* division, replacing the half-compass *Récit* of the Classic instruments, and the division was placed under an expression pedal capable of a great dynamic range. A huge *crescendo* could be created by coupling the manuals together, by employing the expression pedal, and by moving in succession from *Récit* to *Positif* to *Grand Orgue*. Ventils which allowed the organist to add or take off groups of stops (especially the chorus reeds of each division) provided additional means of building smooth *crescendi* and *decrescendi*.

The most successful Cavaillé-Coll sounds were the chorus reeds which dominated the entire ensemble, the smooth strings, the smaller solo reeds, and the warm full-bodied harmonic flutes. The favorite registration combinations of the French school featured these sounds, the best ones available on the Cavaillé-Coll instruments. For loud compositions, one drew all the chorus reeds and foundation stops on all divisions and coupled these together. Or, one began with the foundations and gradually added the chorus reeds of each division through the use of the reed ventils. For soft pieces, even lengthy ones, one favored the *gambe* and *voix céleste*. Solo melodies were played on a flute stop(s) or a reed, especially the *hautbois* or *trompette* of the *Récit*. These standard combinations seemed to satisfy most French organists. Only a few attempts to create unusual, original registrations were made prior to Messiaen's experiments in the 1930's and after.

As an orchestral instrument, the Cavaillé Coll organ was far removed from the traditional organ aesthetic. Yet, paradoxically, it was a chief stimulus for the production of "serious" organ composition. Now that Cavaillé-Coll had demonstrated the feasibility of the organ as a vehicle for Romantic expression, organists could more readily envision the organ as a concert instrument. At the same time, they began to replace the trivial transcriptions played at mass by liturgical music, or more properly, by genuine attempts at liturgical expression.

The specification which follows shows the Cavaillé-Coll organ of the Basilique Ste-Clothilde in its original state, as Franck knew it.

GRAND ORGUE

Montre 16'
Bourdon 16'
Montre 8'
Flûte harmonique 8'
Bourdon 8'
Gambe 8'
Prestant 4'
Octave 4'
Quinte 2⅔'
Doublette 2'
Plein jeu
Bombarde 16'
Trompette 8'
Clairon 4'

POSITIF

Bourdon 16'
Montre 8'
Flûte harmonique 8'

Ex. 14. Saint-Saëns, *Fugue*, m. 1–5.

Bourdon 8'
Gambe 8'
Salicional 8'
Prestant 4'
Flûte octaviante 4'
Quinte 2⅔'
Doublette 2'
Trompette 8'
Clairon 4'
Clarinette 8'

RECIT

Viole de gambe 8'
Flûte harmonique 8'
Bourdon 8'
Voix célestes 8'
Flûte octaviante 4'
Octavin 2'
Trompette 8'
Basson-Hautbois 8'
Voix humaine 8'
Clairon 4'

PEDALE

Bourdon 32'
Contrebasse 16'
Flûte 8'
Octave 4'
Bombarde 16'
Basson 16'
Trompette 8'
Clairon 4'

This was not one of Cavaillé-Coll's largest instruments, but tonally it was one of his finest achievements. The largest ones were the 5-manual organs at St-Sulpice, at Notre-Dame, and at St-Ouen in Rouen. One should note that the *Récit* at Ste-Clothilde was atypically small, although still very expressive. Cavaillé-Coll usually preferred a large *Récit*, sometimes with as many as 19 or 20 stops.

The French organist with the most original personality in the latter 19th century was César Franck (1822-1890). He wrote 12 large organ works, plus a number of short pieces for harmonium or small organ. The harmonium pieces, published under the title *L'Organiste*, are nondescript, scarcely distinguishable from works by Boëllmann, Dubois and others of that ilk. In contrast are the strikingly original 12 compositions for *Grand Orgue*. Their melodies are typically small in range, and a very personal chromaticism pervades each work. Modulations, for which Franck felt an irresistible passion, occur in rapid succession. Intimately linked to the tonal resources of his instrument, Franck's compositions often arose out of his improvisations at Ste-Clothilde. He was less of a virtuoso, and more a poet, than Saint-Saëns, Widor, or Guilmant, his leading contemporaries. Franck's pedal parts, for ex-

ample, are usually not very taxing, and the manual parts, too, generally require more sensitivity and intelligence than they do virtuosity. This modest, introspective man was particularly effective in compositions which expressed his natural melancholy. One should remember that Franck was not a born Frenchman, but a Belgian of Flemish descent. This may partially explain his concern for form. Using the *passacaglia* form for his *Choral No.* 2 would scarcely have occurred to a typically French organist. Moreover, the depth and profound expressiveness of Franck's music was highly extraordinary, a unique phenomenon in Parisian circles.

His *Six pièces* (*Fantaisie in C, Grande pièce symphonique, Prélude, fugue et variation, Pastorale, Prière, Finale*) date from the early years of his appointment as organist at Ste-Clothilde. The *Grande pièce symphonique*, as its title implies, is an organ symphony, reflective of current attitudes toward the orchestral organ. Sonata form was used for the first movement. The second movement is a lyric *Andante*. It is followed by an *Allegro* third movement and a *Finale*.

The *Fantaisie in A*, the *Cantabile*, and the *Pièce héroique* date from a later period, and the *Trois Chorals* are the final works of his lifetime. According to legend, Franck had been heard to say, "Before I die, I am going to write some organ chorales, just as Bach did, but with quite a different plan."[1] Anyone who knows the Franck *Chorals* realizes that they are not only a summation of everything he had said before, but a profound development of previous ideas. Majestic and eloquent, the *Chorals* contrast overpoweringly with the aimless ramblings and silly transcriptions which had passed for organ music earlier in the century.

Alexander Guilmant (1837-1911), organist at Ste-Trinité, and Charles-Marie Widor (1844-1937), organist at St-Sulpice, where he presided over an exceptionally large Cavaillé-Coll, channelled their compositional energies toward the creation of large concert works for the organ. Most important among Guilmant's compositions were his organ sonatas. Widor's major works were his organ symphonies. For both musicians, the organ was a great symphonic instrument upon which compositions of monumental scope should be performed. The following examples from Guilmant's *Sonate No.* 1 shows the two main themes of movement one — a rhythmical first theme contrasted with a lyric second theme, in the traditional sonata manner.

(Examples 15a, 15b)

Large sections of massive sound dominate in Guilmant's sonatas and Widor's symphonies. Fast pedalwork (including double pedalling), rapidly alternating 16th-note chords in the manuals and typical toccata figurations over a pedal solo are other features. They applied, actually, the flashy technique of the piano school to the organ. With Widor and Guilmant, the style traits of the late Romantic and early modern French school of organ playing were definitively established.

Despite their preoccupation with the concert *repertoire*, neither man was indifferent to the cause of liturgical music. Guilmant wrote several volumes of liturgical pieces, although these are certainly not his best compositions. Widor, too, paid tribute to the liturgical tradition by employing liturgical themes in his final symphonies, the *Symphonie gothique* (1895) and the *Symphonie romane* (1900).

Both were also active in promoting forgotten works of early composers. Guilmant's most enduring contribution was the compilation and edition of works of the old French masters, published in the *Archives des maîtres de l'orgue* series and in the *Ecole classique*

de l'orgue. Widor's collaboration with Schweitzer in editing the first five volumes of the Bach organ works was also a substantial contribution.

Less significant contemporaries were Théodore Dubois (1837-1924), Eugène Gigout (1844-1925), and Léon Boëllmann (1862-1897). Each wrote a considerable quantity of service music. Their works are often agreeably melodious, but suffer from a glaring lack of subtlety. Only a very select number of their compositions is acceptable today.

Louis Vierne (1870-1937), student of Guilmant and Widor, and the most widely acclaimed French organist of the early 20th century, brought the symphonic style to its apogee. Inspired by the gigantic, 5-manual organ at Notre-Dame where he was organist, Vierne composed six organ symphonies, expansively laid out, with interminable *crescendi*. His early symphonies are late-Romantic, with Franckian chromaticism. His later symphonies, becoming progressively more difficult, are in the Impressionistic idiom and, finally, the post-Impressionistic idiom of the 1920's. Ranking in importance immediately after his symphonies are the *Pièces de Fantaisie*, brief pieces grouped into four suites. Approximately three to five minutes in length, these miniatures reveal Vierne at his best — imaginative and witty. Among their fanciful titles are *Etoile du soir, Clair de lune, Fantômes,* and *Carillon de Westminster.* Vierne's effectiveness in evoking an at-

Ex. 15a. Guilmant, *First Sonata,* m. 20-28.

Ex. 15b. Guilmant, *First Sonata,* m. 93-100.

mosphere is seen in this excerpt from *Gargouilles et Chimères* (Gargoyles and Chimera) of the *4e Suite.*

(Example 16)

Among other organists active in the 19th-early 20th centuries were Marie-Joseph Erb (1858-1944), composer of sonatas and pieces on Gregorian themes, and Augustin Barié (1883-1915), who is remembered for his cyclical symphony.

Some of the Franck pupils were also active in the organ world — Vincent D'Indy, Gabriel Pierné, Guy Ropartz, Charles Tournemire, etc. Excepting Tournemire, the organ works of these men are rarely performed today. Their most enduring contribution to organ music was their promotion of Franckian ideals. They preached restraint and a respect for good craftsmanship at a time when the worship of technique was getting out of hand. D'Indy (1851-1931), stern and uncompromising, was the leader of the Franck circle. Together with Bordes and Guilmant, he founded in 1896 a church music school called the *Schola Cantorum.* Rapidly usurping leadership from the *Conservatoire,* the *Schola Cantorum* was for four decades the chief training ground for French organists and choir directors. It stressed the preservation and study of old polyphonic works (16th century, etc.) and the creation of new liturgical works of high quality.

Charles Tournemire (1870-1939), the only Franck student for whom organ was a major creative outlet, became organist at Ste-Clothilde in 1898. With Gregorian themes as his major inspiration, Tournemire composed an enormous body of liturgical organ music. His *L'Orgue mystique,* a monumental collection of 255 pieces, arranged in cycles for all occasions of the Catholic calendar, represents the culmination of all efforts to renew liturgical organ music since the mid-19th century. The gentle, atmospheric harmonies and the relaxed meter of Impressionism became, under Tournemire's hands, the perfect companion for the irregular rhythms and subtly flowing melodies of Gregorian chant. In Tournemire's music one finds iridescent harmonies mystically suspended in the air. In other works there is impetuosity and a fiery quality as dramatic as anything to be found anywhere in the modern French school. The following excerpt from the *Fantaisie* of the *Cycle de Noël,* No. 7: *Epiphania Domini,* from *L'Orgue mystique,* is illustrative. The thematic material is derived from the Gregorian "Litany of the Saints."

(Example 17)

Ex. 16. Vierne, *Gargouilles et Chimères,* m. 7-15.

Ex. 17. Tournemire, *Cycle de Noël,* No. 7: *Epiphania Domini,* 5th movement, m. 68-71.

As with Franck, Tournemire's style was intimately connected with the extraordinary Cavaillé-Coll at Ste-Clothilde, an instrument less brilliant than the Cavaillé-Colls at St-Sulpice or Notre-Dame, but more poetic. The effectiveness of Tournemire's music is largely dependent on the right organ sound and on so-called "cathedral acoustics." In addition, it is essential that Tournemire's music be played with *rubato,* as though it were being re-improvised.

Approximately contemporary with Tournemire was Marcel Dupré (1886-1971), who rose to the front ranks in the 1920's. Student of Guilmant and Widor, he continued the symphonic tradition of the late-Romantics. In contrast to Tournemire, many of Dupré's most significant works were written for concert performance — preludes and fugues, symphonies, etc. There are some Impressionistic harmonies in Dupré's music, but the luminous atmosphere of the Impressionists was not his true idiom. The contour of his phrases is much too regular for

that, and the use of counterpoint often determined his choice of harmonies. His major compositions are technically difficult, and in his own playing and teaching, he stressed technical perfection above all else. Throughout his long lifetime he remained a leading influence in France.

A number of minor figures might also be cited, including the Impressionists Henri Mulet (1878-1967) and Ermand Bonnal (1880-1944). Mulet's *Esquisses Byzantines,* written in memory of the Basilique Sacré-Coeur in Montmartre, are a collection of programmatic pieces. Bonnal's works include an organ symphony and pieces evocative of the French countryside. Roger Ducasse (1873-1954) and Jacques Ibert (1890-1962) also made token contributions to the literature for organ. Joseph Bonnet (1884-1944), one of the foremost organists of the period, was important as an editor, but his own compositions have not endured.

In the period following World War I some of the leading neoclassicists took a brief interest in organ composition. Erik Satie (1866-1925), the musical parodist, wrote a *Messe des pauvres* for organ (plus choir in the *Kyrie*). The work is furnished with satiric performance instructions in the typical Satie manner. Arthur Honneger (1892-1955), member of the famed *Les Six,* wrote two organ pieces. Darius Milhaud (1892-   ) wrote several pieces, thin-textured, with a markedly linear emphasis, clearly neo-classical. Francis Poulenc (1899-1963), the master of brief, lighthearted, ironic pieces, was the only member of *Les Six* who produced a major organ work. His *Concerto* for organ, strings, and timpani (1939) shows his great melodic gift and has become one of the most popular works of the modern *repertoire.* Albert Roussel (1869-1937), who turned toward neo-classicism in the latter years of his life, supplied a *Prélude et fughetta.* Together with other neo-classical works, this *Prélude et fughetta* is evidence of the revival of historical forms characteristic of the 1920's and '30's.

Another neo-classicist, but one for whom organ was a major compositional outlet, was Maurice Duruflé (1902-   ). His impressive body of organ compositions reveals remarkable melodic charm and fantastically dramatic qualities. Though few in number, his organ works are monumental in scope. All of them belong to the realm of concert, rather than liturgical, music. For the performer, they present many technical difficulties; for the listener, they have an immediate appeal. The *Scherzo,* op. 2, an early work, is reminiscent of Debussy — a reminder that Duruflé was a student of Vierne and Tournemire. In other works, or movements of works, the neo-classicist's preoccupation with formal clarity and counterpoint predominates, although the harmonies may still be quite lush. The following

excerpt from *Prélude et fugue sur le nom d'Alain* shows one of several appearances of canon in this work.

(Example 18)

The fugue has two subjects. The exposition of the first subject is followed by an exposition of the second, after which both subjects are treated alternately or simultaneously throughout the remainder of the work.

Jean Langlais (1907-   ), a contemporary of Duruflé, has enriched the modern repertory with many effective compositions — suites, liturgical paraphrases, etc. A number of his most characteristic works are neo-classical, although he has subsequently composed in other styles as well. Whatever the style, his works are melodically attractive and colorful. Gregorian chant and the Catholic liturgy have been major sources of inspiration for him. His compositions belong to the most frequently performed organ works of this century. His works being sufficiently well-known, no example will be quoted here.

Becoming a formative influence in the 1930's, Olivier Messiaen (1908-   ) is by far the most fascinating figure in a period when there were many good organists in France. His compositions are theological, which, as he explains it, means that they reveal theological verities — the end of time, the glorified body, the Holy Trinity, etc. His works are not abstract as one might expect, but are intensely sensuous since man can perceive truth only through "the prison of his flesh." Thus, in the *Alléluias sereins* of *L'Ascension,* for example, long trills and joyful rhythmic figures sound against a background of languid sonorities played on the *voix*

Ex. 18. Duruflé, *Fugue sur le nom d'Alain,* m. 105-108.

céleste, gambe, and *bourdon* of the *Récit.*

(Example 19)

Born of his Christian faith, Messiaen's music is intended to be a mirror of the entire cosmos. The exotic elements present in his music constitute no end in themselves, but are a consequence of his universalism. Inspired by the Greek modes, by Gregorian chant, the Hindu *ragas,* the rhythm of the stars and atoms, and the song of birds, Messiaen found music in all the movements of the universe. His studies led him to the creation of modes with limited transpositions, to non-retrograde rhythms, and other inventions. Since his non-retrograde rhythms revolve around a fixed point, temporal diversity is perpetually absorbed in the unity of the eternal present. A static quality results, which opponents attack for its monotony. Admirers of Messiaen, on the other hand, extol this very quality as a victory over the limitations of time and the temporal.

Messiaen's most accessible organ compositions date from the 1930's and '40's. They include, among other works, his large suites, *L'Ascension, La Nativité du Seigneur,* and *Les Corps glorieux.* As with many other compositions from the modern French school, the success of Messiaen's organ music is heavily dependent upon a good acoustical situation. The effects of infinity and of timelessness are nearly impossible in an acoustically dead room where one is constantly aware of the point from which the musical sounds originate. An organ of at least moderate size is also essential, since the right colors are absolutely vital. Even in his early works, Messiaen's registrations were sometimes extraordinary. In *Les Mages,* from *La Nativité* (1936), the pedal solo calls for *flûte* 4′, *prestant* 4′, *nazard* 2 2/3′, and *tierce* 3 1/5′. Note the absence of a fundamental. The manual accompaniment is soft. The right hand, which has a relentlessly plodding figure, employs a 16′ stop, but the left hand uses *gambe* 8′ and *flûte* 4′. Messiaen opened a whole new realm of color possibilities for the organ world.

Messiaen's language has never ceased to evolve. The *Messe de la Pentecôte* (1951), the *Livre d'orgue* (1952), the *Verset pour la Fête de la Dédicace* (1961), and *Les Méditations sur le Mystère de la Sainte-Trinité* (1973) represent further stages in his musical thought. Influenced by his student, Boulez, and by other young avant-gardists, Messiaen began to apply the principle of total serialization to his previous musical researches. His well-known infatuation with bird songs also figures prominently in his later compositions. In addition, experiments in sound have led him to try still more adventuresome registration combinations, registrations which are an absolute antithesis to the former French practice of pulling out handfuls of stops and then altering the registration by gradually adding to or subtracting from it. Taking the *Chants d'oiseaux* from the *Livre d'orgue* as an example, one sees two sets of unorthodox registration alternating throughout the piece. The first is as follows: *Récit: cymbale, bourdon* 16′; *Pos.: clarinette* and *quintat on* 16′; G. O.: *bourdon* 8′; *Péd.: flûte* 4′. The second, commencing seven

Ex. 19. Messiaen, *L'Ascension,* part II: *Alléluias sereins,* m. 40–42.

measures later, is: *Récit*: *flûte* 4′, *octavin* 2′, *bourdon* 16′; *Pos.*: *flûte* 4′, *nazard* 2 2/3′, *tierce* 1 3/5′; *G.O.*: *plein jeu*, *clairon* 4′; *Pèd*: *violoncelle* 8′.

(Example 20)

His most recent work, *Les Méditations sur le Mystère de la Ste-Trinité*, is based on an extended musical alphabet, which hàs musical equivalents for the 26 letters of the standard alphabet. One and a half hours in length, the work employs recurring musical motifs representing such phrases as "to be" and "to have" alternating with fragments of bird songs.

Influenced. by Messiaen, as well as by Tournemire, was Jehan Alain (1911-1940). Alain's music is highly emotional. His incessant repetition of rhythmic patterns (often dance rhythms) creates a deliberately irra

tional effect. *Litanies* provides the most famous example of this rhythmic reiteration, but there are others, such as *Joies*, the first of the *Trois danses*.

(Example 21)

These ostinato-type rhythms bear a recognizable Alain stamp of individuality. They have enormous vitality and a certain breathlessness, nervousness, which the composer underscores by frequent manual and registration changes.

In smaller, contemplative pieces, Alain is very much the mystical poet. Concerned with musical humanism, he focused on man's interior universe, as opposed to Messiaen who attempts to relate to the entire cosmos. For Alain, music was the spontaneous expression of the inner, psychological self. The titles and captions to his works often reveal his personal orientation. He pre

Ex. 20. Messiaen, *Livre d'orgue*, part IV: *Chants d'oiseaux*, m. 1-4, 8-11.

Ex. 21. Alain, *Joies*, m. 54-56.

faced *Le Jardin suspendu,* for example, with the following note: "Le Jardin suspendu, c'est l'ideal perpetuellement poursuivi et fugitif le l'artiste, c'est le refuge inaccessible et inviolable." (The Hanging Garden is the artist's ideal, continuously and fugitively pursued; it is the inaccessible and inviolable refuge). To the *Première Fantaisie* he appended a verse from the *Rubáiyát,* which talks about asking the heavens how fate can guide us through the shadows of life and receiving as reply, "Suis ton aveugle instinct" (Follow your blind instinct). Like Tournemire, Alain insisted that his music should be played freely, without a strict metronomic beat. It should flow like a running brook.

Others who concerned themselves with an inwardly directed musical humanism were Jean-Yves Daniel-Lesur (1908-   ), a member of *La Jeune France,* and Jean-Jacques Grunenwald (1911-   ). *La Jeune France* was an association formed in 1936 for the purpose of re-relating music to life, and particularly to man. The founding members, Baudrier, Messiaen, Jolivet, and Daniel-Lesur, repelled by the abstract tendencies then in fashion, affirmed their belief in a reincarnation of music in man. Music, for them, had a human vocation.

The two most innovative members of the group were Messiaen and Jolivet. The others, despite their high-flown goals, confined themselves mainly to compositional techniques already in existence. André Jolivet (1905-   ), linked in beliefs with Messiaen, found inspiration in the music of primitive peoples. For him, music is a magical expression, an incantation. His *Hyme à l'universe* is energetic and rhythmically somewhat complex.

A number of other composers, most of them organists, likewise added to the literature for organ. Gaston Litaize (1909-   ), influential organ pedagogue, wrote many liturgical works. Others include: A. Fleury, E. Barraine, J. Demessieux, M-L. Girod, R. Falcinelli, A. Reboulot, M. Paponaud, M. Boulnois, and Henriette Puig-Roget.

In the last two or three decades, interest in organ composition has sharply declined in France. Messiaen's most gifted students turned their talents to other fields, ones not connected with tradition or the church. The other prominent organ composers of his generation likewise had very few significant followers. The great spurt of compositional activity which had characterized the first half of the century has spent itself, particularly with respect to organ. Moreover, the latest movement in French organ circles (since the 1960's) focuses primarily on a re-discovery of old instruments and on developing new instruments which often uncompromisingly ignore the needs of Romantic literature and of much of the 20th century *repertoire.* Thus organists in their 40's and younger tend to concentrate on furthering the cause of historical organ building rather than on organ composition.

The works of Jean Guillou (1930-   ) have probably attracted more attention in recent years than those of any other French organist of his generation. Guillou favors relentlessly reiterated chords and irregular accents. Bravura pieces are his specialty.

(Example 22)

The organ compositions of Jacques Charpentier (1933-   ) are attractive, although unadventuresome when one considers their date of composition. More progressive are Guiseppe Englert (1927-   ), Jean-Claude Henry (1934-   ) and Xavier Darasse (1934-   ). However, very little organ music by them has been published.

EDITIONS

Note: 1. If no city is listed, the place of publication is Paris. 2. Not all entries are complete. For minor composers, the list of works has been deliberately restricted.

Alain: *L' Oeuvre d'Orgue,* 3 vols., Leduc, 1943. Vol. I: *Suite, Trois danses.* Vol. II: *Variations sur un thème de Clément Jannequin, Le Jardin suspendu, Deux danses à Agni Vavishta, Litanies,* etc. Vol. III: *2 Préludes, 2 Fantaisies,* etc. Three pieces (*Variations sur un thème de Clément Jannequin, Le Jardin suspendu, Litanies*) from vol. II are also available in a separate collection. *Deux Chorals,* Hérelle, 1938.

Barié: *Symphonie,* op. 5, Durand. *Trois pieces,* op. 7, Durand.

Barraine: *Prélude et Fugue,* Durand, 1929. *2ème Prélude et Fugue,* Durand, 1930.

Ex. 22. Guillou, *Saga No. 2*, m. 122–125.

Boëllmann: *Douze pièces*, op. 16, Leduc, 1890. The same, ed. Bedell, New York, E. B. Marks. *Suite gothique*, op. 25, Durand, 1915. The same, New York, G. Schirmer; Opa-Locka (Fla.), Kalmus; Glen Rock, J. Fischer; New York, E. B. Marks. *Suite No. 2*, op. 27, Leduc, 1896. *Offertoire sur des Noëls*, Durand, 1898. *Six Characteristic Pieces*, ed. Rowley, London, Ashdown Ltd., 1948. *Toccata in D Minor*, ed. Rowley, London, Ashdown Ltd., 1948. *Communion*, Leduc. ORG. & ORCH.: *Fantaisie dialoguée*, op. 35, Durand. Additional publications by Durand, Enoch et Cie., etc.

Boëly: *Pièces d'orgue pour le service liturgique*, 2 vols., ed. Dufourcq, Schola Cantorum. The same, under the title *Liturgical Service*, 2 vols., Opa-Locka (Fla.), Kalmus. Several volumes of his organ music were published by Costallat. They are usually no longer available. The *Fantaisie et Fugue in B♭* is in Bonnet's *Historical Organ Recitals*, vol. 3, New York, G. Schirmer.

Bonnal: Publications by Durand and Leduc.

Boulnois: *Symphonie*, Lemoine. Pieces in various *Orgue et Liturgie* collections, Schola Cantorum.

Charpentier: *L'Ange à la Trompette*, Leduc, 1962. *Six Offertoires*, Leduc. *Cinq Offertoires*, Leduc. *Messe pour tous les Temps*, Leduc. *Répons*, Leduc.

Darasse: *Organum I*, Salabert. Also represented in *L'Organiste liturgique*, Bk. 42, Schola Cantorum.

Demessieux: *Six Etudes*, Bornemann, 1946. *7 Méditations sur le Saint-Esprit*, Durand, 1947. *Twelve Chorale Preludes on Gregorian Chant Themes*, Boston, McLaughlin & Reilly. *Triptyque*, Durand. *Prélude et Fugue*, Durand. *Répons pour le temps de Pâques*, Durand. *Te Deum*, Durand, 1959. ORG. & ORCH.: *Poème pour org. et orchestre*, op. 9, Durand, 1952.

D'Indy: *Prélude et petit canon*, op. 38, Durand, 1894. *Vêpres du commun des martyrs* (8 antiphons), op. 51, Durand, 1899. *Prélude en e♭ min.*, op. 66, Durand, 1911.

Dubois: *Dix pièces pour Grand Orgue*, Heugel. *12 pièces*, Leduc, 1886. The same, ed. Morse, New York, G. Schirmer, 1901. Also Opa-Locka (Fla.), Kalmus. *10 pièces pour Orgue et Harmonium*, Leduc, 1889. The same, ed. Harker, New York, G. Schirmer. *Messe de Mariage*, Leduc, 1891. The same, ed.

Guenther/Cronham, New York, E. B.
Marks. 12 *pièces nouvelles*, Leduc, 1893.
The same, ed. Alphenaar, New York,
E. B. Marks. *Six Pieces* (selected from
the 1893 publication), ed. Noble, Glen
Rock, J. Fischer. *Seven Pieces*, London,
Novello.

Ducasse: *Pastorale*, Durand.

Dupré: Principal publishers are Leduc,
H. W. Gray (New York), and Bornemann. *Trois Preludes et Fugues* (B,
f, g), op. 7, Leduc, 1912. *Scherzo*, op.
16, Leduc, 1919. *Fifteen Pieces Founded
on Antiphons*, op. 18, H.W.G., 1920.
Cortège et Litanie, op. 19, Leduc, 1923.
Variations sur un Noël, op. 20, Leduc,
1922. *Suite Bretonne*, op. 21, Leduc,
1924. *Symphonie-Passion*, op. 21, Leduc, 1924. *Lamento*, op. 24, Leduc, 1926.
Deuxième Symphonie pour orgue, op.
26, Sénart (now Salabert), 1929. *Sept
pièces*, op. 27, Paris/New York, Borne-
mann/H. W. G. *Seventy Nine Chorales*,
op. 28, H.W.G., 1931. *Le Chemin de la
Croix*, op. 29, Durand, 1932. *Trois élévations*, op. 32, Hérelle, 1935. *Poème
héroique*, op. 33, H.W.G. *Angelus*, op.
34, Hérelle, 1938. *Trois Préludes et
Fugues* (e, Ab, C), op. 36, Paris/New
York, Bornemann/H.W.G., 1940. *Evocation*, op. 37, Bor., 1942. *Le Tombeau
de Titelouze*, op. 38, Paris/New York,
Bor./H.W.G., 1942/43. *Suite*, op. 39,
Bor., 1944. *Offrande à la Vierge*, op.
40, Bor., 1945. *Deux Esquisses*, op. 41,
Bor., 1946. *Paraphrase sur le Te Deum*,
op. 43 (in *The Modern Anthology*, ed.
McKay Williams, H.W.G.). *Vision*, op.
44, Bor., 1947. *Miserere mei*, op. 46,
Bor. *Psaume XVIII*, op. 47, Bor., 1950.
Six Antiennes pour le temps de Noël,
op. 48, Bor. 24 *Inventions*, 2 vols., op.
50, Bor. *Triptyque*, op. 51, Bor. *An-
nonciation*, op. 56, Bor. *Choral et
Fugue*, op. 57, Bor. *Trois Hymnes*, op.
58, Bor. *Two Chorales*, op. 59, New
York, Galleon Press. *Eight Short Preludes on Gregorian Themes*, Boston,
McLaughlin & Reilly. *Two Chorales*,
H.W.G. ORG. & INSTRUMENTS:
Symphonie (g minor), op. 25, for org.
& orch., Sénart (now Salabert), 1927/
28. *Concerto* (e min.), op. 31, for org.
& orch., Bor., 1943. *Quartet*, op. 52, for
violin, viola, 'cello, & organ, H.W.G.
Sonata (a min.) for 'cello and organ,
H.W.G. *Cortège et Litanie*, arr. for org.
& instr's, Leduc. *Poème héroique*, arr.
for org. & instr's, H.W.G. Various pieces
for organ and piano, pub. by Leduc
and H.W.G.

Duruflé: *Scherzo*, op. 2, Durand, 1931.
*Prélude, adagio et choral varié sur le
thème du Veni Creator*, op. 4, Durand,
1931. *Suite*, op. 5, Durand, 1934. *Prélude et Fugue sur le nom d'Alain*, op.
7, Durand, 1943.

Englert: *Palaestro 64 pro Organo*, London, C. F. Peters, 1972.

Erb: *Trois Sonates*, Brussels, Otto
Junne, 1908; Leduc, 1921; Sénart (now
Salabert), 1930. Additional publications
by Janin (Lyon), Schwann (Dussel-
dorf), Boston Music Co. etc.

Falcinelli: *Petit Livre de Prières*, op.
24, Bornemann, 1948. *Cinq Chorals
d'orgue*, op. 28, Bornemann. *Rosa mystica*, op. 29, Schola Cantorum. *Cor Jesu
Sacratissimum*, Editions musicales trans-
atlantiques, available through Th.
Presser (Bryn Mawr).

Fleury: *Allegro symphonique*, Hérelle
(now Philippo), 1928. *Prélude et
Fugue*, Hérelle, 1931. 24 *pièces pour
org. ou harmonium*, Hérelle, 1933. *Postlude*, Hérelle, 1935. *Prélude, Andante
et Toccata*, Lemoine, 1935. *2ème Prélude et Fugue*, Lemoine. *Première Symphonie*, Lemoine, 1947. *Deuxième Symphonie*, Lemoine, 1949. Additional publications by Editions de l'Organiste
(Nantes), Les Editions ouvrières
(Paris), etc.

Franck: *Oeuvres complètes*, 4 vols., Du-
rand, 1862, 1878, 1892. *Oeuvres pour
Orgue*, 4 vols., ed. Dupré, Bornemann.
Orgelwerke, 4 vols., ed. Barblan, Frank-
furt C.F. Peters. Other editions: G.
Schirmer, Ars Nova, and Kalmus. 3
Chorales, ed. Viderø, Copenhagen, W.
Hansen. The same, ed. Bonnet, Glen
Rock, J. Fischer. *L'Organiste* (harmo-
nium pieces), 2 vols., ed. Tournemire,
Enoch et Cie. The same, in 4 vols., ed.
Schuitema, Hilversum, Harmonia-Uit-
gave. *L'Organiste*, 1 vol., ed. Duruflé
Durand. Contains selected harmonium
pieces.

Gigout: *Six pièces*, Durand, 1881. *Grand
choeur dialogué* from *Six pièces* is
available separately, by Durand and by
G. Schirmer (New York). *Dix pièces*,
Leduc, 1892. *Album grégorien*, 2 vols.,
Leduc, 1895. The same, entitled *Gregorian Album*, 2 vols., ed. Alphenaar,
New York, E. B. Marks. *Nouveau recueil de douze pièces*, Leduc, 1912. *Gig-*

100

out Album, 3 vols., London, J. W. Chester, 1922. *Douze pièces*, Amsterdam, Seyffart, 1923. ORG. & ORCH.: *Grand choeur dialogué*, orchestrated by Ropartz, Durand. Numerous additional publications by Durand, Leduc, and Enoch et Cie.

Girod: *Suite sur le psaume 23* (*Orgue et Liturgie*, Bk. 64), Schola Cantorum. Additional pieces in other *Orgue et Liturgie* collections.

Grunenwald: *Suite I*, Leduc, 1938, *Suite II*, Leduc, 1938. *Quatre élévations*, Salabert, 1939. *Berceuse*, Salabert. *Hymne aux Mémoires héroiques*, Salabert, 1941. *Hymne à la splendeur des Clartés*, Salabert, 1941. *Hommage à Josquin des Pres*, Bornemann. *Cinq pièces pour l'Office divin*, Rouart, 1951. *Messe du Saint-Sacrament* (*L'Organiste liturgique*, Bk. 26), Schola Cantorum. The same, Opa-Locka (Fla.), Kalmus. *Sonate*, Salabert. ORG. & ORCH: *Fantaisie en dialogue* pour Orgue et Orchestre, Cologne, Gerig Verlag, 1966. Additional pieces in *Orgue et Liturgie* collections.

G u i l l o u : *Fantaisie*, Leduc. *Sinfonietta*, Leduc. *Toccata*, Leduc. *18 Variations*, Leduc. *Sagas*, Leduc. *La Chapelle des abîmes*, Leduc. ORG. & PIANO: *Colloques No. 2*, Leduc. ORG. & ORCH.: *Inventions*, Leduc. *Deuxième Concerto* for org., strings, percussion, Leduc. *Troisième Concerto* for org., strings, Leduc.

Guilmant: *8 Sonates*, Mainz, Schott S. Nos. 1-6 also published by G. Schirmer (New York). *Noëls*, op. 60, 4 vols., Mainz, Schott S. *Pièces dans différents styles*, 18 vols., Mainz Schott S. Vols. 1, 2, 3, 4 & 7 are available. *18 pièces nouvelles*, op. 90, Mainz, Schott S. *Cantique et Noëls*, op. 93, Mainz, Schott S. *L'Organiste liturgique*, op. 65, 10 vols., Mainz, Schott S. Vols. 1-4 are available. *L'Organiste pratique*, 12 vols., Mainz, Schott S. 8 vols. are available. *The Practical Organist* (selected pieces from *L'Organiste pratique*), 3 vols., ed. Warren, New York, G. Schirmer. *Sept morceaux*, London, Novello. *Orgel-Album*, vol. 3, ed. Carl, Mainz, Schott S. ORG. & ORCH.: *Symphonie No. 1*, Mainz, Schott S. *Symphonie No. 2*, Mainz, Schott S. Additional publications by G. Schirmer.

Henry: *Chaconne*, Leduc, *Thalle*, Leduc. Plus pieces in various *Orgue et Liturgie* collections, Schola Cantorum, and in *L'Organiste liturgique*, Bk. 42, Schola Cantorum.

Honegger: *Two Pieces for organ: Fugue and Chorale*, London, J.W. Chester, 1917.

Ibert: *Trois pièces pour orgue*, Heugel, 1920.

Jolivet: *Hymne à l'Universe*, New York, Boosey & Hawkes, 1961.

Langlais: *Adoration des Bergers*, Schola Cantorum, 1929. *Trois poèmes évangéliques*, Hérelle (now Philippo), 1932. *Trois paraphrases grégoriennes*, Hérelle, 1934. *24 pièces pour orgue ou harmonium*, 2 vols., Hérelle, 1939/42. *Première Symphonie pour orgue*, Hérelle, 1944. *Neuf pièces*, Bornemann, 1945. *Deux Offertoires pour tous les temps*, Durand, 1944. *Fête*, New York, H.W. Gray, 1946. *Suite brève*, Bornemann, 1947. *Suite médiévale*, Salabert, 1947. *Suite francaise*, Bornemann, 1948. *Incantation pour un jour saint* (in *Orgue et Liturgie*, Bk. 1), Schola Cantorum. *Four Postludes*, Boston, McLaughlin & Reilly, 1950. *Hommage à Frescobaldi*, Bornemann, 1951. *Folkloric Suite*, Chicago, FitzSimons Co. *In die Palmarum*, Schola Cantorum, 1954. *Organ Book*, Philadelphia, Elkan Vogel. *Huit pièces modales*, Phillippo, 1956. *Prélude au Kyrie "Orbis Factor,"* Brussels, Prestant, 1956. *Triptyque*, London, Novello, 1957. *Three Characteristic Pieces: Hommage to John Stanley*, London, Novello, 1957. *Office pour la Fête de la Sainte-Famille* (in *Organum in Missa Cantata*, Freiburg, Christophorus Verlag). *Miniature*, New York, H.W. Gray. *American Suite*, New York, H.W. Gray, 1959. *Trois Méditations sur la Sainte Trinité*, Philippo, 1962. *12 petites pièces*, Schola Cantorum, 1962. *Essai*, Bornemann, 1962. *Prelude on "Coronation,"* London, Novello, 1963. *Hommage à Rameau*, Philadelphia, Elkan Vogel, *Poem of Life*, Philadelphia, Elkan Vogel, 1964. *Poem of Peace*, Philadelphia, Elkan Vogel. *Poem of Happiness*, Philadelphia, Elkan Vogel. *Trio Sonata*, New York, H. W. Gray. *Livre Oecumenique*, Bornemann. *Offrande à Marie*, Consortium musicale. ORG. & INSTRUMENTS: *Piece in Free Form* for str. quartet and org., New York, H.W. Gray. *Concerto* for org. and orch. May be rented from H.W. Gray.

Lesur: *In Paradisum*, Leduc, 1933. *La vie intérieure*, Lemoine, 1934. *Scène de la Passion*, Leduc, 1935. *Cinq hymnes*, Leduc. 1936.

Litaize: 12 *pièces*, 2 vols., Leduc, 1939. *Prélude et danse fuguée*, Leduc. *Messe basse pour tous les temps (Orgue et Liturgie*, Bk. 42), Schola Cantorum, 1948. *Grande Messe pour tous les temps (Orgue et Liturgie*, Bk. 29, together with a mass by Lebègue), Schola Cantorum, 1949. 5 *pièces liturgiques*, Schola Cantorum. *Messe de la Toussaint (L'Organiste liturgique*, Bk. 47), Schola Cantorum. 24 *Préludes liturgiques*, 3 vols. (*L'Organiste liturgique*, Bks. 1, 4, 9), Schola Cantorum. ORG. & INSTRUMENTS: *Cortège* for org. & brass (*Orgue et Liturgie*, Bk. 9, together with a work by Gagnebin), Schola Cantorum. Additional pieces in various collections.

Messiaen: *Diptyque*, Durand, 1930. *Le Banquet céleste*, Leduc, 1934. *Apparition de l'Eglise éternelle*, Lemoine, 1934. *L'Ascension*, Leduc, 1934. *La Nativité du Seigneur*, 4 vols., Leduc, 1936. *Les Corps glorieux*, 3 vols., Leduc, 1942. *Messe de la Pentecôte*, Leduc, 1951. *Le Livre d'Orgue*, Leduc, 1952. *Verset pour la Fête de la Dédicace*, Leduc, 1961. *Les Méditations sur le Mystère de la Sainte-Trinité*, Leduc, 1973.

Milhaud: *Petite Suite*, M. Eschig. *Neuf Préludes*, Heugel. *Pastorale (Contemporary Organ Series* No. 9), New York, H.W. Gray. *Sonata (Contemporary Organ Series* No. 23), New York, H.W. Gray.

Mulet: *Esquisses Byzantines*, Leduc. *Tu es petra* (No. 10 in *Esquisses Byzantines*) is available separately. *Carillon-Sortie*, Schola Cantorum.

Paponaud: Several pieces in *Orgue et Liturgie* collections, Schola Cantorum. Other publications by Lemoine, Philippo and Hérelle.

Pierné, Gabriel: *Trois pièces*, op. 29, Durand, 1895. *Chorale, Offertoire*, Leduc, 1907. *Fugue*, Bornemann, 1912.

Pierné, Paul: *Toccata*, Lemoine. *Canon*, Hérelle.

Poulenc: *Concerto* (g min.) for org., str. orch. and timpani, Rouart-Lerolle (now Salabert), 1938.

Reboulot: *Cinq pièces pour la messe de requiem (L'Organiste liturgique*, Bk. 15: *Pièces funèbres*), Schola Cantorum. Additional pieces in various *Orgue et Liturgie* collections.

Roget: *Deux prières*, Lemoine, 1934. *Cortège funèbre*, Durand, 1935. ORG. & ORCH.: *Montanyas del Rosello* (symphonic diptyque), Leduc, 1934. Other pieces in *Orgue et Liturgie* collections.

Ropartz: *Deux Chorals*, Salabert. *Au pied de l'Autel* (100 liturgical pieces) 2 vols., Salabert. *Sur un thème breton, Intermède, Fugue*, Schola Cantorum. *Introduction et Allegro moderato*, Durand. 3 *Méditations*, Durand. *Rapsodie sur deux Noëls*, Durand. Plus other publications.

Roussel: *Prélude et fughetta*, op. 41, Durand.

Saint-Saëns: *Six Préludes et Fugues*, op. 99 & 109, 2 vols., Durand. The same, ed. Alphenaar, New York, E.B. Marks Co. The same, Opa-Locka (Fla.), Kalmus. 3 *Rapsodies sur des Cantiques bretons*, op. 7, Durand. The same, Kalmus (Opa-Locka) and G. Schirmer (New York). *Bénédiction nuptial*, op. 9, Durand. The same, G. Schirmer (New York). *Elévation ou Communion*, op. 13, Durand. *Fantaisie*, op. 101, Durand. Also by Kalmus (Opa-Locka). *Marche religieuse*, op. 107, Durand. 7 *Improvisations*, op. 150, Durand. *Troisième Fantaisie*, op. 157, Durand. ORG. & ORCH.: *Symphonie No. 3*, Durand. *Cyprès et Lauriers*, op. 156, Durand. Additional publications by Durand.

Samazeuilh: *Prélude*, Durand, 1917.

Satie: *Messe des Pauvres*, Salabert.

Tournemire: *L'Orgue mystique*, op. 55-57, Heugel, 1927-36. Contents: 51 books (255 pieces) for the liturgical year. Portions of *L'Orgue mystique* have also been published by World Library of Sacred Music (Cincinnati). *Andantino*, op. 2, Leduc, 1894. *Sortie*, op. 3, Leduc, 1894. *Pièce symphonique*, op. 16, Schola Cantorum, 1899. *Variae preces*, op. 21, Lyon, Janin, 1904. *Triple Choral*, op. 41 (*Orgue et Liturgie*, Bk. 54), Schola Cantorum, 1962. The same, Opa-Locka (Fla.), Kalmus. 3 *poèmes*, op. 59, Lemoine, 1933. *Sei Fioretti*, op. 60,

Hérelle, 1954. *Cinq Noëls,* Schola Cantorum. *Petites fleurs musicales,* op. 66, Schola Cantorum, 1935. *Sept Poèmes-Chorals* (7 tone poems on the Seven Last Words), op. 67, M. Eschig, 1935-37. *Postludes libres,* op. 68, M. Eschig, 1935. *Symphonie-Choral,* op. 69, Mainz, Schott S., 1939. *Symphonie sacrée,* op. 71 *(Orgue et Liturgie,* Bk. 44), Schola Cantorum, 1960. The same, Opa-Locka, Kalmus. *Suite évocàtrice,* op. 74, Bornemann, 1943. *Deux Fresques symphoniques sacrées,* op. 75/76, M. Eschig, 1943. 5 *Improvisations,* reconstructed by M. Duruflé, 2 vols., Durand, 1958. Plus other publications.

Vierne: *Symphonie No.* 1, Hamelle, 1899. The same, ed. Bedell, New York, E.B. Marks, and Opa-Locka (Fla.), Kalmus. *Symphonie No.* 2, Hamelle, 1903. The same, ed. Alphenaar, E.B. Marks, and Opa-Locka, Kalmus. *Symphonie No.* 3, Durand, 1912. *Symphonie No.* 4, New York, G. Schirmer, 1914. *Symphonie No.* 5, Durand, 1925. *Symphonie No.* 6, Lemoine, 1936. *Messe basse,* Schola Cantorum, 1913. 24 *pièces en style libre,* 2 vols., Durand, 1914. *Pièces de fantaisie,* 4 vols., Lemoine, 1926/27. *Messe basse pour les défunts,* Lemoine, 1936. *Triptyque,* Lemoine. *Trois Improvisations,* reconstructed by M. Duruflé, Durand. ORG. & INSTRUMENTS: *Marche triomphale pour le centenaire de Napoléon,* for org., brass and timpani, Salabert, 1921. *Adagio de la Troisième Symphonie,* Durand. Plus various other publications.

Widor: 8 *Symphonies,* nos. 1-4, op. 13, nos. 5-8, op. 42, Hamelle. The same, ed. Alphenaar, New York, E.B. Marks. Also by Kalmus (Opa-Locka). *Symphony No.* 5 is also published by G. Schirmer (New York). *Symphonie gothique,* op. 70, London, Schott. The same, New York, E. B. Marks. *Symphonie romane,* op. 73, Hamelle. The same, Opa-Locka, Kalmus. *Suite latine,* Durand. *Trois nouvelles pièces,* Durand. ORG. & ORCH.: *Sinfonia sacra,* op. 81, Hamelle. *Troisième Symphonie* pour l'orgue et orchestre, op. 69, Hamelle. Additional publications by Hamelle, etc.

Collections

Anthology of Nineteenth Century Organ Music, ed. Drinkwater, Glen Rock, J. Fischer. Contents: works or movements of works by Boëly, Gigout, Gounod, Guilmant, Lefébure-Wély, Lemmens, Saint-Saëns, Tournemire, Widor, plus German and English composers.

French Masterworks for Organ, ed. Schreiner, Glen Rock, J. Fischer. Works by Vierne, Widor, Mulet, Gigout, Dupont, R. Vierne.

Historical Organ Recitals, vol. V: Modern Composers, ed. Bonnet, New York, G. Schirmer. Composers from Franck to Reger.

Pièces romantiques ignorées (L'Organiste liturgique, Bk. 17), Schola Cantorum. Pieces by Mendelssohn, Berlioz, Franck, etc.

20 *pièces pour Grand Orgue,* Durand. Works by Boëllmann, Bossi, Boulay, Busser, Catherine, Franck, Gigout, D'Indy, Pierne', Saint-Saëns, etc.

The *Orgue et Liturgie* series published by the Schola Cantorum has numerous volumes in which 20th century French composers are represented. The following is a selected list.

Orgue et Cuivres (Orgue et Liturgie, Bk. 9). Contains *Cortège* for org., 3 trpts., 3 trbns., by Litaize and *Sonata da Chiesa* (for Easter) for org. & trpt. by Gagnebin.

Au saint Sacrement (O et L, Bk. 18). Pieces by Boulnois and Girod.

La Fugue au XXe siècle (O et L, Bk. 20). Litaize, Girod, Grunenwald, Hodeir.

L'Orgue néo-classique (O et L, Bk. 33). Reboulot, Falcinelli, Rolland, Cellier, Revel, de la Casinière.

Le Tombeau de Gonzalez (O et L, Bk. 38). Cellier, Litaize, Grunenwald, Girod, O. Alain, Robert, etc.

Noëls variés (O et L, Bk. 40). Villard, Bourdon, Bouvard, Doyen, Fleury, Joulain, Paponaud. The same, under the title *Christmas Music,* Opa-Locka, Kalmus.

There is also a series of five *Orgue et Liturgie* collections devoted to specific parts of the liturgy: *Préludes à l'Introit (O et L,* Bk. 48); *Offertoires (O et L,* Bk. 52); *Elévations (O et L,* Bk. 57);

*Communions (O et L, B . 62) ; Sorties
(O et L, Bk. 75.* The principal contributors to these collections are A. Alain,
O. Alain, Boulnois, Camonin, Falcinelli, Fleury, Henry, Jacob, Joulain, Paponaud, Plé, Robert.

NOTES

[1] Laurence Davies, *César Franck and
His Circle*, Boston, Houghton Mifflin
& Co., p. 244.

MUSICAL SOURCES

Ex. 14. Saint-Saëns: 3 *Preludes and Fugues*, op.
99, Opa-Locka, Kalmus, p. 15.
Ex. 15a and 15b. Guilmant, A.: *First Sonata*, pp.
3, 5. Copyright © 1916 G. Schirmer, Inc. Used by
permission.

Ex. 16. Vierne: *Pièces de Fantaisie*, 4e *suite*, p. 29.
Copyright 1927 Henry Lemoine et Cie. Used by
permission of the publisher. Theodore Presser Co.,
sole representative U.S.A.
Ex. 17. Tournemire: *Cycle de Noël*, No. 7:
Epiphania Domini (*L'Orgue mystique*). Copyright
1929 Heugel et Cie. Used by permission of the
publisher. Theodore Presser Co., sole represent-
ative U.S.A.
Ex. 18. Duruflé: *Prélude et Fugue sur le nom
d'Alain*, p. 22. Copyright 1943 Durand et Cie.
Used by permission of the publisher. Theodore
Presser Co., sole representative U.S.A.
Ex. 19. Messiaen: *L'Ascension*, part II: *Alléluias
sereins*, pp. 6, 7.
Ex. 20. Messiaen: *Livre d'orgue*, part IV: *Chants
d'oiseaux*, p. 13.
Ex. 21. Alain: *L'Oeuvre d'orgue*, vol. I, p. 17.
Ex. 22. Guillou: *Sagas*, pp. 15, 16.

All organ works of J. Alain J. Guillou, and O.
Messiaen (except *Diptyque* and *Apparition*) are
published by Alphonse Leduc & Cie, 175 rue
Saint-Honoré, 75001 Paris, France, owners and
publishers for all countries.

6

England

 HE history of English organ music can be traced in detail from the time of the early Tudor composers in the first part of the 16th century. In contrast to the scant material available from earlier periods in England (the 14th-century Robertsbridge Codex, believed to be of foreign origin, and the 15th-century Douce Manuscript 381, which contained only a single organ composition), several sources have been preserved from the 16th century. They include Brit. Mus. Ms.29996 (the largest collection), Add. Ms.30513 (known as the *Mulliner Book*), Add. Ms.15233, and Brit. Mus. Roy. App. 56.

The Tudor school of organ playing rose to prominence shortly after Dionysio Memo, organist of San Marco, Venice, visited England in 1516 and performed for the king. While there is no proven connection, Memo's visit may well have stimulated the surge of interest in organ music in early 16th-century England. Most English organ music of this period was liturgical. The standard Tudor repertory consisted of *cantus firmus* versets for hymns, antiphons, offertories, and other liturgical works. In general, mass versets figured less prominently in England than on the continent, while psalm and Magnificat versets were totally lacking in the Tudor school. Some of the organ pieces from this period were mere reductions of motet scores; others were original organ compositions, such as the faburden pieces in Brit. Mus. Add. Ms. 29996[1].

Two basic types of composition can be distinguished. The one was strictly contrapuntal. The other employed abstract figurations. The contrapuntal pieces, although not exactly bursting with originality, were often well-balanced and unified. Compositions belonging to the other type were generally less successful. Even the best composers of the time, once they started with an abstract figuration, repeated it mechanically, almost without variation, until they drained it of all vitality. Although stiff and pedantic, these compositions have considerable historical significance because they led to the lively figurations of the imaginative Virginalist school.

The most important composer of the Tudor school was also its earliest member — John Redford, who died in 1547. Liturgical *cantus firmi* form the basis for most of his works. His writing, generally in 2- or 3-parts, is somewhat archaic by comparison with that of leading contemporaries on the continent. In the following example, a fragment of the *cantus firmus* sounds in the tenor voice, and the 5-note figuration in the soprano is dutifully repeated in this voice (and sometimes in the others) right to the final measure of the composition.

(Example 1)

Active during approximately the same period was Thomas Preston (c.1500?-1564). In addition to offertories and an antiphon, he wrote a setting of the Proper of the mass for Easter Sunday. In other countries, it was common practice to write or improvise organ versets for the Ordinary of the mass, but nowhere was it usual to provide organ versets for the Propers. Another unusual appearance at this time was an organ mass by Philip ap Rhys, which has the distinction of being the only complete setting of the mass Ordinary by an English composer of this period.

Ex. 1. Redford, *Eterne rex altissime*, m. 1-5.

After mid-century, the foremost representatives of the Tudor school were Thomas Tallis (c.1505-1585) and William Blitheman (c.1510-1591). Their most important organ works were hymns, antiphons, and offertories, many of which were preserved in the *Mulliner Book*. Allwood, Carlton, Coxsun, Farrant, Shelbye, Taverner, and several others also wrote organ music.

(Example 2)

Unfortunately, only a short time after English liturgical organ playing had come into flower, its growth was stunted by political and religious strife in England. Following Henry VIII's Act of Supremacy (1534), organ playing came under suspicion as one of the "idolatrous practices" associated with the Roman church. In many Anglican churches, organ playing was forbidden, and organs were destroyed.

Under Queen Elizabeth, who reigned from 1558 to 1603, the negative attitude toward organ playing was somewhat relaxed. Still, the single place where organ playing was actively encouraged was the Chapel Royal, and not the churches throughout the country. At the court, organ playing couldn't begin to compete with virginal music. Although musicians of that day did not differentiate sharply between music for one keyboard instrument and another, as we do today, it is obvious that the instrument which unleashed the Elizabethans' imagination was the virginal, and not the organ. Moreover, the spectacular flowering of the arts which prevailed under Elizabeth's patronage was essentially a secular phenomenon. The many manuscripts and printed books dating from this period are first and foremost collections of virginal music. The few true organ pieces they contain are incidental. Pieces entitled *Voluntary*, *Verse*, and *Point* seem, in general, well-suited to the organ and were probably intended primarily for this instrument. The titles *Voluntary* and *Verse* refer to the function that these pieces would perform within the church service. The title *Point* means "point of imitation," thus indicating a work in imitative counterpoint.

As for the dances and song variations with which the Elizabethan collections abound, these were, of course, essentially virginal music. The short, intonation-like preludes which constitute another part of the repertory were likewise stylistically aligned with the stringed keyboard instrument rather than with the organ. Of the numerous *cantus firmi* compositions (*Fantasies*, etc.) dating from this period, many have features definitely idiomatic to the virginal. Often the *cantus firmi* were taken from Gregorian chant. In such cases, one concludes that the works were played either on virginals or on organs in private residences, since Gregorian chant had no place in the Anglican service.

Of the leading Elizabethan composers, William Byrd (1543-1623) and John Bull (1562/63?-1628) each wrote some music intended for the organ. John Bull's early organ works were in the Tudor style, with the *cantus firmus* in long note values standing in opposition to a succession of dry formulae in the other voice(s). His late organ works, presumably written after he had moved to the continent, reveal, on the other hand, considerable contrapuntal mas-

Ex. 2. Tallis, *Hymn: Iste confessor*, m. 1-4, 19, 20.

tery and more imagination. His set of variations on the Dutch sacred folk song, *Laet ons met herton reyne,* is one of the earliest examples (in any country) of music containing directions for organ registration.

(Example 3)

Peter Philips (1560/61-1628), who traveled extensively in Europe and then settled in Antwerp, later in Brussels, will be discussed with the composers of the Low Countries in another chapter.

As far as one has been able to ascertain, 16th-century organists had to be content with one-manual instruments, having only Diapason and Flute stops. The earliest two-manual specification dates from 1613, at Worchester Cathedral. Two-manual instruments of the first half of the 17th century had a Great and a Chaire organ, but the specifications did not go beyond Diapasons and Flutes. There were no independent pedal stops. One doesn't know if they had pedal pull-downs, or if these first appeared later in the century. As organs were used primarily to accompany choral singing and to play modest voluntaries during the service, small instruments were quite adequate.

Two of the earliest organists who composed specifically for the two-manual organ were John Lugge and Orlando Gibbons. Lugge (c. 1587-c. 1647), organist at the Cathedral of Exeter, wrote three voluntaries for "double organ," as the two-manual instrument was called. Gibbons (1583-1625) wrote a *Fancy for a double orgaine.*

(Example 4)

Some other organists were active in the first half of the 17th century (Benjamin Cosyn, John Robinson, John Reading, John Barrett, etc.), but they are not particularly important as composers. Thomas Tomkins (1571-1656) also contributed several organ pieces, but in the outmoded Tudor style of Redford, Tallis, and Blitheman. These works contrast sharply with Tomkins' virginal pieces which were definitely up-to-date. The religious and political turmoil of the country may well have influenced Tomkins to compose as he did. In 1644 Parliament passed an ordinance which specifically ordered the abolishment of organs, together with other superstitious monuments and practices. Organs and choir books were now destroyed with a vengeance, choirs were disbanded, and church musicians were left without employment, penniless. It was during this tragic period, the final decade of his life, that Tomkins wrote his organ works. One wonders if he might not have been deliberately attempting to preserve the English organ tradition in the face of the Puritans' assault on culture.

After the Restoration of the monarchy (1660), organ music again entered the church. Obviously, a number of new organs had to be built and others repaired after the treatment they had received during the Commonwealth years. It was during this Restoration era that the famous Father Smith took the lead in English organ building and iniated several far-reaching changes. He added solo stops, such as Cornet, Sesquialtera, and Trumpet, and sometimes a mixture, thereby establishing a new taste in English organ building. He frequently built 3-manual instruments. The type of instrument which he created remained standard for well over a

Ex. 3. Bull, *Salve regina,* vs. 1, m. 1-5, 7, 8.

Ex. 4. Lugge, *Voluntary No.* 2, m. 69-71.

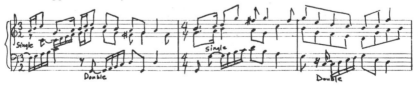

century. The only significant change was the addition of a Swell division during the 18th century. The specification of the organ which he built for the Banqueting House Chapel in London in 1699[2] is quoted below.

GREAT
GG(no GG#) to c³
53 notes

Open Diapason 8'
Hohl Flute 8'
Principal 4'
Nason Flute 4'
Twelfth 2-2/3'
Fifteenth 2'
Block Flute 2' (from c#)
Sesquialtera III
Cornet (from c#') III
Trumpet 8'

CHAIRE
GG(no GG#) to c³
53 notes

Stopped Diapason 8'
Principal 4'
Flute (from c') 8'
Cremona 8 '
Vox Humana 8'

ECHO
g(no g# ?) to c³
29 notes

Open Diapason 8'
Principal 4'
Cornet II
Trumpet 8'

One should remember that not all English organs of this period had three divisions. As a matter of fact, most organists had to be satisfied with one- or two-manual instruments. On small instruments, the solo ranks were frequently divided into bass and descant, so that one could play both accompaniment and solo on the same manual. Pedal stops were still absent, although pulldowns were found on some instruments. However, pedal playing, except in a most rudimentary form, simply did not exist in England prior to the 19th century.

Although the church services didn't demand any elaborate organ music, the new instruments themselves must have inspired organists to compose in a more interesting, less serious, fashion than had previously prevailed. Matthew Locke (c. 1630-1677), primarily known as a composer of vocal church music, wrote some organ pieces, seven of which have been preserved in his keyboard collection entitled *Melothesia* (1673). In the "Advertisements to the Reader" with which Locke prefaces the collection, he lists the major ornaments employed by English keyboardists. Although this is often overlooked today, skillful embellishments were just as essential for English organ music of the 17th century as they were for virginal music. Christopher Gibbons (1615-1676) and Benjamin Rogers (1614-1698) also wrote a few organ pieces. Noteworthy in their works are echo effects and an imaginative use of ornamentation.

(Example 5)

John Blow (1649-1708), the most significant keyboardist since the Elizabethan masters, wrote quite a number of organ works — preludes, voluntaries, verses, fugues. Unity is often lacking in his compositions, yet there is more depth than could customarily be found in English organ music of this period. He learned to display the solo stops of the organ in an attractive manner, and he developed a skillful way of handling echo effects. The excerpt which follows has been taken from his *Echo Voluntary in G*, which was written for a 3-manual organ. The Great Cornet was to be used as the primary solo stop. Answering it was the Cornet of the Echo organ. Intervening interludes and accompanimental parts were played on the Diapasons of the Chaire organ.

(Example 6)

The banality which too often accompanies Echo compositions is successfully avoided in this particular case. Blow knew just the right moment to vary the rhythmic and melodic patterns of the echo fragments. Then, in addition,

Ex. 5. Chr. Gibbons, *Voluntarie*, m. 15-20.

Ex. 6. Blow, *Echo Voluntary in G*, m. 25–29.

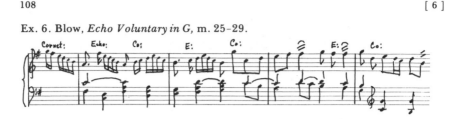

he contrasted these with points of imitation in the Diapason interludes.

Considered one of the foremost masters of his time, Blow relinquished his organ position at Westminster Abbey in 1680 so that his most gifted pupil, Henry Purcell (1659-1695), could succeed him. Certainly, Purcell did take English music to new heights of greatness, but he did not make a major contribution to organ music. The most famous organ pieces formerly attributed to him have for some years been known to be arrangements, to be compositions by someone else, or to be of at least dubious authorship. Some believe the *Voluntary on Old* 100th may have been composed by Blow. Regardless of who wrote it, this voluntary, written for an organ with divided stops (descant and bass) and no pedal, is a unique work, since English organists did not normally write liturgical settings during this period.

Purcell wrote only a handful of organ pieces, some of which are short and not particularly impressive. His *Voluntary in G*, however, is a noble work, and his Voluntary for Double Organ is quite dramatic. Among other things, the *Voluntary for Double Organ* may indicate an acquaintance with the music of Frescobaldi. In style, it has little in common with the 18th-century organ music of Walond, Boyce, Greene, and company, who employed an even metrical pulse and melodies with very regular contours. Purcell's voluntary, as shown in the following excerpt, has a more free melodic line and is extensively embellished.

(Example 7)

In the early 18th century, in the generation after Purcell, voluntaries, two movements in length, increasingly replaced the one-movement voluntary which had been standard up to that time. In the voluntaries of William Croft (1678-1727), for example, there is often a slow introduction, followed by a fast, contrapuntal movement. Somewhat later, after Handel had placed his unmistakeable stamp on English music, specific Handellian trademarks show up in most of the mid-18th century English voluntaries.

Before discussing Handel and his followers, however, one would like to note an English organist who differed significantly from his contemporaries, Thomas Roseingrave (1690-1766), who studied for some years in Italy (1710-1718?). He spent considerable time with Domenico Scarlatti. The unusual modulations, chromatic melodies, and freely-handled dissonances in Roseingrave's organ works clearly indicate Scarlatti's influence.

George Frideric Handel (1685-1759) came to England to produce Italian opera, that most fashionable form of music during the first quarter of the 18th century. As is commonly known, he began writing oratorios after Italian opera had fallen out of favor. It was intended to provide a diverting change at intermission time. Scored for chamber orchestra and organ or harpsichord, the concertos are gay, lighthearted pieces containing some virtuoso elements. Handel himself presided at the organ, and he naturally improvised much in addition to what he had sketched on the page. Today, in performing these works, an organist has the option of elaborating on the score (especially during repeated sections), of improvising cadenzas and

Ex. 7. Purcell, *Voluntary for Double Organ*, m. 23–26.

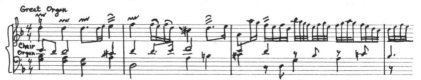

sometimes entire movements.

Handel was one of the earliest composers to write organ concertos.[3] This new form became especially beloved in England, although it was not unknown elsewhere. J. G. Graun (1702/03-1771) and C. P. E. Bach (1714-1788), musicians at the court of Frederick the Great, both composed organ concertos. The French composers, Michel Corrette (1709-1795) and Claude-Bénigne Balbastre (1727-1799) did likewise. And later, the Viennese Classical composers produced several examples in this form.

The immense popularity of Handel's organ concertos stimulated a new creative period in English organ composition. In contrast to the sober voluntaries of the previous century, English organ compositions of the Handellian and post-Handellian eras were gay and secular in character. Conceived primarily as concert music, the best examples of organ music from the mid- and latter-18th century have a strong, rhythmic sense and an exuberant melodic line. Handel's cosmopolitan style — an amalgamation of Italian, German, and English characteristics — formed the model for the new style. This was applied equally to concertos for organ and orchestra and to voluntaries for organ alone. Some voluntaries were now three or four movements in length, although the two-movement voluntary continued its supremacy.

Maurice Greene (1695-1755), contemporary and long-time friend of Handel, wrote a number of voluntaries which clearly reflect the Handel style. His *Voluntary No. 10 in D Minor*, for example, is a two-movement work (*Largo* and

Allegro) consisting of a majestic French overture and a spritely fugue.

(Examples 8a, 8b)

William Boyce (1710-1779) and William Walond (1725-1770), two other skillful composers of the late Baroque, each wrote several voluntaries which characteristically consist of a broad, stately first movement, followed by a fast one. The second movement would be either fugal or would feature a solo stop (Cornet, Trumpet, etc.), sometimes with echo effects. One of Boyce's most captivating works is his *Voluntary No. 1 in D Major*, from which the following two quotations have been taken.

(Examples 9a, 9b)

William Felton (1714-1769), equally under Handel's influence, wrote 32 concertos for organ or harpsichord. Although all of them were published during his lifetime, only a few are available today. The modern editions, unfortunately, are arrangements for organ alone, rather than the actual concertos for organ and orchestra.

Thomas Arne (1710-1778) and John Stanley (1713-1786), two other successful composers, united elements of the Handel manner with transitional features of the pre-Classical, or Gallant style. Arne wrote six concertos for organ and chamber orchestra (strings and 2 oboes, usually). Actually, these concertos, like those of Handel, Felton, etc., were written for any keyboard instrument, and not exclusively for organ. This fact was nearly always indicated on the title page. Since a few registration indications were given, however,

Ex. 8a. Greene, *Voluntary No. 10 in D Minor,* 1st mov't, m. 1-4.

Ex. 8b. Greene, *Voluntary No. 10 in D Minor,* 2nd mov't, m. 1-4.

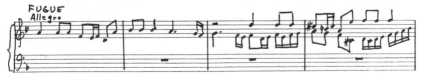

Ex. 9a. Boyce, *Voluntary No. 1 in D Major,* 1st mov't, m. 1-5.

Ex. 9b. Boyce, *Voluntary No. 1 in D Major,* 2nd mov't, m. 1-8.

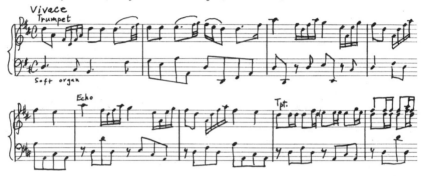

one assumes that Arne, like Handel, preferred to use the organ. An excerpt from Arne's *Concerto No. 5* follows.

(Example 10)

Crossing of the hands and frequent manual changes for echo effects make this a virtuoso piece, for the performer. The listener, however, perceives the work simply as a charming piece, moving the emotions agreeably, without any strain on the intellect.

The works of John Stanley often have the same attractive, deceptively simple quality. Some of his compositions are obviously late Baroque, while others have definitely moved into the Gallant style. His contribution to English organ literature is considerable. He published in 1775 *Six Concertos for the Organ, Harpsichord, or Forte Piano; with accompanyments for two violins and a bass.* He also wrote three sets of 10 voluntaries each, published in 1748, 1752, and 1754. Most of the voluntaries are two movements in length, although there are some 3- and 4-movement voluntaries as well. Echos are amply present in the majority of his compositions. In the two-movement works, the first

Ex. 10. Arne, *Concerto V,* 1st mov't, m. 52-59.

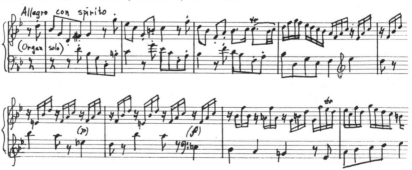

movement is normally an *Adagio* played on the Diapasons. The second movement is quick in tempo and features a solo stop, most often Trumpet or Cornet, sometimes Stopped Diapason or Flute. Stanley's writing for solo stops is very idiomatic. The Trumpet solos really sound like fanfares, and the Cornet solos move rapidly up and down, exploiting the brilliance of the Cornet timbre. In addition, Stanley composed some examples of the type of work known as the *Full Voluntary*. For the *Full Voluntary*, one uses the complete Diapason chorus of the Great organ from beginning to end.

(Examples 11, 12)

Several other composers contributed organ concertos and voluntaries during the late Baroque and Gallant eras. John Keeble (1711-1786) appears to have been a gifted composer. Unfortunately, not much of his music is available today. A small assortment of pieces by Keeble, by John Alcock, Jonathan Battishill, John Bennett, Thomas Dupuis, and other composers of the time can be found in various collections of 18th-century English organ music.

At this point it is necessary to point out that far too much 17th- and 18th-century English organ music has been arranged "for modern organ," as the expression goes. What this means essentially, is that the lowest voice part has been assigned to the pedals and one or usually two inner voices have been added. The entire concept of the piece changes when it is so arranged. The original charm and freshness is lost. If, to add to the offense, the performer succumbs to the temptation to use a big 16' sound in the pedal and a nearly Full organ sound for the solo voice he will have bloated the poor composition beyond recognition.

One additional composer made a significant contribution to English organ literature of the latter 18th century, Charles Wesley (1757-1834). He wrote *Six Concertos for the Organ or Harpsichord,* his opus 2. Written while Wesley was still very young, these works were clearly modelled after the compositions of John Stanley. They represent one of the last appearances of the Gallant style in English organ music. The works of the other two Wesleys, Samuel and Samuel Sebastian, will be discussed later.

EDITIONS

Alcock: 4 *Voluntaries (Tallis to Wesley* series, XXIII) .*

Ex. 11. Stanley, *Voluntary V1,* 2nd mov't, m. 1-4.

Ex. 12. Stanley, *Concerto in C Minor,* 1st mov't, m. 18-24.

Arne: ORG. & ORCHLSTRA: *Concerto V* (g minor) for org., strings, and 2 oboes, ed. A. de Klerk, Kassel, Nagels Verlag. The same, arr. for organ alone, in *English Organ Music of the 18th Century*, II, ed. Butcher ,London, Hinrichsen. *Concerto No. 4 in Bb*, arr. for organ alone by A. Farmer, London, The Faith Press, Ltd. *Organ Solos from the Concertos*, ed. Buchey, London, Hinrichsen. These are concerto movements which were intended to be played on the organ alone, sometimes with improvised cadenzas.

Bennet: *Voluntaries IX and X*, ed. Johnstone, London, Novello.

Blow: *Complete Organ Works*, ed. Shaw, London, Schott. *Selected Organ Works*, ed. Butcher, London, Hinrichsen. *Two Voluntaries*, ed. McLean, London, Novello.

Boyce: 4 *Voluntaries* (D, g, C, a) , ed. Phillips (*Tallis to Wesley* series, XXVI) .* *Two Voluntaries* (a, d), ed. Pearson, London, Hinrichsen. *Two Voluntaries*, London, Novello. *Introduction and Trumpet Tune* (*Voluntary No. 1 in D*) , London, Hinrichsen.

Bull: *Keyboard Music*, 2 vols. (*Musica Britannica*, XIV, XIX) , London, Stainer & Bell. *Selected Works* (*Tallis to Wesley* series, XXXVII) .* *Five Pieces from the Flemish Tabulatura*, Wilhelmshaven, Heinrichshofen Verlag, out of print. *Noëls flamands* (*L'Organiste liturgique*, Bk. 60) Paris, Schola Cantorum.

Byrd: *Keyboard Music*, 2 vols., ed. A. Brown (*Musica Britannica*, XXVII, XXVIII) , London, Stainer & Bell, Ltd., 1971. *Keyboard Works*, 3 vols. (*The Collected Works of William Byrd*, ed. Fellowes, vols. XVIII-XX) , London, Stainer & Bell, 1937-50. In both the *Musica Britannica* edition and the Fellowes' edition, virginal pieces predominate, but there are a few organ pieces. *Forty-five Pieces for Keyboard Instruments*, ed. Tuttle, Paris, L'Oiseau Lyre, 1940. *Eight Organ Pieces*, ed. Ledger, London, Hinrichsen. *Selected Works* (*Tallis to Wesley* series, VIII) .*

Clarke: *Trumpet Voluntary* (often erroneously attributed to Purcell), arr. Ratcliffe, London, Novello. The same, in an edition by Ars Nova (Goes, Netherlands) . Various other arrangements

of the same piece are still published under Purcell's name.

Cosyn: *Three Voluntaries*, ed. Steele, London, Novello.

Croft: *Voluntaries for Organ*, ed. Simpson, London, Hinrichsen, 1956. Published individually, the voluntaries are: *Andante* (C) ; *Andante and Allegro Maestoso* (D) ; *Fugato* (C) ; *Fugato* (d) ; *Introduction and Fugato* (D) ; *Introduction and Fugato* (d) .

Felton: *Concerto*, op. 1 #5 (e) , arr. for organ alone by West, London, Novello, 1904. *Concerto*, op. 2 #3 (Bb) arr. for org. alone by Biggs, New York, H. W. Gray, 1942. *Concerto in Bb*, arr. for org. alone by McLean, London, Oxford University Press. Several arr. of individual movements are also available by Cramer (London) and by Oxford University Press (London) .

Gibbons, Christopher: *Keyboard Compositions*, ed. Rayner (*Corpus of Early Keyboard Music*, XVIII) , Dallas, American Institute of Musicology, 1967.

Gibbons, Orlando: *Complete Keyboard Works*, 5 vols., ed. Glyn, London, Stainer & Bell, 1924/25. *Keyboard Music*, ed. Hendrie (*Musica Britannica*, XX) , London, Stainer & Bell, 1962. In both the Glyn edition and the *Musica Britannica* edition, virginal music predominates, but there are a few organ pieces. *Nine Organ Pieces* from the *Musica Britannica* edition have been reprinted separately by Stainer & Bell. *A Fancy for a Double Orgaine*, *Voluntary*, *Fantasy from "Parthenia"* (*Tallis to Wesley* series, IX) .* *Ten Pieces* (*from the Virginal Book of Benjamin Cosyn*) , arr. for org. with ped., by Fuller-Maitland, London, J. & W. Chester, 1925.

Greene: 3 *Voluntaries*, Set I (f, Bb, b) (*Tallis to Wesley* series, IV) .* 4 *Voluntaries*, Set II (G, Eb, c, d) (*Tallis to Wesley* series, XV) .* *Voluntary in C Minor*, ed. West, London, Novello, 1961. *Voluntary XIII*, ed. Emery, London, Novello.

Handel: ORG. & ORCHESTRA: 12 *Orgelkonzerte*, op. 4, op. 7 (*G. F. Händels Werke*, ed. Chrysander, XXVIII) , *Deutsche Händelgesellschaft*, Leipzig, Moeck, 1858-1903. *Orgelkonzerte*, op. 4, ed. Matthaei (*Hallische Händel-Aus-*

gabe, Series IV, vol. 2), Kassel, Bären-reiter/Leipzig, Deutscher Verlag für Musik, 1955. *Orgelkonzerte,* op. 4 & 7, ed. Seiffert, Leipzig, Breitkopf & Härtel, 1924-28. *Orgelkonzerte,* op. 4 & 7, ed. Walcha, Mainz, Schott, 1940-43. 6 *Orgelkonzerte,* ed. de Lange, Frankfurt, C. F. Peters, c. 1953. There are also arrangements of the concertos for organ alone by Matthaei (Bärenreiter), by Keller (W. Müller Verlag), by Dupré (Bornemann), by Lang and Bower (Novello), by Phillips (Hinrichsen) and others. Other pieces for organ or harpsichord can be found in the complete editions of Handel's works, as well as in the following editions. 6 *Fugen,* ed. Hellmann, Wiesbaden, Breitkopf & Härtel. 6 *Fugues or Voluntaries,* Set I, ed. Phillips *(Tallis to Wesley* series, XII).* 4 *Voluntaries,* Set II *(Tallis to Wesley* series, XIX).* 18 pieces for mechanical clock were printed in W. B. Squire, "Handel's Clock Music," *Musical Quarterly,* V, 1919, pp. 538-552. *Pieces for a Musical Clock,* ed. Spiegl, London/Mainz, Schott, apparently out of print.

Locke: *Organ Voluntaries,* ed. Dart *(Complete Keyboard Works,* Bk. 2), London, Stainer & Bell, 1957. 7 *Voluntaries from "Melothesia" (Tallis to Wesley* series, VI).*

Lugge: *Three Voluntaries for Double Organ,* ed. Jeans/Steele, London, Novello, 1956.

Purcell: *Harpsichord and Organ Music,* ed. Squire/Hopkins *(The Works of Henry Purcell,* VI) Purcell Society, London, Novello, 1895. New edition: *Organ Works,* ed. McLean, London, Novello, 1957. *Three Voluntaries* (A, d, C) *(Tallis to Wesley* series, X).* There are many arrangements of the *Trumpet Tune, Trumpet Voluntary,* etc., including: arr. Biggs (Mercury Music), arr. H. Grace (Schott), arr. Buszin (Concordia), arr. Dupré (Bornemann), arr. Peasgood (Novello). Also, *Sonata in C* (from *Sonatas of Three Parts,* no. 6), arr. Dalton, London, Novello. *Sonata for Trumpet and Organ* (in D Major), arr. Arnold, St. Louis, Concordia. The *Voluntary on the 100th Psalm Tune* is also available in various publications, usually with poor editing.

Redford: Complete works were published in C. F. Pfatteicher, *John Redford, Organist and Almoner of St. Paul's Cathedral* . . . Kassel, Bärenreiter, 1934.

Robinson: *Voluntary in A Minor,* ed. S. Jeans, London, Novello, 1966.

Rogers: *Voluntary,* ed. S. Jeans, London, Novello.

Roseingrave: *Compositions for Organ and Harpsichord,* ed. D. Stevens, University Park, Penn., Pennsylvania State University Press, 1964. *Fifteen Voluntaries and Fugues,* ed. Butcher, London, Hinrichsen, out of print. *Ten Organ Pieces,* ed. P. Williams, London, Stainer & Bell, 1961.

Stanley: *Voluntaries for the Organ,* 3 vols. (Facsimile reproduction of the 18th century edition of 30 voluntaries), London, Oxford University Press. 10 *Voluntaries,* op. 5 *(Tallis to Wesley* series, XXVII); 10 *Voluntaries,* op. 6 *(Tallis to Wesley* series, XXVIII); 10 *Voluntaries,* op. 7 *(Tallis to Wesley* series, XXIX).* *Three Voluntaries from Opera Quinta* (nos. 2, 5, 9) *(Tallis to Wesley* series, XI).* *Twelve Diapason Movements from the Voluntaries (Tallis to Wesley* series, XXXIV).* Individual voluntaries, usually arranged for organ with pedal, are published by Novello (London). *Flute and Trumpet Tunes,* arr. for org. with pedal by Wyton, N.Y., Carl Fischer. Individual pieces also available by Cramer (London). ORG. & STRINGS: *Organ Concerto in A,* ed. Le Huray, London, Oxford University Press. *Organ Concerto in c,* ed. Le Huray, London, Oxford University Press.

Tallis: *Complete Keyboard Works,* ed. Stevens, London, Hinrichsen, 1953. 3 *Hymn Verses and 4 Antiphons (Tallis to Wesley* series, II).* *Four Pieces, Partly from the Mulliner Book (Tallis to Wesley* series, III).*

Tomkins: *Keyboard Music,* ed. Tuttle *(Musica Britannica,* V), London, Stainer & Bell, 1955. Contents: primarily virginal music. *Nine Organ Pieces,* ed. Tuttle/Dart, London, Stainer & Bell. *Three Hitherto Unpublished Voluntaries,* ed. Stevens *(Tallis to Wesley* series, XVII).*

Walmisley: *Organ Pieces (Tallis to Wesley* series, XXXVI),* out of print. Some publications by Novello, likewise out of print.

Walond: *Three Cornet Voluntaries* (e, d, G), Set I *(Tallis to Wesley* series,

XX) .* *Three Cornet Voluntaries* (G, d-D, d), Set II (*Tallis to Wesley* series, XXXII) .* *Introduction and Toccata*, London, Cramer.

Wesley, Charles: ORG. & STRINGS: *Concerto IV* (C Major) , ed. Finzi, London, Hinrichsen, 1956.

Collections

Alte englische Orgelmeister, ed. Phillips (*Liber Organi*, X, gen'l ed. Keller). Mainz, Schott. Compositions by Alwoode, Blow, Boyce, Byrd, O. Gibbons, Greene, Purcell, Redford, Stanley, Tomkins, S. Wesley.

Altenglische Orgelmusik, ed. D. Stevens, Kassel, Bärenreiter. Compositions from the Tudor school: Allwood, Blitheman, Coxsun, Preston, Redford, Ph. ap Rhys, Strogers, Taverner, Thorne, White.

Altenglische Orgelmusik: Die Orgelstücke aus der Parthenia (1621) *und London Ms 29996* (1647) (*Cantantibus Organis*, Bk. 16, gen'l ed. Kraus) , Regensburg, Verlag Fr. Pustet.

Alte Orgelmusik aus England und Frankreich, ed. Fl. Peeters, Mainz, Schott. Contents: 35 pieces (some of which are virginal pieces) by Clarke, Croft, Byrd, Blow, Bull, O. Gibbons, Stanley, Purcell, Tallis, P. Philips, and several French composers.

Blow and His Pupils Reading and Barrett: 3 Unpublished Voluntaries (*Tallis to Wesley* series, XXI) .*

Contemporaries of Purcell, London, Hinrichsen. Contents: 16 pieces (organ and virginal) by 17th c. composers — D. Purcell, Barrett, Blow, Clarke, Croft, Eccles, Loeillet.

Early Tudor Organ Music, 2 vols., ed. Caldwell (*Early English Church Music VI, X*), London, Stainer & Bell. Vol. I: *Music for the Office*. II: *Music for the Mass*.

English Keyboard Music of the XVIII and XIX Centuries, ed. Tubbs, Glen Rock, J. Fischer. Works by S. Long, Greene, Th. Adams, and Ch. Wesley.

English Organ Music of the Eighteenth

Century, 2 vols., ed. Butcher, London, Hinrichsen. Vol. I: Handel, *Organ Concerto in g*, arr. for org. alone; Dupuis, *Introduction and Fugue in D;* Stanley, *Voluntary in a;* Boyce, *Voluntary No.* 1 *in D, Voluntary No.* 4 *in g.* Vol. II: Walond, *Voluntary in G;* Keeble, *Andante, Largo and Fugue in G;* Arne, *Organ Concerto No.* 5, arr. for org. alone.

English Organ Music of the 18th Century, vol. 1, ed. Phillips, London, Hinrichsen. Contents: voluntaries by Stanley, Boyce, Travers, Walond, James, Dupuis.

Mulliner Book, ed. D. Stevens (*Musica Britannica*, I) , London, Stainer & Bell, 1951.

5 Organ Pieces, Wilhelmshaven, Heinrichshofen's Verlag. Contents: works by Blytheman, Newman, Redford, Sheppard, Tallis.

Old English Album (*Masterpieces of Organ Music* series, ed. Hennefield/ Mead/White, Bk. CXXIII) , New York, The Liturgical Music Press. Contents: works by Alwood, Gibbons, Redford, Tye.

Old English Organ Music for Manuals, 6 vols., ed. Trevor, London, Oxford University Press, 1965 —. Vol. I: Keeble, Croft, Goodwin, Camidge, Travers, Battishill, Arne, Heron, Ch. Wesley, Alcock, Boyce, Walond, Bennett, Burney. Vol. II: Alcock, Battishill, Bennett, Boyce, Dupuis, Goodwin, Greene, Hayes, Heron, Keeble, Linley, Roseingrave, Stanley, Thorley, Travers, Wesley. Vol. III: Camidge, Boyce, Alcock, Arne, Hine, James, Bennett, Greene, Dupuis, Walond, Bennett, Goodwin. Vol. IV: Bennett, Boyce, Travers, S t a n l e y, Greene, Worgan, Walond, Burney, Heron, Wesley, Goodwin, Hine. Vol. V: Greene, Shepherd, Berg, Pepusch, Selby, Purcell, anonymous, Long, Travers, Alcock, Tallis. Vol. VI: Alcock, anonymous, Alwood, Croft, Gibbons, Goodwin, Greene, Heron, Long, Redford, Stubley, Tallis.

Preludes and Fugues by Dupuis (g) , *Keeble* (C) , *Travers* (c) (*Tallis to Wesley* series, XXII) .*

Ten 18th Century English Voluntaries, ed. Peek, St. Louis, Concordia.

The 3 Wesleys: 3 Pieces, Set I (Tallis to Wesley series, V).*
The 3 Wesleys: 3 Pieces, Set II (Tallis to Wesley series, XXIV).*

Three 18th-Century Voluntaries, ed. Campbell, London, Oxford University Press. Works by Boyce, Greene, Stanley.

Three Organists of St. Dionis Backchurch, London: Philip Hart, Charles Burney, John Bennet (Tallis to Wesley series, XXXV).*

Trumpet and Organ Voluntaries, London, Musica Rara. Works by Croft, Walond, Stanley, Alcock, Handel, Dupuis.

Twelve Voluntaries, New York, Galaxy. Contents: works for organ or harpsichord by Boyce and Greene.

Voluntaries by Boyce (G), Stanley (d), Walond (E) (Tallis to Wesley series, I).*

MUSICAL SOURCES

Ex. 1. The Mulliner Book, ed. Stevens, p. 22. Copyright 1951. The Musica Britannica Trust, London. Used by permission of Galaxy Music Corporation, sole U.S. agent.
Ex. 2. Thomas Tallis: Complete Keyboard Works, ed. Stevens, p. 34. Copyright 1953 C. F. Peters.
Ex. 3. John Bull: Keyboard Music, I (Musica Britannica, XIV), p. 118. Copyright 1960. The Musica Britannica Trust, London. Used by permission of Galaxy Music Corporation, sole U.S. agent.
Ex. 4. John Lugge: Three Voluntaries for Double Organ, p. 10.
Ex. 5. Reproduced from Gibbons, Christopher, Keyboard Compositions (CEKM 18).   ©

Copyright 1967 by the American Institute of Musicology/Hänssler-Verlag, Neuhausen-Stuttgart, W. Germany. Used by permission.
Ex. 6. John Blow: Two Voluntaries, ed. McLean, p. 6.
Ex. 7. Henry Purcell: Organ Works, ed. McLean, p. 8.
Exs. 8a, 8b. Maurice Greene: Four Voluntaries (Tallis to Wesley, XXV) ed. Phillips, p. 9. Copyright Hinrichsen Edition. Used by permission of C. F. Peters.
Exs. 9a, 9b. Dr. William Boyce: Four Voluntaries (Tallis to Wesley, XXVI) ed. Phillips, pp. 5,6. Copyright Hinrichsen Edition. Used by permission of C. F. Peters.
Ex. 10. Thomas Arne: Concerto V, ed. de Klerk, p. 9.
Ex. 11. John Stanley: Voluntary VI (Facsimile edition), p. 19.
Ex. 12. John Stanley: Concerto in C Minor, ed. LeHuray, p. 2.

ABBREVIATIONS

* Tallis to Wesley series, gen'l ed. Phillips, London, Hinrichsen.

NOTES

[1] Hugh Miller, "Sixteenth-Century English Faburden Compositions for Keyboard" in MQ 26:1 (1940), 50-64.
[2] The specification is taken from the preface to John Blow, Two Voluntaries, ed. H. McLean.
[3] The reader is reminded that the "organ concerti" of Handel's contemporaries, J. S. Bach and J. G. Walther, were something quite different. They were arrangements for organ alone of works originally composed for orchestra (without organ).

ENGLAND IN THE 19TH AND 20TH CENTURIES

The major organist in England in the early 19th century was Samuel Wesley (1766-1837), who was a tireless champion of the music of Johann Sebastian Bach. Introducing the English to the organ and choral works of Bach was indeed one of his best achievements. He was also acclaimed as a great organist. As for his own compositions, most are not really spectacular. One work, a piece entitled *Full Voluntary*, shows a certain Bach influence. Most of the others have lovely melodies, seemingly artless in their simplicity, with rather naive accompaniment.

(Example 13)

Next in prominence, during the first half of the 19th century, were Thomas Adams (1785-1858), whose style was often flamboyant, Samuel Sebastian Wesley (1810-1876), who sometimes wrote in a pianistic fashion (see his *Choral Song in C*), and Thomas Attwood Walmisley 1814-1856). Thomas Attwood (1765-1838) and William Russell (1777-1813) also wrote a few organ pieces.

Mendelssohn was a frequent visitor to England from 1829 until 1847, the year of his death. His works were well-received, and he found the musical climate of England most congenial. Be-sides conducting his own compositions (symphonies, oratorios, etc.), he gave organ concerts in which he played the Bach organ works, among other things. He and Samuel Wesley, both Bach proponents, had one opportunity to meet and to perform for each other in 1837, the year of Wesley's death. Mendelssohn naturally promoted his own organ works as well, and the effect of this can be seen in much English composition of the 19th century. Basil Harwood (1859-1949), although miles apart from Mendelssohn in quality, wrote two organ sonatas, a form first brought to prominence for organ composition by Mendelssohn. William Thomas Best (1826-1897), also under Mendelssohn's influence, adopted various elements of his style.

(Example 14)

Best was the leading concert organist in England in the latter part of the 19th century. His organ compositions are rhythmically attractive and tuneful, as the previous example illustrates. But, organ composition was not his major business. What he enjoyed most was playing transcriptions of popular oratorio choruses, operatic arias, symphonies, etc. For these, he was famous.

Ex. 13. Samuel Wesley, No. 11 from *12 Short Pieces*, m. 1-8.

Ex. 14. W. T. Best, *All People That On Earth Do Dwell* (Theme in the Tenor), m. 1-8.

Organ transcriptions were common all over Europe in the 19th century, but the English seemed particularly enamoured of them. Sometimes not a single genuine organ work could be found on a 19th-century English organ program.

An enormous change took place in English organs during this period. The active pedal line shown in the previous musical excerpt, for example, would have been inconceivable in England a century earlier, since 18th-century organs had only pull-downs, or often no pedalboard at all. Mendelssohn's concert tours did much to convince the English of the need for an independent pedal division. It was also at least partially from Mendelssohn that the English acquired a desire for large instruments incorporating some of the features of continental organs. The more progressive organ builders (William Hill, Edmund Schulze, Henry Willis) began to change the entire concept of the English instrument from that which it had been in the 17th and 18th centuries. They not only introduced an independent pedal division, but they made the Swell organ second in importance to the Great, while reducing the importance of the Choir. When possible, they included a Solo division with big reeds. Large Diapason tone became customary, and the entire organ possessed a greater variety of colors.

Unfortunately, the English Romantic organ was flagrantly distorted near the end of the century through all sorts of excesses due largely to the influence of Robert Hope Jones. As Clutton and Niland so aptly put it, Jones was "an electrical engineer by trade who unfortunately strayed into organ building, to which he first applied an electric action of more ingenuity than reliability and then a tonal system of tasteless vulgar-

ity."[1] Thanks to him, organists and organ builders alike became obsessed with the idea of technically "improving" the organ through an ever increasing number of sub- and super-octaves, couplers, pistons, multiple expression pedals, and every conceivable accessory. Of course, one could never get enough stops, either. English organs of this vintage have some of the longest stoplists in the world. One wonders if this preoccupation with size and with control over the most minute gradations of color and volume did not perhaps place the organist in a position where he expended all his time and energy manipulating pistons, expression and crescendo pedals, etc., so that he could ignore the inherent dullness of the compositions he was playing. That most English service music of the 19th and first half of the 20th centuries was extraordinarily unimaginative is a well-known fact. There were, of course, some notable exceptions, and these will be discussed shortly.

In the area of concert music, England's famous symphonist, Sir Edward Elgar (1857-1934), wrote one major work for organ, the *Sonata in G Major* (1896). Most of the other organ works commonly attributed to him are nothing more than arrangements of some of his orchestral compositions. His four-movement sonata has frequent key and meter changes, as is typical for Elgar, and a variety of rhythmic patterns. Some sections of the work are extremely pianistic, a somewhat detracting factor. The work gives the performer superabundant opportunities to bathe in one orchestral color after another. Organists who like to program Guilmant and Widor sonatas, or similar works, might consider Elgar's sonata for a change of pace.

(Example 15)

Ex. 15. Elgar, *Sonata*, mov't 1, m. 1-8.

Given Elgar's stature in the musical world, one would have expected a rash of organ sonatas in England in the early 20th century. But, such was not the case. True, Sir Charles V. Stanford (1852-1924) did compose five sonatas for organ, but he was an exception. His colleagues, Sir Charles H. H. Parry 1848-1918) and Charles Wood (1866-1926) generally contented themselves with short pieces for the church service. One example of a larger work by Parry, his *Toccata and Fugue* (*The Wanderer*), will be quoted here because it shows the German influence which still hovered over English organ music. The chromaticism of this toccata bears a great resemblance to that of Reger, and the fugue is a typical German Romantic fugue in the Mendelssohn manner.

(Example 16)

As is generally known, these three — Stanford, Parry, and Wood — were leaders of the movement which reformed English church music. It was largely due to their efforts that the sentimentality and lack of refinement of most 19th-century English choral music was replaced by better craftsmanship and a finer sensitivity to word setting. In their organ works, as well, these men concentrated on good craftsmanship, but they didn't reach the level of inspiration that they attained in their best choral compositions.

The case is similar with several other names which can be . cited. Ralph Vaughan Williams (1872-1958) contributed a few short works for organ. As agreeable as these works may be, they stand on the periphery of his creative activity. In fact, arrangements, rather than original organ compositions, constitute a sizeable portion of that which is commonly considered to be his organ music. Harold Darke, (1888-1977) also left a few pleasant organ pieces, as did the song writer, John Ireland (1879-1962). Ireland's organ works are rather pianistic. Frank Bridge (1879-1941), noted for his fine chamber music, wrote some short organ pieces and a sonata.

Herbert Howells (1892-   ) is perhaps the only one among the leading English composers who has devoted considerable attention to the organ. In addition to a number of short pieces for service use (psalm preludes, etc.), he has written two sonatas and a 4-movement partita, the latter composed in 1971. His interest in organ music spans

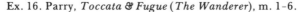

Ex. 16. Parry, *Toccata & Fugue* (*The Wanderer*), m. 1-6.

his entire adult life. The following example from *Sarabande (In Modo Elegiaco)*, composed c. 1940, has a melancholy impressionism which is typical of much of Howells' music. This example also illustrates the ingenious, little rhythmic twists which have become an integral part of his style. His latest organ work, *Partita* (25 minutes in length) is somewhat more modern, but it still clearly recognizable as a Howells composition.

(Example 17)

Ralph William Downes (1904-   ) Michael Tippett (1905-   ), and Benjamin Britten (1913-1977) made only token contributions to organ literature, but their pieces are worth performing.

(Example 18)

The bulk of organ music heard in English churches was written, of course, not by famous composers, but by men who were organists by trade. Among the most popular representatives of this group during the first half of the century were George Oldroyd (1886-1951),

Ex. 17. Howells, *Saraband (In Modo Elegiaco)*, m. 1-8.

Ex. 18. Downes. *Paraphrase on "O Filii et Filiae,"* m. 1-6.

Alec Rowley (1892-1958), Eric Thiman (1900-1974), and Percy Whitlock (1903-1946). With the exception of such rhythmic pieces as Whitlock's *Toccata* (from his *Plymouth Suite*), much of their music is characterized by an easy melodiousness and smoothly flowing lines. Often it is quite solemn and sub-dued. It is nearly always pleasant and undisturbing. Under the hands of less gifted organists than those mentioned, English service music was not merely pleasant and undisturbing, it was totally innocuous. It seemed to possess a self-effacing quality, as if the organist were constantly reminding himself that the glory of the Anglican church was its choral tradition, against which he had no right to compete.

In attempting to round out the picture of English organ music during the first half of the 20th century, it is essential to recall the fact that a large number of English organists emigrated to the United States and Canada. While not relinquishing their British orientation usually, the most important among these men took such prominent positions in America, that it will be more convenient to discuss them in a separate chapter, with the Americans.

Since the 1950's organ playing and organ building have changed drastically, due largely to the infiltration of ideas from the continent. The instrument which spear-headed the movement was the organ in Royal Festival Hall built in 1954 by Harrison and Harrison. Best described as neo-classic, the instrument represents a synthesis of Baroque and Romantic characteristics, and includes French reeds and German-influenced principal choruses. It was conceived as an instrument which should be capable of playing practically all organ literature. At first it met with stormy opposition. After all, how many English organists of the 1950's were interested in clarity in the individual voice parts? And the total effect of the instrument was much too aggressive for them. Gradually, however, the all-purpose, neo-classic instrument became the most common type for new instruments in Great Britain. Now, in the 1970's, after the horizon has been broadened still more, one can find other types of organs, as well, even a fair number of trackers.

As the instruments changed, so, too, did the approach toward organ playing and composition. Many continental practices were either imitated directly or were integrated into the English manner. The influence of Messiaen has been especially strong (see Preston's *Alleluyas* for an obvious example). One notes also the impact of the French neo-classicists (Langlais, etc.), of the German neo-Baroque composers, of Hindemith, and of other individuals who were already historically established on the continent. Although there are some notable exceptions (soon to be mentioned), most British organ composers of today are still somewhat conservative by comparison with leading continental composers.

There is as yet no one composer, or group of composers, who dominates the scene in Great Britain. There is no one who forms a rallying point, the way Messiaen did in France, or Distler and Hindemith did in Germany. One can only mention individual British composers and their contributions.

Two of the most imaginative composers are certainly Iain Hamilton (1922-   ), a Scotsman now living in the United States, and Malcolm Williamson (1931-   ), an Australian by birth. They stand apart from the rank and file of British organ composers because they are writing in a more contemporary idiom than most. In Hamilton's music, the various techniques of the serial school, together with some aspects of aleatoric composition, are most effectively combined with constantly changing organ colors and volume levels. His music is well-constructed, carefully thought-out. His most famous organ work is probably the *Paraphrase of the Music for Organs in "Epitaph for this World and Time."* Inspired by an apocalyptic text, the work is violently evocative of "the war in heaven" that the Book of Revelations describes.

(Examples 19a, 19b)

Williamson has written several works for organ. Often a mystical aura pervades his compositions (such as *Vision of Christ-Phoenix*), but the mood is heavily dependent on a good acoustical environment. In a dry room, parts of his music may sound trite. In all honesty, one is compelled to add that his writing is uneven. There is a sizeable discrepancy between his best works and his weakest ones. Williamson's *Symphony* is a major work, one of the most original organ compositions to appear in England in recent years.

(Examples 20a, 20b)

Less well-known, but equally imagina-

Ex. 19a. Hamilton, *Paraphrase of the Music for Organs in "Epitaph for this World and Time,"* excerpt from p. 8.

Ex. 19b. Hamilton, *Paraphrase* . . . , excerpt from p. 9.

Ex. 20a. Williamson, *Symphony,* mov't 6: *Paean,* m. 1–5.

Ex. 20b. Williamson, *Symphony,* mov't 6: *Paean,* m. 84–88.

tive and adventuresome, is Sebastian Forbes (1941-), a fine craftsman, who has written several very effective modern pieces in the last few years. An excerpt from his *Tableau* follows.

(Example 21)

A composer whose music has a wider, more popular appeal is William Matthias (1934-). One might wish for more subtlety in some of his pieces, but in all of them there is a bouncy vitality which is undeniably atractive. His language is not up-to-date, but his music is enjoyable (particularly the *Toccata Giocosa* and the *Invocations*).

(Example 22)

Other composers of interest include: Francis Jackson (1917-), a very conservative musician whose best work is probably his *Sonata in G Minor;* Peter Racine Fricker (1920-), (now living in the United States), who has drawn upon various elements of the French and German tradition without slavishly imitating any one; Francis Routh (1927-); Alun Hoddinott (1939-), whose compositions include a concerto for organ and orchestra; Kenneth Leighton (1929-); Peter Hurford (1930-); Peter Dickinson (1934-);

Nicolas Maw (1935-), whose *Essay for Organ* is a 5-movement serial composition, extremely intricate and cerebral; Simon Preston (1938-); John McCabe (1939-).

(Examples 23, 24, 25)

EDITIONS

Attwood: several publications by Novello, now out of print.

Best: *Introduction, Four Variations and Finale on "God Save the Queen,"* op. 29, London, Hinrichsen. The same, under the title, *Prelude on America,* Boston, Boston Music Co. *Christmas Fantasies on English Carols,* Opa-Locka, Kalmus. 12 *Short Preludes on English Psalm Tunes,* Opa-Locka, Kalmus. Plus publications by Novello (London) and Augener (London) which are out of print.

Bridge: *Organ Pieces,* 2 bks, London, Boosey & Hawkes. Bk. II is out of print. The *Adagio in E* from Book II is published separately by H. W. Gray (New York). Additional publications by No-

Ex. 21. Forbes, *Tableau,* m. 44–48.

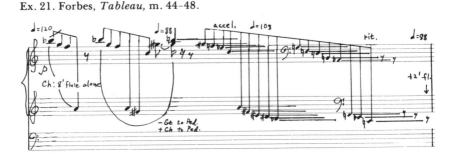

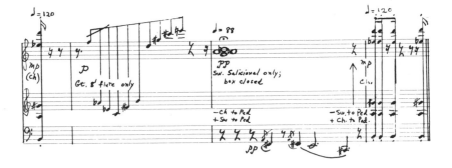

Ex. 22. Mathias, *Invocations*, m. 32-36.

vello (London) and Curwen (London) are out of print.

Britten: *Prelude and Fugue on a Theme of Vittoria* (1947), London, Boosey & Hawkes.

Darke: *A Meditation on Brother James' Air*, London, Oxford University Press. *Fantasy*, London, Oxford University Press. *Three Chorale Preludes*, op. 20, London, Novello. *Bridal Processional*, London, Chappell, out of print. *Rhapsody in E*, London, Stainer & Bell, out of print.

Dickinson: Publications by Novello (London) . *Postlude on "Adeste Fideles,"* 1964. *Three Statements*, 1966. *Paraphrase I* (1967), 1969. ORG. & INSTRUMENTS: *Fanfares and Elegies,* for 3 trpts, 3 trbns, and organ, 1967.

Downes: *Jubilate Deo*, New York, H. W. Gray. *Paraphrase on "O Fillii et Filiae,"* London, Hinrichsen.

Elgar: *Sonata in G*, op. 28, Leipzig, Breitkopf & Härtel, 1896. New Copyright, London, British and Continental

Ex. 23. Fricker, *Toccata*, *"Gladius Domini,"* m. 29-34.

Ex. 24. Preston, *Alleluyas*, m. 1-3.

Ex. 25. McCabe, *Dies Resurrectionis*, m. 1.

Music Agencies, Ltd., 1941. *Andante Espressivo* (from the *Sonata*), New York, H. W. Gray. 11 *Vesper Voluntaries*, pub. in 1891, have been reprinted under the title, *Suite for Organ*, London, Chappell. Also available are arrangements of various orchestral works, or movements.

Forbes: Publications by Oxford University Press (London). *Sonata*, 1970. *Haec Dies*, 1971. *Capriccio*.

Fricker: *Chorale*, London, Schott, 1957. *Pastorale*, London, Schott, 1961. *Wedding Processional*, London, Schott, 1961. *Ricercare*, op. 40, London, Schott, 1966. *Praeludium*, London, Oxford University Press, 1971. *Six Short Pieces*, Minneapolis, Augsburg. *Toccata Gladius Domini*, Minneapolis, Augsburg, 1971. *Intrada*, London, Faber Music Ltd., 1974.

Hamilton: *Fanfares and Variants* (1960), London, Schott, 1965. *Aubade* (1965), Bryn Mawr, Theodore Presser, 1971. *Threnos: In Time of War* (1966), Bryn Mawr, Theodore Presser, 1970. *Paraphrase of the Music for Organs in "Epitaph for this World and Time,"* Bryn Mawr, Theodore Presser, 1972.

Harwood: Publications by Novello (London), unless otherwise indicated. *Sonata No.* 1 in c-sharp minor, op. 5, London, Schott. *A Quiet Voluntary for Evensong, Dithyramb*, op. 7. *Communion in F on the Hymn Tune "Irish,"* op. 15, no. 1. *Interlude in D*, op. 15, no. 2. *Paean*, op. 15, no. 3. *Short Postlude for Ascensiontide on the old 25th Psalm Tune*, op. 15, no. 4. *Requiem aeternam*, op. 15, no. 5. *Andante tranquillo in E-flat on the Hymn Tune "Bedford,"* op. 15, no. 6. *Capricco*, op. 16. *Two Sketches in A and F*, op. 18, nos. 1, 2. *Three Cathedral Preludes*, op. 25. *Sonata No. 2 in F-sharp minor. Christmastide (Fantasia)*, op. 34. *Rhapsody*, op. 38. *In an Old Abbey*, op. 32. *Wedding March*, op. 40. *Three Preludes on Anglican Chants*, op. 42. *Voluntary in D-flat*, op. 43. *Processional*, op. 44. *Three Short Pieces*, op. 45. *In Exitu Israel*, op. 46. *Toccata*, op. 49. *Lullaby*, op. 50. *Prelude, Larghetto, and Finale*, op. 51. *An Album of Eight Pieces*, op. 58. ORG. & ORCH.: *Concerto in D*, op. 25. Additional publications by Oxford University Press (London) (now out of print).

Hoddinott: ORG. & ORCH.: *Organ*

Concerto (1967), London, Oxford University Press, 1968.

Howells: Publications by Novello (London), unless otherwise indicated. *Three Psalm-Preludes*, Sets I and II, op. 32. *Sonata. Six Pieces (Sine Nomine; Sarabande for the Morning of Easter; Master Tallis' Testament; Fugue, Chorale and Epilogue; Sarabande; Paean). Siciliano for a High Ceremony. Partita* (1971). *Rhapsody No.* 1 *in D flat*, London, Stainer and Bell. *Rhapsody No.* 2 *in E flat*, London, Stainer and Bell. *Rhapsody No.* 3 *in C sharp minor*, London, Stainer and Bell.

Hurford: *Five Short Chorale Preludes*, London, Oxford University Press, 1958. *Five Verses on a Melody from the Paderborn Gesangbuch*, London, Oxford University Press, 1960. *Suite: Laudate Dominum*, London, Oxford University Press, 1961. *Two Dialogues*, London, Novello. *Passingala*, London, Novello.

Ireland: *Elegiac Romance*, Novello. Plus other publications by Novello and by Stainer & Bell which are out of print.

Jackson: Publishers are Novello (London) and Oxford University Press (London). *Division on "Nun danket,"* Nov. *Three Pieces (Procession; Arabesque; Pageant)*, Nov. *Toccata, Chorale and Fugue*, Nov. *Toccata-Prelude on "Wachet auf,"* Nov. *Impromptu for Sir Edward Bairstow on his Seventieth Birthday*, OUP. *Sonata in G. Minor*, op. 35, OUP, 1971. *Sonata Giocosa*, OUP, in preparation.

Leighton: *Et Resurrexit*, London, Novello. *Festival Fanfare*, New York, Carl Fischer. *Improvisation*, London, Novello. *Prelude, Scherzo and Passacaglia*, London, Novello. 1964.

Mathias: Publisher is Oxford University Press (London). *Partita*, op. 19, 1962. *Variations on a Hymn Tune ("Braint")*, 1963. *Invocations*, op. 35, 1967. *Toccata Giocosa*, op. 36, no. 2, 1968.

Maw: *Essay for Organ*, London, Boosey & Hawkes.

McCabe: *Dies Resurrectionis*, London, Oxford University Press, 1964. *Johannis-Partita* (1964), London, Novello, 1965.

Sinfonia (1961) , London, Novello, 1966. *Elegy* (1965) , London, Novello, 1967.

Oldroyd: *Three Liturgical Preludes,* London, Oxford University Press, 1938. *Three Liturgical Improvisations,* London, Oxford University Press, 1948. *Two Evening Responds,* London, Oxford University Press, out of print. Additional publications by Augener (London) are out of print.

Parry: Publisher is Novello (London) , unless otherwise indicated. *Elegy. Seven Chorale Preludes* op. 186 & 205, in 2 sets, 1912/1916, copyright renewed 1940/ 1944. *Fantasia and Fugue* (G Major), 1913. *Bridal March and Finale. Scherzo in F,* London, E. Ashdown. *Three Chorale Fantasies* (1915) . *Toccata and Fugue* (*The Wanderer*) , 1921.

Preston: *Vox Dicentis,* London, Novello, 1973.

Ridout: *The Seven Last Words,* London, Oxford University Press, 1968. *Two Pictures of Graham Sutherland,* London, Oxford University Press, 1970.

Routh: *The Manger Throne (A Meditation on the Divine Mystery of the Incarnation)* , op. 3, London, Boosey & Hawkes. *Fantasia,* London, Hinrichsen. *Five Short Pieces (Prelude; Compline Hymn; Chorale and Variation; Voluntary; Fantasia on an Easter Alleluia),* London, Hinrichsen.

Rowley: Major publishers are Novello (London) and Edw. Ashdown (London) *Benedictus,* Nov. 2 *Paean,* Nov. *Second Benedictus,* Nov. *Christmas Suite,* Nov. *Fantasia on "Veni Emmanuel,"* Nov. *Five Improvisations,* Nov. *Sonatina,* Nov. *Symphony in B Minor,* Nov., out of print. *Symphony No. 2 in F,* Nov., out of print. *Toccata (Moto Perpetuo)* , Nov. *Triptych,* Nov. *Triumph Song. Chorale Preludes on Famous Hymn Tunes,* 5 vols., E. Ash. Vol I: Lent; II: Easter, Ascension; III: Christmas, Advent, Passion, Whitsuntide, Harvest; IV: General; V: Various Occasions, including Saints' Days and Weddings. *A Book of Voluntaries,* E. Ash. *A Fantasy of Happiness,* E. Ash. *Keltic March,* E. Ash. *Pavan,* E. Ash. *Rhapsody,* E. Ash. *Heroic Suite,* E. Ash. *Suite,* E. Ash. *Chorale Preludes* (4 Seasonal Improvisations) , London, Hinrichsen. *The Sixty-fifth Psalm* (Thanksgiving) , New York, H. W. Gray.

ORG. & ORCH: *Concertina* for organ and string orch., London, United Music Publishers. *Meditation* for organ and string orch., London, Hinrichsen. Additional publications by Joseph Williams (London) are out of print.

Russell: *Voluntaries (Tallis to Wesley* series, XVI), London, Hinrichsen, out of print.

Stanford: *Fantasia and Toccata in d,* London, Stainer & Bell. *Six Occasional Preludes,* 2 bks., London, Stainer & Bell. *Six Short Preludes and Postludes,* 2 sets, op. 101, 105, London, Stainer & Bell. Numerous additional publications by Stainer & Bell, by Novello (London) , by G. Schirmer (New York) , by Breitkopf & Härtel (Leipzig) , and by Augener (London) are now out of print, including the sonatas.

Thiman: Major publishers are Novello (London), J. Curwen & Sons (London), and G. Schirmer (New York) . *Canzona,* Nov. *Eight Interludes,* 3 sets, Nov., 1946, 1948, 1952. *Four Choral Improvisations,* Nov. *Four Quiet Voluntaries,* 2 sets, Nov. *Improvisation on "Crimond,"* Nov. *March for a Pageant,* Nov. *Postlude on "Adeste Fideles,"* Nov. *Postlude on Harwood's "Thornbury,"* Nov. *Three Pieces (Meditation on "Slane"; Pavane; Postlude a la Marcia)* , Nov. *Times and Seasons,* 2 sets of 5 pieces each, Nov. *A Tune for a Tuba,* Nov. *Four Improvisations,* J. Cur. *Preludes and Voluntaries,* 3 bks, J. Cur. *Six Pieces in Various Styles,* 2 sets, J. Cur., 1960. *Four Offertories Founded on "The Modes,"* J. Cur., 1965. *Four Miniatures,* G. Sch. *Four Occasional Pieces,* G. Sch. *Three Meditations,* G. Sch. Additional publications by G. Schirmer are out of print. *Pastorale in E.,* London, Hinrichsen. *Varied Accompaniments,* London, Oxford University Press. *By Verdant Pastures,* New York, H. W. Gray. *Sequence in Miniature,* New York, H. W. Gray. *Varied Harmonizations of Favorite Hymn Tunes,* New York, H. W. Gray, *Interludes in Miniature,* London, Ascherberg, Hopwood & Crew (now Chappell) , 1963.

Tippett: *Preludio al Vespro di Monteverdi,* London, Schott, 1947.

Vaughan Williams: Publisher is Oxford University Press (London) , unless otherwise indicated. *Three Preludes Founded* on Welsh Hymn Tunes (Bryn Calfara, Rhosymedre, Hyfrydol). London, Stainer & Bell. Prelude and Fugue in C Minor (1921), 1930 (rental). Two Preludes on Welsh Hymn Tunes (1956), 1964. Variations on "Aberystwyth," arr. Byard. A Vaughan Williams Organ Album, 1964. Contents: 8 pieces, including arrangements. Some of these pieces, such as the Greensleeves arrangement, are also published separately by OUP.

Wesley, Samuel: 12 Short Pieces (Tallis to Wesley, series, VII), London, Hinrichsen. Air and Gavotte from 12 Short Pieces have also been published separately as Vol. XVIII of the Tallis to Wesley series. Voluntary (D), London, Hinrichsen. An Old English Melody, London, Hinrichsen. Three Short Pieces: Air and Gavotte, ed. Ramsey, London, Novello, 1961. Two Short Pieces in A Minor, ed. Ramsey, London, Novello, 1961. TWO ORGANS: Duet for Organ, ed. Emery, London, Novello. Additional publications by J. B. Cramer (London). Plus numerous old publications, no longer available.

Wesley, S. S.: Publications by Novello (London) unless otherwise indicated. Fourteen Organ Pieces by S. Wesley and S. S. Wesley, ed. Marchant, London, Wickins, 1909, out of print. Andante in E Minor (Tallis to Wesley series, XIII), London, Hinrichsen. Andante (G), London, Hinrichsen. Choral Song and Fugue in C, ed. Emery. Air Composed for Holsworthy Church Bells, and Varied. Introduction and Fugue in c♯, ed. Ley. Larghetto in f♯, ed Chambers. National Anthem with Variations. Selection of Psalm Tunes with Pedal Obligato, ed. West.

Whitlock: Publisher is Oxford University Press London). Five Short Pieces (Allegretto, Folk Tune, Andante tranquillo, Scherzo, Paean), 1930/1958. Four Extemporizations (Carol, Divertimento, Fidelis, Fanfare). Reflections (After an Old French Air, Pazienza, Dolcezza). Seven Sketches on Verses from the Psalms, 2 bks. Six Hymn Preludes, 2 bks. Salix. Toccata (from "Plymouth Suite"), 1939. A Sonata, the complete Plymouth Suite, and Two Fantasy-Chorals are out of print.

Williamson: Vision of Christ-Phoenix, London, Chappell, 1962. Resurgence du Feu, London, Chappell. Elegy — J.F.K.,

London, Jos. Weinberger, Ltd., 1964. Fons Amoris, London, Novello, 1965. Epitaphs for Edith Stillwell, London, Joe. Weinberger Ltd., 1968. Symphony, London, Novello, 1971. Peace Pieces (1971), London, Jos. Weinberger, 1972.

Wood: Sixteen Preludes Founded on Melodies from English and Scottish Psalters, 2 vols., London, Stainer & Bell, 1912. Prelude on " Carey's," London, Stainer & Bell, out of print.

Collections

Collections are important in English organ literature, especially modern, since the best pieces of certain composers have sometimes been published in collections together with compositions of other composers, rather than separately. As Oxford University Press (London) has published a large number of collections, the abbreviation, OUP, will be used for their publications. Many more English collections could be cited, but the following are some of the best.

An Album of Postludes, OUP, 1964. 7 pieces by Englishmen and others: R. Douglas, P. Van de Weghe, A. Cooke, D. Johnson, F. Jackson, C. S. Lang, Wm. Mathias.

An Album of Praise, OUP. 6 pieces by Peeters, G. Jacob, G. Dyson, N. Gilbert, H. Willan, P. Hurford.

An Album of Preludes and Interludes, OUP, 1961. 8 pieces by A. Cooke, Wm. Hunt, Chr. Morris, Tomlinson, Hurford, G. Phillips, P. de Maleingreau, C. S. Lang.

A Book of Hymn Tune Voluntaries, OUP. Works by Ley, Murrill, Slater, Rowley, Oldroyd, Coleman.

A Book of Simple Organ Voluntaries, OUP. Works by Oldroyd, Sumsion, Ley, Darke, Murrill, Coleman.

A Christmas Album, OUP. 6 pieces by Burton, Thiman, Jackson, Gibbs, Bush, Campbell.

A Festive Album, OUP. 6 pieces by Jackson, Armstrong, Gibbs, Coleman, Guest, Bush, Campbell.

An Easy Album, OUP, 1956. 6 pieces by Willan, Gibbs, Coleman, Darke, Watson, Thiman.

ASecond Easy Album for Organs: Six Pieces by Contemporary British Composers, OUP. Contents: pieces by Harris. Drayton, Ridout, Rutter, Sumsion, Lord.

Ceremonial Music, 2 bks., OUP Bk. 1: Pieces by Willcocks, Hurford, Jackson, Purcell, Clarke, Stanley. Bk. 2, ed. by Dearnley, contains nothing but arrangements.

Easy Modern Organ Music, 2 bks., OUP, 1971. Bk. 1: Hoddinot, *Intrada;* Leighton, *Fanfare;* Mathias, *Chorale;* Brown, *Nocturne;* McCabe, *Pastorale;* Cooke, *Impromptu.* Bk. 2: Ridout, *Processional; Joubert, Prelude on Picardy;* Orr, *Elegy;* Fricker, *Trio;* Gardner, *Prelude in G Minor;* Forbes, *Ite, missa est, Deo gratias.*

Festal Voluntaries, 6 vols., London, Novello. Vol. I: Works for Advent; Vol. II: Christmas & Ephiphany; Vol. III: Lent, Passiontide & Palm Sunday; Vol. IV: Easter; Vol. V: Ascension, Whitsuntide & Trinity; Vol VI: Harvest. Composers represented: Rowley, Jackson, Langstroth, Thiman, Gilbert, Slater, Ratcliffe, etc.

3 Meditations for Organ, London, Hinrichsen. Works by Brydson, Marshall, Middleton.

Moaern Urgan Music, 3 bks., OUP, 1965-1974. Bk. 1: Kelly, *Exultate;* McCabe, *Nocturne;* Hoddinot, *Toccata;* Preston, *Alleluyas;* Whettam, *Fantasia;* Mathias, *Processional.* Bk. 2: 5 pieces by composers from various countries: Leighton, *Paean;* Roberts, *Dialogue;* Langlais, *Prelude on "Coronation,"* Heiller, *Ecce lignum crucis;* Mushel, *Toccata.* Bk. 3: Brown, *Scherzo;* Forbes, *Tableau;* Hoddinot, *Sarum Fanfare;* Johnson, *Trope on "Cante Tuba;"* Mews, *Gigue de Pan.*

Music Before Service, London, Novello, Contents: Barlow, *Passion Music;* Dickinson, *Dirge;* Leighton, *Elegy;* McCabe, *Prelude;* Ratcliffe, *Threnody.*

Preludes — Interludes — Postludes, 9 vols., ed. Phillips, London, Hinrichsen. Works by 20th c. English composers and others: Willan, Andriessen, Peeters, Reger, Campbell, Milner, Phillips, Arnell, etc.

Samuel Wesley and Dr. Mendelssohn: 3 Organ Fugues (*Tallis to Wesley* series, XIV) , London, Hinrichsen.

Selected Pieces for the Organ, 2 vols., London, Novello. Vol. I: Works by Stewart, Faulkes, Ross, Meale, Waters, Foster, Hailing, S. Wesley, Higgs, Wadely, Blair. Bk. II: Hollins, Higgs, Greenhill, Rowley, Darke, Brewer, Lemare, Fletcher, Coleman, Stanford.

The 3 Wesleys: 3 Pieces, Set. I (*Tallis to Wesley* series, V), London, Hinrichsen.

The 3 Wesleys: 3 Pieces, Set II (*Tallis to Wesley* series, XXIV) , London, Hinrichsen.

Two-Stave Voluntaries by Modern Composers, 2 bks., London Novello. Vol. I: Works by Coleman, Lang, Rowley, Ratcliffe, Statham. Vol. II: Eldridge, Harker, Harris, Hutchings, Thiman.

NOTES

[1]Clutton and Niland, *The British Organ*, London, Batsford, Ltd,4/1969,p.106

MUSICAL SOURCES

Ex. 13. Samuel Wesley: 12 *Short Pieces* (*Tallis to Wesley* series, VIII), ed. Phillips, p. 16. Copyright Hinrichsen. Used by permission of C. F. Peters.

Ex. 14. W. T. Best: 12 *Short Preludes*, Kalmus Ed., p. 50.

Ex. 15. Elgar: *Sonata*, p. 3, © 1896. Reproduced by permission of EMI Music Pub. Ltd. 138-140 Charing Cross Road, London, Eng.

Ex. 16. Parry: *Toccata and Fugue* (*The Wanderer*), p. 1.

Ex. 17. Howells: *Saraband* (*Six Pieces for Organ*, No. 5), p. 1.

Ex. 18. Downes: *Paraphrase on "O Filii et Filiae,"* p. 1. Copyright Hinrichsen. Used by permission of C. F. Peters.

Exs. 19a & 19b. Hamilton: *Paraphrase of the Music for Organs in "Epitaph for this World and Time,"* pp. 8, 9. Copyright 1972 Theodore Presser Co. Used by permission of the publisher.

Exs. 20a & 20b. Williamson: *Symphony*, mov't 6: Paean, pp. 47, 53.

Ex. 21. *Modern Organ Music*, Bk. 3 (OUP), p. 24.

Ex. 22. Mathias: *Invocations*, p. 2.

Ex. 23. Fricker: *Toccata "Gladius Domini,"* p. 8. Copyright 1971 Augsburg Publishing House.

Ex. 24. *Modern Music*, Bk. 1, p. 17.

Ex. 25. *McCabe: Dies Resurrectionis*, p. 1.

7

The Low Countries

THE major contribution of the Netherlands, during the early history of organ playing, was the development of the type of Renaissance instrument known as the "Brabant organ" (named after the Netherlands province). From the 14th century on, organ building was a major industry in the Netherlands. Organ builders from the northern part of the country, and especially from the northern part of Brabant, have been credited with some highly significant innovations. (The province of Brabant actually belonged to the southern provinces, politically and economically, but, with respect to organ building, it was aligned with the north Netherlandish type rather than with the southern, or Flemish, type).

The spring chest is believed to have originated in the Netherlands, as well as certain flute stops, particularly those of the *quintaton* type. By the middle of the 16th century, most of the basic forms of pipes which exist today could be found on north Netherlandish instruments. While an increase in stop types was common throughout Europe in that century, the manner in which the Brabant builders organized these stops is particularly significant. The *Hoofdwerk* (Great Organ) was housed together with *Pedaal*, *Bovenwerk* (like the German *Oberwerk*), and *Borstwerk* (*Borstwerk*). Together they formed one large complex in which all of the stop families were represented. Opposing this was the *Rugwerk* (*Rückpositiv*) which was placed in a separate case some distance from the main body of pipework and which likewise contained members of all stop families. The *Pedaal* usually had some stops for *cantus firmus* use (*Nachthoorn 2′*, *Trombet 8′*, etc.) and the *Hoofdwerk* could be coupled to it. Brabant builders, greatly in demand in

foreign countries, exercised a particularly profound influence on organ building in north Germany. It is significant for the later history of organ music (17th century) that the major working territory of these Renaissance Netherlandish builders coincided roughly with the territory in which Sweelinck's influence was later felt.

In the southern part of the Low Countries (that area which corresponds roughly to present-day Belgium), organ building moved in a different direction. The south Netherlandish Renaissance organ, or Flemish Renaissance organ as we may also call it, was enclosed within a single case and often had no more than one manual with appended pedal. Independent pedal stops were rare. When the organ did have a second division, it was a *Borstwerk* rather than a *Rugwerk*, implying that it had a smaller variety of stops and did not require a case placed apart from the *Hoofdwerk*. Flemish organ builders did not have as wide a sphere of influence as did the northern builders. However, some of them moving to Normandy in the late Renaissance and early Baroque periods, were active in the early formation of the French baroque instrument.

As already indicated, the development of the well-balanced, colorful Brabant instrument was, in the organ field, the most far-reaching contribution made by the Lowlands during the Renaissance era. One would expect, then, to find organ compositions of high artistic merit dating from the same period. Strangely, however, musicians in the Low Countries were late in establishing an independent keyboard style. Several of the great Flemish polyphonic masters (Willaert, etc.) played the organ, but their organ playing generally consisted of transcriptions from vocal literature. Not until the latter half of the 16th century do we see Flemish musicians beginning to develop an idiomatic keyboard style. Moreover, musicians who did write in a keyboard style were not those who stayed at home in the Low Countries, but rather ones who took positions in important centers elsewhere: Jacques Buus (d. 1565), employed in Venice and Vienna; Giovanni (Jean de) Macque (c.1550-1614), active in Rome and Naples; Samuel Mareschal (1554-1640), who lived in Basel; Simon Lohet (c. middle 16th c. - 1611), a member of the Stuttgart court; Karel (Charles) Luython (1557/58-1620), employed at the imperial courts in Vienna and Prague. Within the Low Countries, however, native organists prior to Sweelinck were not able to free themselves from the domination of the vocal polyphonic style.

During approximately the same period (the latter 16th century), a few prominent foreign organists took up residence in the Low Countries. Of their number, John Bull (1562/63-1628) and Peter Philips (1560/61-1628) are the most significant. Francesco Guami, an Italian who was organist at the Brussels court, is also noteworthy as a carrier of the Venetian style to Flanders. John Bull, a virtuoso keyboardist, probably did more than anyone else to promote the use of English virginal forms and techniques in the Lowlands. His compatriot, Peter Philips, also contributed. Having lived as a religious exile in Italy, Spain, and France before settling in Brussels and Antwerp, Philips brought not only his native tradition, but techniques acquired in other countries as well.

These men prepared the soil for Sweelinck's remarkable creativity. At the same time, they may have learned some things from Sweelinck. Certainly, they benefited from their acquaintance with the remarkably progressive Netherlandish organs. In Bull's fantasia on *Laet ons met hertyn reyne,* for example, the composer was clearly inspired by Netherlandish organs since he specified the use of stops typical of such organs

— stops which were non-existent in England at this time.

In Jan Pieterszoon Sweelinck (1562-1621), Netherlandish organ music found its first significant representative of native birth. Sweelinck's works reflect the polyphonic heritage of the great Netherlandish choral composers, while at the same time revealing the absorption of foreign keyboard traditions. Certain aspects of the Spanish variations technique *(Diferencias)* and possibly the restrained Spanish handling of instrumental counterpoint seem to have influenced him. The figurations of the English virginal style, together with English variation techniques, are, in some compositions, quite apparent. The *ricercar* form and the contrapuntal keyboard style of the Venetians can likewise be seen in some of his works. While it is significant that he brought together such highly diversified elements, Sweelinck's real greatness derives from the fact that he carried these styles and techniques further, to a new height of development. Some of his large *fantasias* and *ricercare,* for example, are related to the monothematic Italian *ricercar,* but go beyond their model in that they already contain the essence of the fugue, namely: the theme is not only presented and repeated, but developed contrapuntally. The following example from the *Fantasia Chromatica* shows a use of *stretto.*

(Example 1)

In Sweelinck's *echo fantasias* — a separate category from the great *fantasias* — Venetian antiphonal devices have been applied to organ playing. Composed of repeated phrases employing contrasting dynamics and colors, the *echo fantasias* appear designed to display the varied colors and multiple manuals of the north Netherlandish organ. In Italy organists could only respond to the choir, or alternate with a group of instrumentalists or with another organ in the same church. Sweelinck, on the other hand, with a more diversified instrument at his dis-

Ex. 1. Sweelinck, *Fantasia Chromatica,* m. 55-61.

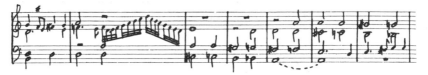

posal, could make a variety of echo and contrast effects on a single instrument, simply by moving from one manual to another. The main organ in the *Oude Kerk* of Amsterdam, where Sweelinck was organist, had the following specification during his lifetime.[1]

Rückpositiv

Principal 8
Quintadena 8
Octave 4
Sifflöte
Gedackt 4
Mixture
Scharf
Krummhorn 8
Baarpyp 8 (a reed)
Schalmei 4

Hauptwerk

Principal 16
Octave 8
Mixture
Scharf

Pedal

Trumpet 8
Nachthorn

Oberwerk

Principal 8
Gedackt 8
Offenflöte 4
Nasard 2 2/3
Gemshorn 2
Sifflöte
Terzzimbel
Trumpet 8
Zink (8, treble?)

In another area, that of toccata composition, Sweelinck's work was likewise important since it formed a link between the early Italian and the North German toccata styles. In the free sections of his toccatas, Sweelinck drew upon the Spanish and English traditions, employing broken chords, repeated tones, and running passagework in parallel thirds and sixths, with both hands (instead of the right hand alone) being actively engaged in executing the figuration.

In addition to the already mentioned works, Sweelinck wrote variations on German chorale tunes, on secular songs, and on dances.

A slightly younger contemporary of Sweelinck was the Brussels court organist, Pieter Cornet (1593-1626). While only a few works by Cornet have been preserved, they indicate that he was an artist of high stature. Contrary to Sweelinck who lived in the Calvinist part of the Lowlands, Cornet, a resident of the Catholic, southern part, wrote liturgical music, in addition to pieces for non-liturgical use. In his hymn versets one sees a warmth of expression and a certain mysticism. Two of the major influences on Cornet were the Italian *ricercar* tradition and the English virginal school. His *fantasias*, in particular, are a witness to his skill in combining formal aspects of the *ricercar* with style traits of the virginal school.

(Example 2)

Another contemporary of Sweelinck was Henderick Speuy (c. 1575-1625) who published in 1610 a collection entitled *De Psalmen Davids gestelt op het Tabulature van het Orghel en de Clavecymbel* (The Psalms of David Notated in Organ and Clavichord Tablature). Each of the psalms in this book was arranged as a Bicinium, with the *cantus firmus* (one of the Calvinist psalm tunes) appearing in either soprano or bass, or alternating between the two parts. Other compositions of the early 17th century have been preserved in the *Liber Fratrum Cruciferorum Leodiensium*. This manuscript, published in Guilmant, *Archives des Maîtres de*

Ex. 2. Cornet, *Fantasia 3 Toni*, m. 1-8, 11-13.

l'Orgue, X, contains works by A. Gabrieli, Merulo, Sweelinck, Gerardus Scronx, William Brown, and a number of anonymous composers who appear to have belonged to the Netherlands school of organ playing. Several of the compositions (one by Scronx and others by anonymous composers) bear the title *Echo.* They testify to the Netherlanders' interest in organ colors and contrasts in registration.

In the latter half of the 17th century, the small number of surviving manuscripts leads one to believe that interest in organ music was probably declining in the Low Countries. In the Catholic south, the only significant organ composer of whom we have knowledge was Abraham van den Kerckhoven (1627-1701/02), organist at the royal court in Brussels. Like Cornet, the foremost Flemish organist during the first part of the century, Kerckhoven wrote both liturgical and non-liturgical pieces. Among his preserved works are a large number of versets, a mass, fantasies, fugues, and preludes and fugues.

(Example 3)

In the Protestant north, there was one organist worthy of note during this period, Anthoni van Noordt (d. 1675). He wrote a *Tabulatuur-Boek van Psalmen en Fantasyen,* published in 1659. His psalm settings were based on Sweelinck's variations, and his fantasies were monothematic compositions pointing toward the fugue as it developed under the hands of later Baroque composers.

As is commonly known, Sweelinck's students in the Netherlands never attained more than provincial significance. His true disciples — those who were able to expand upon his achievements — were the north and middle German organists who came to Amsterdam to study with him (Scheidt, J. Praetorius, Scheidemann, Schildt, etc.). There may be several reasons why the Sweelinck tradition flourished better on German soil than in the Netherlands. But, a chief reason was certainly the fact that the Lutheran church in Germany encouraged liturgical organ playing, while the Calvinist, or Reformed, church did not. After Calvinism had become the state religion for the northern provinces in 1578, organ playing was unequivocally banned from the Reformed church service. Fortunately, the Dutch were so proud of their magnificent organs that they refused to let these instruments be destroyed by religious fanatics, as was done in other parts of Europe, especially Switzerland and England. In the Netherlands, the municipal government assumed jurisdiction over the use and preservation of organs, and organists became civil employees totally independent of the church. They performed full-length public recitals following the Sunday morning and Sunday afternoon church services, and at other times during the week, but they did not play at all during the worship service itself. This explains why Sweelinck ignored liturgical music, while concentrating on toccatas, fantasies, and variations. His *Choralbearbeitungen,* by the way, should not be mistaken for liturgical pieces. The German melodies on which these works were based were not sung in the Calvinist service, and it is impossible that Sweelinck could have used these *Choralbearbeitungen* for any liturgical purpose.

By mid-17th century, organ playing had gradually re-entered the Reformed service, although it was still regarded with suspicion in several localities. The organist was now allowed to play pieces, or improvisations, based on the psalms sung by the congregation. No other literature was permitted during the service.

In the following centuries, the 18th and 19th, Dutch organists continued to play for church services, but found themselves less in demand as concert artists. Organ building still flourished, but Dutch organists of the 18th and 19th centuries produced little literature which could stand alongside the best organ music from Germany, France, or Belgium.

Ex. 3. Kerckhoven, *Fantasia,* m. 1-10.

At the beginning of the 20th century, a general cultural revival lent new artistic significance to all areas of music, including organ music. Then, about 1930, the Organ Reform movement made its way into the Netherlands, increasing in momentum after World War II. In addition to stimulating the appreciation of historic organs and old organ music, the Organ Reform guided organ builders toward the creation of many neo-Baroque instruments of superior quality.

Organ composition, too, was stimulated by the cultural revival and, more particularly, by the Organ Reform. Both liturgical music and concert works are well represented in Dutch organ music of the 20th century. Hendrik Andriessen (1892-   ), Anton van der Horst (1899-1965), Jacob Bijster (1902-1958), and Henk Badings (1907-   ) have been major figures, especially during the first half of the century. Andriessen often combined German Romantic style traits with French Impressionism.

(Example 4)

Several of his pieces are contemplative in mood. The works of van der Horst and Bijster range from Romantic compositions to those in a fairly modern

idiom, such as van der Horst's *Suite in Modo Conjuncto,* based on a scale of alternating tones and semitones. Badings, less conservative than many Dutch composers, has experimented with a variety of techniques. In his concert works, the organ is often combined with another instrument (oboe, flute, viola, timpani, guitar, etc.). An excerpt from his *Orgelconcert* follows.

(Example 5)

Another influential organist and teacher is Albert de Klerk (1917-   ). While some of his compositions show an indebtedness to his teacher, Andriessen, others reflect his deep interest in old organs and historical forms. Among the other Dutch organ composers to be noted are: Bernard van den Sigtenhorst Meyer (1888-1953); Marius Monnikendam (1896-1977); Jaap Vranken (1897-1956); Cor Kee (1900-   ); Jan Nieland (1903-1963); Kees van Baaren (1906-1970); Jan Mul (1911-   ); Herman Strategier (1912-   ); Louis Toebosch (1916-   ); Piet Post (1916-   ); Willem Vogel (1920-   ); Piet Kee (1927-   ); Bernard Bartelink (1929-   ); Jaap Dragt (1930-   ). Careful craftsmanship is usually present in the com-

Ex. 4. Andriessen, *Concerto per organo e orchestra,* mov't 1 (organ part), m. 1-6.

Ex. 5. Badings, *Orgelconcert,* mov't 1 (organ part), m. 165-173.

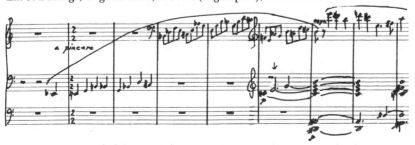

positions of the 20th century Dutch organ school.

Turning now to that part of the Lowlands which constitutes modern-day Belgium, one notes that, in Sweelinck's day, a definite kinship had existed between organ playing in the southern provinces and that in the northern ones, despite the difference in instruments. By the late 17th century, however, this was less true. Some organists in the southern provinces continued to build on the polyphonic tradition of Sweelinck and Cornet (Mathias van den Gheyn, 1721-1785, for example), but others looked increasingly toward France. Among the latter group were Lambert Chaumont (c. 1635-1712) and Babou, his contemporary at Liège. In Chaumont's *Pièces d'Orgue sur les 8 tons* (1695), the style, forms, ornaments, and registration of the Parisian school of Lebègue and Nivers are particularly well-expressed.

(Example 6)

The composer even followed the French practice of providing instructions for registration and a table of ornaments. During the 18th century, this emulation of the French manner continued to prevail.

In the 19th century, cultural ties with France were still strong, but were no longer one-sided. In a period when sentimental melodies and trite programmatic pieces were the French organist's usual fare, it was a Belgian, Nicolas-Jacques Lemmens (1823-1881), who began crusading for a more idiomatic use of the organ and for a return to liturgical writing. True, in some works he did not completely relinquish pianistic accompaniment, march rhythms, and other traits typical of mid-19th century French organ music. However, in several works he exhibits considerable restraint and sometimes employs Gregorian chant.

(Example 7)

As a pedagogue, Lemmens' influence was extremely far-reaching. The fluent pedal and manual technique of the French school of the late 19th and 20th centuries can be traced back largely to Lemmens, who stressed technique at a time when it was sorely needed. For decades, Lemmens' *Ecole d'Orgue* was the standard method book at the Paris and Brussels conservatories. Charles-Marie Widor and Alexandre Guilmant, Lemmens' two most prominent pupils, built upon his ideas and transmitted them to several generations of French organists.

Among Lemmens' Belgian students, Alphonse-Jean-Ernest Mailly (1833-1918) and Joseph Callaerts (1838-1901) were the most important in their day. However, their writing was rather superficial and they did not make as great an impact as did Widor and Guilmant.

At this point, one would also like to recall that it was another Belgian, Cèsar Franck (1822-1890), who gave the French school an additional transfusion later in the century. Usually considered as a

Ex. 6. Chaumont, *Prélude* (*Premier ton*), m. 1-5.

Ex. 7. Lemmens, *Grand Fantasia in E Minor*, m. 1-4, 48, 49.

Frenchman, Franck was not typically French, since, in addition to being born in Belgium, he had a Dutch father and a German mother. His Germanic background coupled with his Parisian training and experience, produced a unique personality. A discussion of his contributions will be omitted at this point, since they were mentioned in an earlier chapter.

In the 20th century, the alliance with French organ music continued. The works of Joseph Jongen (1873-1953) and Paul de Maleingreau (1887-1956), Walloon composers, illustrate this particularly well.

(Example 8)

They both employed the symphonic style, which Guilmant, Widor, and Vierne brought to its apex, and they were unmistakeably influenced by the French Romantic instrument.

Flor Peeters (1903-   ), who is of Flemish origin, presents a more diversified picture. On the one hand, he has been undeniably touched by the liturgical mysticism of Tournemire and by the rhythmic fluidity of Gregorian chant. Some of his most successful works have grown out of the French Catholic liturgical framework. At the same time, Peeters feels a distinct kinship with the old Netherlandish masters, with north

European instruments, and with the Protestant organ tradition. These influences are particularly noticeable in the numerous chorale and hymn preludes which he has composed in recent years.

(Example 9)

To complete the picture of Belgian organ composition in the 20th century, one adds: Charles Hens (1898-1967); Pater J.M. Plum (1899-1944); Gabriel Verschraegen (1919-   ); Pierre Froidebise (1914-1962). In the realm of organ building, there has been less activity in Belgium than in the Netherlands in the present century.

EDITIONS

Note: All van Rossum publications (Utrecht) are now handled by Muziekuitgeverij Herman Zengerink (Utrecht).

Andriessen: Publications by van Rossum (Utrecht), unless otherwise indicated. *Premier Choral* (1913). *Deuxième Choral* (1916-1965). *Troisième Choral* (1920), Paris, Leduc. *Quatrième Choral* (1952). *Toccata* (1917). *Sonata da chiesa* (1927). *Passacaglia* (1929). *Sinfonia* (1940). 24 *Intermezzi*, 2 vols. (1943). *Thema met variaties* (1949). *Quattro studi* (1953).

Ex. 8. Jongen, *Toccata,* m. 1-3.

Ex. 9. Peeters, *Partita: Jesu, Dulcis Memoria,* mov't 2, m. 1, 2; mov't 8, m. 1, 2.

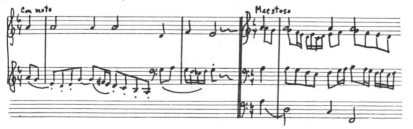

136 [7]

Suite (1960). *Advent to Whitsuntide,* vol. I, London, Hinrichsen. *Fête Dieu,* Amsterdam, Annie Bank. ORG. & INSTRUMENTS: *Concerto* for Organ and Orchestra, Amsterdam, Donemus. *Pezzo Festivo* for org., 2 trpts., 2 trbns., Amsterdam, Donemus.

Badings: Publications by Donemus (Amsterdam). *Toccata* (1929). *Preludium* (1938). *Preludium en Fuga No.* 1 (1952). *Preludium en Fuga No.* 2 (1952). *Preludium en Fuga No.* 3 (1953). *Preludium en Fuga No.* 4 (1956). *Variations on a Mediaeval Dutch Theme* (1969). ORG. & INSTRUMENTS: *Canzona* for oboe and organ (1938). *Fuga* for flute, oboe, violin, viola, and organ (1938). *Intermezzo* for violin and organ (1938). *Concerto* for organ and orchestra. *Concerto No.* 2 for organ and orchestra. *Passacaglia,* timpani and organ (1958). *It Is Dawning in the East,* organ and guitar. *Dialogues,* flute and organ. *Quempas* for violin and organ (or viola and organ) (1967). *Canzona* for C trumpet and organ, 1971.

Bartelink: *Partita piccola super Lumen ad revelationem gentium,* Utrecht, van Rossum. *Toccata per organo,* Utrecht, van Rossum. *Preludium, Trio en Fuga* (1960), Amsterdam, Donemus. *Musica pro offertorio et sub communione,* Hilversum, Gooi et Sticht, 1970.

Bijster: Major publisher is Ars Nova (Goes). *Variaties op een oud Nederlands Lied* (1934), Amsterdam, Nieuwe Muziekhandel. *Variaties en Dubbelfuga over het Valeriuslied "Merck toch hoe sterck"* (1935), Amsterdam, Nieuwe Muziekhandel. *Passacaglia* (1935), Amsterdam, Nieuwe Muziekhandel/revised ed. (1954), New York, Metro Music Co. *Fantasie in Kerkstijl over Psalm* 68 (1945), A.N. *Toccata* (1945), A.N. *Fantasie over "Komt nu met zang"* (1947), A.N. *Paraphrase over "Gelukkig is het land"* (1947), A.N. *Deuxième Choral voor orgel* (1948), Amsterdam, Broekmans & van Poppel. *Variaties over "Komt wilt U'Spoeden naar Bethlehem"* (1934), Amsterdam, Nieuwe Muziekhandel. 2 *Voorspelen voor orgel zonder pedaal: Psalmen* 51 *en* 65:1 (1948), A.N. *Triptyque pour Orgue* (1949), Amsterdam, Broekmans & van Poppel. *Variaties voor Orgelove r het oud Nederlandse Lied "Stort tranen uyt, schreyt, luyde! weent en treurt!"* (1950), A.N. *Ricercare* (1951), Amsterdam, Alsbach. 6 *Harmonische Variaties voor Orgel* (1953), Hil-

versum, Harmonia Uitgave. 10 *Impressies voor harmonium* (1954), Amsterdam, Broekmans & van Poppel. 8 *Psalmen met voorspelen met obligaat pedaal:* Ps. 27, 42, 62, 100, 103, 121, 36, 138 (1954), A.N. 2 *Koraalbewerkingen voor orgel manualiter: Prelude en Fughetta over "Vaste Rots van mijn behound" en Ricercare over "Heem mijn leven, last het Heer"* (1957), A.N. *Koraal, trio, introductie en fuga over "Meester, men zoekt U wijd en zijd"* (1958), A.N.

Callaerts: Publications by Schott Frères, Brussels. 24 *pièces,* in 2 series, 4 bks. to each series. *Première sonate en ut mineur. Deuxième sonate en la majeur. Pièces pour orgue. Morceau de concert* (Offertoire). *Symphonie pastorale.* 6 *morceaux pour orgue. Grande fantaisie de concert.* ORG. & INSTRUMENTS: *Concerto* for organ and orchestra.

Chaumont: *Livre d'orgue,* ed. Hens/ Bragard (*Monumenta Leodiensium musicorum*), Liège, Editio Dynamo, 1939. *Pièces d'orgue sur les huit tons,* ed. Ferrard, Paris, Heugel.

Cornet: All but 2 of Cornet's perserved works can be found in vol. X of *Archives des Maîtres de l'orgue,* ed. Guilmant, Paris, Durand, 1910.

Dragt: Publisher is Ars Nova (Goes), unless otherwise indicated. 5 *Koraalpreludes,* Series I (1955), Amsterdam, Alsbach & Doyer. 5 *Koraalpreludes,* Series II (1956), Amsterdam, Alsbach & Doyer. *Gezang* 103 (1957). *Psalm* 38: kleine partita (1958). 3 *Koraalpreludes* (Ps. 1, Ps. 62, "Now Thank We All Our God") (1959). *Variaties over "Nu zijt wellecome"* (1960). *Partita: Psalm* 103 (1962). 4 *Koraalpreludes* ("Vater unser," "Veni Creator," "Christe, qui Lux es et dies," Psalm 23) (1964). *A Mighty Fortress* (1966). *Cortège* (1966), appeared as enclosure in *De Praestant,* Oct. 1968, no. 4. *Diptyque* (1966), Hilversum, Harmonia-Uitgave. *Herr Jesu Christ, dich zu uns wend* and *Psalm* 146 (1966). *Psalm* 122: *Preludio e fuga con corale* (1966). *Choralfantasie: Was Gott tut, dass ist wohlgetan* (1966), appeared as enclosure in *Het Orgelblad,* Jan./Feb. 1971. *Deux Noëls* (1969/70), Hilversum, Harmonia-Uitgave. *Prelude I, Trio, Prelude II* (1969), appeared as enclosure in *Organist en Eredienst,* Mar./Apr./ May, 1970.

Gheyn, van den: *Morceaux fugués,* ed.

van Elewyck and Lemmens, Brussels, Schott Frères, 1865. *Recueil de productions légères*, Brussels, Schott Frères.

Guillet: *Fantaisies*, 4 bks. (*L'Organiste liturgique*, bks. 33, 37, 49, 50), Paris, Schola Cantorum. *Fantasies*, 1 vol., Opa-Locka, Kalmus. Also see *MMB* IV under "Collections."

Horst, van der: *Suite in Modo Conjuncto* (1943), Goes, Ars Nova. *Partite diverse sopra "O Nostre Dieu, et Seigneur amiable"* (Ps. 8) (1947), Goes, Ars Nova. *Variazioni sopra la sinfonia della cantata "Christ lag in Todesbanden" di Giov. Seb. Bach,* op. 64 (1954), Amsterdam, Donemus. *Etude de concert,* op. 104 (1963), Amsterdam, Donemus. ORG. & INSTRUMENTS: *Concerto per Organo Romantico* with orchestra, op. 58 (1952), Amsterdam, Donemus. *Concert pour orgue et orchestre à cordes dans le style baroque,* Amsterdam, Donemus.

Jongen: *Quatre pièces* (Offertoire, Communion, Pastorale, Offertoire), op. 5, Liège, Muraille, 1894-96. *Trois pièces,* Brussels, Schott Fr., 1908. *Quatre pièces* (Cantabile, Improvisation-Caprice, Prière, Choral), op. 37, Paris, Durand, 1911. *Deux pièces,* op. 38, Arras, Procure générale, 1911. *Offertoire pour harmonium,* Paris, Sénart, 1911. *Deux pièces* (Prélude élégiaque, Pensée d'automne), op. 47, London, Augener, 1915. *Deux pièces* (Chant de Mai, Menuet-Scherzo), op. 53, London, J & W Chester, 1917. *In Mèmoriam,* op. 63, Brussels, Ledent-Malay, 1919 (now Paris, Lemoine). *Sonata éroica,* op. 94, Paris, Leduc, 1930. *Toccata,* op. 104a, Paris, Lemoine, 1935. *Petit Prélude,* Brussels, Centre Belge de Documentation musicale, 1941. *Scherzetto et Prière,* op. 108, London, Oxford University Press, 1938. *Prélude et Fugue,* op. 121, Brussels, Centre Belge de Documentation musicale, 1941. ORG. & INSTRUMENTS: *Hymne* for organ and string orchestra, op. 78 (1924), Brussels, Centre Belge de Documentation musicale, 1924. *Symphonie concertante* for organ and orchestra, op. 81 (1926), Brussels, Cranz, 1933. *Humoresque* for cello and organ, op. 92 (1930), Brussels, Centre Belge de Documentation musicale. *Alleluia* for orchestra and organ, op. 112 (1940), Brussels, Centre Belge de Documentation musicale.

Kee, Cor: Major publisher is Ars Nova (Goes). *Avondzang,* Amersfoort, Willemsen. *Een vaste Burg,* A.N. *Fantasie over "De Heer is God,"* A.N. *Fazen* (Phases), Amsterdam, Donemus. *Feestpostludium*: *Dankt, dankt nu allen Gott,* A.N. *Inleidend orgelspel over "Van U zijn alle dingen,"* A.N. *3 Inventionen,* Amsterdam, Donemus, 1967. *Kerstmuziek,* A.N. *Kleine Partita op een oud Nederlands lied,* A.N. *Onze Psalmen en Gesangen,* Naarden, Seyffardt. *Partita: Jezus leeft,* Amsterdam, Alsbach. *Partita over Psalm* 106, A.N. *Partita over Ps.* 116, A.N. *Postludium op Psalm* 145 en *Preludium op Psalm* 22 (for Lent & Easter), A.N. *Psalm* 24, Amersfoort, Willemsen. *Psalm* 33, Amersfoort, Willemsen. *Psalm* 43, Amersfoort, Willemsen. *Psalm* 31 en *Psalm* 57, A.N. *Psalm* 46 en *Psalm* 47, A.N. *Psalm* 84, Amersfoort, Willemsen. *Psalmen,* 3 vols., Amsterdam, Alsbach. *3 Psalmen* (Ps. 17, 105, & 123), A.N. *6 Psalm Tune Preludes,* New York, Edition Musicus. *14 Psalmen,* Amsterdam, Alsbach. *2 kleine partita's over Ps.* 26 en *Ps.* 33, A.N. *2 preludes en fuga's,* A.N. *Scheepvaart onder Jezus hoede,* Amsterdam, Alsbach. *Reeksveranderingen* in 4 secties, I en II (Serial permutations), Amsterdam, Donemus. *Variaties op "Merck toch hoe sterck",* Amsterdam, Alsbach. *Variatie-Postludium en Reks-Postludium,* Amsterdam, Donemus. *U kan ik niet missen,* Amsterdam, Alsbach. *Suite,* Amsterdam, Donemus.

Kee, Piet: *Inleidend orgelspel over "God is tegenwoordig",* Goes, Ars Nova. *Four Manual Pieces,* Amsterdam, Donemus. *Partita: Gott ist gegenwärtig,* London, Hinrichsen. *Triptych on Psalm 86,* London, Hinrichsen, 1964. *Two Pieces* (Fantasy on "Sleepers Wake"; "Passion Chorale"), London, Hinrichsen. ORG. & INSTRUMENTS: *Music and Space* (1969), rondo for two organs and brass, Amsterdam, Donemus.

Kerckhoven: *Werken voor orgel,* ed. J. Watelet (*Monumenta Musica Belgicae,* II), Vereeniging voor Muziekgeschiedenis, Antwerp, De Ring, 1933. Contains nearly all the preserved works of Kerckhoven.

Klerk, de: *Inventionen* (1945), Goes, Ars Nova. *Octo fantasiae super themata gregoriana* (1954), Utrecht, van Rossum. *Prelude en fuga* (1940), Utrecht, van Rossum. *Postludium,* Amsterdam, Annie Bank. *Ricercare: hommage à Sweelinck* (1950), Utrecht, van Rossum. *Sonata* (1942), Amsterdam, Donemus. 10

Orgelwerken, 2 vols., (1946), Amsterdam, Editions Heuwekemeijer. *Variaties op "O Jesu soet,"* Amsterdam, Annie Bank. 12 *Images,* Amsterdam, Annie Bank. ORG. & INSTRUMENTS: *Concerto* for organ and orchestra, Amsterdam, Donemus. *Concerto* for organ and brass (2 hrns., 2 trpts., 2 trbns.), Amsterdam, Donemus, 1967.

Lemmens: *Pièces d'orgue,* Mainz, Schott. *Oeuvres inédites,* I, Leipzig, Breitkopf & Härtel, 1883. 3 *pièces* (Communion, Quatuor, Prélude), Paris, Hamelle. 10 *Prières,* Paris, Hamelle. *Sonata No.* 1 (Pontificale), London, Novello. *Sonata No.* 2 (O Filii), London, W. Paxton. *Sonata No.* 3 (Pascale), London, Novello. *Grand Fantasia in G Minor,* London, Novello. *Fanfare,* New York, H. W. Gray. *Grand Fantasia in E Minor* (The Storm), New York, G. Schirmer.

Mailly: Publications by Schott Fréres (Brussels), unless otherwise indicated. *Sonate,* op. 1. *A la chapelle. Méditation. Grand choeur. Elégie. Recueillement pour orgue ou harmonium.* 6 *morceaux caractéristiques,* op. 3. *Trois morceaux,* Paris, Lemoine. ORG. & INSTRUMENTS: *Sérénade francaise* for flute and harmonium, or flute, piano and harmonium. *Méditation* for violin and organ (also a version for violoncello and organ).

Maleingreau: *Deux pièces (Post partum Virgo, Ego sum panis vivus),* op. 3 Paris, Philippo. *Opus Sacrum,* 2 vols., op. 10 & 22, Paris, Sénart. Vol. I: Christmas; vol. II: Lent. *Suite,* op. 14, Paris, Durand. *Offrandes musicales,* op. 18, London, J. & W. Chester. *Toccata,* op. 18, no. 3, London, J. & W. Chester. *Symphonie de Noël,* op. 19, London, J. & W. Chester. *Symphonie de la Passion,* op. 20, Paris, Sénart (now Salabert). *Symphonie de l'Agneau mystique,* op. 24, Paris, Leduc, 1926. *Préludes à l'Introit,* 7 bks., op. 25, Paris, Sénart (now Salabert). Vol. I: Christmas; II: Easter; III: Pentecost; IV: Ordinary of the Saints' Days; V: Feasts of the Virgin; VI: Propers of the Saints' Days; VII: Supplement. 18 *Elévations liturgiques,* op. 27, Paris, Philippo. *Messe de Pâques,* op. 31, Paris, Philippo. *Méditation pour le temps Pascal,* Paris, Philippo. *Messe du jour de Noël,* Paris, Philippo. *Messe du jour de l'An,* op. 30, Paris, Philippo. *Messe de la Toussaint,* op. 30, no. 2, Paris, Philippo. *Ite missa est,* Paris, Philippo. *Suite Mariale* (4 paraphrases of hymns to the Virgin), op. 65, London,

Oxford University Press. *Suite,* op. 71, London, Oxford University Press, 1937. *Diptych for All Saints,* Glen Rock, J. Fischer. *Préludes de Carême,* London, Oxford University Press. *Si Consurrexit,* Paris, Durand.

Monnikendam: *Choral* (1951), Amsterdam, Annie Bank. *Cortège,* Utrecht, van Rossum. *Marcia funèbre* (1959), Amsterdam, Donemus. 10 *Inventiones* (1959), Amsterdam, Donemus. 12 *Inventions for Organ,* Cincinnati, World Library of Sacred Music. 12 *More Inventions for Organ,* Cincinnati, World Library of Sacred Music. *Sonata da chiesa* (1961), Utrecht, van Rossum. *Tema con Variazione per la Notte di Natale,* Amsterdam, Annie Bank. *Toccata* (1936), Amsterdam, Annie Bank. *Toccata,* New York, C. F. Peters, 1970. ORG. & INSTRUMENTS: *Concerto* for org. and brass (2 trpts, 2 trbns) (1956), Amsterdam, Donemus. *Concerto* for org. and orch. (1968), Amsterdam, Donemus. *Concerto* for org. and string orchestra, Amsterdam, Donemus. *Intrada and Sortie* for organ, 2 trpts, 2 trbns, Cincinnati, World Library of Sacred Music. *Overture* for organ and orchestra, Amsterdam, Donemus. *Rodena* for timpani and organ (1960), Amsterdam, Donemus.

Mul: *Choral joyeux* (1956), Amsterdam, Donemus. *Sonata,* Amsterdam, Annie Bank.

Noordt: *Tabulatuur-Boek van Psalmen en Fantasien,* ed. Seiffert (Vereeniging voor Noord-Nederlandse Muziekgeschiedenis, XIX), Leipzig, Breitkopf & Härtel, 1896/new edition, Amsterdam, Alsbach, 1957. *Psalmbearbeitungen,* ed. Pidoux, Kassel, Barenreiter, 1954.

Peeters: Major publishers are: C. F. Peters (Frankfurt/New York); H. W. Gray (New York); McLaughlin & Reilly (Boston); Lemoine (Paris); Schott (abbrev., Sch.) (Mainz); Schwann (abbrev., Schw.) (Düsseldorf). *Four Improvisations on Gregorian Melodies,* op. 6, McL. & R. *Symphonic Fantasy on an Eastern Gregorian Alleluia,* op. 13, H.W.G. *Monastic Peace,* op. 16a, McL & R. *Variations and Finale on an Old Flemish Song,* op. 20, Philadelphia, Elkan Vogel. *Toccata, Fugue and Hymn on "Ave Maris Stella,"* op. 28, Lem. *Flemish Rhapsody,* op. 37, Sch. *Elégie,* op. 38, Lem. 10 *Orgelchoräle über altflämische Lieder,* op. 39, Sch. *Passacaglia und Fuga,* op. 42, Sch. *Suite modale,* op.

43, Lem. *Sinfonia per Organo* (4 movts.) , op. 48, Lem. *Aria,* op. 51, Amsterdam, Edition Heuwekemeijer. *Concert Piece,* op. 52a, Pet. *Thirty-five Miniatures,* op. 55, McL & R. *Variations on an Original Theme,* op. 58, Philadelphia, Elkan Vogel. *Four Pieces* (Morning Hymn, Gavotte antique, Nostalgia, Legend), op. 59, H.W.G. *Lied Symphony,* 5 vols., op. 66, Pet. *30 Chorale Preludes on Well-Known Hymns* (Lutheran hymn tunes) , 3 vols., op. 68, 69, 70, Pet. *Four Pieces* (Hymn, In Memoriam, Largo, Finale) , op. 71, McL & R. *3 Praeludien und Fugen,* op. 72, Sch. *30 Chorale Preludes on Gregorian Hymns,* 3 vols., op. 75, 76, 77, Pet. *Manuale* (15 Easy Pieces) , op. 78, Schw. *2 Chorale Preludes,* op. 81, London, Novello. *Praeludium, Canzona e Ciacona,* op. 83, London, Novello. *Solemn Prelude,* op. 86c, London, Hinrichsen Ed. *Festival Voluntary,* op. 87, London, Oxford University Press. *16 Praeludien und Hymnen,* op. 90, Schw. *30 Short Chorale Preludes on Well-Known Hymns,* op. 95, Pet. *Sixty Short Pieces* (w/o ped.) , H.W.G. *Hymn Preludes and Postludes for the Church Year,* 24 vols., op. 100, Pet. Vol. I: Advent through Epiphany; II: Lent & Easter; III: Ascentiontide, Pentecost, Holy Trinity; IV: Minor Festivals; V: All Saints', Memorial Day, etc.; VI: Worship, Adoration, Praise; VII: Matins, Lauds, etc.; VIII: Holy Scriptures and Propagation of the Word; IX: Holy Baptism, Holy Communion; X: The Church, The Holy Ministry, Ordination, etc.; XI: The House of God, Dedications and Anniversary; XII: The Lord's Day, Beginning and Close of Worship; XIII: Repentance, Faith and Redemption; XIV: The Kingdom of God, Missions; XV: Confirmation, Christian Education; XVI: Sanctification and the Christian Life; XVII: Christian Stewardship and Service; XVIII: Contemplation, The Inner Life, Comfort, Trust; XIX: Prayer, Intercession & Supplication; XX: Pilgrimage, Conflict & Victory; XXI: Death, L i f e Everlasting, Commemoration; XXII: Harvest and Thanksgiving; XXIII: Marriage, The Home and Family; XXIV: City and Nation, The World, Doxology. *Partita on "Almighty God of Majesty,"* op. 109, McL & R. *Praeludiale* (16 manual pieces), op. 114, Schw. *Six Lyrical Pieces,* op. 116, H.W.G. *10 Inventionen,* op. 117, Schw. *Partita on a Plainchant Hymn* (Urbs Beata) , London, Hinrichsen. ORG. & INSTRUMENTS (OR VOICE) : *Speculum Vitae,* poem for org. and high voice in 4 movts., op. 36, Pet. *Concerto for Organ and Orchestra,* op. 52 (also arr. for org. & piano by the composer) , Pet. *Concerto for Organ and Piano,* op. 74, H.W.G. *Entrata Festiva* for organ, 2 trpts., 2 trbns. (timpani and unison chorus ad lib.) , op. 93, Pet. *Chorale Fantasy on "Christ the Lord Has Risen"* for org., 2 trpts., 2 trbns. op. 101, H.W.G. Additional pieces in various contemporary collections.

Speuy: *Psalm Preludes,* ed. Noske, Amsterdam, Editions Heuwekemeijer, 1962.

Strategier: *Preludium, intermezzo en thema met variaties* (1939), Utrecht, van Rossum. *Ritornello capriccioso* (1944) , Utrecht, van Rossum. *Thirty Short Inventions,* 3 vols., Boston, McLaughlin & Reilly. *Toccatina* (1951) , Utrecht, van Rossum. *Tweede Passacaglia* (1946) , Utrecht, van Rossum. *3 kleine Trio's,* Goes, Ars Nova.

Sweelinck: *Opera omnia,* Vol. I (*The Instrumental Works*) , fascicles I,II,III, Amsterdam, Vereniging voor Nederlandse Muziekgeschiedenis, 1968. Contents of Fasc. I: Keyboard Works — Fantasias and Toccatas, ed. Leonhardt. Fasc. II: Keyboard Works — Settings of Sacred Melodies, ed. Annegarn. Fasc. III: Keyboard Works — Settings of Secular Melodies and Dances; Works for Lute, ed. Noske. *Werken voor Orgel en Clavecimbel,* I, ed. Seiffert, Vereniging voor Nederlandse Muziekgeschiedenis, 's-Gravenhage & Liepzig, Nyhoff/Breitkopf & Härtel, 1894 (contained 36 keyboard pieces)/2nd ed., 1943 (expanded to include 69 pieces) /3rd ed., Amsterdam, Alsbach & Co., 1957, with a supplement of 5 additional pieces edited by Annegarn, 1958. *Opera Organis Concinenda,* 2 vols. (*Musica Antiqua Batava,* nos. 700 & 701) , Vereniging voor Nederlandse Muziekgeschiedenis, The Hague, Editio Musico. *Opera Organis Concinenda,* 2 vol., ed. Engels, Wiesbaden, Breitkopf & Härtel. *Ausgewählte Orgelwerke,* 2 vols., ed. Hellmann, Frankfurt, Peters, 1957. *Choralbearbeitungen,* ed. Moser-Fedtke, Kassel, Bärenreiter, 1956. *Liedvariationen,* ed. Doflein, Mainz, Schott, 1935. *Werken voor Orgel of clavecimbel uit het "Celler Klavierbuch 1662,"* ed. J.H. Schmidt, Amsterdam, Vereniging voor Nederlandse Muziekgeschiedenis, 1955.

Vogel: All publications by Ars Nova (Goes) , unless otherwise indicated.

Bicinia (Psalmen). *Een roze fris ontloken* (Lo, How a Rose). *Fantasie: Jezus leeft, en wij met Hem; Orgelkoraal: Jezus leven van mijn leven. Heft op Uw hoofden; Psalm 43. Heil'ge Geest daal tot ons neer; Psalm 22. Liturgische Suite* I, II. *Muziek voor lijdenstijd en Pasen* (Music for Lent & Easter). *Partita: Christus is opgestanden. Partita: Wij loven U o God* (Te Deum Laudamus). *Prelude: Psalm 122; Partita: Psalm 121. Psalmenmuziek* (psalms 24, 25, 62, 96, 100, 116, 139, 143). *3 Preludes en Fugas. Toccata: Psalm 150. Trio-sonatine. Eenvoudige orgelkoraalen,* Hilversum, Harmonia Uitgave.

Collections

Werken voor Orgel (*Monumenta Musicae Belgicae,* IV), Vereeniging voor Muziekgeschiedenis, Antwerp, De Ring, 1938. Contents: works by Ch. Guillet, Jean de Macque, and Ch. Luyton.

Werken voor Orgel (*Monumenta Musicae Belgicae,* VI), Vereeniging voor Muziekgeschiedenis, Antwerp, De Ring, 1938. Contents: works by Dieudonné Raick and Charles Joseph van Helmont.

Liber Fratrum Cruciferorum Leodiensium (*Archives des Maîtres de l' Orgue,* X), ed. Guilmant/Pirro, Mainz, Schott, 1910. Contents: works by A. Gabrieli, Merulo, P. Philips, Sweelinck, Scronx, Wm. Brown, Cornet, etc.

Altniederländische Meister (*Early Flemish Masters*), ed. Peeters, Mainz, Schott, 1938. Contents: 21 pieces by Sweelinck, van den Kerckhoven, de Macque, Cornet, van Helmont, Luython, & Guillet.

Les Maîtres anciens Néerlandais (*Old Netherlandish Masters*), 3 vols., Paris, Lemoine. Bk.1: Ockeghem, Obrecht, Isaac, Willaert, des Pres, de Monte, Sweelinck, Cornet, van den Kerckhoven, de Macque, Loeillet, Rayck, Baustetter, Fiocco. Bk.2: Obrecht, Dufay, Brumel, Isaac, des Pres, Willaert, Lassus, de Macque, Luython, Philips, Cornet, Scronx, Sweelinck, van Noordt, Guillet, van den Kerckhoven, Loeillet, Fiocco, Rayck, van den Gheyn. Bk. 3: Dufay, Obrecht, Isaac, des Pres, Willaert, Lassus, de Macque, Luython, Philips, Cornet, Scronx, Sweelinck, van den Kerckhoven, Loeillet, van Meert, Rayck, van den Gheyn. (Note: not all of these are original organ compositions).

Anthologia pro Organo, 4 vols., ed. Peeters, Mainz, Schott. Contents: an international selection of organ pieces from the 13th through 18th centuries, with several Netherlandish composers represented.

46 Choräle für Orgel von J.P. Sweelinck und seinen deutschen Schülern, ed. Gerdes, Mainz, Schott S., 1957. Contents: Chorale settings by Sweelinck, J. Praetorius, Schildt, etc.

Cantantibus Organis, 6 vols., Utrecht, van Rossum. Vol. I: Banchieri, Pachelbel, Havingha, Vranken, Kee, Micheelsen, Langlais, Eraly, Strategier, de Klerk, Verschraegen. II: Titelouze, Frescobaldi, Chaumont, Andriessen, Hens, Walcha, Peeters, Badings, Huybrechts, v. Koert, de Klerk, Verschraegen. III: Sweelinck, Rossi, v.d. Kerckhoven, Lübeck, Klotz, Verschraegen, Hallnäs, Peeters, de Klerk, D'Hoir. IV: Sweelinck, v.d. Kerckhoven, Lopez, Zipoli, Hens, Schroeder, De Laet, Froidebise, De Brabanter, Joris, Roelstraete, Bartelink. V: Banchieri, Anonymous, Usper, Praetorius, Absil, v.d. Hooven, Sulyok, De Brabanter, Verschraegen, D'Hoir, Dubois.

Dutch Keyboard Music of the 16th and 17th Centuries, ed. Curtis (*Monumenta Musica Neerlandica,* III), Amsterdam, Vereniging voor Nederlandse Muziekgeschiedenis, 1961. Contents: primarily pieces for the stringed keyboard instruments, with a few possibly for organ.

Hollandsche Koraalkunst, Zaandam, Bureau van Uitgave "Nederlandsche Orgelmuziek." Works by Sweelinck, Speuy, van Noordt, G.G. van Blankenburg, Bastiaans, Zwart.

Old and Contemporary Masters, Vol. III, ed. de Klerk, Amsterdam, Annie Bank. 18 pieces by contemporary Dutch composers.

Preludes- Interludes- Postludes, Vol. II, ed. Phillips, London, Hinrichsen. Works by Andriessen, Peeters, Reger.

Six Communion Pieces by Six Dutch Composers, Cincinnati, World Library of Sacred Music. Works by Smit, Monnikendam, H. Andriessen, J. Andriessen, Weegenhuise, van Koert.

18 eenvoudige Orgelwerken van hedendaagse Componisten, Vol. III, Hilversum, Gooi et Sticht. Work by E. Stam, M. Pirenne, H. Strategier, A. de Klerk, B. Kahmann, and M. Dijker.

Muziek voor Kerk en Huis, 24 books to date, Naarden, Alsbach & Co. Easy works on sacred melodies. The composers are generally not well-known.

Edition Ars Nova (Goes) also has several collections of preludes on psalm tunes. Most of the composers represented are unknown outside of the Netherlands.

NOTES

[1]Sweelinck, *Opera Omnia*, vol. I, fascicle I, p. xiii.

MUSICAL SOURCES

Ex. 1. Sweelinck: *Opera omnia*, vol. I, fasc. I, p. 2.
Ex. 2. *Archives des Maitres de l'Orgue*, X, p. 192.
Ex. 3. *Monumenta Musicae Belgicae*, II, p. 57.
Ex. 4. Andriessen: *Concerto per organo e orchestra*, pp. 1, 2. Copyright Donemus. Used by permission of C.F. Peters.
Ex. 5. Badings: *Orgelconcert*, p. 15. Copyright Donemus. Used by permission of C.F. Peters.
Ex. 6. Chaumont: *Pièces d'orgue sur les 8 Tons*, p. 1. Copyright 1970 Heugel et Cie. Used by permission of the publisher. Theodore Presser Co., sole representative U.S.A.
Ex. 7. Lemmens: *Grand Fantasia in E Minor*, pp. 1, 6.
Ex. 8. Jongen: *Toccata*, p. 1. Copyright 1937 Henry Lemoine et Cie. Used by permission of the publisher. Theodore Presser Co., sole representative U.S.A.
Ex. 9. Peeters: 30 *Chorale Preludes on Gregorian Hymns*, III. pp. 20, 25. Copyright 1954 C.F. Peters. Used by permission.

8

Scandinavia

HE musical history of Denmark and Sweden has been, for the most part, connected with, and dependent on, developments in the leading musical countries of Europe. In the 16th and 17th centuries, the Danish and Swedish countries employed many foreign musicians, including such prominent figures as John Dowland and Heinrich Schütz (both under the patronage of Christian IV of Denmark). Works most frequently performed at the courts were foreign in origin—Netherlandish, Italian, German, or English. In the late 18th and 19th centuries, the German influence became particularly strong, with Swedish and Danish musicians frequently going to Germany for their musical training. In our present day, ties with Germany and other European countries have continued, but Scandinavian musicians are no longer always content to be the followers. Sometimes they are the actual pacesetters, as will be seen in the discussion of modern Swedish organ music.

In Norway, where there was neither a court, an aristocracy, nor a wealthy middle class to subsidize the arts in earlier times, anonymous folk music was the major musical outlet until at least the mid-19th century. Then, after the rise of nationalism, musical compositions which were consciously Norwegian in character, although often under the influence of German Romanticism, began to make their appearance. The nationalist composers had generally only a slight interest in organ music, and even today, organ composition and organ building receive little attention in Norway.

In Finland, the case is still more extreme. Since there was relatively little musical creativity of note in Finland prior to the establishment of national independence in 1917, it is not surprising to learn that the earliest organ works

which the Finns claim as their own are two pieces by Jean Sibelius. After the mid-20th century, a few additional composers have begun writing sporadically for the organ.

Returning to Denmark and Sweden and to the Baroque era, one notes again the overshadowing influence of the Netherlandish-German organ culture. Several German organists were employed in Sweden, among them, Anders Düben, the Sweelinck student who became court organist in Stockholm in 1620, and Christian Ritter, who worked in Stockholm in the late 17th century. Approximately a century later, the Abbot George Joseph Vogler served as Hofkapellmeister at the Swedish court, and other names could be cited up to the present day. In Denmark, the list of German organists during the Baroque time would include: Johann Lorentz; Lorenz and Daniel Schroeder; Daniel Berlin. As for native Danish and Swedish organists of the same period, only a few names are known to us, although the Danes can claim one organist of great eminence: Diderik Buxtehude (c. 1637-1707). Buxtehude has already been discussed with the north German school, since he spent the majority of his professional years in Germany. Still, one should remember that he is believed to have been born in Denmark, in Helsingborg, and that he maintained contact with musicians in Denmark and Sweden after moving to Germany.[1]

Preserved organ works by Baroque composers in Denmark and Sweden, either foreigners or native composers, are rare. However, it is certain that there was considerable organ playing since most churches in these countries had organs. According to a report made by Abraham Hülphers in 1773, there were, at that date, nearly 500 church organs in Sweden alone.[2] The type of instrument built in Denmark and Sweden followed closely the major trends of northern Europe. In the 16th century, for example, the Brabant organ type was important in Denmark and Sweden, while in the 17th and 18th centuries, German organs, particularly the north German type, predominated. Foreign craftsmen were imported to build these instruments. Not until the late 17th century do we have record of native organ builders in Denmark and Sweden. And, then, they did not strive to create an independent style. Rather, they modelled their instruments on those of the Germans. While the most common model was the north German instrument, some Swedish builders of the 18th century also turned to Gottfried Silbermann for inspiration.

Organists in Denmark and Sweden, and in Norway as well, followed more or less the liturgical practices of Lutheran Germany. The Scandinavian countries had adopted Lutheranism in the 16th century and thus naturally looked to Germany for leadership in the development of liturgy and liturgical music. Many of the German chorale tunes were taken over by the Scandinavian churches, too.[3] Thus, although we have little direct evidence to indicate how the many magnificent Baroque instruments were used in Denmark and Sweden, we would imagine that organ practices in the north followed basically those of Protestant Germany, with *Choralvorspiele* to introduce the chorales and the possibility of alternation between organist and congregation during the singing of the chorales.

Later, in the 19th century, Romanticism affected both the instruments and the manner of playing in the Scandinavian countries in much the same way

that it did in the major countries of Europe. Organ composition was not yet a prominent activity for Scandinavians in the 19th century, but a few did begin writing for the organ. In Denmark, Johann Peter Emilius Hartmann (1805-1900) and Niels Gade (1817-1890), leading composers among the Danes, each wrote organ compositions in the German Romantic manner (sonatas, fantasies, funeral marches, etc.). Gade's compositions, in particular, are well-constructed and show an affinity for Mendelssohn, with whom he became acquainted during his (Gade's) years as assistant conductor for the *Gewandhaus* in Leipzig.

(Example 1)

Otto Malling (1848-1915), another Dane, also wrote organ music.

In Norway, Ludvig Lindemann (1812-1887), a Bach admirer, composed organ music clearly under the German influence. His style was not appreciated by his countrymen, who considered it heavy and ponderous. In Sweden, on the other hand, the influence of César Franck and the French Romantics made itself felt in the music of Emil Sjögren (1853-1918). A protracted Romanticism was continued into the 20th century by two other Swedes, Oskar Lindberg (1887-1955) and Otto Olsson (1879-1964). Lindberg's primary orientation was French, while Olsson was apparently influenced by both the German and French schools. Olsson's *Praeludium og Fuga* (d♯ minor) illustrates his craftsmanship and melodic inventiveness.

(Example 2)

Since the advent of modern organ music, Swedish composers have taken an increasing active interest in the organ. A lively joy i n experimentation has characterized their music, especially that

Ex. 1. Gade, *Tre Tonestykker, No. 3*, m. 1–7.

Ex. 2. Olsson, O., *Preludium og Fuga, No. 3* (dis-moll), m. 9–12.

of the last two decades. Contrary to the previous situation in which Scandinavian composers followed other Europeans, Swedish composers are now among the pathfinders, at least in avant-garde circles. To trace their history, one looks back to Hilding Rosenberg (1892-1962), the spiritual father of modern Swedish music, who began to write for the organ in the 1940's. A study of the Bach contrapuntal style, together with experiments in atonality, polytonality, etc., led Rosenberg to the evolution of his own linear style, which though cool and reserved, is still expressive. His *Toccata — Aria pastorale — Ciaccona* (1952), quoted here, is an excellent example of his mature writing. It is less extreme than the early revolutionary compositions[4] which gained him notoriety in the 1920's.

(Example 3)

His contemporary, Gottfrid Berg (1889-1970), also wrote organ works noted for their linear qualities. Other composers from the same, and from the next, generation likewise wrote for the organ, mainly *Gebrauchsmusik*: Gunnar Thyrestam (1900-   ); Gustav Carlman (1906-1958); Torsten Sörenson (1908-

); Valdemar Söderholm (1909-   ).

From the generation of composers born around 1920, several became students of Rosenberg. The influence of this provocative teacher stimulated a healthy surge of composition of all types. A linear style was characteristic for the Rosenberg disciples in the 1940's and '50's. Later, some of them turned to serial and aleatoric composition. Some formed the "Monday Group," which used to meet on Mondays during the 1940's to discuss the compositions and theories of Hindemith and other contemporary composers. From the "Monday Group" both Sven-Erik Bäch (1919-   ) and Göte Carlid (1920-53) have written a few pieces for organ.

A path in a different direction was taken by Torsten Nilsson (1920-   ), whose early works incorporated Gregorian chant tradition with elements adopted from the styles of Messiaen and Distler.[5] Several successful organ works resulted from this particular snythesis. More recently, Nilsson has turned to cluster writing and an aleatoric style.

(Example 4)

Another composer to whom one would like to draw attention is Stig Gustav

Ex. 3. Rosenberg, *Toccata—Aria pastorale—Ciaccona*, m. 4–6.

Ex. 4. Nilsson, T., *Nativitas Domini* from *Septem improvisationes,* pp. 2, 3.

Schönberg (1933-), who has written many works for organ. His *Lacrimae Domine* (1958), quoted here, is considered to be one of his best.

(Example 5)

Siegfried Naumann (1919-), another leading Swedish composer, has recently published an extremely modern work for organ and percussion, *Bombarda,* which has aroused considerable interest. Other composers one might mention are: Arne Mellnäs (1933-); Bo Nilsson (1937-); Roland Forsberg (1939-).

During the 1960's, the composer Bengt Hambraeus (1928-) became the major force in Swedish organ music. A musicologist as well as a composer (specialties: 16th-century lute music and Baroque organ music), Hambraeus early began a path of exploration parallel with the work of Ligeti and others on the continent. Some of his experiments may even antedate Ligeti's. *Constellations I — II — III,* composed fairly early in his career (1958-'61) was among his first attempts to realize his dream of "a fan-

tastic space-organ beyond all boundaries."[6] *Constellations I* is an organ piece; *Constellations II* is an electronic elaboration of it; *Constellations III* is a new organ work combined with the tape of No. II. One sees here sonority for its own sake, with little perceptible forward motion. It was Hambraeus' interest in expanding sonoral resources that led him to develop unconventional methods of playing the organ and unusual combinations of stops. In this author's opinion, subtlety and originality distinguish Hambraeus' music from the average products of the avant-garde school and make it worthy of wider recognition. Organists interested in acquainting themselves with his style might find it useful to begin with his *Tre Pezzi (Movimenti, Monodia, Shogaku)* which are easier to read than some of his works.

(Example 6)

Another brilliant Swedish organ composer is Jan Morthenson (1940-). Like Hambraeus, he has been an innova-

Ex. 5. Schönberg, S. G.: *Lacrimae Domini,* m. 118-121.

Ex. 6. Hambraeus, *Shogaku,* m. 59, 60.

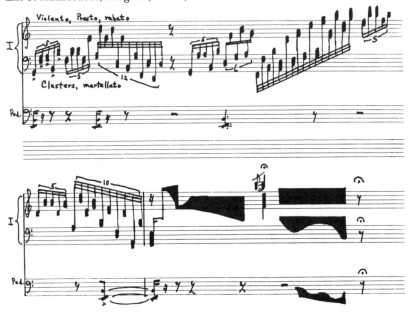

tor in search of a new language. In his compositions, *Pour Madame Bovary* and *Eternes,* for example, the performers work almost exclusively with the stop knobs, drawing them out to varying degrees, and altering the wind pressure. Certain tones are sustained on the keyboard, through the use of wedges or weights, but almost no other use is made of the keyboard, as such. The performers play on the stop knobs, rather than on the keyboard. (Obviously, such techniques work only on a mechanical instrument.)

(Example 7)

In his latest works, Morthenson has added theatrics to musical composition.

Ex. 7. Morthenson, *Pour Madame Bovary,* the beginning.

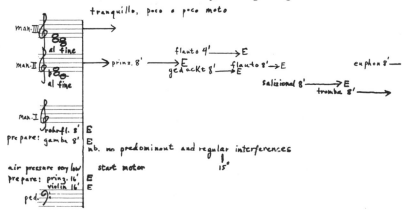

While one can find quite a number of performers and composers engaged in similar techniques throughout the western world, not all of them impress one with their intelligence as Morthenson does.

The chief spokesman in Sweden for this type of organ music is Karl-Erik Welin, who has been a prominent concert organist since the early 1960's. His interpretations of radical organ music, especially that which may be described as "instrumental theatre," have been extremely influential, both in Sweden and on the continent.

One stresses in this survey the most radical compositions and composers because these are the ones which are most significant in Sweden. Organ music of this type probably carries proportionately more weight in Sweden than in almost any other country. In connection with this, one should remember that Swedish churches no longer play much of a role in the spiritual life of the people, but rather concentrate on being a cultural force. Organ concerts are encouraged in the churches, which are viewed primarily as concert halls. Major organ composers generally write little music for use in the church service, but focus on concert works devoid of religious significance.

Returning now to Denmark and surveying the scene earlier in the century, one notes that the famous symphonist, Carl Nielsen (1865-1931), became interested in the organ during his last years. In addition to short organ works, he composed one large organ composition entitled *Commotio*, written in the year of his death. Linear, yet symphonic in scope, *Commotio*, like many other Nielsen works, is based on a synthesis of contrapuntal techniques of the post-war era with the extended harmonic tradition of the post-Romantic style. In a letter to Emelius Bangert, Nielsen stated that he intended, in *Commotio*, to stick to strict form and firm counterpoint with repression of "all personal feelings."[7]

(Example 8)

Other transitional figures, bridging the Romantic and modern eras, would include Knut Jeppesen (1892-   ) and Rued (Rud) Langgaard (1893-1952). Jeppesen's *Intonazione boreale*, said to be influenced by Nielsen's *Commotio*, shows the composer's interest in historical forms and techniques, such as triple fugue and passacaglia. The style is not, however, strictly neo-baroque. It still relies somewhat on a Romantic harmonic structure.

(Example 9)

Ex. 8. Nielsen, *Commotio*, m. 352-355.

Ex. 9. Jeppesen, *Intonazione boreale*, m. 184-187.

Niels Otto Raasted (1888-1966), a disciple of Max Reger, continued the post-Romantic tradition far into the 20th century. He was a very active organ composer, writing many *Choralbearbeitungen* and sonatas in the Reger manner. Some of his later works also employ slightly modern elements.

(Example 10)

There has been no actual modern school of organ playing and organ composition in Denmark, such as one finds in Sweden. However, the following composers have written for the organ: Flemming Weis (1898-   ); Leif Kayser (1919-   ); Leif Thybo (1922-   ); Bernhard Lewkovitch (1927-   ). Lewkovitch's 65 *Orgelkoraler*, short chorale preludes for the church service, are tastefully written, yet easy to play.

(Example 11)

Other good and representative examples of 20th-century Danish service music may be found in the 47 *Orgelkoraler af nutidige Dansk Komponister*, edited by Johnsson.

Among the musical explorers, the radicals, in Denmark, Per Nørgaard (1932-   ) and Bent Lorentzen (1935-   ) have shown some interest in organ music. Lorentzen's music is graphically notated, while Nørgaard's, although more traditionally notated, has a complex organization, is rather cerebral and not easily approachable.

In the area of organ building, the Danes have achieved high distinction, with their instruments being much in demand in other countries. While their main orientation has been toward Germany, it would be unfair to think of Danish organ builders as mere followers. The firm of Marcussen & Søn, for example, was one of the first to wholeheartedly embrace the ideals of the *Orgelbewegung* earlier in this century. Danish builders have remained in the front ranks ever since.

In Norway, which was, until recently, rather isolated from the main currents of Europe, the most common approach to organ composition has been strongly conservative. Even the violent musical upheaval which shook most European countries in the 1920's caused scarcely a ripple in Norway. Only one composer, Fartein Valen (1887-1952), took up nontonal writing prior to the 1950's. Combined with a veneration for Bach's music, Valen was led through his interest in atonal principles to develop an austere polyphonic style. Having no real followers in Norway, he has remained an isolated figure in that country.

Other Norwegian composers, such as Arild Sandvold (1895-   ), remained tied to the Romantic tradition, although Sandvold did sometimes combine Ro-

Ex. 10. Raasted, *Orgelsonate No. 3*, mov't 1, m. 1-4.

Ex. 11. Lewkovitch, *Op alle some pa jorden bor*, m. 1-5.

mantic harmonies with neo-Baroque techniques. Conrad Baden (1908-) and Knut Nystedt (1915-), two other traditionalists, have written several pieces for church use.

In recent years, Egil Hovland (1924-) has attracted attention for works of an avant-garde nature, such as his *Elementa pro Organo*.

In Finland, organ music is essentially a mid- and latter-20th century phenomenon. The first published collection of Finnish organ music did not appear until 1955. There are no composers working extensively in organ composition, but a few individual compositions may be singled out for their quality. One thinks particularly of the *Exsultate* (1954) of Erik Bergman (1911-) and the *Magnificat* (1969) of Juoko Linjama (1934-). The latter work was conceived after the composer had withdrawn from serial writing and was engaged in "the rediscovery of the triad . . ."[8] The *Ricercata* (1971) of Erkki Salmenhaara (1941-) and the serial composition, *ta tou theou* (1967) of Einojuhani Rautavaara (1928-) should also be mentioned. Earlier in the century, Jean Sibelius (1865-1957) wrote two pieces of funeral music for the organ. In general, one can describe Finnish organ composition as being definitely conservative. The collection, *Organum Fennicum*, edited by Raitio, provides a cross-section of organ composition in Finland.

EDITIONS

Note: The following abbreviations are used throughout. NMS= Nordiska Musikförlaget (Stockholm). W.H.= Wilhelm Hansen (Copenhagen). NMO= Norsk Musikforlag (Oslo). Works followed by the abbreviation, ms STIM, are manuscripts available in photocopy from the Swedish Music Information Center (Stockholm).

Westerlund publications have been taken over by Fazer (Helsinki). Publications by the Svenska Kyrkans Diakonistyrelse Bokförlag are now available through Verbum (Stockholm).

Bäck: *O altitudo I* (Organ Music for Trinity Sunday) (1967), NMS. ". . . for Eliza"* (1971), with ad. lib. tape, NMS, 1972.

Baden: Publications by Edition Lyche (Drammen/Oslo), except where noted otherwise. 12 *Orgelkoraler. Toccata, Chorale and Fugue on "Korset vil jeg aldri svike."* 4 *Koralforspill.* 5 *Orgelkoraler. Toccata, Choral, and Fugue on "Lux Illuxit." Fantasi og fuge over "Ljoset yver landet dagna,"* NMO. *Partita: Den Herre Krist i dødens bänd*, ms available through Ed. Lyche. *Ricercare: Eg veit i himmerik ei borg*, ms available through Ed. Lyche. *Partita over Folketonem "Jeg ser deg, o Guds Lam, a sta,"* Oslo, Norsk Musikforlag, 1974.

Bentzon: *Variationer*, op. 103, W.H., 1965.

Berg: 5 *Koralpartitor: Befall i Herrens händer* (1930); *I denna ljuva sommartid* (1941); *Lov vare dig, o Jesu Krist* ( ); *O gode ande, led du mig* (1943); *Vi tacka dig, o Jesu god* (1939), NMS. Sold individually. *Canzona* (1949), Stockholm, Eriks Förlag. *Preludio e fughetta*, Stockholm, Eriks Förlag. 8 *Koralförspel* (1939-1953), NMS.

Bergman: *Exsultate*, op. 43 (1954), Helsinki, Westerlund, 1954/Fazer, 1967.

Buxtehude: See chapter on German organ music.

Carlid: *Orgelstycke* (1951), Stockholm, Edition Suecia, 1964.

Carlmann: *Fantasia Gotica* (1940), NMS. *Fantasia Ostinata* (1947/49), NMS, 1951.

Forsberg: *Liten svit* (1959), Stockholm, Svenska Kyrkans Diakonistyrelse Bokförlag (Verbum). *Musica solenne* (1960), Stockholm, Verbum. *Passacaglia* (1960), Mantorp, Noteria AB, 1966. *Variationer över "Ecce novum gaudium"* (1966), Stockholm, Verbum, 1971. *Partita: Ingen hinner fram* (1967), Klockrike, Noteria AB. *Koralmotiv*, Stockholm, Verbum. Photocopies of additional works in ms are obtainable from STIM.

Gade: *Orgelkompositioner*, ed. Lindholm, W.H., 1969. *Fantasi over "Love den herre"* (Praise to the Lord), with obbligato trpt. and trbn. parts, W.H.

Hambraeus: *Liturgia pro organo (Introitus, Litania, Choral, Alleluia, Amen)*, op. 3 (1951-52), Stockholm, Svenska Kyrkans Diakonistyrelse Bokförlag (Verbum). *Koralförspel*, op. 4 (1947-49), ms STIM. *Toccata pro tempore pente-costes,* op. 12/2 (1948), ms STIM. *Introitus et Triptychon,* op. 19, ms STIM. *Musik för Orgel,* op. 24 (1950), NMS. *Permutations and Hymn,* op. 36 (1953), ms STIM. *Constellations I-II-II* (1948/ '59/'61), NMS, 1974. *Interferenser* (1961/ 62), Stockholm, Edition Suecia, 1972. *Tre Pezzi* (1966/67), Minneapolis, Augsburg, 1973. Contents: *Movimenti; Monodia; Shogaku. Nebulosa* (1969), ms STIM. ORG. & INSTRUMENTS OR VOICE: *Psalmus CXXIII* (Latin, Swedish, English), soprano and organ, Stockholm, Eriks Förlag. *Concerto för orgel och cembalo* (1947-51), NMS.

Hartmann, J.P.E.: *Samlige Orgelvaerker,* ed. with a preface and critical comments by J. E. Hansen, Copenhagen, Samfundet, 1968.

Hedwall: *Chaconne* (1951/57), NMS, 1960. *Partita: Den blomstertid nu kommer* (1955), NMS, 1956. *Partita: Christe qui lux es* (1955), NMS. *Partita: Att bedja är ej endast att begära* (1956), NMS, 1960. *Svit* (1959), Stockholm, Verbum. *In Memoriam* (1961), NMS, 1969. Photocopies of several unpub. mss (chorale settings, etc.) are obtainable from STIM.

Hovland: *Elementa pro Organo* (5 pieces), op. 52 (1965), NMO, 1968. *Partita: Lord God, Thy Glorious Name and Honour,* op. 56 (1967), NMO 1967. *5 Koralforspill,* NMO. *100 Salmeforspill,* Drammen/Oslo, Ed. Lyche. *Orgelkoraler,* bks. 1-3, Drammen/Oslo, Ed. Lyche. *Orgelkoraler,* bks. 4 & 5, NMO, 1970/'73.

Janacek, Bedrich: *Liten Partita och Ricercare över "Vart flyr jag för Gud och hans eviga lag,"* NMS. *2 Orgelkoraler,* Mantorp, Noteria AB. *3 Passionskoraler,* NMS. *Two Chorale Preludes,* London, Oxford University Press.

Jeppesen: *Preludium och Fuga* (e), NMS. *50 Koralforspil,* W.H., 1957. *Intonazione Boreale,* W.H., 1958. *Passacaglia* (1956), W.H., 1965.

Kayser: *3 Improvvisazioni,* op. 7 (1942), W.H., 1943. *Parafrase,* op. 10, Copenhagen, Skandinavisk Musikforlag, 1947. *Variations on "In Dulci Jubilo,"* op. 14, W.H., 1948. ORG. & VOICE: *3 salmi*

per contralto e organo (1956), Copenhagen, Samfundet, 1956.

Langgaard: *Toccata,* W.H. *Fantasia patetico,* W.H.

Lewkovitch: *65 Orgelkoraler* (1972), W.H., 1973. ORGAN AND VOICES: *A Danish Church Mass,* for organ and choir, W.H.

Lindberg: *Marcia funèbre,* NMS, 1928. *Sonata* (g), op. 3 (1924), NMS, 1973. *Gammal fäbodpsalm,* NMS, 1941. Also arr. for organ and violin or 'cello. *4 Orgelkoraler,* NMS, 1944. *Orgelkoral: Den signade dag,* NMS, 1949. *Variationer över en gammal dalakoral,* NMS, 1949. *Bröllopsmusik,* NMS. *Partita: När stormens lurar skalla,* NMS, 1954. *3 Orgelkoraler,* Stockholm, Carl Gehrmans Musikförlag. *Introitus solemnis,* NMS, 1957. *Old Hymn from Dalecarlia,* NMS. *Musik till Jobs bok,* ms STIM.

Lindemann: *36 fugerte praeludier,* 4 bks., NMO. *34 salmemelodier av Kingos Gradual 1699,* NMO. *Musik till "Den nye Høimesse-Liturgi,"* NMO. *Kroningsmarsch* (1873), NMO. *54 Praeludier for orgel,* bk. 2, NMO.

Linjama: *Magnificat,* op. 13 (1969), Helsinki, Fazer, 1973.

Lorentzen: *Intersection.* (1970), W.H., 1971. *Puncta* (1973), WH..

Malling: *Aus dem Leben Christi,* op. 63, 2 bks., W.H. *Christus* (3 Pieces from op. 63), W.H. *Kirkearets festdage,* op. 66, 2 bks., W.H. *Requiem for orgel,* op. 75, bk. 1, W.H. *Easter Morning,* New York, H.W. Gray. *Der Tod Christi,* W.H. *Kristi fødsel,* W.H.

Mellnäs: *Fixations* (1967) New York, C.F. Peters. Also ms STIM. *Disparitions* (1971), NMS, 1973.

Møller: *60 Forspil til Salmemelodier,* op. 27, Copenhagen, Skandinavisk Musikforlag, 1946. *Orgel-Te Deum,* op. 56 (1949), Copenhagen, Samfundet, 1949. *Orgel-Fantasi no. 6,* op. 53, W.H., 1955.

Morthenson: *New Organ Music* (1961-1973), NMS, 1974. Contents: *Some of these . . .* (1961); *Pour Madame Bovary* (1962); *Encores* (1962); *Eternes*

(1964); *Decadenva I* 1968); *Farewell* (1970/1973). The individual works were previously published separately.

Naumann: *Strutture,* op. 9 (1963), ms STIM. ORG. & INSTRUMENTS: *Bombarda* for organ and percussion instruments, NMS, 1974.

Nielsen, Carl: 29 *Short Preludes,* op. 51, W.H., 1930. *Commotio,* op. 58 (1931), Copenhagen, Samfundet, 1932/²1971. *Fest Praeludium ved arhundredskiftet,* W.H., 1963. 2 *Posthumous Preludes,* W.H.

Nilsson, Bo: *Stenogramm* (1959), NMS.

Nilsson, Torsten: *Partita: Av djupets nöd* (1950), NMS, 1960. *Communiomusik* (1960), NMS, 1973. *Introduktion och passacaglia* (1963), ms STIM. *Kyrie-Variationen und Fuge über zwei Zwölftonmelodien* (1964), ms STIM. 7 *Improvisationes* (1964-67), Stockholm, Edition Suecia, 1970/71. Contents: *Magnificat; Nativitas Domini; Epifania; Crucifigatur; Resurrexit; Ascensio; Linguae tamquam ignes.* Sold separately. *Ski 'zein II* (1969), ms STIM.

Nørgaard: *Partita Concertante,* op. 23 (1958), W.H., 1969. *Canon* (1970-72), W.H., 1974.

Nystedt: *Variasjoner over den norske folktone: Med jesus vil eg fara,* op. 4 (1940), NMO. *Introduzione e Passacaglia,* op. 7 (1945), Oslo, Edition Musikk-Huset. *Toccata,* op. 9 (1941), Drammen/Oslo, Ed. Lyche. *Deus Sancta Trinitas,* op. 28 (1951), Drammen/Oslo, Ed. Lyche. *Fantasia trionfale,* op. 37 (1955), Drammen/Oslo, Ed. Lyche. *Partita: Hos Gud er idel glede,* op. 44, Drammen/Oslo, Ed. Lyche. *Pièta,* op. 50, Drammen/Oslo, Ed. Lyche. *Resurrexit,* op. 68, NMO, 1974. *Christ the Lord Is Risen,* Minneapolis, Augsburg. *Partita: In Heaven Is Joy,* New York, C.F. Peters. *Bryllupsmarsj,* Drammen/Oslo, Ed. Lyche. *The Happy Christmas Comes Once More,* Minneapolis, Augsburg. *Tu es Petrus,* op. 69, Oslo, Norsk Musikforlag, 1975.

Olsson, Otto: *Miniatyrer,* op. 5, Stockholm, Körlingsförlag. *Meditation* (e), op. 16b, Stockholm, Elkan & Schildknecht. *Suite* (G), op. 20, London, Augener. *Fantasi och fuge över "Vilove dig, o store Gud,"* op. 29 (1909), Stockholm, Körlingsförlag. *Gregorianska melodier* (6 pieces), op. 30 (1910), Stockholm, Carl

Gehrmans Musikforlag. 12 *Orgelstycken över koralmotiv,* op. 36 stockholm, Körlingsförlag. *Sonata in E,* op. 38, London, Augener. *Preludium och fuga* (c♯), op. 39, W.H. 10 *Variations on the Dorian plainsong "Ave Maris Stella,"* op. 42, London, Augener. Also ms STIM. 5 *Trios,* op. 44, London, Augener. 6 *Pieces on Old Church Songs,* op. 47, London, Augener. *Credo symphoniacum,* op. 50 (1918), Stockholm, Elkan & Schildknecht. *Preludium och fuga* (f♯), op. 52 (1919-1920), W. H. *Preludium och fuga* (d♯), op. 56, W.H., 1940. *Adagio* (D-flat), Stockholm, Elkan & Schildknecht. *Berceuse, Sestetto och Fantasia chromatica,* London, Augener. *Lätta koralpreludier,* Stockholm, Körlingsförlag. *Praeludium,* W.H. *Suite för orgelharmonium: Preludium-Sarabande-Trio-Adagio-Marsch. Stockholm, M. Th.* Dahlström.

Parviainen: *Partita koraalista: Halleluja nyt soikohon,* Helsinki, Fazer. *Toccata et fuga* (1958), Helsinki, Fazer, 1968. 10 *pientä urkurkoraalia* (10 short organ chorales), Helsinki, Fazer.

Raasted: 12 *Orgelkoraler,* op. 8, bks. 1 & 2, W.H. *Orgelfantasi over "Krist stod op af Døde,"* op. 10, W.H. *Sonate,* op. 16, W.H. *Partita: Af dybsens nød,* op. 20, W.H. *Orgelsonate No. 3,* op. 33 (1922), Leipzig (now Munich), F.E.C. Leuckart, 1922/23. 24 *Organ Chorales,* 2 vols., op. 46, Leipzig (now Wiesbaden), Breitkopf & Härtel. 18 *kleine Präludien,* op. 48, W.H. 18 *Orgelkoraler,* op. 58, W.H. *Orgelmesse,* op. 82, W.H. *Requiem,* op. 100, W.H., 1957. 40 *Orgelkoraler,* op. 108, W.H.

Rautavaara: *Ta Tou Theou,* op. 30 (1967), Helsinki, Fazer, 1968. *Toccata per Organo,* op. 59 (1971), Helsinki, Fazer, 1975.

Rosenberg: *Fantasia e Fuga* (1941), NMS, 1954. *Praeludio e Fuga* (1948), NMS, 1954. *Toccata- Aria pastorale- Ciaccona* (1952), NMS, 1974. *Koralvariationer: Lover Gud i himmelshöjd* (1965), Stockholm, Eriks Förlag.

Salmenhaara: *Toccata per organo,* Helsinki, Fazer. *Ricercata* (1971), copyright by the composer, 1971.

Salonen: *Two Partitas* (1942), Leipzig (now Wiesbaden), Breitkopf & Härtel.

Variationer och fuga över en finsk koral:
Liksom vandraren i längtan, op. 7, (1943)
Stockholm, Carl Gehrmans Musikforlag.
Passacaglia (f) (1944), Stockholm, Carl
Gehrmans Musikforlag. *Toccata,* op. 24,
Helsinki, Westerlund (F azer). 10 *Chorale Preludes* (1959), Helsinki, Westerlund (Fazer). 61 *Organ Chorales* (1965),
Helsinki, Fazer. *Partita from a Finnish
chorale: Lapuan taisteluvirsi,* op. 34
(1963), Helsinki, Fazer, 1963. *Missa de
tempore,* op. 42 (1970), Helsinki, Fazer,
1971.

Sandvold: *Orgelsonate* (f), op. 9, NMO.
*Variasjoner over norsk folketone, "Eg
veit i himmerik ei borg"* (1960), NMO,
1960. *Variasjoner over norsk folketone,
"Herre, jeg hjertelig önsker a fremme
din aere,"* (1960), NMO. 25 *Pre og Post-
ludier over koralmotiv* (1960), NMO,
1960. *Preludium og Dobbeltfuge* (a),
NMO, 1966. 2 *Orgelstykker: Fuga in g,
Adagio in a,* NMO, 1966. *Introduksjon
og passacaglia,* NMO. 6 *Improvisasjoner
over folketoner fra "Den nye koralbo-
ken,"* NMO. 2 *Orgelstykker over tema
av Jos. Haydn: Fantasi, Toccata,* NMO.
ORGAN METHOD: *Orgelskole,* 2 vols.,
NMO.

Schönberg, Stig Gustav: *Partita: Att
bedja Gud han Själv oss bjöd* (1952),
ms STIM. *Toccata concertante I* (1954),
NMS, 1957. *Duo per organo* (1957),
Stockholm, Svenska Kyrkans Diakonistyrelse Bokförlag (Verbum). *Trio per
organo* (1957), Stockholm, Svenska Kyrkans Diakonistyrelse Bokförlag (Verbum). *Interludium* (1957), ms STIM.
Preludium (1957), ms STIM. *Solo*
(1957), ms STIM. *Lacrimae domini*
(1958), NMS, 1973. *Festmusik för orgel*
(1958), Stockholm, Svenska Kyrkans Diakonistyrelse Bokförlag (Verbum). *Liten
kammarmusik för orgel* (1962), Stockholm, Svenska Kyrkans Diakonistyrelse
Bokförlag (V e r b u m). *Variationer*
(1962), ms STIM. *Toccata, variation och
fuga över ett tema av Buxtehude* (1964),
ms STIM. 10 *sma preludier för orgel*
(1965), Stockholm, Svenska Kyrkans Diakonistyrelse Bokförlag (Verbum). *Preludium och fuga* (1966), ms STIM. *Variationer över en värmländsk folkvisa*
(1966), ms STIM. *Koralfantasi: Var Gud
är oss en väldig borg* (1968), ms STIM.
Toccata concertante II (1968), ms STIM.
Adagio, Stockholm, Eriks Förlag. ORG.
& INSTRUMENTS: *Bereden vag för
Herran,* chorale prelude for 2 trpts, horn,
trbn, & organ, Stockholm, Eriks Förlag.
Also arr. for other slightly different en-

sembles. *Konsert,* for organ and string
orchestra (1962), ms STIM.

Sibelius: *Intrada,* op. 111a, Helsinki,
Fazer. *Surusoitto* (Funeral Music), op.
111b, Helsinki, Fazer.

Sjögren: *Preludium och fuga* (g), op.
4, Stockholm, Huss & Beer. *Legender,*
op. 46, 2 bks., NMS. *Preludium och fuga*
(a), W.H. *Preludium och fuga* (c), op.
posth., NMS.

Söderholm: *Improvisationer över "O du
saliga,"* NMS, 1947. *Praeambel och fug-
etta* (1948), NMS, 1954. *Two Sonatinas*
(1949/1955), NMS, 1973. *Partita: Dig
vare lov och pris, o Krist* (1958), NMS,
1959. *Sonatin Nr. 3* (1960), Stockholm,
Svenska Kyrkans Diakonistyrelse Bokförlag (Verbum). *Sänd ditt kjus och din
sanning* (1960), Stockholm, Svenska Kyrkans Diakonistyrelse Bokförlag (Verbum). *Toccata, Interludium och Fuga*
(1961), Stockholm, Eriks Förlag. *Ave
Crux* (1968), Stockholm, Eriks Förlag.
Toccata (a), Stockholm, Carl Gehrmanns
Musikforlag. *Toccata* (C), NMS, 1973.
4 *Legender för orgel,* Stockholm, Svenska Kyrkans Diakonistyrelse Bokförlag
(Verbum). ORG. & INSTRUMENTS:
Orgelkonsert (B-flat), NMS. *Vaken up!
En stämma bjuder,* for congregation,
trumpet and organ, Stockholm, Eriks
Förlag. Plus many works (sonatinas,
etc.) available in photocopy from STIM.

Sommerfeldt: ORG. & INSTRUMENTS:
Elegy, op. 27, for trumpet and organ
(1971), NMO, 1973.

Sörenson, T.: *Breviarium Musicum* (24
pieces for small organ) (1954), Stockholm, Carl Gehrmans Musikforlag. *Toccata* (1958), Stockholm, Edition Suecia.
Mässatser för orgel (Kyrie, Sanctus, Agnus Dei) (1961-63), Stockholm, Svenska
Kyrkans Diakonistyrelse Bokforlag (Verbum. *Adorazione per organo* (1963),
Stockholm, Eriks Förlag. *Sub communione* (6 pieces) (1966), Stockholm, Verbum. *Dig vare lov och pris, o Krist,*
Stockholm, Eriks Förlag. Plus various
mss available in photocopy from STIM.

Thybo: *Preludio, Pastorale & Fugato,*
op. 11 (1948), W.H., 1950. *Concerto per
organo* (alone) (1953-54), Copenhagen,
Samfundet, 1956.

Thyrestam: *Partita: Dig skall min själ*

sitt offer bära, NMS, 1952. *Psalmus vespertinus,* NMS, 1954. *Tripartita* (1954), ms available from Eriks Förlag (Stockholm). *Toccata och Fuga,* NMS, 1973.

Valen: *Prelude and Fugue,* op. 33, Drammen/Oslo, Ed. Lyche. *Pastorale,* op. 34, Drammen/Oslo, Ed. Lyche.

Viderø: 3 *Koralpartiter,* Copenhagen, Engstrom-Sødring. *Organ Chorales and Psalm Preludes,* 2 bks., Copenhagen, Engstrom-Sødring. 10 *Chorale Preludes and* 10 *Organ Chorales,* Copenhagen, Engstrom-Sødring. *Koralpreludier och orgelkoraler* (for the Swedish chorale book), NMS. *Passacaglia* (1946), W.H., 1946. ORGAN METHOD: *Orgelskole,* W.H., 1963.

Weis: *Concertino for orgel* (1957), Copenhagen, Samfundet. 1961. *Für die Orgel* (1969), Copenhagen, Samfundet.

Collections

Album nordischer Komponisten, 2 vols., ed. P. Gerhardt/M. Reger, W.H., 1921. Contents: Vol. I — Works by Krygell, Cappelen, Sjögren, Svendsen, P. Rasmussen, Hartmann, Lindemann, Matthison-Hansen, Malling. Vol. II — Works by Matthison-Hansen, Amberg, Buxtehude, Grieg, Gade, Malling, C. Nielsen, Neruda, Krygell, Sinding.

Annorlunda Koralförspel, ed. Henrik Jansson, Stockholm, Verbum Forlag. Chorale preludes by: Hallnäs, Hedwall, Helldén, Johanson, T. Nilsson, S.G. Schönberg, Thyrestam.

Koralförspel, 2 vols., ed. R. Andersson/ R. Norrman, NMS. Contents: Vol. I — Works by Berg, Carlman, T. Olsson, Rosenberg, Rosenquist, T. Sörenson. Vol. II — Works by R. Andersson, Berg, Edlund, Franzén, Lindroth, Norrman, T. Olsson, Rosenberg, Rosenquist, Runbäck, T. Sörenson, Thyrestam.

Musica Organi, Vol. III, ed. Henry Weman, NMS. Vol. III contains works by Scandinavian composers grouped according to country: Danish composers — Andersen, Emborg, Jeppesen, Möller, Raasted, Rung-Keller; Finnish composers — Bergman, Haapalainen, Salonen, Stenius; Norwegian composers — Baden, Nielsen, Nystedt, Sandvold; Swedish composers — Berg, Fryklöf, Johansson,

Lindberg, D. Olson, O. Olsson, Rosenberg, Runbäck, Söderholm, Sörensen, Thyrestam, Wikander.

Organum fennicum, ed. J. Raitio, Helsinki, Fazer, 1973. Contains works by: Stenius, Sibelius, Kuusisto, Raitio, Parviainen, Johansson, Mononen, Haapalainen.

47 *Orgelkoraler af nutidiger danske komponister,* ed. Bengt Johnsson, W.H., 1957. Contains works by: E. Andersen, K. Høgenhaven, J. Maegaard, T. Nielsen, P. Nørgaard, I. Nørholm, P. Olson, E. Sark, L. Thybo.

Orgelmusik vid Högmässans Avslutning (Organ Music for the Conclusion of High Mass or Morning Service), ed. Runbäck, NMS. Compositions by: Berg, Hägg, D. Olson, Runbäck, Söderholm.

Orgelmusik vid Jordfästning (Organ Music for Funeral Services), ed. Runbäck, NMS. Compositions by: Andersson, Berg, Cederwall, Lundborg, D. Olson, T. Olsson, Runbäck, Sjögren, Söderholm, Wikander, Aehlén.

Orgelmusik vid vigsel (Wedding Music), ed. Runbäck, NMS. Compositions by: Berg, Bjärbäck, D. Olson, Runbäck, Söderholm.

Postludio, Helsinki, Fazer. Organ music for the liturgical year, including: 38 chorale preludes by old masters; 26 chorale preludes by Sulo Salonen.

Pro Organo, 5 vols., ed. Karlsen/Nielsen, Drammen/Oslo, Edition Lyche. 298 chorale settings, most of them by the Norwegian composers, Rolf Karlsen and Ludwig Nielsen; some by older composers.

NOTES

[1] Horton, *Scandinavian Music: A Short History,* 63.
[2] Hülphers, A., *Historisk Afhandling om Musik och Instrumenter . . . jemte Kort beskrifning öfwer Orgwerken i Sverige* (1773), as cited in Horton, op. cit., 111.
[3] Horton, *op. cit.,* 33.
[4] Chamber music, etc., not organ music.
[5] Cnattingius, *Contemporary Swedish Music,* 66.
[6] *Ibid,* 5.
[7] Yoell, *The Nordic Sound,* 159.
[8] From the pamphlet, *Juoko Linjama,* printed by the Finnish Music Information Centre (Helsinki).

MUSICAL SOURCES

Ex. 1. Gade: *Orgelkompositioner*, p. 11.
Ex. 2. Olsson, O.: *Praeludium og Fuga i dis-moll*, p. 3.
Ex. 3. Rosenberg: *Toccata — Aria pastorale — Ciaccona*, p. 1.
Ex. 4. Nilsson, T.: *Nativitas Domini*, pp. 2, 3.
Ex. 5. Schönberg, S.G.: *Lacrimae Domini*, p. 9.

Ex. 6. Hambraeus; *Tre pezzi*, p. 17. Copyright 1973 Augsburg Publishing House.
Ex. 7. Morthenson, *New Organ Music*, p .15.
Ex. 8. Nielsen: *Commotio*, p. 21. Copyright 1971 Samfundet. Used by permission of C.F. Peters.
Ex. 9. Jeppesen: *Intonazione boreale*, p. 14.
Ex. 10. Raasted: *Orgelsonate No. 3*, p. 2.
Ex. 11. Lewkovitch: *65 Orgelkoraler*, p. 66.

9

Switzerland

HE presence of organs and organ playing in Switzerland can be established from the Middle Ages, especially in monasteries such as those at St. Gall, Einsiedeln, and Engelberg.[1] One of the oldest European organs still in partially playable condition is located in Switzerland, in the town of Sion. This organ dates from the early 15th century and was rebuilt in 1718. Foreign organ builders often worked in Switzerland, and occasionally Swiss organ builders were given contracts for instruments in neighboring territories, as far away as Mainz and Milan.[2]

The 15th and early 16th centuries (the pre-Reformation era) constituted a period of cultural expansion for the Swiss. Several German organists were employed in Switzerland, including one of the leading south German "colorists," Hans Kotter (c.1480/84-1541). Swiss musicians, on the other hand, often took employment abroad. The illustrious Ludwig Senfl (c.1486-1542/43), who became one of the most famous musicians in all of the German-speaking territory, was a Swiss by birth. Among Swiss organists who remained in their homeland, the most prominent was Fridolin Sicher (1490-1546), student of Hans Buchner and organist at St. Gall. He wrote a keyboard tablature in the early decades of the 16th century. With respect to both contents and style, this tablature resembles Souh German tablatures of the period and indicates that Sicher was acquainted with keyboard practices beyond the Swiss borders. From the vocal models used for the intabulations in this tablature, one judges that he was well acquainted with polyphonic works of the great European masters. Thus, musical life in Switzerland, particularly in the German-speaking part, was by no means isolated from the main cultural trends of Europe. Rather, it reflected major developments elsewhere.

The cultural growth and expansion which characterized the 15th century, and the beginning of the 16th, was abruptly broken off and reversed by the Protestant Reformation. The Reformers, in an attempt to purge the church of anything which might remind them of Rome, forbade all music except unison singing and the simplest 4-part music, note against note. Gone were the contrapuntal motets, the organ improvisation, and all of the rich and varied forms of musical expression which had previously been used in the service of the church. Many organs were destroyed or removed. Fortunately, in Basel, organ music was again tolerated from the year 1560. But, apparently the organist was restricted to playing preludes, postludes, and interludes; he did not provide organ accompaniment to the congregational singing.[3] In many other towns, no organ playing of any kind was permitted until the end of the 17 century. In Geneva, in the principal church of St. Pierre, the organ was still silent as late as 1756. When the organ did find its way back into Swiss Protestant services, it was at first prohibited from accompanying the congregational singing and was restricted to less important parts of the service. In Zürich, the exceptionally strict church leaders could not bring themselves to accept organ accompaniment until the 19th century, and around 1900 one could still find several congregations which sang unaccompanied in 4-parts.[4]

In an atmosphere where congregational participation was encouraged above all else and where artistic elaboration was viewed with suspicion, it is not surprising to find a dearth of interesting musical personalities. Samuel Mareschal (1554-1640), a native of Belgium and resident of Basel, constitutes a minor exception. He composed a sizeable, although unimaginative, volume of psalm and chorale settings. Instrumental compositions based on the Huguenot psalms were rare at that time, so Mareschal's settings are not typical expressions of the Calvinist spirit.

In the centuries that followed, musical creativity continued to be sparse. In the 19th century, foreign musicians, particularly Germans, tried to stimulate interest in the musical arts in Switzerland, and by the end of that century a few native musicians were able to carry on this pioneering labor.[5] Of Swiss musicians active at the turn of the century, the interesting one for the study of organ music is Otto Barblan (1860-1943). Having studied and taught in Germany, Barblan returned to Switzerland to become leader of a movement to revive interest in the music of J. S. Bach. Among his own compositions, noteworthy are the *Passacaglia,* op.6, in which he quotes the countersubject of Bach's *Passacaglia and Fugue,* and the *Chaconne über BACH,* op.10.

(Example 1)

His use of historical forms is an indication of his basic orientation.

As the 20th century progressed, it became apparent that the newly-awakened musical consciousness of the Swiss was developing with unusual vigor. Interest in organs and organ music gained momentum, and some of the foremost Swiss composers became involved in organ composition. Moreover, the previous German domination of Swiss musical life was now tempered by an acquaintance with, and admiration for, French music. Swiss music of the 20th century has dipped into both the German and French musical experiences, in degrees which vary from one composer to the next. There has been no concerted movement to develop a distinctive Swiss style. Nationalism of any kind is almost impossible to trace in Switzerland.[6]

Henry Gagnebin (1886-1960) is an example of a Swiss who belongs by family descent and by training to both the German and French cultures. Having studied in both Berlin and Paris, he returned to Switzerland where he was for many years director of the Geneva conservatory. Four volumes of organ settings based on the Huguenot psalter are his major contribution to organ music. The Lutheran *Choralbearbeitungen* of Bach were his model.

Frank Martin (1890-1974), probably Switzerland's most outstanding composer, was likewise not a member of a single national school, but took impulses from both the German (12-tone) and the French traditions, and especially from J. S. Bach. "The Bach *Passions* signify for me the strongest musical impression of my life," he said.[7] He composed a *Sonata da chiesa* for viola d'amour and organ (1938), a *Passacaille* for organ alone (1944-54), and, more recently, a 3-movement work for orchestra and organ entitled *Erasmi Monumentum* (1969). In the *Passacaille* he used a traditional form and tradition-based counterpoint (canon, etc.), but infused them with new elements: a chromatic ostinato theme which has a 12-tone implication; the occasional use of harmonies recalling the flavor of Ravel or Stravinsky; the use of dodecaphonic devices such as scattering the theme in multiple voices (m.65ff.).

(Example 2)

Arthur Honegger (1892-1955), whom the Swiss claim as one of their greatest composers, belongs more properly to the French school and has already been dis-

Ex. 1. Barblan, *Passacaglia,* p. 9, m. 2-4.

Ex. 2. Martin, *Passacaglia*, m. 1-14.

cussed in a previous chapter. Other
notable contemporaries of Martin who
wrote for the organ are Willy Burkhard
(1900-1955) and Conrad Beck (b.1901),
both from the German-speaking part of
Switzerland. Their contrapuntal style
is more severe than Martin's and stands
largely under the shadow of the German neo-Baroque movement. Their
works have sometimes been described
as being "like the wood-cut with its often harsh accentuation and intentional
aridity."[8]

(Example 3)

Other organ composers of that generation include: Rudolf Moser (b.1892);

Walter Geiser (b.1897); Albert Moeschinger (b.1897); Paul Müller-Zürich
(b.1898). As was true with the works
of their contemporaries in France and
Germany, the Romantic idiom predominated in some of their compositions,
while in others the transition had been
made to the objectivity of the post-war
era.

Bernard Reichel (b.1901), friend and
colleague of Frank Martin, contributed
several organ works, of which the *Concerto* for organ and strings is notable.
Like Martin, he retained the construc-
tive principle of Schönberg's aesthetic
but allowed himself the liberty to com-

Ex. 3. Burkhard, *Choral-Triptychon*, mov't 2, m. 37-41.

bine this with other techniques. Adolph Brunner (b.1901), active in the renewal of Protestant church music in Switzerland, contributed a set of variations under the title *Pfingstbuch* (Pentecost Book). Additional service music has been written by: Hans Studer (b.1911); Albert Jenny (b.1912); Oswald Jaeggi (b.1913); Heinz Wehrle (b.1921); Ernst Pfiffner (b.1922). In some works an alignment with German organ music is most apparent. In other compositions, different influences may be present, as in Wehrle's *Vision "Le Rideau divin,"* where the Messiaen imprint is unmistakeable.

(Example 4)

Klaus Huber (b.1924), one of the few Swiss composers to write for organ in the serial manner, has contributed works which have been praised for their fine construction and sense of color. His *Cantus cancricans,* of which a part is quoted here, is a crab canon.

(Example 5)

Jacques Wildberger (b.1922), known for dodecaphonic works, has written five pieces for organ. Rudolf Kelterborn (b.1931), a Swiss by birth, but employed in Germany, and Hans Ulrich Lehmann (b.1937) have each contributed within the aleatoric genre.

The organs of Switzerland, like the

Ex. 4. Wehrle, *Vision 'Le rideau divin,'* m. 1-4.

Ex. 5. Huber, *Cantus Cancricans,* m. 1-3, 26-28.

composers, reflect the major trends of neighboring countries, especially Germany and France. The principal chorus most frequently corresponds to a German principal chorus, while reeds are often French in design and voicing. Also French-inspired is the practice of mounting the *Cornet* immediately behind the organ facade. Careful workmanship, for which the Swiss are famous, has brought Swiss organ building to a position of world prominence.

EDITIONS

Barblan: *Andante mit Variationen*, op.1, Leipzig, Rieter - Biedermann. *Gebet*, Zürich, Hug & Co. 6 *Hymnen*, Zürich, Hug & Co. *Hymne solennel*, Zürich, Hug & Co. *Deuil*, Zürich, Hug & Co. *Quand même*, Zürich, Hug & Co. *Cinq pièces*, op. 5, Frankfurt, C. F. Peters, 1946. *Passacaglia*, op. 6, Frankfurt, C. F. Peters, 1946. *Chaconne über BACH*, op. 10, Munich, Leuckart. 4 *Stücke*, op. 21, Frankfurt, C. F. Peters, 1946. *Drei Stücke für Orgel*, op. 22, Augsburg, A. Böhm & Sohn. *Toccata*, op. 23, Zürich, Hug & Co. *Variationen und Tripelfuge über BACH*, op. 24, Zürich, Hug & Co. 4 *Pièces*, op. 26, Geneva, Edition Henn.

Beck: *Sonatine* (1927); Mainz, Schott. 2 *Praeludien für Orgel* (1932), Mainz, Schott. *Choralsonate* (1938), Mainz, Schott. ORG. & INSTRUMENTS: *Improvisation über ein lothringisches Verkündigungslied*, for cello and organ (1945), Mainz, Schott.

Bovet: *Pièces d'orgue* (psalms, chorales, free works), Zürich, Edition Eulenburg, 1972. TWO ORGANS: *Petite Suite de concert sur des Psaumes Huguenots*, op. 14, published by the composer. ORG. & INSTRUMENTS: *Sonata da chiesa*, op. 15, for oboe d'amore and organ, published by the composer.

Brunner: *Pfingstbuch für Orgel* (Variations: Nun bitten wir), Kassel, Bärenreiter. *Kleine Partita: Nun freut euch, lieben Christen g'mein*, Stuttgart, Hänssler.

Burkhard: Publications by Bärenreiter (Kassel), unless otherwise indicated. *Praeludium und Fuge*, op. 16a, 1932. *Variationen: Aus tiefer Not*, op. 28, no. 1, (1930), Mainz, Schott. *Variationen: In dulci jubilo*, op. 28, no. 2 (1930), Mainz, Schott. *Fantasie*, op. 32 (1931), Mainz, Schott. *Partita: Grosser Gott, wir loben Dich* (1932). *Partita: Wer nur den lieben Gott lässt walten* (1932). *Orgelstücke aus der "Musikalischen Uebung*, op. 39. *Sonatine*, op. 52 (1938). *Fantasie und Choral: Ein feste Burg*, op. 58 (1939). *Choral Triptychon: Ich steh an deiner Krippe hier; O Mensch, bewein; Christ lag in Todesbanden*, op. 91, 1953. ORG. & INSTRUMENTS: *Konzert*, for org., strings and brass, op. 74 (1945). *Dankeshymne* for organ and orchestra, op. 75 (1945). *Canzone*, for 2 flutes and piano, or organ, op. 76a.

Gagnebin: *Carillon*, Paris, Leduc. *Pastorale*, Paris, Leduc. *Pièces d'orgue sur des Psaumes Huguenots*, 4 vols., Geneva, Edition Henn, 1947-51. *Toccata*, Vienna, Doblinger; *Prière*, Geneva, Edition Henn. *Six pièces d'orgue*, Paris, Les Editions Ouvrières. ORG. & INSTRUMENTS: *Sonata da chiesa per la Pasqua* (for Easter), for trpt. and organ (*Orgue et Liturgie*, Bk. 9), Paris, Schola Cantorum. *Sonata da chiesa per la Natale* (for Christmas), for oboe and organ, published by the author.

Geiser: *Fantasie I*, op. 17a, Kassel, Bärenreiter. *Christ lag in Todesbanden*, op. 17b, published by the composer. *Sonatine*, op. 26 (1939), Kassel, Bärenreiter. *Fantasie II*, op. 28, Kassel, Bärenreiter. ORG. & INSTRUMENTS: *Konzertstücke* for organ and chamber orchestra, op. 30, Kassel, Bärenreiter.

Huber, Klaus: *In Memoriam Willy Burkhard* (1955), Kassel, Bärenreiter. *In te Domine speravi* (1964), Kassel, Bärenreiter. *Invention: In Dich hab' ich gehoffet, Herr*, Mainz, Schott. *Cantus Cancricans* (1965), Kassel, Bärenreiter.

Jaeggi: *Invocation: Kyrie, orbis factor* (1950), Heidelberg, W. Müller Verlag, 1957. *Orgelsuite Nr. 1 über gregorianische Themen*, Heidelberg, W. Müller, 1960. *Kleine Orgelsuite Nr. 2 über gregorianische Themen*, Freiburg, Christophorus Verlag. *Kleine Orgelsuite Nr. 3*, Freiburg, Christophorus Verlag.

Jenny: *Präludium* Zürich, Eulenburg. *Vorspiel*, Zürich, Eulenburg. *Zwischenspiel*, Zürich, Eulenburg. *Orgelheft V: Pfingstkreis*, Lucerne, Edition Cron. 2 *Choralvorspiele: Tollite portas; Dies sanctificatus*, Lucerne, Edition Cron.

Kelterborn: See the chapter on German Literature.

Lehmann: *Noten für Orgel* (1964-66), Mainz, Ars Viva Verlag, 1967. ORG. & INSTRUMENTS: *Sonata da chiesa*, violin & org. (1971), Cologne, Gerig Verlag.

Mareschal: *Selected Keyboard Works*, ed. J.-M. Bonhote (*Corpus of Early Keyboard Music, XXVII*), Dallas, American Institute of Musicology, 1967.

Martin: *Passacaille* (1944-54), Vienna, Universal Edition, 1956. ORG. & INSTRUMENTS: *Sonata da chiesa* for viola d'amour and organ or for flute and organ (1938), Vienna, Universal Edition. *Erasmi Monumentum* (3 movt's) for full orchestra and organ (1969), Vienna. Universal Enition.

Moeschinger: *Introduktion und Doppelfuge*, op.17 (1929), Mainz, Schott. Several works in manuscript.

Moser: *Dorische Rhapsodie*. op. 18, no. 2 (1921), Paris, Leduc. *Choralvorspiele*, op. 26 (1924-27), Leipzig, Breitkopf u. Härtel. *Passacaglia*, op. 30, no. 1, Gertrud-Moser-Verlag. *Fantasie und Fuge* (G), op. 30, no. 2, Gertrud-Moser-Verlag. *Suite: Der Tag, der ist so Freudenreich*, op. 54, no. 1 (1932), Zürich, Hug & Co. *Suite: Veni sancte spiritus*, op. 54, no. 2 (1937), Zürich, Hug & Co.

Müller-Zürich: *Toccata I* (C), op. 12 (1925), Mainz, Schott. *Praeludium und Fuge* (e), op. 22a (1934), Mainz, Schott. *Canzone* (e), (1936), published by the composer. *Toccata II* (D), op. 38 (1943), New York, H. W. Gray. *Toccata III* (a), op. 50 (1952), Mainz, Schott. *Choralfantasie: Ach Gott vom Himmel sieh darein*, op. 56 (1955), Kassel, Bärenreiter. *Passacaglia*, op. 65, Zürich, Hug & Co. *Canzone*, Zürich, Eulenburg. *Fantasia*, Zürich, Eulenburg. ORG. & INSTRUMENTS: *Konzert* for organ & str. orch., op. 25 (1935), Mainz, Schott. *Fantasie und Fuge*, for violin & org., op. 45 (1949), Zürich, Hug & Co. *Choraltoccata: Fin' feste Burg*, op. 54, no. 1, for 2 trpts, 2 trbns, & org. (1953), Kassel, Bärenreiter. *Choralfantasie: Wie schön leuchtet der Morgenstern*, op. 52, no. 2, for 2 trpts, 2 trbns, & organ (1953), Kassel, Bärenreiter.

Pfiffner: *Toccata* (1957), Vienna, Doblinger. *Meditationen: O Lamm Gottes unschuldig*, Berlin, Merseburger. 2

Stücke für Orgel: *Fantasie*; *Toccata II*, Zürich, Eulenburg. *Choralesonate I*, Lucerne, Edition Cron. *Choralsonate: Mitten wir im Leben sind*, op. 64/65, published by the composer. *Choralsonate II: In Memoriam Papae Joannis XXIII*, published by the composer. *Fantasie*, published by the composer. *Praeludium*, Zürich, Eulenburg. *Et Exaltavit Humiles*, Lucerne, Edition Cron.

Reichel: *Toccata pour Noël*, published by the composer. *3 Variations*, published by the composer. *Aria et 2 variations*, Geneva Edition Henn. *Prelude*, Zürich, Eulenburg. *11 Chorales* (1942), Kassel, Bärenreiter. *Quatre Pièces pour l'avant*, published by the composer. ORG. & INSTRUMENTS: *Concerto*, organ & str. orch., op. 51 (1946-50), Geneva, Edition Henn. *Concertino*, for piano and organ, Kassel, Bärenreiter. *Invocation*, for trpt. and organ, published by the composer.

Studer: *Freie Orgelstücke*, Zürich, Eulenburg. *Choralfantasie: Ach Gott im Himmel, sieh darein*, published by the composer. *Toccata, Aria und Fuge*, published by the composer. *3 Orgelchoräle*, published by the composer. ORG. & INSTRUMENTS: *Petite fantasie pastorale* (1952), for flute and organ, Kassel, Bärenreiter. *Konzert* for organ and orch., published by the composer.

Wehrle: *4 Orgelstücke* (*Aria variata; Chant de Paix; Fanal; Sons d'Orgue*), Zürich, Eulenburg, 1970. *Choralmusik II: O Heiland, reiss die Himmel auf* (1967), Zürich, Eulenburg, 1973. *2 Orgelstücke: Le Rideau divin; Requiem* (1954/71), Zürich, Eulenburg, 1974.

Wildberger: *5 Stücke* (1966), Cologne, Gerig Verlag.

Collections

Pièces cultuelles, Geneva, Edition Henn. A collection of pieces for the church service by J. Binet, G. Doret, H. Gagnebin, J. Lauber, B. Reichel, E. Schmidt, R. Vuataz.

Zeitgenössische Orgelmusik im Gottesdienst (Contemporary Organ Music for Liturgical Use), ed. by the Zürich Organistenverband, Zürich, Edition Eulenburg, 1970. Contains 72 short pieces by contemporary composers, most of them Swiss. Germans, French, and Belgians also represented.

NOTES

[1] Jakob, "Introduction to Swiss Organ Building," *ISO Information*, No. 7, Dec. 1971, p. 53.
[2] *Schweizer Muskibuch*, p. 54.
[3] *Ibid*, p. 69.
[4] *Ibid*, p. 70.
[5] *Der Schweizerische Tonkünstlerverein* 1900-1950, p. 250.
[6] Hartog, *European Music in the Twentieth Century*, p. 152.
[7] Billeter, *Frank Martin*, p. 33.
[8] 40 *Contemporary Swiss Composers*, p. 47.

MUSICAL SOURCES

Ex. 1. Barblan: *Passacaglia*, p. 9. Copyright 1946 C.F. Peters. Used by permission.
Ex. 2. Martin: *Passacaglia*, p. 1. Universal Edition. Used by permission of European American Music.
Ex. 3. Burkhard: *Choral-Triptychon*, p.6.
Ex. 4. Wehrle: *Vision "Le Rideau divin,"* pp. 1,6. Copyright 1974 Edition Eulenburg. Used by permission of C.F. Peters.
Ex. 5. Huber: *Cantus Cancticans*, pp.3,7.

10

Bohemia and Present-day Czechoslovakia

HE early history of organ playing in the kingdom of Bohemia (comprising Bohemia, Moravia, and sometimes a part of Silesia) was aligned with organ playing in south Germany and the area that is now Austria. Bohemia and Austria were so often under the same rule, the Habsburgs, that they participated in a mutual culture. For absolute historical accuracy, organ music of the old Bohemian masters should be placed together in one section with organ music of the Austrians and south Germans. I have chosen to list Bohemian organ music separately because later developments, especially in modern-day Czechoslovakian music, have taken paths quite independent of Austrian and German music.

During the Renaissance era, organ playing was one of the many arts cultivated by the imperial Habsburg court at Prague. Organ playing was not generally practiced elsewhere throughout the kingdom, except in Catholic churches and monasteries. After the Hussite Revolution (1419-1436), the common people of Bohemia usually ignored instrumental music, while devoting themselves fervently to singing, especially in unison. Thus, the musical practices of the Habsburg court, which was Catholic not only in religion but also in artistic taste, was completely divorced from the music of the common people. At the court, all kinds of elaborate choral and instrumental music were encouraged, including organ music. Foreign musicians from several countries were employed there, with first the Flemish and later the Italians in positions of dominance. Among those recruited for service in the emperor's *cappella* was the Flemish keyboardist, Karel Luython (c.1557/58-1620). Also under the emperor's patronage was the famous

Hans-Leo Hassler (1564-1612) who held the title, "Organist to the Emperor," an honorary designation not requiring residence in Prague. In the 16th century, Prague was truly an international music center.

In the 17th century, Prague lost some of its importance as Vienna became the permanent residence of the emperor. With the court no longer residing in Prague, the responsibility for promoting organ playing and organ building in Bohemia passed to the Catholic churches and monasteries. Particularly active were the Jesuits, who considered organ music, and indeed all art, as tools to further the cause of the Counter-Reformation. There is relatively little documented information about organ playing in Bohemia in the 17th century. Yet one assumes that Bohemian organ music passed through the same stages as Austrian organ music, since Vienna, during the 17th century, set the style for musical practice in Prague. This means that organ playing in Bohemia submitted first to aspects of the Venetian style and then, in the mid-17th century, to the influence of Frescobaldi.

Like Bohemian music, old Bohemian organs followed the same format as organs in Austria and south Germany. Organists who are familiar with the 17th-century south German instrument will have a good picture of Bohemian organs dating from the same period. Following the strong Italian influence which appeared near the end of the 16th century, mutations and reeds (especially the latter) were reduced in number. Principal stops predominated, and the prevailing quality of the instruments was mild and gentle. Most organs were fairly small, having one or two manuals with pedal. Later, during the course of the 18th century, instruments were often enlarged, following general European trends. A deficiency in reeds and mutations, however, continued to characterize organs in the Habsburg realm.

Few names of Bohemian organ composers prior to the 18th century have survived, with the exception of Arnolt Schlick, author of the famous *Spiegel der Orgelmacher und Organisten,* published in Mainz in 1511. Schlick (born c.1450-1460; died after 1520) is generally considered a member of the south German organ school, and one of its foremost leaders, but he was born in Bohemia and spent the larger portion of his life there. The kingdom of Bohemia produced numerous other fine musicians, both in that century and in successive centuries, but the best ones often took positions in foreign countries: Johann Stamitz, founder of the Mannheim school; J. Myslivecek; A. Reicha; F. X. Richter, etc. Charles Burney, the music historian, reported in *The Present State of Music in Germany, the Netherlands, and United Provinces* (1775), that the Bohemians had the reputation of being the most musical people of Germany, or perhaps, of all Europe.[1]

The first native Bohemian organist to build up a tradition of organ music in his country was Bohuslav Cernohorsky (1684-1742). Only a few of his organ works are extant. As illustrated by the opening measures of the *Toccata in C,* Cernohorsky wrote in the post-Frescobaldian, south German manner.

(Example 1)

Upon first hearing one might even mistake this work for a pedal toccata of Pachelbel. There are no folk elements such as one has come to expect from Romantic and modern Czech compositions. Rather, this is a true product of the south German school.

Cernohorsky had many students and followers, of whom one of the best was certainly Johann Zach (1699-1773). His preserved organ works consist of four preludes and two fugues. Josef Seger (Seeger) (1716-1782), the most famous Bohemian organist of the following generation, may also have been a student of Cernohorsky, although this is not certain. Seger's works (toccatas, fugues, preludes, fantasies, etc.) are in a late Baroque style and reveal excellent craftsmanship. The opening measures of his *Prelude in Eb* are quoted here.

(Example 2)

J. S. Bach was acquainted with Seger's compositions and is reputed to have held them in high esteem.[2]

A younger contemporary of Seger, Frantisek Xaver Brixi (1732-1771), is

Ex. 1. Cernohorsky, *Toccata,* m. 1-3.

Ex. 2. Seeger, *Prelude in Eb Major,* m. 1-4.

noteworthy for three concerti for organ and chamber orchestra. Brixi is one of the precursors of the Classical idiom,[3] and his concerti foreshadow organ concerti of a famous Austrian contemporary, Franz Joseph Haydn. Johann Stamitz (1717-1757) also wrote a concerto for organ and string orchestra.

Throughout most of the 19th century, organists were content to imitate the style handed down to them from Cernohorsky and Seger. Of course, the first part of the 19th century was artistically a low period for organ composition almost anywhere in Europe. But, in Bohemia, the condition was aggravated by the fact that many of the best Bohemian musicians had been leaving their homeland for better occupational opportunities elsewhere. The organists who remained in Bohemia in the 19th century were generally not that country's most gifted musicians.

With the advent of Romanticism in the mid-19th century, there arose a longing for an independent national culture. Similar to the situation in Norway, Sweden, Poland, Hungary, and other countries, the birth of a national consciousness provided an enormous incentive to artistic creativity. Organ music did not benefit from the patriotic spirit as quickly nor as directly as did orchestral, vocal, or chamber music. Yet, by the 20th century at least, organ music was beginning to reap the rewards of Bohemian nationalism.

Following the example furnished by symphonic and choral literature of the Romantic era, composers of organ music in the 20th century began taking their inspiration from the rich fount of folk melodies and rhythms which abound throughout Czechoslovakia. At first, they were not willing to relinquish the Romantic idiom, yet, later, they found it possible to combine modern composi-

tional techniques with their national heritage.

In the years following World War I and the establishment of the first Czechoslovakian Republic, Prague was a meeting place for avant-garde musicians from all over Europe. One need only think of Alois Haba's experiments with quarter- and sixth-tone composition to realize that Prague was very progressive during the 1920's and '30's. This progressive character did not yet, however, affect organ composition, which lagged behind other compositional areas. One very encouraging fact, however, was present: composers who themselves were not organists began taking an interest in organ composition, indicating that they considered the organ to be a suitable concert instrument, and not exclusively a church instrument.

One of the most spectacular compositions from the '20's and '30's was the *M'sa Glagolskaja* (Glagolitic Mass) of Leos Janácek (1854-1928). It is particularly interesting for us because of the two fiery organ solos it contains. One solo is a part of the *Credo*. The other forms the *Postludium* to the mass. This work represents the continuation of a centuries-old tradition in Austria and Bohemia, that of using both orchestra and organ to accompany a choral mass. A unique feature of this particular mass, however, is the bravura character of the sections allotted to the organ alone. They have no counterpart in other Mass literature.

(Example 3)

A chief promoter of organ music in the early 20th century was B.A. Wiedermann (1883-1951), probably more significant as a teacher than as a composer. At mid-century, Jiri Reinberger (b. 1914) became a prime force behind contemporary organ composition and his-

Ex. 3. Janacek, *Orgelsolo aus der 'Festlichen Messe,'* m. 142-147.

torical organ study. As editor of several collections — old Bohemian, Romantic, and modern Czech—he has made a large quantity of organ music available to his countrymen and to organists in other countries.

In recent decades, Czech composers have received government subsidization, and their creative efforts have been substantially encouraged. Competitions are held to select the best compositions and best performers, which then appear at the Prague Spring Festivals. The most successful organ works written in Czechoslovakia in the last two decades have generally been works prepared for these festivals. The leading contributors to organ literature have been: Karel Janecek (b. 1903), , Miloslav Kabeláč (b. 1908): Karel Reiner (b. 1910); Klement Slavicky (b. 1910); Milos Sokola (b. 1913); Otmar Macha (b. 1922); Petr Eben (b. 1929). With the exception of Eben, none of these has written extensively for the organ, but each has written at least one or two very fine works. All of them, excepting Kabeláč, have relied heavily on folk melodies and rhythms and have worked in a style which is an outgrowth of post-Romanticism. In general, Czech organ compositions are

meant for concert, not liturgical, use. They are often virtuoso pieces, often symphonic, and can best be realized on an organ which is able to accommodate Romantic literature. Examples are here provided for each of the composers mentioned.

(Examples 4-9)

The 3-volume collection, *Nuove Composizioni per Organo,* from which these examples have ben taken, provides a superb cross section of modern Czech organ music.

The outstanding organ composer among the Czechs is Petr Eben, who differs from his compatriots in that he has chosen to recall the liturgical heritage of the organ. For Eben, the organ is not solely a concert instrument. He frequently employs Gregorian chant, even in his *Concerto* for organ and orchestra, entitled *Symphonia gregoriana.* Like other Czech composers, he often uses folk idioms, and occasionally a touch of jazz is present. The rhythmic vitality typical of his work is illustrated in the following example, an excerpt from the *Moto ostinato* of his *Hedelni Hudba* (Sunday Music).

(Example 10)

Ex. 4. K. Janecek, *Toccata,* m. 1-8.

Ex. 5. Kabelac, *Ctyri Preludia,* no. 4, the beginning.

Ex. 6. Reiner, *Tri Preludia,* no. 1, m. 9-12.

Ex. 7. Slavicky, *Invokace,* m. 1-4.

Ex. 8. Sokola, *Passacaglia quasi Toccata na Tema BACH,* m. 49-50, 53-54.

Ex. 9. Macha, *Smutecni Toccata,* m. 53-54.

Ex. 10. Eben, *Moto ostinato*, m. 1-4.

Another example, this one taken from the fourth movement of the suite *Laudes*, shows a rapid interchange between chords on one manual and those on another, a favorite device with Eben. (Example 11)

EDITIONS

The official American agent for most Czechoslovakian publications is Boosey & Hawkes, Inc. (New York).

Brixi: Together with works by Zach, organ works by Brixi are in *Orgelwerke altböhmische Meister*, vol. III, ed. Quoika, Wiesbaden, Breitkopf & Härtel, 1948. ORG. & INSTRUMENTS: *Orgelkonzert* (F) for org., strings, 2 horns, & basso continuo, ed. Racek/Reinberger (*Musica Antiqua Bohemica*, Series I, vol. 26), Prague, Suprahon. Available on loan. *Zwei Konzerte*, for organ and orchestra (*Musica Antiqua Bohemica*, Series I, vol. 75), Prague, Suprahon.

Cernohorsky (Czernohorsky): *Composizioni per organo*, ed. Helfert/Michálek (*Musica Antiqua Bohemica*, Series I, 3), Prague, Supraphon. *Orgelwerke altböhmische Meister*, vol. I, ed. Quoika, Wiesbaden, Breitkopf & Härtel, 1948.

Eben: *Hedèlní Hubda* (Sunday Music) (1958), Prague, Artia-Státní nakladatelstvi, 1963. *Laudes* (1964) is part of the collection, *Nuove Composizioni per organo*, II, Prague, Panton. ORG. & INSTRUMENTS: *Symphonia gregoriana*: *Concerto per organo ed orchestra* (1954), Prague, Panton, 1961.

Janácek, Leos: *Orgelsolo aus der "Festlichen Messe,"* Vienna, Universal Edition, 1929.

Kopelent: *Halleluja per Organo* (1967), Cologne, Gerig Verlag, 1968.

Luython: Together with works by Charles Guillet and Giovanni Macque, Luython's preserved works are in *Monumenta musicae belgicae*, IV, ed. Watelet, Antwerp, De Ring, 1938.

Seeger (Seger): *Acht Toccaten und Fugen*, ed. Albrecht (*Organum*, series IV, no. 22), Lippstadt, Kistner u. Siegel, 1949. *Composizioni per organo*, 2 vols. (*Musica Antiqua Bohemica*, vols. 51, 56), Prague, Supraphon. *Orgelwerke altbömische Meister*, vol. II, ed. Quoika, Wiesbaden, Breitkopf & Härtel.

Ex. 11. Eben, *Laudes*, mov't 4, m. 153-158.

Slavicky, Klement: *Fresky* (Frescoes) (1957), Prague, Státní hudebni nakladatelstvi, 1962.

Stamitz: ORG. & INSTRUMENTS: *Konzert in c* organ and string orchestra, ed. H. Schubert, Mannheim, Mannheimer Musikverlag.

Wiedermann: *Tre composizioni* (1912/1920/1931), Prague, Artia-Státní nakladatelstvi, 1951. *Tri chorálové predehry* (3 choral overtures) (1919/1927/1928), Prague, Hudebni Matice Umelecké Besedy, 1944. *Notturno*, London, United Music Publishers, 1954.

Zach: Together with works by Brixi, Zach's complete works in *Orgelwerke altböhmische Meister*, vol. III, ed. Quoika, Wiesbaden, Breitkopf & Härtel, 1948.

Collections

A Century of Czech Music, 2 bks., ed. Paukert, Chicago, H. T. FitzSimons, 1965. Bk. 1: works by Cernohorsky, Seeger, Brixi, Kuchar and Rejcha. Bk. 2: Seeger, Cernohorsky, Zach, Brixi, Vanhal.

Classici boemici per organo, ed. Reinberger (*Musica Antiqua Bohemica*, Series I, vol. 12). Prague, Artia-Státni nakladatenství. A survey of 18th- and early 19th-century music. Composers represented: Cernohorsky; Zach; J. I. Linek; J. K. Kuchar; K. Kopriva; A. Rejcha; K. F. Pic; Seeger; Vanhal; and Brixi.

Musica Bohemica per Organo, 3 vols., ed. Reinberger, Prague, Artia-Stání nakladatelství, 1953/56/58. A survey of organ works from the Romantic period through the mid-20th century. Vol. I: Smetana; Dvorak; Musil; Janácek; Foerster; Klicka; Tregler; Novák; Wiedermann; Michálek. Vol. II: Vycpálek; Tichy; Blatny; Kvapil; Zelinka; Hába; Chlubna; Broz; Hlobil; Janácek. Vol. III: Krejcí; Kabelác; Tynsky; Slavicky; Hawlík; Sokola; Vrána; Hanus; Hurník; Eben.

Nuove Composizioni per Organo, 3 vols., Prague, Panton-Státní nakladatelství, 1958/1966/ ? . Vol. I contains: *Moto*

ostinato, P. Eben; *Invocazione*, E. Hlobil; *Toccata*, K. Janecek; *Fantasia*, M. Kabelác; *Ciaccona*, M. Sokola; *Fantasia e Toccata*. J. Zimmer. Vol. II: *Laudes*, P. Eben; *Ctyri Preludia* (Four Preludes), M. Kabelác; *Smutecni* Toccata (Mourning Toccata), O. Macha; *Tri Preludia* (3 Preludes), K. Reiner; *Invokace* (Invocation), K. Slavicky; *Passacaglia quasi Toccata na téme BACH* (Passacaglia quasi Toccata on the Theme BACH), M. Sokola. Vol. III: *Rapsodia*, J. Feld; *Musica Aspera*, M. Istvan; *Affresco Sinfonico*, V. Kalabis; *Capriccio*, I. Rezác; *Via del Silenzio*, L. Sluka.

Orgelkompositionen alter böhmischer Meister (*Musica Viva Historica*, XXI) Prague, Supraphon.

Orgelwerke altböhmische Meister, 3 vols., ed. Quoika, Wiesbaden, Breitkopf & Härtel, 1948-55. Vol. I: works of Cernohorsky: II: Seeger; III; Zach and Brixi.

Slovenska organova tvorka (Slovakian Organ Music), 2 vols., Bratislava, Slovensky Fond. Works by Slovakian composers of the first half of the 20th century. Composers included: Moyzes; Bella; Babusek; Albrecht; Ocenás; Zimmer; Kardos.

NOTES

[1]Scholes, ed., *Dr. Burney's Musical Tours in Europe*, II, p.131.
[2]*Musik in Geschichte und Gegenwart*, XII, p. 462.
[3]Helfert, *Geschichte der Musik in der Tschechoslovakischen Republik*, trans. Steinhard, p.20.

MUSICAL SOURCES

Ex. 1. *A Century of Czech Music*, II, p. 5.
Ex. 2. *A Century of Czech Music*, II, p. 3.
Ex. 3. Janacek: *Orgelsolo aus der "Festlichen Messe,"* p. 7. Universal Edition. Used by permission of European American Music.
Ex. 4. *Nuove Composizioni per Organo*, I, p. 28.
Ex. 5. *Nuove Composizioni per Organo*, II: *Ctyri Preludia*, p. 5.
Ex. 6. *Ibid*, II: *Tri Preludia*, p. 2.
Ex. 7. *Ibid*, II: *Invokace*, p. 3.
Ex. 8. *Ibid*, II: *Passacaglia quasi Toccata na Tema BACH*, p. 7.
Ex. 9. *Ibid*, II: *Smutecni Toccata*, p. 9.
Ex. 10. Eben: *Nedelni Hudba*, p. 23.
Ex. 11. *Nuove Composizioni per Organo*, II: *Laudes*, p. 37.
Ex. 1 and 2 are used by permission of the copyright owners, H. T. FitzSimons Co., Inc.

11

Hungary

N Hungary during the Renaissance era, the courts, churches and monasteries cultivated organ music along with the other arts. Some noted European musicians resided in Hungary. Adrian Willaert, for one, spent seven years in Buda. We know, too, of the presence of organs in that country from at least the 15th century.[1]

In the 16th and 17th centuries, when organ music was making great strides in other countries, political chaos in Hungary made cultural development impossible. First, there were wars with the Turks, then the Turkish occupation. Then the country was partitioned (1606) and later there were wars with the Habsburgs who wanted to recover part of their empire.

By the 18th century, organ building and playing were again able to make limited progress, although organ music never occupied more than a peripheral role in Hungarian cultural life. One Hungarian organist seems to have attained some recognition outside his own country — Johann Francisci (1691-1758). He travelled in Austria and Germany, made the acquaintance of Mattheson and earned the reputation of being an excellent organist.[2] Since the kingdom of Hungary was part of the Habsburg empire at this time, it, like Bohemia, participated in the imperial culture which had its center at Vienna. Thus, Hungarian music (art music, not folk music) followed basically the practices of the leading Austrian masters. Some Hungarian noble families became active patrons of music. Chief among them was the Esterházy family, who counted in its employ, F. J. Haydn, Ignatz Pleyel and J. N. Hummel. At least one of Haydn's organ concerti, if not more,

was written while he was living in Hungary at the Esterházy residence.

In the 19th century, the taste for music spread to the middle classes. Several institutions and schools were founded for the study of music. The latter part of the century also saw the rise of nationalism in Hungary, with corresponding attempts to escape the hegemony of Austrian and German music. Nationalism provided direction to Hungarian musical creativity in general, but did little, or nothing, for organ music.

Franz (Ferencz) Liszt (1811-1866) became a symbol of the new national self-respect, a hero to subsequent generations of Hungarians. His organ music, however, contains no specifically Hungarian elements and is, rather the embodiment of the German Romantic spirit. Liszt did not write for the organ while living in Hungary. One supposes that his interest in organ music was awakened by experiences in Germany and France where he became aware of the organ's potential for Romantic expression. His organ compositions had an immediate impact on the organ situation in Germany, but not until later did they provoke a small interest in organ music within his own country.

In the 20th century, the chief creative personalities in the Hungarian musical world have been, of course, Béla Bartók (1881-1945) and Zoltán Kodály (1882-1967). Bartók did not compose for the organ, but his spirit overshadows composers who did try their hand at organ composition. Kodály, the other father of 20th-century Hungarian music, wrote a few organ works, including a simple organ mass in 8 movements, *Organoedia*. The direct compositional antecedent of his well-known *Missa brevis, Organoedia* is restrained, predominantly contrapuntal music, with no touch of the folk elements that one associates with Kodály.

(Example 1)

In recent years, several other composers have increased the number of Hungarian organ compositions on the market, but no one appears as a personality on the international scene. The secular element is particularly marked in some of their works, as in the *Bagatelles* of Rudolf Maros (b. 1917). Here the integration of folk and art styles, which was a trademark of Bartok's writing, is in evidence.

(Example 2)

In contrast, certain other composers have preferred forms and styles traditionally associated with the organ. Examples are the *Introduzione, passacaglia e fuga* of Erzsébet Szónyi and the *Praeludium et fuga* of Zoltán Gárdonyi.

(Example 3)

Gyorgy Ligeti (b. 1923), who spearheaded the avant-garde movement as it entered the organ scene in the 1960's, has not been included in this survey since he has not been associated with

Ex. 1. Kodály, "Introitus" from *Organoedia*, m. 29-35.

Ex. 2. Maros, *Bagatelles*, no. 1: *Preludio*, m. 1-5.

Ex. 3. Szönyi, *Introduzione, Passacaglia e fuga*, m. 1-4.

the land of his birth for many years. One should more properly consider him part of the German-speaking world. Judging from the selected organ pieces available in the state-published 3-volume collection of Hungarian organ music (*Magyar Orgonazene*), Ligeti's style of writing has had little impact on organ music within his native land.

EDITIONS

The official American agent for Hungarian publications is Boosey & Hawkes, Inc. (New York).

Kodaly: *Organoedia* (Organ mass), ed. M. Hall, London, Boosey & Hawkes, 1947. *Pange Lingua,* Vienna, Universal Ed. "Preludium" from the *Pange Lingua* is available separately, Vienna, Universal Ed.

Ligeti: See The chapter on Germany.

Liszt: See the chapter on Germany.

Magyar Orgonazene (Hungarian Organ Music), 3 vols., Budapest, Editio Musica, 1966/1969/1969. Vols. 1 & 2 were edited by S. Pecsi, vol. 3 by F. Gergely. Contents — Vol. I: *Introduzione, passacaglia e fuga,* E. Szönyi; *Sonata,* F. Hidas. Vol.

II: *Fantázia;* S. Jemnitz; *Négy Orgonadarab* (4 pieces: Dirge, Study, Lullaby, Toccatina), P. Kadosa; *Canephorae* (5 pieces: Maestoso, Andante, Leggierissimo, Lento, Allegro moderato), F. Farkas; *Bagatelles* (5), R. Maros. Vol. III: *Alleluja,* G. Perényi; *Preludium et Passacaglia,* Z. Gárdonyi; *Halleluja,* J. Kapi-Králik; *Two Hungarian Pastorales,* G. Lisznyai-Szabó; *Epilogue (B-A-C-H),* E. Huzella; *Partita,* I. Koloss; *Te Deum,* I. Sulyok.

Additional works by Gardónyi, Jemnitz, Sulyok, and Szönyi have been published by Editio Musica (Budapest).

NOTES

[1]Kaldy, *A History of Hungarian Music,* p. 16.
[2]*Ibid,* p. 28.

MUSICAL SOURCES

Ex. 1. Kodaly: *Organoedia,* p. 2. Copyright 1947 Boosey & Hawkes. Reprinted by permission.
Ex. 2. *Magyar Orgonazene,* II, p. 37. Copyright 1969 Editio Musica, Budapest. Reprinted by permission of Boosey & Hawkes.
Ex. 3. *Magyar Orgonazene,* I, p. 7. Copyright 1966 Editio Musica, Budapest. Reprinted by permission of Boosey & Hawkes.

12

Poland

HE first preserved sources of organ music in Poland date from the 16th century, the most important being: the *Tablature of Johannes of Lublin* (c. 1540) ; the *Cracow Tablature* (c. 1548) ; the somewhat later *Warsaw Musical Society Tablature* (c. 1580) . The first, the *Lublin Tablature,* has the distinction of being, by far, the largest 16th-century organ book in all of Europe. Opening with a treatise on setting liturgical *cantus firmi* for the organ, the *Lublin Tablature* contains intabulations of vocal works (the bulk of its contents) , dances, hymn settings, and preambles.

(Example 1)

Similar types of compositions can be found in the *Cracow Tablature.* The *Warsaw Musical Society Tablature* concentrates on liturgical forms (Mass, sequence, hymn) for *alternatim* use and does not have any independent keyboard pieces or secular compositions. With the notable exception of compositions by Mikolaj of Cracow and a few believed to be authored by Jakub Sowa,[1] most works in these early tablatures are unsigned. According to Golos, there is good reason to believe that the anonymous composers were Polish, since the melodies used for the *cantus firmi* in the organ settings seem to have been taken from Polish diocesan plainchant of the day. In addition, there are organ setting of Polish hymns, with inscriptions in the same language.[2]

Cracow, the royal residence, was the principal site of artistic life in Poland in the 16th century. Desiring to promote sacred music, King Sigismund I created in 1543 a chapel at Wawel (the Castle and Cathedral in Cracow) which was to be the Polish equivalent of the Sistine Chapel. The most famous Polish musicians were connected with the Wawel chapel. In fact, to be employed there, it was necessary to be Polish and not a foreigner.[3] The chapel repertory included Polish compositions and the great choral works of the Netherlandish, French, and Italian masters.

At the king's private chapel, which was not the same as the Wawel chapel, a large group of foreign musicians was employed, with Italians predominating. During the Renaissance, then, musicians in Poland cultivated a native tradition, while at the same time participating in an international European culture. For all its cosmopolitan character, Polish

Ex. 1. Anonymous, *Preambulum in D Minor,* m. 1–5.

Renaissance music was not a mere slavish imitation of musical practices in western Europe. Distinctively Polish features were preserved in much of the music, as can readily be seen in the Polish folk dances in the early tablatures.

As for organs and organ playing, references to the instrument date back to the 12th century. Significant is the fact that the first Polish builder known by name, Jan Wanc of Zywiec, constructed already in 1381 an organ with pedalboard.[4] The Lublin and Cracow tablatures likewise refer to the use of the pedal, an unusual feature in 16th-century tablatures. Since, at this early period, pedal playing was normally associated only with the German school, these pedal indications seem to reveal an alignment with German organ practice. Polish instruments, moreover, were constructed along the same lines as the Netherlands-North German organs, with fully-developed Great and Positive divisions and an independent pedal division intended for polyphonic playing. In addition to Polish organ builders of repute, craftsmen from the Netherlands and North Germany often built instruments in Poland.

German organists also were known to take employment in Poland. One of these was the former Sweelinck student, Paul Siefert (1586-1666), who was organist at the Warsaw court from 1616-1623. Still another witness to the presence of the German organ-playing tradition in Poland is found in a 17th-century manuscript, the *Pelplin Organ Book* (c. 1630), or more specifically in some organ pieces which were appended to this manuscript in the latter part of the 17th century. These added works include chorale settings by North German organists, Ewaldt, N. Hasse, H. Scheidemann, and F. Tunder. Not preserved in any German sources, these works would be unknown to us were it not for the *Pelplin Organ Book.*[5]

The German influence in organ playing declined, in the latter years of the 16th and in the 17th century, in favor of the Italian style. A struggle between partisans of the Italian art and of the German art, with Marco Sacchi and Paul Siefert as leaders of the two camps, was finally resolved with the acknowledged victory of the Italians.[6] Since many aspects of Polish cultural life had already gone over to the Italian style, it is no wonder that organ music should follow. Moreover, when one considers that the neighboring north and middle German

schools of organ playing were thoroughly Protestant, one can understand why Polish organists, spurred on by the Counter-Reformation, should find it necessary to reaffirm their ties with Italy.

Several Italian keyboardists were employed in Poland. The first whose name is known to us is Diomedes Cato (born c. 1570; died after 1615). Tarquinio Merula (d. after 1652), acknowledged to be one of Italy's leading musicians, also spent some years in Poland as organist to the king. During the same period, it was common practice for Polish organists to go to Italy to study. We know that at least three Poles studied with the great Girolamo Frescobaldi.[7] His influence on their writing and that of their contemporaries in Poland is unmistakeable.

As early as 1591, we find a Polish manuscript written in Italian keyboard notation, the *Gdánsk* MS 300. Of subsequent manuscripts containing music in the Italian style, notable is the *Warsaw Tablature* (c. 1680), which contains many beautiful compositions in the Frescobaldian and post-Frescobaldian manner. Johannes Podbielski and Piotr Zelechowski are two of the composers represented in this manuscript. Most of the other composers have remained anonymous. Their anonymity, however, shouldn't lead one to think that they were second-rate. Judging from their compositions, there were highly sensitive craftsmen among the anonymous composers of Poland.

(Example 2)

The domination of Polish organ music by the Italian style, observable from the latter years of the 16th century, naturally affected the instruments as well. In southern Poland, in particular, reed stops were often eliminated and the pedal was confined to playing the bass line. Organs in this part of the country often bore a close resemblance to instruments of the Austro-Hungarian empire, where the Italian influence had blended with the south German style. In fact, Austrian and Bohemian organ builders were often invited to build instruments for the monastic orders in southern Poland.

In the 18th century, Polish organ music appears to have continued along the lines established in the 17th century.

Ex. 2. Anonymous, *Toccata tertio toni*, m. 1-3, 6.

Unfortunately, only scant information and few works have survived from this period. At the very moment when Baroque music elsewhere was coming into its fullest bloom, in Poland it was already subsiding due to unfavorable political and economic conditions. The frequent victim of invasions and wars for control of her territory and her throne, Poland in the 18th century did not have the stability to nurture the musical arts. Almost no music was printed during this time, and the few examples of organ music which have survived indicate that this art, like others, was in a state of decline.

In the latter part of the 19th century, some organists took up the problem of raising the standards in organ music and thereby prepared the way for a rebirth of interest in the organ and its music. The most prominent recitalist and composer of organ music in Poland in the late 19th and early 20th centuries was Mieczyslaw Sursynski (1860-1924), who received his training in Berlin, Leipzig, and Regensburg. Sursynski was one of several Polish organists who rooted their compositional style in the German Romantic tradition. Still other Poles looked to Paris for inspiration. Feliks Nowowiejski (1877-1946), for example, wrote nine organ symphonies, clearly indicating a French alignment. There seems to have been no attempt to develop a distinctively Polish Romantic school of organ music. Rather, composers followed the major trends of Germany and France.

Although the Romantic style of organ composition persisted in Poland beyond the point where it was common in France and Germany, recent generations of Polish composers have contributed works in modern idioms. While some of these composers have a national rather than an international significance, their compositions are nonetheless interesting. Golos, in his article, "Modern Organ Music in Poland,"[8] singles out: *Sonata* and *Passacaglia* by Boleslaw Szabelski (b. 1896) ; *Sonata* by Augustyn Bloch (b. 1929) ; four *Concerti* for organ and orchestra by Tadeusz Machl (b. 1922) , *Etude No. 5* by the same composer; *Sonata in F-sharp Minor* and *Duet* for piano and organ by Tadeusz Paciorkiewiecz (b. 1916) ; *Organ Sonata, Variations, Toccata*, three *Trios, Prelude* and *Meditation* by Kasimierz Jurdzinski (1894-1960) ; and *Praeludium in B-flat Minor* by B. Wallek-Walewski. These works, he says, are outstanding. For listing of additional compositions and composers, the reader is referred to the above-mentioned article.

(Example 3)

In recent years, organ festivals, such as those held yearly at Oliwa and Kamién Pomorski, have supported the

Ex. 3. Machl, "Entree" from *Mini-suita*, m. 1-6.

art of organ playing and organ composition through competitions and recitals. The prize-winning compositions of the 1968 Organ Competition in Kamién Pomorski have been published in an anthology entitled *Polska wspolczesna miniature organowa* (*Contemporary Polish Organ Miniatures*). Representing a variety of modern styles (both in graphic and standard notation), they provide a glimpse of the wide range of expression utilized by contemporary Polish composers. Two examples from the collection follow.

(Examples 4, 5)
Contemporary Polish organ composi-

tion embraces both the most up-to-date techniques as well as some of the more traditional ones. This is not surprising since, for a number of years, progressive trends in music have received ample recognition in Poland.

In addition to organ music composed for competitions and public performances, service music for the church is being written, as well. Stanislaw Kisza's conservative settings of familiar chorale melodies are examples of service music which succeeds in being artistic, while remaining simple.

(Example 6)

Ex. 4. Gorecki, *Kantata*, m. 148-150.

Ex. 5. Hawel, *Studium*, m. 65-67.

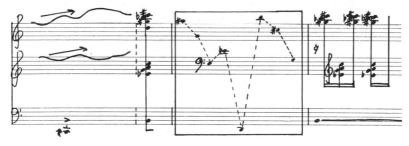

Ex. 6. Kisza, *Interludia*, no. 15, m. 1-5.

EDITIONS

N o te : P.W.M. = Polskie Wydawnictwo Musyczne (Polish Music Publishing House). Edw. B. Marks Corp. is the official American agent for Polski Wydawnictwo Musyczne, with Belwin Mills being the current distributor for E. B. Marks.

Anonymous: *Anonim (Miniatury organowe,* no. 21), Cracow, P.W.M. Contains a paraphrase of Psalm 43 by a 17th century anonymous composer.

Bloch, A.: *Sonata organowa* (1954), Cracow, P.W.M., 1965.

Jablonski, H.: *Tryptyk na organy,* Cracow, P.W.M., 1966.

Jurdzinski, K.: *Sonata* (1972), Cracow, P.W.M., 1965. *2 tria* (1943), Cracow, P.W.M., 1946. *Trio nr 3* (1945), Cracow, 1946. *Passacaglia i Elegia,* C r a c o w, P.W.M,. 1971.

Kisza, S.: *Interludia organowe,* Cracow, P.W.M., 1967.

Kozlowski, A.: *Male preludia organowe,* Cracow, P.W.M., 1964.

Machl, T.: *Etiuda nr 5 (Miniatury organowe,* no. 3), Cracow, P.W.M. *Kompozycja w pieciu czesciach,* Cracow, P.W.M., 1967. *Mini-suita,* W a r s a w, Agencja autorska, 1974.

Nowowiesjski, F.: *Pièces pour orgue,* Paris, Procure générale de Musique, 1922. *Fantazja polska (Miniatury organowe,* no. 20), Cracow, P.W.M.

Paciorkiewiecz, T.: *Sonata na organy* (1946), Cracow, P.W.M., 1966.

Pietrzak, B.: *4 kontrasty na organy,* Cracow, P.W.M., 1964.

Podbielski, J.: *Preludium (Wydawnictwo Dawnej Muzyki Polskiej* series, no. 18), Cracow, P.W.M. *Passacaglia* (d) *Elegia (Miniatury organowe,* no. 44), Cracow, P.W.M.

Rohaczewski, A.: *Canzona (Wydawnictwo Dawnej Muzyki Polskiej* series, no. 43), Cracow, P.W.M.

Serocki, K.: *Fantasia elegiaca* for organ and orchestra, Cracow, P.W.M., 1972.

Surzynski, M.: *Utwory na Organy* (Selected Organ Works), ed. Rutkowski, Cracow, P.W.M., 1954. *Trio na organy,* op. 20 no. 10; *Tria,* op. 21, Cracow, P.W.M., 1954. *Improwizacje na temat "Swiety Boze,"* Cracow, P.W.M., 1958.

Szabelski, B.: *Sonata* (1943), Cracow, P.W.M., 1966. *Largo* (from the sonata) *(Miniatury organowe,* no. 31), Cracow, P.W.M.

Wallek-Walewski, B.: *Preludium (Bb) (Miniatury organowe,* no. 30), Cracow, P.W.M., 1962.

Zelechowski, P.: *Fantasia (Wydawnictwo Dawnej Muzyki Polskiej* series), Cracow, P.W.M., in preparation.

Collections

Among anthologies of old Polish music, the most readily available are the scholarly editions, found in most university libraries. The most common ones are listed here. There are also a few practical editions (anthologies) of old Polish organ music.

Anonim Utwory z Warszawskiej Tabulatury Organowej z XVII w (Organowe Miniatury, no. 39), ed. C. Sikorski, Cracow, P.W.M., 1969. Contents: works by anonymous composers from the Warsaw Tablature of the 17th c.

Dawna polska muzyka organowa (Old Polish Organ Music), ed. J. Grubich, Cracow, P.W.M., 1968. Contents: works by 16th and 17th century composers— Mikolaj of Cracow, M. Leopolita, D. Cato, J. Sowa, A. Rohaczewski, P. Zelechowski, J. Podbielski and several anonymous.

Johannes of Lublins Tablature of Keyboard Music, 6 vols., ed. J. R. White (*Corpus of Early Keyboard Music,* VI/ 1-6), Dallas, American Institute of Musicology, 1964-67.

Keyboard Music from Polish Manuscripts, 4 vols., ed. J. Golos/A. Sutkowski (*Corpus of Early Keyboard Music,* X/ 1-4), Dallas, American Institute of Musicology, 1965-67. Vol. I: organ chorales by N. Hasse & Ewaldt. II: organ chorales by H. Scheidemann & F. Tunder. III: fantasias from Gdansk Ms. 300. IV: organ music by D. Cato, J. Podbielski, M.

Wartecki, P. Zelechowski and anonymous composers.

Music of the Polish Renaissance, ed. Z. Lissa/J. Chominski, Cracow, P.W.M., 1955. Contains several organ pieces from the Lublin Tablature, as well as instrumental, choral, lute and harpsichord music.

Muzyka w dawnym Krakowie (Music in Old Cracow), ed. Z. Szweykowski, Cracow, P.W.M., 1964. Selected works from the 15th through 18th centuries (keyboard and lute pieces, choral works, instrumental pices.)

Tabulatura organowa cysterow z Pelpline, facsimile and transcription, 10 vols., ed. S u t k o w s k i/Osostowicz-Sutkowska (*Antiquitates Musicae in Polonia*, I-X), Warsaw/Graz, Akademische Druck- und Verlagsantalt, 1967.

Tabulatura Warszawskiego towarzystwa musycznego, ed Golos (*Antiquitates Musicae in Polonia*, XV), Warsaw/Graz. Akademische Druck- und Verlagsanstalt, 1967. Transcription of the Warsaw Musical Society Tablature.

Z polskiej muzyki organowej XVIw (Polish Organ Music, 16th Century), ed. J. Golos, Cracow, P.W.M., 1966. Contents: selected works from the Lublin Tablature, the Cracow Tablature of c. 1548, and the Warsaw Musical Society Tablature. Editor's commentary in both Polish and English.

As for anthologies of Romantic organ compositions, most are out of print. Representative works by the following Romantic composers, W. Rychling, A. Sokulski, A. Freyer, S. Moniusko, and W. Zelenski, are available in P.W.M. publications (*Miniatury organowe*, nos. 37, 38, 41, 42). See also Surzynski and Nowowiesjski entries above.

For 20th-century compositions, note the following collections.

Polska wspolczesna miniatura organowa: '68 *Kamien Pomorski* (Contemporary Polish Organ Miniature: '68 Kamien Pomorski), Cracow, P.W.M., 1975. Contents: *Kantata*, H. M. Gorecki; *Al fresco*, B. Petrzak; *In memoriam*, W. Gniot; *Spotkania*, M. Dziewulska; *Studium*, J. W. Hawel; *Passacaglia*, A. Glinkowski.

Polska wspolczesna miniatura organowa, 1939-68 (Contemporary Polish Organ Miniatures, 1939-68), Cracow, P.W.M., in preparation. Contents: *Toccata*, 3 *Tria*, K. Jurdzinski; *Tryptyk*, H. Jablonski; *Czesc II z Sonatyx*, A. Bloch; *Aria i Finale z Tryptyku*, M. Sawa.

Zbior preludiow na organy (Anthology of Organ Preludes), ed. F. Raczkowski, Warsaw, 1960. Contents: 64 *preludia na tematy piesni*, J. Furmanik; 9 *preludiow*, T. Jarzecki; *Fantazja f-minor na organy solo* (1919), K. Gorski; *Wariacje na organy*, *Toccata i fuga*, J. Janca; *Parafraza i preludium na organy lub fisharmonie* (1940) and *Preludium*, K. Jurdzinski; *Preludium na temat Asperges me i Alleluja, Jezus zyje*, and *Fuga*, H. Makowski; *Preludia na Kyrie, Sanctus, Benedictus, Agnus Dei*. H. Nowacki; *Offertoire*, op. 7, no. 2, and *Preludium na temat "Juz slonce wschodzi ogniste*, F. Nowowiejski; *Preludia*, M. Sawa; *Trio*, op. 48, *Entrata, In memoriam, Fughetta, Wariacje na temat "Jesu Chryste*," op. 50, M. Surzynski; *Tria organowe, Interludia*, E. Walkiewicz; 5 *preludiow na tematy piesni koscielnych*, S. Wroclawski; and other works.

NOTES

[1]Golos ed., *Z polskiej muzyki organowej XVIw*, editor's note, p. 53.
[2]*Ibid*, 53.
[3]Opienski, *La Musique polonaise*, 39.
[4]Golos, "An Historical Survey of Organbuilding in Poland until 1900," THE DIAPASON, Apr., 1976, p .1.
[5]See *Corpus of Early Keyboard Music*, X, vols. 1, 2.
[6]Opienski, *op. cit.*, 61.
[7]Golos, "Old Polish Organ Music," *Polish Music*, III, no. 2, 1968, 4.
[8]Golos, "Modern Organ Music in Poland," *Polish Music*, III, no. 3, 1968, 17.

MUSICAL SOURCES

Ex. 1. *Music of the Polish Renaissance*, p. 63.
Ex. 2. *Anonim utwory z "warszawskiej tabulatury organowej z XVII w,"* p. 16.
Ex. 3. Machl: *Mini-suita*, p. 3.
Ex. 4. *Polska wspolczesna miniatura organowa*, p. 14.
Ex. 5. *Ibid*, p. 58.
Ex. 6. Kisza: *Interludia organowe*, p. 18.

* * * * * * *

The author wishes to thank Dr. Jerzy Golos who supplied materials for the discussion of Polish organ music.

13

The United States

HE history of organs and organ playing in the British colonies in America can be traced from the 18th century. Religious motivation was high during the early colonial period, yet organ music did not generally occupy an important place within the American religious or cultural experience. Among the separatist groups from England (the Puritans and some groups of Pilgrims), psalm singing was practiced with genuine fervor, but without organ accompaniment.[1] If reinforcement for the singing was needed, some instrument other than the organ was employed. Like the Calvinists in England, the American separatists regarded the organ part of the "Popish" ceremonialism which should be driven from their worship at any expense. An example of the Puritan attitude is furnished by the often-cited case of the chamber organ which Thomas Brattle willed in 1713 to the Brattle Street Church, Boston, of which he had been a founding member. The Brattle Street Church, a Puritan congregation, refused his gift, so the organ was donated to King's Chapel of the same city. There, too, prejudice was so great that the organ remained seven months on the porch of the church before it was unpacked, and after its installation it was severely criticized.[2]

The Anglican congregations, less numerous in New England than the separatists, did allow organs in the church. However, they often couldn't afford to buy an instrument, so organs were not plentiful. Quite naturally, the first instruments in the Anglican churches were imported from England. They had no pedal stops or pedalboard, following the English tradition, and the majority of these instruments had but one manual. The music played on these organs was English in style, some of it composed on English soil, some of it in America.

For the Anglican service, it was customary that the organist accompany the congregational singing and provide short voluntaries. In some of the more prominent New England Anglican churches, the organ even acquired a limited concert status in the late 18th century. When programs of sacred music were presented in the churches, organ concerti were sometimes included, although choral and instrumental ensembles were obviously the main attraction. Composers featured on such programs included Handel, Maurice Greene, C.P.E. Bach, Thomas Arne, William Felton, occasionally Mozart or Haydn—in other words, the same composers who were most sought-after in England. Organists who emigrated here (William Selby, Francis Linley, and others) sometimes performed their own works as well. Examples of their compositions can be found in *A Century of American Organ Music* (1776-1876), two volumes, edited by Barbara Owen. The excerpt which follows was taken from Linley's *Trumpet Voluntary,* a work wholeheatedly in the English tradition.

(Example 1)

In the southern colonies, the only city which appeared to take an interest in organs and organ music was Charleston, the cultural center of the south. Karl Theodore Pachelbel, son of Johann Pachelbel, was organist in Charleston, at St. Philip's church, from 1737 until his death in 1750. Another resident of this city was an English keyboardist, Peter Valton, the reputed composer of *Six Sonatas for Harpsichord or Organ, with Violin Obbligato.*[3] As is to be expected in a new city located in a rude, as yet uncultivated country, Charleston-

Ex. 1. Linley, *Trumpet Voluntary*, m. 1-6.

ians took great pride in maintaining the "correct" tradition of the mother country, in this case, England. There was as yet no thought of creating music which would be distinctively American.

In the middle colonies, emigrants from other European countries brought their own musical traditions and did their best to nourish these on American soil. The Germans and Swedes who settled mainly in Pennsylvania, and the Moravians who came there somewhat later (c.1740), had a considerable appreciation for music. They considered organ music so important that even their smallest rural churches had organs. The Swedish church *Gloria Dei* in Philadelphia is notable for providing the earliest recorded use of an organ in colonial America. In 1703, this congregation borrowed a portable organ to be used with strings, woodwinds, brass, and percussion to provide festive music for a pastoral ordination. The Moravians likewise encouraged the use of the organ with other instruments, although they apparently took a dim view of the organist playing solo repertory. The Germans, too, brought with them a tradition of liturgical organ playing. The type of organ building which predominated in the part of the country where they settled was naturally not English, but German. The instruments of David Tannenburg and other German organ builders working in Pennsylvania constitute an important chapter in the history of the American organ. Unforunately, almost no organ literature has been preserved from the Germanic settlers in Pennsylvania. Moreover, these immigrant groups made no attempt to mingle with the English-speaking colonists, so their exceptional music culture had little impact on the mainstream of American life. It remained an isolated phenomenon.

In the first half of the 19th century, the portions of the country which had been most strongly under the English influence continued to look to England for direction. An increasing number of

the dissenting churches reluctantly agreed to install organs to aid the congregational singing, although the straitlaced atmosphere in these churches was scarcely conducive to the development of an artistic level of service playing. In the Anglican, or Episcopal, churches, meanwhile, the organist continued to provide introductions and interludes to the singing, and played voluntaries at specified points in the service.[4]

By the mid-19th century, printed collections of voluntaries had begun to appear, so that the organist had the possibility of playing composed music in addition to his own improvisations. By the latter half of the century, it had also become customary to add preludes and postludes to the service. The most popular organ works of European composers, such as Mendelssohn and Lemmens, became standard prelude-postlude material. At the same time, transcriptions from the orchestral, operatic, and oratorio world found their way into the church service. In playing transcriptions, American organists were following the example of British organists whose repertory at that time was heavily weighted with transcriptions.

The latter half of the 19th century also saw the rise of greater interest in the organ as a concert instrument. In this connection, there was a gradual demand for larger instruments with a complete pedalboard and with the full chorus of stops needed to perform the works of the European masters. Interest in developing a fine manual and pedal technique became a matter of genuine concern for the first time, and organ playing, in general, came to be viewed as an artistic experience rather than a mere utilitarian one.

When a large concert instrument was desired for the Boston Music Hall, the contract was given, not to an English firm, but to E. F. Walcker of Ludwigsburg, Germany. This instrument which was installed there in 1863, not only provided a fine example of Romantic organ building, but focused attention on the German school. In the years following this installation, other fine Romantic instruments by American builders appeared along the eastern coast.

The English orientation in organ building and organ playing was in process of being supplanted by a German influence. The Boston Music Hall organ was certainly decisive in bringing about this change. Another factor promoting this condition was the immigration to America at mid-century of large numbers of German-speaking people, who included in their number many skilled musicians. These musicians rapidly took leading positions in orchestras and other musical organizations and made Americans aware of the latest developments on the European continent.

As a result, when American organists first decided to go to Europe to study, they chose Germany as the country where they would complete their musical education. It was New Englanders first of all who made this pilgrimage to Germany. When they returned, they faced the difficult task of educating, not only their students, but their audiences. The most successful of these new American concert organists found it necessary to include on their programs—alongside organ works of Bach and Mendelssohn —transcriptions of Rossini arias, perhaps, or a chorus from the *Messiah*, as well as some orchestral overtures.

John Knowles Paine (1839-1906), who became professor of music at Harvard, spent four years of study in Berlin. Upon his return, he worked indefatigably to establish a higher level of professionalism in American organ playing. His organ compositions show his admiration for the German masters and were a studied attempt to overcome the "handicap" of being American. The craftsmanship in these works is solid, but the ideas are not original.

(Example 2)

Dudley Buck (1839-1909), who became one of the most popular concert artists in his day, also served an apprenticeship in Germany. His organ compositions, which were well-received during his lifetime, but seem a bit too obvious today, include the first organ sonata written by an American. Following these men came George W. Chadwick (1854-1931), a pupil of Haupt, of Jadassohn and of Rheinberger in Germany, and Arthur W. Foote (1853-1937), who received his German training from the hand of John Knowles Paine. The list of German-trained New England composers continues with Horatio Parker (1863-1919), who did much to establish a high level of craftsmanship in American choral music. Of his works for organ, an excerpt from his tuneful *Introduction and Fugue in E Minor* is quoted here.

(Example 3)

To the list of musical pioneers should be added the name of Lowell Mason (1792-1872), who earlier in the century had succeeded in introducing music instruction into the public schools and who had been a fervent crusader for higher standards in hymn singing and choral music. Although he wasn't an organ composer, his contribution paved the way for later accomplishments in organ music.

Charles Edward Ives (1874-1954), the first strikingly original American composer, was a student both of Parker and of Dudley Buck. As his well-known *Variations on America* attests, Ives was one of the first Americans who consciously attempted to create a distinctively American music. Finding inspiration in Yankee folk and popular music, he felt free to use these elements without altering them to conform to the standards of European art music. In his search for vigor and vitality, he used polytonality, polyrhythms and a variety of other unheard-of techniques before they were employed in Europe. Himself an organist, Ives wrote a number of organ pieces in his early years, but most of them have not been located. His *Variations on America* is a saucy, irreverent work, with sardonic allusions to New England musical experience— the town bands in parade, the village organist improvising on a sentimental hymn, etc.

(Example 4)

Up to this point, only New Englanders have been mentioned in the list of notable organists and teachers of the 19th century. This is understandable if one remembers that New England, particularly Boston, was the intellectual capital of America at that time. The intellectual climate in other regions of the United States was not yet ready to nourish organ playing as an artistic expression. For most congregations, it was sufficient if the organist

Ex. 2. Paine, *Concert Variations on the Austrian Hymn,* variation 1, m. 1-3.

Ex. 3. Parker, *Introduction and Fugue in E Minor,* m. 1-4.

Ex. 4. Ives, *Variations on "America,"* m. 75-79.

could support, rather than hinder, the singing of the hymns. True, organs were being built all over the continent to serve the needs of new congregations. A look at the number of organs mentioned in Orpha Ochse's *History of the Organ in the United States* is staggering. Yet, in most cases, there was little organ literature to go with these instruments. The organist improvised most of what was needed for the service. One should mention the presence in the midwest of the German organ virtuoso and teacher, Wilhelm Middelschulte (1863-1943), who did the same kind of musical ground-breaking in Chicago, Milwaukee, and Detroit that Paine, Buck,

Parker, and their colleagues had done in New England. However, Middelschulte didn't move to Chicago until 1891, and the effects of his labors were not felt until the 20th century.

By the turn of the present century, New York had become a cultural center vying with Boston, and several organists of note could be found there as well as in New England. At about the same time, the German domination of American music was in process of being supplanted by an admiration of all things French. The concert tours made to this country by Alexandre Guilmant in the final years of the 19th century ushered in a new phase in American organ playing. In New York City, an institution for the training of organists and choir directors was established in 1899 under the name Guilmant Organ School. It was the first institution of its kind in the United States.

The leading American organists no longer chose to complete their education in Germany, but went rather to Paris, where they studied with Guilmant, Widor, D'Indy, or Vierne. Among the earliest Americans to study organ in Paris was Clarence Dickinson (1873-1969), who prefaced his French studies by a year in Berlin. Eric Delamarter (1880-1953), Seth Bingham (1882-1972), Edward Shippen Barnes (1887-1958), David McKay Williams (1887-1978) and Garth Edmundson (1895-1971) were other prominent American organists who had their training in France. The impact of the French school shows up repeatedly in the toccatas, organ symphonies, and atmospheric character pieces of these composers writing in the early decades of the century. Not only were forms and compositional techniques largely determined by what was done in Paris, but registration, too, followed as much as possible the patterns of the French school. Delamarter's *The Fountain*, for example, is an adaptation of French impressionism.

(Example 5)

It would be a mistake, however, to think that France was the only country which left its imprint on the budding American organ school of the early 20th century. England, which no longer had much influence in the realm of concert music, still exercised a normative influence in the area of service playing.

English church musicians had been imported for large church positions since colonial days, and this importation continued in the 20th century. T. Tertius Noble (1867-1953), Roland Diggle (1887-1954), and T. Frederick H. Candlyn (1892-1964) are but a few of the English organist-choirmasters who took prominent positions in America in the first decades of the 20th century. Choir schools and boy choirs, which had been introduced into America in the 19th century, received added significance as choir schools were set up at the Cathedral of St. John the Divine, at St. Thomas' Church, and at other important establishments in the early decades of the 20th century. Thus, the English worship service concept, with choral music at its core and the organist in a subsidiary role, became part of the American experience. American organists looked to Paris for direction in concert music, but the way they played a church service was determined by practices inherited from England. The Parisian manner of playing the organ mass was obviously not transferable to Protestant American soil.

Some of the American Catholic churches imported organists and choir directors from Italy, such as Pietro Yon (1886-1943), who became organist at St. Patrick's Cathedral, and Father Carlo Rossini (b. 1890), organist at St. Paul's Cathedral, Pittsburgh. "Devotional music" practiced by most Catholic organists in America earlier in this century was deplorably insipid. However, some of Yon's concert pieces, for example his *Sonata Cromatica*, are not devoid of interest.

A large quantity of service music, especially for Protestant churches, was produced in the early decades of the century. Composers mentioned earlier

Ex. 5. Delamarter, *The Fountain*, m. 4-5.

(E. S. Barnes, G. Edmundson, S. Bingham, etc.) were regular contributors. Others one should mention are Joseph Clokey (1890-1960), Philip James (b. 1890) and H. Everett Titcomb (1884-1969). While the last three did not study abroad, they wrote in a manner which showed the influence of both the French and English schools.

At this point, it becomes necessary to mention the contribution of some men who were professional composers, rather than professional organists or organist-choirmasters. One would mention, first, certain composers who studied in Paris with Nadia Boulanger, herself an organist, and with Vincent D'Indy; they are Aaron Copland, Roy Harris, and Walter Piston. These composers, and others who studied with them in Paris, brought back to America the aesthetic of Igor Stravinsky, the ideas of neo-classicism, and the ideals of Erik Satie. However, the significant thing is that these composers, unlike those who had gone to Germany in the 19th century, no longer felt a compulsion to slavishly imitate whatever was most successful in Europe. Rather, living and studying in Paris was for them a liberating, liberalizing experience. It opened their eyes to possible explorations into the American musical experience. For the first time, a substantial group of composers (as opposed to an isolated individual, such as Ives) became concerned with the idea of creating a distinctively American music.

Virgil Thomson (b. 1896) used revivalist hymn tunes to create his particular brand of American organ music. He wrote four sets of *Variations on Sunday School Hymns* ("Shall We Gather at the River," etc.). The satire in these variations, reminiscent of Ives' *Variations on America*, derives from Thomson's belief that music takes itself too seriously. It is this type of composition which earned him the not altogether accurate

label of "the Erik Satie of American music."

Aaron Copland (b. 1900), the year after he returned from Paris, wrote a *Symphony for Organ and Orchestra*, commissioned by Nadia Boulanger for her American concert tour in 1925. Reflective of the composer's neo-classic training, this early work does not yet exhibit the American flavor that one expects to find in his works. In 1940 Copland wrote another work for organ, *Episode*, which is short, but good.

Roy Harris (b. 1898) composed two works for organ and brass. Following his example, a number of other composers not generally associated with the organ began to compose an occasional piece for organ in combination with other instruments.

Walter Piston (1894-1976), another American who received his neo-classical orientation from Nadia Boulanger, differed from the others in that he aimed at an international, rather than a national, style. The mastery of fugal writing for which this theorist has become famous, is evidenced in his *Chromatic Study on the Name of B-A-C-H* (1940). He also wrote a *Partita* for violin, viola, and organ (1944), which incorporates elements of the 12-tone method, and a *Prelude and Allegro* for organ and strings.

(Example 6)

Roger Sessions (b. 1896) is another internationally-minded composer who spent many years abroad, most of them in Florence. His style, which has absorbed many influences, gravitates toward atonal chromaticism and the 12-tone school.[6] Among the best-known of his early compositions were his *Three Chorale Preludes* (c. 1928) for organ, written in what was considered at that time to be a rather austere idiom.

Ex. 6. Piston, *Chromatic Study on the Name of B-A-C-H*, m. 1-7.

Ex. 7. Sessions, *Chorale No. 1*, m. 14-15.

Other well-known American composers also made occasional contributions to organ literature: Wallingford Riegger (1885-1961); Douglas Moore (1893-1969); Quincy Porter (1897-1966); Henry Cowell (1897-1965); Otto Luening (b. 1900).

While these composers were generally attempting to write in an up-to-date language, two others, Howard Hanson and Samuel Barber, were re-discovering romanticism. Hanson (b. 1896) wrote a *Concerto* for organ, strings, and harp, which is unashamedly in a 19th-century idiom. Hanson's main contribution, however, was not his compositions, but, rather, his inauguration of the American Composers' Concerts and the annual Festival of American Music at Rochester. By giving native composers the chance to be heard at a time when American audiences valued only European music, Hanson provided an invaluable service.

Samuel Barber (b. 1910) wrote for organ two chorale preludes in the lyric neo-Romantic style which is characteristic of much of his writing. One of these preludes is based on an old Southern shape-note hymn. Along with other preludes on folk or revivalistic hymns by composers already mentioned, this work represents a part of the search for a distinctively American expression. Later, in 1960, Barber wrote a *Toccata Festiva*

for organ and orchestra, a sizeable work, technically challenging.

(Example 8)

Two other composers who drew on the 19th-century folk hymn heritage were the neo-classicists, Gardner Read (b. 1913) and Richard Donovan (1891-1970). They both succeeded in capturing the quaint tunefulness and primitive character of the original folk melodies.

Leo Sowerby (1895-1968), an organist choirmaster from the midwest, was the first American composer of stature to devote a major portion of his creative output to music for the church, both choral and organ. He worked ceaselessly to elevate the stature of the church musician. He also wrote an impressive number of organ works for recital use. His predilection for contrapuntal textures led him to compose several works in fugue, chaconne, or passacaglia style. His melodies have a directness and frankness which mark them as distinctly American. Basically a traditionalist with a faith in tonality, he made no atempt to keep pace with composers who were looking for new idioms. Early Sowerby works have an impressionistic hue, while later ones are more neo-classic. His registration instructions call for romantic stop combinations. Among his major

Ex. 8. Barber, *Toccata Festiva* (organ score), m. 135-136.

works for organ, the *Symphony in G* illustrates his writing at its best.

(Example 9)

Before following the course of American composers further into the 20th century, it is essential to recall that many of the best minds of Europe came to the United States in the years prior to World War II. The presence in this country of Schoenberg, Stravinsky, Hindemith, Krenek, Bartok, Milhaud, and other masters of international stature had a tremendous impact on the musical life of this nation. Younger American musicians studied with these men and came directly under their influence. Highly significant was the fact that their presence in the United States altered the view of what supposedly constituted Americanism in music. On the one hand, Americans felt less need to imitate what was done in Europe, since the great European masters were now living on American soil. On the other hand, they recognized that American music didn't have to quote a Negro spiritual or a revivalistic hymn nor imitate a jazz pattern in order to qualify as an American composition. The concept of what constitutes a valid American musical expression was broadened to become as multi-faceted as America itself.

In addition to Europeans who emigrated just prior to the Second World War, one should also mention the Swiss-born Ernst Bloch (1880-1959), who moved to the United States in 1917 and became one of the most influential teachers on this continent. His organ compositions include *Six Preludes for the Synagogue* and other pieces for service use.

The number of mainstream American composers contributing to organ literature at the mid-century, and during the decade beyond, continued to expand, although one must admit that they generally wrote only a few pieces for organ. The number of church-oriented musicians who were writing service music, on the other hand, grew by leaps and bounds. They produced countless volumes. In academic circles, the major trends at this time were neo-classicism, neo-romanticism (of the Samuel Barber variety), and a style which, à la Stravinsky, was an assimilation of 12-tone techniques with neo-classical practice. Among composers who worked primarily in church circles, on the other hand, the style was much more tradition-bound, more retrospective.

Paul Creston (b.1906), Norman Dello Joio (b.1913), and Norman Lockwood (b.1906) wrote sizeable concert works for organ with other instruments. Their works represent a conservative brand of neo-classicism. Ross Lee Finney (b.1906), Leslie Bassett (b.1923), and Alvin Etler (1913-1973) also wrote a few pieces for organ solo. Virgil Thomson, who had composed for organ earlier in the century, returned in 1962 with an excellent concert piece on the *Pange Lingua*. Still employing polytonality and some of his other tongue-in-cheek devices, he very effectively seizes the medieval flavor of the chant and displays it in a modern setting, with tone clusters, etc.

(Example 10)

Herman Berlinski (b.1910) provided the earliest Jewish organ music which enjoyed wide circulation in the United States. His works, particularly the earlier ones, are full of atmosphere and descriptive color, finding their point of departure in the rapturous Oriental melismas of Hebrew cantillation. While his style has continued to evolve in recent

Ex. 9. Sowerby, *Symphony,* movement 3: *Passacaglia,* m. 136–140.

Ex. 10. Thomson, *Pange Lingua,* m. 173–177.

years, it is the early liturgical pieces, recalling the Hebraic tradition, which occupy a special place in American organ music.

(Example 11)

Ellis B. Kohs (b.1916) also wrote some variations on Hebrew hymns and, notably, a *Passacaglia* for organ and strings. Samuel Adler (b.1928) likewise wrote a few short works for the synagogue and, more recently, a concert work for organ with percussion.

From still another ethnic background, yet certainly American, is Alan Hovhaness (b.1911), who has substantially added to the literature for organ and other instruments. Identifying with the heritage of his Armenian ancestors, Hovhaness made melismatic melodies of the near-Eastern type and ceaseless repetitions the mainstay of his style.

(Example 12)

A composer who began writing for the organ in the 1940's and who has continued to increase in stature is Vincent Persichetti (b.1915). Using ideas derived from a variety of sources, he is essentially an amalgamator, rather than a pathfinder. His techniques vary from one composition to another. Yet, in all of them, one is struck by his sense of design and his considerable craftsmanship. His *Sonata* has the lean texture of neoclassicism, while his *Shimah B'kohli*

Ex. 11. Berlinski, *The Burning Bush,* m. 16–18.

Ex. 12. Hovhaness, *Sonata for Trumpet and Organ,* rehearsal no. 1.

(Psalm 130) integrates aspects of serialization with more traditional methods. The *Chorale Prelude: Drop, Drop Slow Tears* is an expressive, linear work, rich in canon and other imitative devices, and conveying a deep-felt sense of penitence.

(Example 13)

His *Parable,* to mention just one more, is a colorful, yet rather abstract serial piece, with much use of displaced notes and crushed chords.

Daniel Pinkham (b. 1923) has been a regular contributor, since the 1940's, to the literature for organ with other instruments. His early works are basically neo-classic, later works are frequently in a modified serial technique. During the '70's he entered the tape music scene, combining tape with traditional instruments. In his *Toccatas for the Vault of Heaven* (1972), for organ manuals and tape, the tape features synthetic sonorities in a tinkling, shimmering hue. Another work for organ and tape, *When the Morning Stars Sang Together,* is an effective atmospheric depiction of God speaking to Job out of the voice of the whirlwind. *The Other Voices of the Trumpet* (1971) is a serial composition for organ, trumpet, and tape, for which an excerpt is furnished below.

(Example 14)

Alan Stout (b. 1932) has provided two books of short chorale preludes suitable for the church service (in addition to several other, considerably interesting pieces). Linear music of the highest quality, slightly ascerbic, these works are a most welcome addition to literature for the church service. They speak a contemporary language, but are not difficult to play.

(Example 15)

As is to be expected in a country having more than 250 religious denom-

Ex. 13. Persichetti, *Sonata for Organ,* m. 1-3.

Ex. 14. Pinkham, *The Other Voices of the Trumpet,* for trumpet, organ, and tape, m. 104-106.

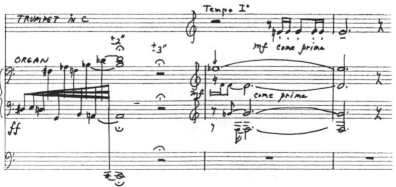

Ex. 15. Stout, *Schmücke dich o liebe Seele*, m. 1-4.

inations, there are more composers writing for the church service and the synagogue than could ever be mentioned in a survey of this type. Numerous competent composers who have enriched the music of their denomination will have to remain unmentioned, although some of them are listed under "Editions." Looking for broad trends, I would mention only a group of musicians associated with the Lutheran liturgy: Jan Bender, Paul Manz, Gerhard Krapf, Ludwig Lenel, Gerald Near, and others. The block impact of their work has caused a broadening and raising of standards in liturgical music. An excerpt from Lenel's *O Christ, Thou Lamb of God* is given below.

(Example 16)

The fact that most of these men are located in the midwest is an indication of the state of affairs in the latter half of the 20th century where leadership in organ and church music is no longer the exclusive property of the eastern United States. One can find in a surprising number of localities across the nation a genuine interest in good organs and quality organ music. On the west coast, moreover, the Los Angeles County AGO chapters have promoted their regional composers by publishing the works of these composers in a volume known as *The California Organist,* with several volumes appearing each year.

Concert music for the organ has in recent years received a new infusion of life as contemporary composers discovered that the organ is a kaleidoscopic source of exciting new sounds. William Albright (b. 1944) has probably done more than any other American composer in the '70's to promote the organ as a contemporary concert instrument. Timbre is one of his primary considerations, and he favors beauty of sound over bizarre or startling effects. His registrations call for lush, full sounds requiring a large organ and a reverberant room for their adequate realization. His use of color is often intimately connected with his manipulation of texture to generate form. To attain the desired textures, he requires the organist to employ non-traditional methods of organ playing through the use of palms, forearms, etc. At the same time, he does not turn his back on the organ's tradition. A hallmark of his style is, actually, a juxtaposition of old and new. His music is full of allusions to historical organ styles, many of them very amusing. Much of the communicative ability of his style is due to the delightful conflicts which arise when historical allusions are presented within a contemporary framework.

(Example 17)

Another work which owes much of

Ex. 16. Lenel, *O Christ, Thou Lamb of God,* m. 1-6.

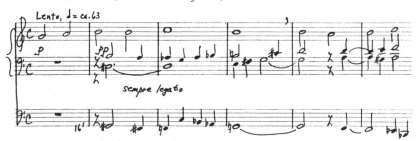

Ex. 17. Albright, *Organbook II*, mov't 3: *Last Rites*, beginning of organ score.

its popularity to the juxtaposition of normally incompatible materials is the *Black Host* (1967) of William Bolcom (b. 1938). Scored for organ, percussion, and tape, this work is a giant collage combining carnival music, a Genevan psalm tune, theatre organ and rock. There is a nightmarish quality about the work. At the same time a sly humor is present which tells us that the composer is not taking himself too seriously. This music bears a "made-in-America" label. It is inconceivable that it could have been the product of any other culture.

A work which allows the organist and his assistants considerable free play is the *Four Etudes* (1969) of Lukas Foss (b. 1922). In this aleatoric work, the assistants "interfere" with the performance of the organist by playing tone clusters at the extremes of the keyboard and by drawing and retiring stops in an erratic fashion.

Among the major contributors to organ music utilizing tape is Richard Felciano (b. 1930). Unlike some composers for whom the tape is merely a background surface, Felciano is intent on creating a sonic synthesis which goes beyond the scope of the traditional instruments without negating them. He was also one of the first American composers to bring electronic music and multi-media productions into the church. Musicians who have used in church his works for organ and tape have found them to be effective vehicles for worship. For some listeners, his particular integration of natural musical sounds with pre-recorded ones can produce a near ecstatic effect.

The number of other composers who have written for organ and tape is too long to allow one to discuss all of them here. Besides, as this is a new genre, it is not possible to have much historical perspective on this subject. Among works which have attracted a fair amount of attention, however, one would certainly want to mention Ronald Perera's *Reverberations*, Richard Stewart's *Prelude for Organ and Tape*, Robert Jones' *Sonata for Worship No. 6*, Herbert Bielewa's *Quodlibet SF 42569*, and Elliott Schwarz's *Prisms*.

Works which appear even more estranged from tradition are the experimental compositions of such people as Heidi von Gunden, Robert Cogan, Pozzi Escot, Gary White, and David Cope. For them, sound has been completely divorced from its historical commitment to logical arrangement, to progression, development, or formal design. The organ is treated as a sound source, and all parts of it are shamelessly explored, often in combination with far-out tape effects.

At the same time, one can find more sober compositions in a more readily comprehensible style written by young composers, such as Rudy Shackelford (b. 1944), Richard Toensing (b. 1940), Thomas Janson (b. 1947), David Isele (b. 1946), or Stuart Smith (b. 1948). In their writing, an emphasis on solid craftsmanship is combined with an imaginative use of organ color. Shackelford's *Canonic Variations: Vom Himmel hoch*, for instance, is satisfying intellectually and, at the same time, it is charming, listenable music.

(Example 18)

Organists who try to keep abreast of new developments may be interested to know that Elizabeth Sollenberger, asso-

Ex. 18. Shackelford, *Canonic Variations: Vom Himmel hoch,* mov't 1, m. 1-2.

ciated with the Hartt College Annual Contemporary Organ Music Festival, has a selected list of 20th-century organ compositions which she regularly updates to include the most recent works. One would also like to speak a word of appreciation to the Hartt Festival for generating a good deal of interest in organ composition in the past decade. It is at least partly due to the efforts of this festival that an impressive number of composers not formerly associated with the organ have begun to view the organ as a viable vehicle for expressing contemporary ideas.

Works which are not yet published can often be obtained from the Composers Facsimile Edition (New York). There are also two series which specialize in modern organ works. One is the Contemporary Organ Series of H. W. Gray (now Belwin-Mills). The other is a series bearing the same name, published by Hinshaw Music, Inc.

EDITIONS

Adler, Samuel: *Two Meditations,* New York, Mercury Music. *Toccata, Recitation and Postlude,* London, Oxford University Press. *Welcoming the Sabbath,* New York, Transcontinental Music Publishers. ORG. & INSTRUMENTS: *Xenia: A Dialogue for Organ and Percussion,* Minneapolis, Augsburg.

Albright, William: *Juba,* Bryn Mawr, Elkan-Vogel, 1968. *Pneuma,* Bryn Mawr, Elkan-Vogel, 1969. *Chorale Partita in an Old Style on "Wer nur den lieben Gott lässt walten,"* Bryn Mawr, Elkan-Vogel. *Organbook I,* Paris, Jobert. ORG. & TAPE: *Organbook II,* Paris, Jobert, 1973.

Barber, Samuel: *Chorale Prelude on "Silent Night,"* New York, G. Schirmer, 1961. *Wondrous Love: Variations on a Shape-note Hymn* (1959), New York, G. Schirmer, 1959. ORG. & ORCH.: *Toccata Festiva,* op. 36 (1960) for organ and full orchestra, New York, G. Schirmer, 1961. Also exists in a version for organ, strings, trumpet & timpani (op. 36a).

Barlow, Wayne: *Three Christmas Tunes,* St. Louis, Concordia. *Voluntaries on the Hymn of the Week,* 3 vols., St. Louis, Concordia. Vol. I: Advent, Christmas, Epiphany; II: Septuagesima to Good Friday; III: Easter to Trinity Sunday.

Barnes, Edward Shippen: *Deux pièces,* op. 5 *(Prélude solennel, Offertoire),* Paris, Durand. *Petite Suite,* op. 23, Paris, Durand. *Suite No. 2,* op. 25, Boston, Boston Music Co. *Third Suite,* op. 39, New York, G. Schirmer. *Allegro risoluto,* New York, H. W. Gray. *Symphony I,* New York, G. Schirmer. *Festal Prelude in G Minor,* New York, Carl Fischer. *Song for Organ,* New York, Carl Fischer. ORG. & PIANO: *Duetto pastorale,* Melville (N.Y.), Belwin-Mills. *Reverie,* Melville, Belwin-Mills.

Bassett, Leslie: *Four Statements,* New York, American Composers Alliance. *Toccata,* New York, American Composers Alliance. *Organ Voluntaries,* New York, American Composers Alliance.

Bender, Jan: Major publisher is Concordia (St. Louis). *Kleine Choralvorspiele zum Gottesdienstlichen Gebrauch,* op. 2, 3 vols., Kassel, Bärenreiter. *Vesper I (Partita: "Now Rest beneath Night's Shadow"),* op. 5, Kassel, Bärenreiter. *Toccata, Aria and Fugue,* op. 6, no. 1, Conc. *Twenty Short Organ Pieces,* op.

6. no. 2. Conc. Processional on "All Glory, Laud and Honor," op. 6, no. 3, Conc. *Chorale Fantasy on "Awake, My Heart, with Gladness,"* op. 6, no. 4, Conc. *Six Variations on a Theme by Daniel Moe,* Minneapolis, Augsburg. *Tabulatura Americana (New Organ Settings),* op. 22, 3 vols., Conc. *Partita : Our Father Thou in Heaven above,* op. 25, Minneapolis, Augsburg. *Festival Preludes on Six Chorales,* op. 26, Conc. *Triptych,* op. 33, Conc. *6 Variations on a Theme by Hugo Distler,* op. 38, Springfield (Ohio), Chantry Music Press. *Introduction, Fugue and Variations on "Kremser,"* op 41, Nashville, Abingdon. *O God, Lord of Heaven and Earth,* Minneapolis, Augsburg. *Four Variations on "Down Ampney,"* op. 47, Minneapolis, Augsburg. *Missa pro Organo,* op. 52, Berlin, Verlag Merseburg. *Experimentum Organo,* Springfield (Ohio), Chantry Music Press. *A Meditation,* Springfield, Chantry Music Press. *Organ Fantasy and Setting on "Mit Freuden zart,"* Springfield, Chantry Music Press. *Partita: Glorious Things of Thee Are Spoken,* Stewartsville (Mo.), White Harvest Publications. *Organ Partita on "Edwards,"* Stewartsville (Mo.), White Harvest Publications. ORG. & INSTRUMENTS: *Phantasy on "Come, Holy Ghost, God and Lord,"* for organ, 3 trpts, 3 trbns, timp., and cymbals, Conc.

Berlinski, Herman: *From the World of my Father* (1938), New York, Merrymount Music, Inc. (through Presser). *Sinfonia No.* 1, New York, American Composers Alliance. *The Burning Bush* (1956), H. W. Gray, 1957. *Two Preludes for the High Holy Days* (1956), New York, Merrymount, Inc. *Preludes for the Three Festivals* (Shalosh Regolim) (1958), New York, Merrymount Music, Inc. *In Memoriam* (1958), New York, Associated Music Publishers, 1959. *Elegy* (1958), New York, H. W. Gray. *Kol Nidre,* New York, Mercury Music Corp. (now Presser), 1962. *Processional Music,* New York, Mercury Music. *Prelude for the Sabbath (Shovas Vayeenofash),* New York, Transcontinental Music Publications. *Sinfonia No. 3 (Sounds and Motions),* New York, H. W. Gray.

Bielawa, Herbert: *Chorale and Fugue on "Lasst uns erfreuen,"* Nashville, Abingdon. *Four Preludes on Hymns of the Church,* Nashville, Abingdon. 1967.

Fantasy on "Nicaea," (1968), Delaware Water Gap, Shawnee Press. ORG. & TAPE: *Quodlibet SF42569,* New York, H. W. Gray (Belwin-Mills), 1974.

Bingham, Seth: Publications by H. W. Gray (New York), unless otherwise indicated. *Adoration,* op. 9, no. 2. *Aria,* op. 9, no. 5, out of print. *Agnus Dei* (Communion), op. 36, no. 2. *At the Cradle of Jesus* (1943), Glen Rock, J. Fischer. *Baroques* (Suite in 5 movements), op. 41 (1944), New York, Galaxy, 1944. *Bells of Riverside,* op. 36, no. 5, Glen Rock, J. Fischer. *Canonic Etude on "Greensleeves." Carillon de Chateau-Thierry* (1936), out of print. *Chorale Prelude on "St. Flavian,"* op. 9, no. 4. *Counter-theme,* op. 9, no. 6. *The Good Shepherd,* New York, Galaxy, 1966. *Harmonies of Florence,* op. 27 (1929), *He Is Risen* (Fantasy on Easter Themes) *Hymn-Fantasy on "Riverton"* (1957), Evanston, Summy & Birchard *Introit on "Elton,"* (1962), Cincinnati, World Library of Sacred Music. *Nativity Song* (1941). *Night Sorrow,* op. 36, no. 4, Glen Rock, J. Fischer. *Offertory on a Spanish Folk-Song,* Cincinnati, World Library of Sacred Music. *Passacaglia,* op. 40 (1939), Glen Rock, J. Fischer. *Pastoral Psalms* (Suite), op. 30 (1938), New York, Carl Fischer. *Pastorale (Memories of France),* op. 16, *Pioneer America* (Second Suite), op. 26 (1928). *Puritan Procession* from this suite available separately, H. W. Gray. *Prelude and Fugue* (c), op. 9, no. 1. *Prelude and Fughetta* (F), op. 36, no. 1, Glen Rock, J. Fischer. *Prelude on "Festal Song," (Rise Up, O Men of God). Prelude on "St. Kevin,"* (1962), New York, Galaxy. *Good Shepherd,* New York, Galaxy. *Roulade,* op. 9, no. 3. *Seven Preludes or Postludes on Lowell Mason Hymns,* op. 42, 1935. *Sixteen Carol Canons* (from op. 55). *Sonata of Prayer and Praise,* op. 60 (1960). *Suite,* op. 25, New York, G. Schirmer, 1926. *Thirty-six Hymn and Carol Canons,* op. 55 (1952). *Toccata on "Leoni,"* op. 36, no. 3. *Twelve Hymn Preludes,* op. 38, 2 vols., 1942. *Ut queant laxis: Hymn to St. John the Baptist* (1962), New York, C. F. Peters, 1962. *Unto the Hills,* op. 30, no. 1, New York, Carl Fischer. ORG. & INSTRUMENTS: *Concerto in G Minor,* op. 46, for organ & orchestra, H. W. Gray, rental. *Concerto,* op. 57 for organ, snare drum, 3 trpts, 3 trbns, (1954). *Connecticut Suite,* op. 56 (1953), for organ and strings, with optional parts for trpt & trbn, H. W. Gray, rental.

Binkerd, Gordon: *Cantilena* (1955), New York, H. W. Gray. *Organ Service* (Prelude, Offertory, Postlude), Oceanside, Boosey & Hawkes, 1968. *Andante,* New York, Associated Music Publishers. *Arietta,* New York, Associated Music Publishers. *Concert Set* (transcribed by R. Shackelford), Oceanside, Boosey & Hawkes. ORG. & INSTR.: *Studenten-Schmauss* (1962) for organ and double brass choir, Oceanside, Boosey & Hawkes, in preparation.

Bloch, Ernst: *Six Preludes for the Synagogue,* New York, G. Schirmer, 1948. *Four Wedding Marches,* New York, G. Schirmer, 1951. *Processional,* New York, G. Schirmer, 1961. *In Memoriam,* New York, Broude Bros.

Bolcom, William: *Hydraulis,* ed. Albright, New York, E. B. Marks, 1971. ORG. & INSTRUMENTS/TAPE: *Black Host,* for organ, percussion, and tape, Paris, Jobert, 1972. *Praeludium,* for org. & vibraphone, New York, E. B. Marks (rental).

Borowski, Felix: *Adoration,* ed. Whiting, Bryn Mawr, Theodore Presser. *First Suite,* ed. Alphenaar, New York, E. B. Marks. *Prière,* ed. Alphenaar, New York, E. B. Marks. *Sonata No. 1 for Organ,* Glen Rock, J. Fischer. *Second Sonata,* ed. Alphenaar, New York, E. B. Marks. *Suite for Grand Organ,* ed. T. T. Noble, Glen Rock, J. Fischer.

Buck, Dudley: *The Holy Night,* New York, G. Schirmer, 1891/1919. *Star-Spangled Banner Concert Variations,* New York, McAfee Music Co. Many other publications by G. Schirmer, Novello, Ed. Schuberth and others are out of print.

Candlyn, T. Frederich H.: Major publishers are H. W. Gray (New York) and Abingdon Press (Nashville). *Festal Rhapsody on "Christ ist erstanden,"* A. P. *Finale on a Tonic Pedal,* HWG. *Indian Legend,* HWG. *Marche héroique,* HWG. *March of the Three Kings,* HWG. *Prelude on "Darwell,"* A. P. *Prelude on "Divinum Mysterium,"* HWG. *Prelude on "Flavian,"* A. P.

Prelude on "Hyfrydol," A. P. *Prelude on "Mit Freuden zart,"* A. P. *Prelude on "Rockingham,"* A. P. *Prelude on "St. Bernard,"* A. P. *Rhapsody on "Sursum Corda,"* HWG. *Scherzo Caprice,* HWG. *Six Hymn Preludes,* A. P. *Sonata Dramatica,* HWG. *Song of Autumn,* HWG. *Three Christmas Preludes,* A. P. Plus publications by G. Ditson, C. Fischer, and A. P. Schmidt.

Chadwick, George W.: *Elegy,* New York, H. W. Gray. *Fantasia in E-flat,* New York, H. W. Gray. *In Tadaussac Church,* New York, H. W. Gray. *Marche Ecossaise,* New York, H. W. Gray. *Suite in Variation Form,* New York, H. W. Gray, 1923. *Pedalzaione Organistica,* New York, G. Ricordi. Plus publications by A. P. Schmidt and others, now out of print.

Clokey, Joseph W.: Publications are by H. W. Gray (New York), unless otherwise indicated. *Ballade in D. Bell Prelude. Cathedral Prelude. In a Norwegian Village. Légende. Three Mountain Sketches (Canyon Walls; Jagged Peaks; Wind in the Pine Trees). Ten Meditations on Hymn Melodies,* Glen Rock, J. Fischer. *Ten Preludes on Plainsong Kyries,* New York, H. Flammer. *Ten Pieces for Organ* (or piano), Glen Rock, J. Fischer. *Thirty-five Interludes of Hymn Tunes,* Glen Rock, J. Fischer. *A Wedding Suite,* Glen Rock, J. Fischer. *Woodland Idyl.* ORG. & INSTRUMENTS: *Partita in G Major,* for org. & piano, rental only. *Partita in G Minor,* for org. & str. orch., rental only. *Trio* for organ, violin, cello, rental.

Cooper, Paul: *Variants* (1974), London, J. & W. Chester.

Copland, Aaron: *Episode,* New York, H. W. Gray, 1941. *Preamble for a Solemn Occasion,* arr. for organ by the composer, Oceanside, Boosey & Hawkes. ORG. & ORCHESTRA: *Symphony* (1924), Oceanside, Boosey & Hawkes. Also exists in a reduction for organ and piano.

Copley, R. Evan: Publisher is Abingdon (Nashville), unless indicated otherwise. *Chorale Prelude on "Ein feste Burg." Three Chorale Preludes. Eleven Chorale Preludes. Chorale Toccata on "Lasst uns erfreuen,"* New York, H. W. Gray, 1964. *"Out of the Depths,"* New York,

H. W. Gray. *Fifteen Miniatures for the Organ*, Waco, Sacred Word, Inc. *Toccata. Three Preludes and Fugues*, 1967.

Cowell, Henry D.: *Processional*, New York, H. W. Gray, 1944. *Prelude*, New York, Associated Music Publishers, 1958. *Hymn and Fuguing Tune No. 14*, New York, Assoc. Music Publishers, 1962. ORG. & INSTR.: *Grinnell Fanfare* for organ & brass (1941), New York, American Composers Alliance.

Crandall, Robert: *Carnival Suite*, New York, H. W. Gray, 1950.

Creston, Paul: *Suite for Organ*, New York, G. Ricordi, 1960. *Fantasia*, op. 74, New York, G. Ricordi, 1960. *Rapsodia breve*, op. 81, New York, Franco Colombo (through Belwin-Mills). ORG. & INSTR: *Meditation*, op. 21, for org. & marimba, New York, G. Schirmer.

Delamarter, Eric: Major publishers are H. W. Gray (New York) and Witmark & Sons (New York). *Carillon*, HWG. *Chorale Prelude on a Melody by Hassler*, Wit. *Festival Prelude*, Wit., 1945. *The Fountain*, HWG, 1943. *Intermezzo*, HWG. *Gothic Prelude*, New York, G. Schirmer, 1937. *March*, HWG. *Nocturnes*, HWG, 1943. *Stately Procession*, HWG, 1943. *Suite*. Wit., 1945 *Toccatino*, HWG. ORG. & ORCH.: *Concerto No. 1* (E), (1920), HWG, rental. *Concerto No. 2* (A), (1922), HWG, rental.

Dello Joio, Norman: *Five Lyric Pieces*, New York, E. B. Marks. *Laudation*, New York, E. B. Marks, 1965. ORG. & INSTR: *Antiphonal Fantasia on a Theme of Albrici*, for org., brass, & strings (1965), New York, E. B. Marks.

Dickinson, Clarence: All publications by H. W. Gray (New York). *Andante Serioso. Berceuse. Canzona, Exaltation. Intermezzo* (from the "Storm King Symphony"). *The Joy of the Redeemed* (O Quantia Qualia). *Meditation on "Ah, Dearest Jesus." Memories. Old Dutch Lullaby. Preludes on Two Ancient Melodies. Reverie. Romance.* ORG. & INSTRUMENTS: *Exaltation*, arr. for org., harp (or piano), violin and cello. *Meditation on "Ah Dearest Jesus"* is available in following versions: for violin, cello, harp, trumpets, trombones, organ; for violin, cello, harp and organ; for trumpets, trombones and organ. Rental only. *Old Dutch Lullaby*,

for harp and organ. *Storm King Symphony*, for organ & orchestra, rental. *Reverie*, arr. for violin, cello, harp & organ. *The Joy of the Redeemed*, arr. for 2 trpts, 2 trbns, and organ.

Diggle, Roland: Major publisher is H. W. Gray (New York). *Allegrétto Grazioso*, HWG. *In Olden Times*, HWG. *Prelude, Variation and Fugue on "Dundee,"* HWG. *Prologue élégiaque*, New York, E. B. Marks. *Rhapsody Gothique*, HWG. *Scherzo Fantastique*, HWG. *Solemn Epilogue*, Melville, Mills/MCA. *Song of Triumph*, New York, G. Schirmer. *Toccata Gregoriano*, HWG. *Toccata on St. Theodulph*, HWG. *Will o' the Wisp* (Concert Scherzo), HWG. Plus numerous publications by Th. Presser, Ed. Schubert, O. Ditson, J. Fischer, E. H. Morris, and others, now out of print.

Donovan, Richard: *Two Chorale Preludes on American Folk Hymns* (1947), New York, Mercury Music. *Paignon* (1947), New York, H. W. Gray, 1948. *Antiphon and Chorale*, New York, American Composers' Alliance.

Edmundson, Garth: Major publishers are H. W. Gray (New York) and J. Fischer (Glen Rock). *Caravan of the Magi* and *In Silent Night* (from *In Modum Antiquum*), J. F. *Carillon* (from *Christmas Suite No. 1*), HWG. *A Carpenter Is Born* (from *Apostolic Symphony*), HWG. *Chorale Prelude for Christmas* ("Break Forth"), J. F., out of print. *Chorale Prelude on "In dulci Jubilo"*, HWG. *Christmas Suite No. 1*, HWG, 1932. *Christus Advenit* (Christmas Suite No. 2), HWG, 1937. *Christus Crucifixus*, HWG. *Christus Nocte*, HWG, 1941. *Christus Resurrexit*, HWG. *Concert Variations*, HWG. *Easter Spring Song*. J.F. *Eucharistia*, HWG. *For Passiontide*, HWG. *From the Western Church*, HWG. *Gargoyles* (from *Impressions gothiques*), J. F. 1933. *In Modum Antiquum*, 2 vols., J.F. *Oremus*, HWG. *Seven Classic Preludes*, J. F. *Seven Contrapuntal Preludes*, J. F. *Seven Modern Preludes*, J. F. *Seven Polyphonic Preludes*, J. F. *Seven Service Preludes on Seasonal Subjects*, J.F. *To The Setting Sun*, J.F. *Toccata on "Wie schön leuchtet*, HWG. *Vom Himmel Hoch* (from *Christus Advenit*) HWG. Additional publications by J. Fischer, H. W. Gray and Galaxy now out of print.

Elmore, Robert: Major publishers are H.W. Gray (New York) and H. Flammer (New York). *Air*, HWG. *Alla Marcia*, H.F. *Contemporary Chorale Preludes*, Dayton, Lorenz Publishing Co. *Donkey Dance*, HWG. *Fantasy on Nursery Tunes*, H.F. *Meditation on an Old Covenanter's Tune*, HWG. *Night of the Star*, New York, Galaxy. *Prelude: Seelenbrautigan*, ` London, Novello. *Rhythmic Suite* (Pavane, Rhumba), New York, St. Mary's Press (now Gentry Publications/Presser). *Themes for Organ*, Waco, Sacred Word, Inc. *Three Meditative Moments on Moravian Hymns*, H.F. *Three Miniatures*, H.F. *Two Pieces*, HWG. *Two Chorale Preludes*, Bryn Mawr, Elkan-Vogel. ORG. & INSTRUMENTS: *Concerto* for brass, org., & percussion, HWG, 1969. *Fanfare for Easter*, for org., 2 trpts, 2 trbns, perc., H.F. *Festival Toccata* (Easter) for org., 2 trpts, 2 trbns, perc., H.F. *Meditation on "Veni Emmanuel*," for 2 trpts, 2 trbns & organ, Glen Rock, J. Fischer. *Venite Adoremus*, for organ and piano, Glen Rock, J. Fischer.

Etler, Alvin: *Prelude and Toccata* (1950), New York, Associated Music Publishers.

Felciano, Richard: Publisher is E. C. Schirmer (Boston) unless indicated otherwise. *Ekagrata*, for organ, 2 drums, and tape. *Glossalalia*, for tape, baritone (or dramatic tenor), organ, and percussion, Cincinnati, World Library of Sacred Music. *God of the Expanding Universe*, organ and tape, 1971. *I Make My Own Soul of All the Elements of the Earth*, organ and tape, 1972. *Litany*, for organ (manuals alone) and tape, 1971. *Stops*, for organ and tape.

Finney, Ross Lee: *Capriccio*, New York, C.F. Peters. *Five Organ Fantasias*, New York, C. F. Peters.

Foote, Arthur W.: Several publications by A.P. Schmidt, no longer available.

Foss, Lukas: *Four Etudes*, New York, Carl Fischer, 1967.

Gehring, Philip: *Six Hymn Tune Preludes*, St. Louis, Concordia, 1966. *Four Pieces in the Manner of an Organ Mass*, Minneapolis, Augsburg, 1969. *Two Folk-Hymn Preludes for Organ*, Minneapolis, Augsburg.

Goeb, Roger: *Three Processionals* for organ and brass quintet, New York, American Composers' Alliance.

Goemanne, Noel: *Church Windows*, Cincinnati, World Library of Sacred Music. *Fantasia*, Glen Rock, J. Fischer. *Festival Voluntary on "Protexisti*," Glen Rock, J. Fischer. *Rhapsody*, Cincinnati, World Library of Sacred Music. *Six Canzonetti*, Chicago, FitzSimons Co. *March*, Glen Rock, J. Fischer. *Solemn Overture*, Carol Stream (Ill.), Hope Publ. Co. *Sortie on "Easter Hymn*," Bryn Mawr, Presser. *Toccata*, Delaware Water Gap, Shawnee Press. ORG. & INSTRUMENTS: *Fanfare For Festivals*, (3 trpts, timpani, and organ), Carol Stream (Ill.), Agape/Hope Publishing Co.

Hampton, Calvin: *Three Hymn Tunes*, St. Louis, Concordia. *Prelude and Variations on "Old Hundredth*, New York, McAfee Music Co.

Hanson, Howard: *Concerto* for organ, strings, and harp, (1921) New York, Carl Fischer, 1947.

Harris, Roy: *Etudes for Pedals* (1964), Cincinnati, World Library of Sacred Music. ORG. & INSTRUMENTS: *Chorale for Organ and Brass* (3 trpts, horn, 3 trbns), Melville, Mills Music, 1943, rental. *Toccata for Organ & Brass* (3 trpts, horn, 3 trbns), Melville, Mills music, 1944, rental. *Fantasy* for organ, brass (2 trpts, 2 trbns), and timpani, Berlin, Bote und Bock, 1966.

Held, Wilbur: *Flourish*, Bryn Mawr, Th. Presser. *Nativity Suite*, St. Louis, Concordia. *Partita on "O Sons and Daughters*," Minneapolis, Augsburg, 1964. *Preludes and Postludes*, vol. I, Minneapolis, Augsburg. *Processional on "The King's Majesty*," Melville, Belwin-Mills. *Six Carol Settings*, St. Louis, Concordia. *Suite of Passion Hymn Settings*, St. Louis, Concordia. ORG. & INSTRUMENTS: *Built on a Rock*, for 2 trpts and organ, Minneapolis, Augsburg. *Two Traditional Carols* for organ and C instrument, Minneapolis, Augsburg.

Hewitt, James: *The Battle of Trenton*, ed. & arr. by E. P. Biggs, Bryn Mawr, Merion Music, Inc. (Presser), 1974. *The 4th of July: A Grand Military Sonata*, arr J. Spong, Buchanan (Mich.), Electro-Voice, 1968.

Hodkinson, Sydney: *Dolmen-Megalith I*, Bryn Mawr, Theodore Presser. *Menhir-Megalith II* (1973), Bryn Mawr, Theodore Presser. *Talayot-Megalith III* (for organ à 2), Bryn Mawr, Theodore Presser.

Hokanson, Margrethe: *Organ Brevities*, Chicago, Hope Publishing Co., 1965. *A Nordic Reverie*, New York, H.W. Gray. *Three Fleeting Impressions*, Melville, Belwin-Mills.

Hovhaness, Alan: Publications by C.F. Peters (New York). *Bare November Day. Dawn Hymn. Sanahin* (Partita). ORG. & INSTRUMENTS: *Sonata for Oboe and Organ. Sonata for 2 Oboes and Organ. Sonata for Ryuteki and Sho* (Flute and organ), 1968. *Sonata for Trumpet and Organ*, 1963.

Isele, David: Publications by Hinshaw Music (Chapel Hill) in the Contemporary Organ Series. *Heraldings. Macedon Fanfares. Modentum. Prologue and Conjugation. Recitative, Interlogue and Torque. Zorgandum* (Organ duet).

Ives, Charles: *Variations on "America" and "Adeste Fidelis,"* New York, Mercury Music, 1949.

James, Philip: Major publisher is H.W. Gray (New York). *Alleluia-Toccata*, New York, Carl Fischer, 1955. *Christmas Suite*, HWG. *Dithyramb*, HWG. *Festal March "Perstare et Praestare."* HWG. *Fête*, HWG. *First Organ Sonata*, HWG. *Il Riposo*, HWG. *Meditation à Sainte Clothilde*, Philadelphia, Oliver Ditson. *Novellette*, HWG. *Ostinato*, HWG. *Pantomime*, HWG, 1941. *Passacaglia on a Cambrian Bass*, New York, C. Fischer. *Pastorale*, New York, Southern Music Publishing Co, 1955. *Pensée d'Automne*, HWG. *Requiescat in pace* (1949), Evanston, Summy-Birchard, 1957. *Solemn Prelude*, New York, Southern Music Publishing Co., 1955.

Janson, Thomas: *Celestial Autumn*, New York, H. W. Gray, (Belwin-Mills), 1974.

Johnson, David: Publisher is Augsburg (Minneapolis) unless otherwise indicated. *Beautiful Saviour*, New York, H.W. Gray, 1967. *Chorale Prelude on "Ein' feste Burg." Chorale Prelude on "Faith of our Fathers." Chorale Prelude*

on *"Wondrous Love,"* 1965. *Deck Thyself, My Soul, with Gladness*, 1968. *Easy Trios (Music for Worship). Free Harmonizations of 12 Hymn Tunes. Free Hymn Accompaniments for Manuals*, 2 bks. *Fugue à la Gigue. Just As I Am*, Nashville, Abingdon. *Lord, Keep Us Steadfast*, 1967. *Music for Worship for Manuals*, 1969. *Of the Father's Love Begotten (Divinum Mysterium)*, 1967. *Variants on "Earth and All Stars." Variations on "America,"* Phoenix, Trinity Cathedral Press. *Variations on "Love Came Down at Christmas."* ORG. & INSTRUMENTS: *Six Fanfares for Organ and Brass Quartet* (Plus timpani), St. Louis, Concordia. 3 *Festival Pieces*, for brass and organ. *Trumpet Tune in D Major. Three Trumpet Tunes* (C, G♭, and G). *Two Trumpet Tunes* (A, B♭).

Jones, Robert W.: *Sonata for Worship No. 2*, Delaware Water Gap, Shawnee Press. *Sonata for Worship No. 3*, Delaware Water Gap, Shawnee Press. *Toccata on "St. Denio,"* Oceanside, Boosey & Hawkes. ORG. & TAPE: *Sonata for Worship No. 6* (1971), New York, H. Flammer.

Kay, Ulysses Simpson: *Two Meditations*, New York, H. W. Gray

Kohs, Ellis B: *Capriccio* (1948), New York, Mercury Music. 3 *Chorale Variations on Hebrew Hymns*, New York, Mercury Music, 1953. ORG. & INSTRUMENTS: *Passacaglia for organ and strings* (1946), H.W. Gray, 1951.

Krapf, Gerhard: Major publishers are Concordia (St. Louis) and Augsburg (Minneapolis). *All Praise to Thee, Eternal God*, Augs., 1966. *Chorale Prelude on "Ah, Holy Jesus,"* Conc. *Chorale Partita on "Lord Jesus Christ, with Us Abide,"* Conc. *Christmas Sonata da Chiesa*, Glen Rock, J. Fischer. *Come, Your Hearts and Voices Raising*, Augs. *Dear Christians One and All, Rejoice*, Augs., 1970. *Little Christmas Pastorale* (for piano or organ, 4 hands), Augs. *Little Organ Psalter*, New York, C. Fischer. *Partita: Die Guldne Sonne*, Springfield (Ohio), Chantry Press. *Partita: Ein Lämmlein geht*, Conc., 1970. *Partita on "Lobe den Herren,"* Conc., 1965. *Partita on "Mit Freuden Zart,"* Conc., 1965. *Partita on "Wie schon leuchtet,"* Conc. *Partita on "Wachet* auf," Conc. *Reformation Suite,* Conc. *Saviour of the Nations, Come,* Augs. *Sonata I: "Historia Nativitas,"* Conc. *Second Organ Sonata: Thanksgiving,* Glen Rock, J. Fischer. *Third Organ Sonata on Morning Chorales, New York* H.W. Gray. *Totentanz,* Nashville, Abingdon. *Trumpet Tune,* Glen Rock, J. Fischer, 1962. *Various Hymn Settings,* Opa-Locka, Kalmus.

Lemare, Edwin Henry: Of works still available, H.W. Gray is the major publisher (New York). *Andantino in D-flat,* London, Novello. *Concert Gavotte,* HWG. *Dream Frolic,* HWG. *Dream Song,* HWG. *Easter Morn,* HWG. *Folk Song,* HWG. *Inspiration,* HWG. *October Serenade,* HWG. *Romance Triste (Marche funèbre),* HWG. *Second Romance in D-Flat,* HWG. *Twelve Short Pieces,* HWG. *Victory March,* HWG. Numerous other publications by H.W. Gray, Schott, Th. Presser, G. Schirmer, A. P. Schmidt and J. Fischer now out of print. ORG. & INSTRUMENTS: *Caprice orientale* for organ and orchestra, London, Novello, out of print. *Symphonie No. 2* (D Min.), for organ and orchestra, London, Novello, out of print.

Lenel, Ludwig: Publications by Concordia (St. Louis), unless indicated otherwise. *Fantasy on "In the Midst of Earthly Life." Four Organ Chorales,* 1951. *Prelude to the Quempas Carol,* Springfield (Ohio), Chantry Press. *Three Chorale Fantasies on Pre-Reformation Hymns,* 1958. *Two pieces for Organ Based on Ancient Church Melodies.*

Lockwood, Norman: *Fantasy for Reformation Sunday,* Mt. Vernon (New York), Roy Anderson, publisher, 1963. *Processional Voluntary,* Waterloo Music Co. (thru Associated Music Publishers). ORG. & INSTRUMENTS: *Concerto for Organ and Brasses* (2 trpts, 2 trbns), New York, Associated Music Publishers, 1953.

Luening, Otto: *Choral Phantasy for Organ* (1922), New York, American Composers' Alliance. *Choral Vorspiel zu "Christus der ist mein Leben."* (1918), New York, American Composers' Alliance. *Fantasia* (1929), New York, C.F. Peters, 1963. *Fugue and Chorale Fantasy,* Cincinnati, World Library of Music, 1973. *Organ Piece* (1916), New York, American Composers' Alliance.

Maekelberghe, August: Publisher is H. W. Gray (New York), unless indicated otherwise. *De Profundis Clamavi,* 1946. *Fantasia,* Glen Rock, J .Fischer. *Flandria Variations. A Flemish Prayer. Impromptu Etude,* New York, Associated Music Publishers. *Improvisation on "Puer natus est." Let All Mortal Flesh Keep Silence. Night Soliloquy. Plainsong Prelude. Three Hymn Preludes. Toccata. Melody in Blue and Fugue,* Melville, Belwin-Mills, *Triptych.*

Manz, Paul: *Ten Chorale Improvisations,* 6 sets to-date, St. Louis, Concordia. Set I: op. 5, 1962. Set II: op. 7, 1964. Set III: op. 9, 1970. Set IV: op. 10, 1970. Set V: op. 14. Set VI: op. 16. *Ten Short Intonations on Well-known Hymns,* op. 11, Minneapolis, Augsburg, 1970. *Partita on "St. Anne,"* St. Louis, Concordia. ORG. & INSTRUMENTS: *How Lovely Shines the Morning Star,* for oboe and organ, St. Louis, Concordia.

Middelschulte, Wilhelm: *Chromatische Fantasie und Fuge,* Leipzig, Kahnt. *Kanon und Fuge über den Choral "Vater unser,"* Leipzig, Leuckart. *Perpetuum Mobile,* New York/Frankfurt, C. F. Peters. The same, ed. V. Fox, New York, H.W. Gray. *Tokkata über den Choral ein feste Burg,* Leipzig, Leuckart. ORG. & INSTRUMENTS: *Kanonische Fantasie über B-A-C-H und Fuge über 4 Themen von J.S. Bach,* for organ and orchestra, Leipzig, Kahnt. *Konzert über ein Thema von J. S. Bach,* for organ and orchestra, Leipzig, Kahnt.

Moore, Douglas: *Dirge (Passacaglia)* (1939), New York, H.W. Gray, 1941.

Near, Gerald: Publishers are H. W. Gray (New York) and Augsburg (Minneapolis). *Fantasy,* HWG. *Passacaglia,* Augs. 1966. *Preludes on Four Hymn Tunes,* Augs., 1969. *Prelude on Three Hymn Tunes, Augs.,* 1967. *Postlude on "St. Dunstan's,"* Augs., 1968. *Roulade,* Augs., 1965. *Suite,* HWG, 1966. *Toccata,* Augs., 1971. *A Triptych of Fugues,* Augs., 1968. *A Wedding Processional,* HWG.

Newman, Anthony: *Barricades,* New York, G. Schirmer. *Bhajeb,* New York, G. Schirmer. 1974. *Fantasy on La, Fa, Fis* (1969), Boston, McLaughlin &

Reilly. *Fugue on the Kyrie,* Boston, McLaughlin & Reilly.

Noble, T. Tertius: *Fifty Free Organ Accompaniments to W e l l - K n o w n Hymns,* Melville, Belwin-Mills. *Free Organ Accompaniments to 100 Well-Known Hymn Tunes,* Melville, Belwin-Mills. *Two Traditional Hebrew Melodies,* New York, H. W. Gray. *Pastoral Prelude on a Chinese Christmas Carol,* New York, H.W. Gray. *Triumphal March,* New York, H.W. Gray. Numerous other publications by G. Schirmer, Galaxy, A. P. Schmidt, Oxford University Press, Augener, and Stainer & Bell, most of which are out of print.

Paine, John Knowles: *The Complete Works of John Knowles Paine,* ed. Leupold, New York, McAfee Music Co. Other publications by Oliver Ditson, A. P. Schmidt, etc., out of print.

Parker, Horatio: *Introduction and Fugue in E Minor,* Minneapolis, Augsburg, 1974. *Jerusalem,* London, J. B. Cramer & Co. *Quick March* (Duet for Two Organists), Carol Stream (Ill.), Hope Publishing Co. Numerous other publications by G. Schirmer and Novello, now out of print. ORG. & INSTRUMENTS: *Concerto* for organ and orchestra, op. 55, Novello, 1903. A new edition of this Concerto, edited by Robert Hart Baker, is also available. It can be rented from the editor, who can be reached at Yale University.

Perera, Ronald: *Reverberations,* Boston, E. C. Schirmer (Ione Press), 1972.

Persichetti, Vincent: Publisher is Elkan-Vogel (Bryn Mawr). *Chorale Prelude: Drop, Drop Slow Tears,* op 104, 1968. *Do Not Go Gentle,* for pedals alone, 1975. *Fantasy on the Hymn "Holy, Holy, Holy." Parable* (1971). *Shimah B'koli* (Psalm 130), op. 89, (1962), 1963. *Sonata* (1960), 1961. *Sonatine,* for pedals alone, op. 11 (1940), 1955.

Pinkham, Daniel: Publisher is E. C. Schirmer (Ione Press, Boston), unless indicated otherwise. *Canon* (1955) New York, American Composers' Alliance. *Five Voluntaries for Manuals. Four Short Pieces for Manuals. Pastorale on "The Morning Star,"* New York, Galaxy. *Prelude and Chaconne* (1953), New York, American Composers' Alliance. *A Prophecy,* 1971. *Prothalamion* (1955), New York, American Composers' Alliance. *Revelations* (1955) 1965. *Sonata No.* 1 (1944), New York, American Composers' Alliance. *Sonata No.* 2 (1961), New York, American Composers' Alliance. ORG. & INSTRUMENTS/TAPE: *"And The Angel Said",* for Organ and Tape. *Concertante* for organ, brass and percussion, New York, C. F. Peters. *Concertante* for organ, celesta, and percussion, New York, C. F. Peters. *Concertante* for guitar, harpsichord, organ, and percussion, New York, C. F. Peters, rental only. *Concertino* for organ and strings (1947), New York, American Composers' Alliance. *For Evening Draws On,* for English horn, organ and tape. *Gloria,* for organ and brass, Northeaston (Mass), Robert King Music Co. *Liturgies,* for organ, timpani, and tape. *Mourn For The Eclipse of His Light,* for organ, violin and tape. *The Other Voices of the Trumpet,* for organ, trumpet and tape, 1972. *Sonata No.* 1 *for Organ and Strings* (1943), 1964. *Sonata No.* 2 *for Organ & Strings* (1954). *Sonata for two oboes and organ,* New York, C. F. Peters. *Sonata for organ & brass* (1947), New York, American Composers' Alliance. *See That Ye Love One Another,* for organ, and tape. *Shepherds' Symphony,* for 1 or more melody instruments, organ, tape, and optional percussion. *Toccatas for the Vault of Heaven,* for organ and tape, 1972. *Trumpet Voluntary* (1955), New York, American Composers' Alliance. *Variations* for oboe and organ, New York, C. F. Peters. *When the Morning Stars Sang Together,* for organ and tape, 1972. TWO ORGANS: *Signs in the Sun,* New York, C. F. Peters, rental.

Pisk, Paul Amadeus: Publications by American Composers' Alliance (New York), unless otherwise indicated. *Aria Variata. Capriccio. Chorale-Fantasy on "When I Survey the Wondrous Cross." Chorale Prelude: Hast Thou Hidden Thy Face, Jesus (California Organist #47),* Los Angeles, Avant Music. *Improvisation on an American Folk Melody* (1958). *Pastorale. Phantasy on Mexican Folk Songs* (1940). *Prelude, Adagio and Canzona. Prelude, Fugue and Hymn. Processional. Six Choral Preludes for Organ, Op.* 41 (1938). *Sonata,* op. 46 (1940). *Suite in Four Movements, op.* 64.

Piston, Walter: *Chromatic Study on the Name of B-A-C-H* (1940), New

York, H. W. Gray, 1941. ORG. & IN-STRUMENTS: *Partita* for organ, violin and viola (1944), New York, Associated Music Publishers, 1951. *Prelude and Allegro* for organ and strings (1943), New York, Arrow Music press, 1944.

Porter, William Quincy: *Canon and Fugue* (1941), New York H. W. Gray, 1941. *Toccata, Andante and Finale* (1930), New York, H. W. Gray, 1966. *Wedding Prelude and March*, New York, H. W. Gray. ORG. & INSTRUMENTS: *Fantasy on a Pastorale Theme* for organ and strings (1943), New York, American Composers' Alliance.

Powell, Robert: Publisher is Abingdon (Nashville) unless otherwise indicated. *Carol Prelude on "The Snow Lay on the Ground"* (*California Organist* #17), Los Angeles, Avant Music, 1964. *Chorale Prelude on "Angelus." Chorale Prelude on "Bedford." Christmas Organ Fest* (7 carol arrangements), New York, E. B. Marks. *Elegy. Fantasy on "Victimae Paschali." Fifteen Organ Pieces*, Oceanside, Boosey & Hawkes. *Five Short Voluntaries*, Delaware Water Gap, Shawnee Press. *Four Preludes on Early American Tunes. Four Psalm Preludes*, in 2 sets (1962) *Introduction and Passacaglia. Meditation Upon the Passion of Our Lord. Sacred Heart Suite. Service Sonata*, Delaware Water Gap, Shawnee Press. *Six Easter Preludes. Three Miniatures for Organ. Trumpet Tunes and Ayres*, New York, E. B. Marks. *Two Christmas Preludes.*

Read, Gardner: Publications by H. W. Gray (New York), if not indicated otherwise. *Chorale-Fantasia on "Good King Wenceslas." Eight Preludes on Old Southern Hymns* (1951), op. 90, 1952. *Elegiac Aria*, 1969. *Little Pastorale*, New York, Galaxy. *Meditation on "Jesu, meine Freude." Passacaglia and Fugue*, op. 34 (1936), Melville, Belwin-Mills. *Quiet Music*, op. 65a, Nashville, Abingdon. *Six Preludes on Old Southern Hymns*, op. 112. *Suite for Organ*, New York, Transcontinental. *Variations on a Chromatic Ground* (1964), Boston, McLaughlin & Reilly. ORG. & INSTRUMENTS: *Christmas Pastorale*, for organ and violin, New York, Seesaw Music Corp. *De Profundis*, for organ and French horn (1943), New York, Mills/MCA. *Sinfonia da chiesa* (1969) for organ and brass, New York, C. F. Peters.

Riegger, Wallingford: *Canon and Fugue*, op. 33, New York, H. Flammer, 1954. ORG. & INSTRUMENTS: *Fantasy and Fugue* for orchestra and organ (1930/31), New York, American Composers' Alliance.

Roberts, Myron: Publisher is H. W. Gray (New York). *Carillon. Homage to Perotin*, 1956. *Improvisation on the Agincourt Hymn*, 1964. *Improvisation on "God Rest You Merry,"* 1968. *Im Memoriam*, 1949. *Litany*, 1958. *Nova*, 1973. *Pastorale and Aviary*, 1969. *Prelude and Trumpetings*, 1961. *Sarabande*. ORG. & INSTRUMENTS: *Five*, for organ and marimba, New York, Carl Fischer.

Rohlig, Harald: Major publishers are Abingdon Press (Nashville) and Concordia (St. Louis). *Fifteen Preludes*, A. P. *Fifty-five Hymn Intonations A.P. Prelude on "Christ Is Arisen"*, A.P. *Sonata I*, A. P. *Ten Pieces for Organ* A.P. *Thirty New Settings of Familiar Hymns*, A.P. ORG. & INSTRUMENTS: *Concertino* for organ and orch. (strings and 2 trpts), Conc. *Eight Intradas and Chorales* for organ and trumpet, conc. *Fantasy on "O Come All Ye Faithful,"* A.P. *Good Christian Men, Rejoice*, for org., flute, 3 trpts, A.P., 1963. *A Little Shepherd Music*, for organ and flute (or recorder), Conc., 1959. *Now Thank We All Our God*, for 3 trpts and organ, A. P. *Variations on Es kommt ein Schiff geladen,"* Conc. Additional publications by Concordia, Augsburg and Abingdon.

Rorem, Ned: *Pastorale*, New York, Southern Music Publishing Co., 1953.

Ross, William James: *The Way from Earth*, New York, H. W. Gray (Belwin-Mills), 1974.

Schwartz, Elliott: *Five Mobiles* for Flute, Organ, Harpsichord and Tape, Chapel Hill, Hinshaw Music Inc. *Prisms*, for organ and tape, Boston, E. C. Schirmer. *Cycles* and *Gongs* for organ, trumpet, and tape, (1975), Chapel Hill, Hinshaw Music Inc.

Selby, William: *A Lesson for the Organ*, ed. Biggs, New York, Associated Music Publishers. *Two Voluntaries for Organ*, ed. Pinkham, Boston, E. C. Schirmer.

Sessions, Roger: *Chorale No.* 1, New

York, H. W. Gray, 1941, *Three Chorale Preludes,* New York, E. B. Marks, 1934.

Shackelford, Rudy: *Canonic Variations: Vom Himmel hoch,* New York, H. W. Gray (Belwin-Mills), 1975. *Nine Aphorisms,* Chapel Hill, Hinshaw Music. *Sonata,* Chapel Hill, Hinshaw. *Trio Sonata* 1970, Oceanside, Boosey & Hawkes.

Smith, Russell: *Three Chorale Preludes,* New York, H. W. Gray 1965.

Smith, Stuart: *Gifts,* for organ and 2 melody instruments, New York, H. W. Gray (Belwin-Mills). *Two Makes Three* for organ and percussion, New York, H. W. Gray (Belwin-Mills) 1974. *One for Two,* for organ and saxophone, New York, Seesaw. *To All of Those* (1-2 organs), New York, Seesaw.

Sowerby, Leo: Publisher is H. W. Gray (New York), unless otherwise indicated. *Advent to Whitsuntide,* vol. IV, London, Hinrichsen. *Arioso,* 1942. *Behold, O God Our Defender,* 1964. *Bright, Blithe, and Brisk. Canon, Chacony and Fugue,* 1951. *Carillon,* 1920. *Chorale Prelude on a Calvinist Hymn,* Boston, Boston Music Co. 1925. *Chorale Prelude on a Palestrina Fragment,* 1919. *Chorale Prelude on "Palisades,"* 1950. *City of God,* 1965. *Comes Autumn Time,* Boston, Boston Music Co. 1916. *Fanfare,* 1937. *For We Are Laborers Together with God,* 1950. *Interlude* (from *Forsaken of Man*), 1950. *Holiday Trumpets,* London, Novello. *Joyous March,* 1919. *Jubilee,* 1959. *Madrigal,* 1920. *Meditations on Communion Hymns,* 1942 *Pageant,* 1932. *Pageant of Autumn,* 1938. *Passacaglia,* 1973. *Postludium super "Benedictus Es, Domine." Praeludium super "Benedictus sit Deus Pater." Prelude on the Benediction "Ite Missa Est,"* Boston, Boston Music Co., 1916. *Prelude on "Non Nobis, Domine." Psalm* 136, 1965. *Prelude on "The King's Majesty,"* 1945. *Rejoice, Ye Pure in Heart,* 1913. *Requiescat in Pace,* 1926. *Rhapsody* (1949). *Sinfonia Brevis,* 1966. *Sonatina,* 1947. *Suite. Symphony in G,* London, Oxford University Press, 1932. *Ten Preludes on Hymn Tunes,* 1956. *Three Pieces (Preludes-Interludes-Postludes,* vol. IV), London, Hinrichsen. *Toccata,* 1941. *Two Sketches. The Snow Lay on the Ground. A Wedding Processional. Whimsical Variations,* 1952. ORG & INSTRUMENTS: *Ballade,* for org., clarinet, vln, vla, Eng. horn, 1948. *Classic Concerto* for org. &

strings, 1944, rental. Also exists in reduction for piano and organ. *Concert Piece,* for org. & orch., rental. Also in reduction for piano and organ. *Concerto in C Major,* for org. & orch., 1937, rental. *Dialog,* for organ and piano. *Fantasy* for trpt. & organ, 1964. *Festival Musick,* for org., 2 trpts, 2 trbns, timpani, 1955. *Medieval Poem,* for org., and orch. Also in reduction for piano and organ. *Poem for viola* (or violin) and org., 1942.

Stevens, Halsey: *Improvisation on "Divinum Mysterium,"* New York, Peer International Corp., 1955. *Three Short Preludes for Organ,* New York, Peer International Corp., 1959. *Three Pieces,* Editio Helios (thru M. Foster Music Co., Champaign, Ill.). *Soliloquy for Organ,* Editio Helios.

Stewart, Richard: *Prelude for Organ and Tape,* New York, H.W. Gray (Belwin-Mills), 1972.

Stout, Alan: Publisher is American Composers' Alliance (New York), except where indicated otherwise. *Adagio and Toccata,* op. 13. *Communio,* op 30a. *Eight Organ Chorales,* Minneapolis, Augsburg. 1969. *Epilogue,* op. 82. *Forspil over "O Gud vors Lands." Pieta,* op. 7. *Prelude,* op. 16. *Ricercare and Aria,* op. 43a. *Sonata,* op. 62, no. 5. *Study in Densities and Durations,* New York, C.F. Peters. *Three Intonations,* op 15, no. 2. *Three Organ Chorales,* Minneapolis, Augsburg, 1971. *Two Pieces,* op. 6. ORG. & INSTRUMENTS: *Serenity* for cello (bassoon) and organ, New York, C. F. Peters, 1967.

Thompson, Randall: *Twenty Chorale-Preludes, Four Inventions and a Fugue,* Boston, E. C. Schirmer.

Thomson, Virgil: *Fanfare,* (1921), New York, H. W. Gray. *Pange Lingua* (1962), New York, G. Schirmer, 1962. *Passacaglia* (1922), New York, G. Schirmer. *Pastorale on a Christmas Plainsong* (1922), New York H. W. Gray, 1942. *Variations on Sunday School Tunes* (1926-30), New York, H. W. Gray, 1955. Each set of variations is available separately: 1) Come, Ye Disconsolate; 2) There's Not a Friend Like the Lowly Jesus; 3) Will There Be Any Stars in My Crown; 4) Shall We Gather at the River.

Titcomb, Everett: Major publishers are H. W. Gray (New York), Carl Fisher

(New York) , and B. F. Wood (Boston) . *Advent and Christmas.* C.F. *Aspiration,* HWG. *Benedicta Tu,* HWG. *Elegy,* HWG. *Festive Flutes* (Theme from "Vocem Jucunditatis") , HWG, 1958. *Four Improvisations on Gregorian Themes* ("Puer natus est"; "Alleluia nostra"; "Gaudeamus:" "Cibavit eos") , New York, Mills Music, (through Belwin-Mills) . *Hosanna,* through Belwin-Mills. *Improvisation on the Eighth-Psalm Tone,* HWG. *Improvisation on "Oriel,"* C. F., 1963, *Improvisation-Toccata on "Tonus peregrinus,"* New York, H. Flammer. *Pastorale,* HWG. *Pentecost,* B.F.W. *Prelude on "Terry,"* Boston, McLaughlin & Reilly. *Requiem,* HWG. *Rhapsody on Gregorian Motifs,* HWG. *Sortie,* C.F. *Suite in E,* HWG. *Three Short Pieces,* New York, H. Flammer. *Three Short Pieces on Familiar Gregorian Melodies* ("Credo in Unum Deum;" "Regina Coeli"; "Vexilla Regis") , B.F.W., 1940. *Three Short Postludes,* C.F. *Toccata on "Salve Regina,"* HWG. *Two Communions* ("Adoro te"; "Ave verum") , B.F.W., 1943. *Voluntary on "Crimond,"* HWG. *Wedding Day: Improvisation on "O Perfect Love,"* HWG, 1961. *Wedding Processional,* Nashville, Abingdon.

Toensing, Richard: *Sounds and Changes II,* New York, H. W. Gray (Belwin-Mills) , 1975.

Wolff, Christian: *For* 1, 2 *or* 3 *People,* New York, C. F. Peters.

Wright, Searle: *Carol-Prelude on "Greensleeves,"* New York, H. W. Gray, 1954. *Introduction, Passacaglia and Fugue,* New York, H. W. Gray, 1962. *Lyric Rhapsody,* New York, H. W. Gray. *Prelude on "Brother James' Air,"* London Oxford University Press, 1958. ORG. & INSTRUMENTS: *Fantasy on "Wareham,"* for org., 3 trpts, 3 trbns, timpani and cymbals, with optional choral finale, New York, H. W. Gray.

Wuensch, Gerhard: *Aria (California Organist #13)* , Los Angeles, Avant Music. *Sonata breve (California Organist #35)* , Los Angeles, Avant Music. *Toccata piccola (California Organist #4)* , Los Angeles, Avant Music. ORG. & INSTRUMENTS: *Suite for Trumpet & Organ,* Los Angeles, Western International Music.

Wyton, Alec: Major publishers are H.

W. Gray (New York) and H. Flammer. *Christ in the Wilderness,* HWG. *Dialogue: "Praise Him in the Sound of the Trumpet,"* New York, Mercury Music. *Dithyramb,* HWG, 1960. *Fanfare,* HWG, 1956. *Fanfare-Improvisation on "Azmon,"* Nashville, Abingdon. *Fanfare on "Hark, the Herald Angels Sing,"* H. F. *Fanfare on "The Strife Is O'er,* H. F. *Flourish,* New York, Mercury Music. *In Praise of Merbecke* (Suite) , HWG, 1957. *A Little Christian Year,* New York, Carl Fischer, 1964. *March on "St. Patrick's Breastplate,"* H.F. *Music for Lent,* H. F. *Nativity Suite,* H.F. *Prelude on "Come, Holy Spirit,"* H. F. *Preludes on Contemporary Hymns,* Minneapolis, Augsburg. *Prelude on "Forty Days and Forty Nights,"* H.F. *Prelude on "O Come, O Come, Emmanuel,"* H.F. *Preludes, Fanfares and a March for The Liturgical Year,* H.F. *Preludes for "Christian Praise,"* Dayton, Sacred Music Press. *Preludes for Saints and Sinners,* Carol Stream (Ill.) , Hope Publishing Co. *Resurrection Suite,* H.F. *Variants on Earth and All Stars,* Minneapolis, Augsburg. ORG. & INSTRUMENTS: *Concert Piece* for organ and seven untuned percussion instruments, HWG. *Elegy,* for organ and solo instrument (trpt., clarinet, oboe, soprano vocalist) , Cincinnati, World Library of Sacred Music.

Yon, Pietro: Major publisher is J. Fischer (Glen Rock) . *Canto Elegiac,* New York, Galaxy. *Christ Triumphant,* J.F. *Gesu Bambino* (Pastorale) , J.F. *Humoresque,* J.F. *Hymn of Glory,* J.F. *Sonata No.* 1, New York, G. Schirmer. *Sonata No.* 2 (Cromatica) , J.F., 1917. *Sonata No.* 3 (Romantic) , J.F., 1922. Additional publications by G. Schirmer, J. Fischer, and McLaughlin & Reilly. ORG. & INSTRUMENTS: *Concerto Gregoriano,* for organ and orchestra, J.F.

Collections

American Organ Music, 2 vols., ed. Hart, Dayton, Lorenz Publishing Co. Vol. I: Works by S.B. Whitney, J.H. Brewer, L. Sowerby, H. Parker, Jas. H. Rogers, A. Foote, E.E. Truette, G. Edmundson, P. Yon, E. Titcomb, C. Eddy. Vol. II: Works by S. Bingham, Jos. Clokey, Van Denman Thompson, S.E. Rogers, R. Elmore, D. Wehr, D. Johnson, R. Purvis, G. Young, R. Powell, C.A. Peloquin, D. Wood, G. M. Martin.

The Bicentennial Collection of American Keyboard Music, ed. E. Gold, New York, McAfee Music Corp. More piano than organ music, this collection contains works by: Alex. Reinagle, Jas. Hewitt, Fr. Damish, A. Ph. Heinrich, Chas. Grove, S.C. Foster, H.A. Wollenhaupt, L. M. Gottschalk, R. Hoffman, Fr. Brandeis, Geo. W. Chadwick, Edw. McDowell, E. Nevin, H. Loomis, Mrs. H.H.A. Beach, S. Joplin, A. Farwell.

The California Organist, 53 volumes (a publication of the Los Angeles AGO chapters), Los Angeles, Avant Music, 1963—. Vol. 1: Donald Johns, *3 Chorale Preludes,* 1963. 2: Wm. Schmidt, *Two White Spirituals,* 1963. 3: Orpha O'chse and Clar. Mader, *Two Monograms,* 1963. 4: Gerhard Wuensch, *Toccata piccola,* 1963. 5: Geo. Fr. McKay, *Lament for Absalom,* 1963. 6: Henri Lazarof. *Largo,* 1963. : Wm. G. Still, *Elegy,* 1963. 8: Don Stone, *Interlude on "Veni Emmanuel"* and *Procession,* 1963. 9: Clifford Vaughn, *Hymn Prelude on Billings' "When Jesus Wept,"* 1964. 10: Kenneth Lowenberg, *Chorale Prelude on "St. Anne,"* 1964. 11: Rob't Manookin, *Hymn Prelude on "Dennis,"* 1964. 12. Lowndes Maury, *Chorale Aria,* 1964. 13: Gerhard Wuensch, *Aria,* 1964. 14: Geo. Fr. McKay, *Sonata Mistica,* 1964. 15: Rayner Brown. *Liturgical Fugue,* 1964. 16: Tikey Zes, *Processional,* 1964. 17: Robert. J. Powell, *Carol Prelude on "The Snow Lay on the Ground,* 1964. 18: Clar. Mader, *Obbligato for Flutes on an Advent Melody,* 1964. 19: Donald Johns, *Partita on a Passion Chorale,* 1964. 20: Charles Shatto, *Poem,* 1965. 21: Wm. Schmidt, *Phantasy on an American Spiritual,* 1965. 22: Norberto Guinaldo, *Prelude for the Passion of the Lord,* 1965. 23: Harold Owen, *Two Settings of "Picardy,"* 1965. 24: John Biggs, *Aria and Toccata,* 1965. 25: Gilbert M. Martin, *Intercession,* 1965. 26: Matt Doran, *Pastorale,* 1965. 27: Henri Lazarof, *Lamenti,* 1965. 28: Donald Johns, *3 Meditations on the "Nunc Dimittis,"* 1965. 29: Clifford Vaughn, *Service Piece.* 30: Michael E. Young, *Prelude and Fugue in F Major.* 31: Rayner Brown, *Sonatina 18.* 32: C. Griffith Bratt, *Prelude, Little Fugue and Air.* 33: Alma Oncley, *Two Chorale Preludes.* 34: Michael Young. *Prelude and Fugue.* 35: Gerhard Wuensch, *Sonata Breve.* 36: Clar. Mader, Orpha Ochse, Donald Johns, R. Brown, G. Wuensch — *Second Prelude Book.* 37: Kent Smith, *Toccata.* 38: Lucrecia R.

Kasilag, *Evocative.* 39: N. Guinaldo, *Partita.* 40: Owen, *Ouverture dans le styl francais.* 41: Matthews, *Two Christmas Preludes.* 42: Michael Young, *Prelude and Fugue No. 3.* 43: Arthur Hall, *Toccata on C-sharp.* 44: Johns, *Organ Mass.* 45: Clifford Vaughn, *Invocation.* 46: Rayner Brown, *Fugue and Prelude.* 47: Paul Pisk, *Hast Thou Hidden Thy Face, Jesus.* 48: *Pedal Book,* 1967. 49: Jon Polifrone, *Prelude on "In God and Love We Trust."* 50: Geo. Fr. McKay, *A Wedding Processional.* 51: Paul Chihara, *Prelude and Motet on "Veni Domine."* 52: Boris Pillin, *Fugue.* 53: N. Guinaldo, *Ricercare.*

A Century of American Organ Music, 1776-1876, 2 vols., ed. Owen, New York, McAfee Music Corp., 1975. Contents of vol. I: 24 pieces by J. Bremner, Wm. Selby, J. Linley, J.C. Moller, R. Taylor, B. Carr, Th. Lord, B. Cross, Chas. Zeuner, J.C. Beckel, L.H. Southard, J. Zundel, S. Jackson, H.S. Cutler, W.E. Thayer, D. Buck, Geo. W. Chadwick, H. C. Eddy. Vol. II: 23 pieces by Wm. Selby, Benj. Carr, F. Linley, Ch. Hommann, Ch. Zeuner, J. Geo. Schetky, Geo. J. Webb, Jas. C. Beckel, M. Emilio, J. Zundel, S.P. Tuckerman, Geo. W. Morgan, L. Southard, W.E. Thayer, D. Buck, Wm. H. Clarke, S.B. Whitney, A. Foote.

19th Century American Organ Music, ed. Woomer/Beck, Cleveland, the AGO Chapter, 1975. Contents: J.K. Paine, *Concert Variations on the "Austrian Hymn"*; D. Buck, *Concert Variations on the "Star-Spangled Banner"*; plus works by H. Parker, Geo. Chadwick, A. Whiting, A. Wm Foote, Geo. Fr. Bristow.

Contemporary Organ Series, ed. Strickland/Drinkwater, New York, H.W. Gray (now Belwin-Mills), 1941—. Over 50 volumes, a continuing series. 1: Leo Sowerby, *Toccata,* 1941. 2: Roger Sessions, *Chorale No. 1,* 1941. 3: Walter Piston, *Chromatic Study on the Name of Bach,* 1941. 4: Douglas Moore, *Dirge* (Passacaglia), 1941. 5: Bernard Wagenaar, *Eclogue,* 1941. 6: Frederick Jacobi, *Prelude,* 1941. 7: Aaron Copland, *Episode,* 1941. 8: Philip James, *Pantomine,* 1941. 9: Darius Milhaud. *Pastorale,* 1942. 10: Ernst Krenek, *Sonata,* 1942. 11: Seth Bingham, *Pastorale from "Memories of France."* 12: Quincy Porter, *Canon and Fugue.* 13: Arnold Schoenberg, *Variations on a Recitative,* 1947. 14: Virgil Thomson, *Pastorale on a Christmas Plainsong*, 1942. 15: Mrs. H.H.A. Beach, *Prelude on an Old Folk Tune*, 1943. 16: Henry Cowell, *Processional*, 1944. 17: Cecil Effinger, *Prelude and Fugue*, 1946. 18: Richard Donovan, *Paignion*. 19: Gail Kubik, *Quiet Piece*, 1948. 20: Richard Arnell, *Baroque Prelude and Fantasia*, 1948. 21: Mary Howe, *Elegy*, 1948. 22: Homer Keller, *Fantasy and Fugue*, 1949. 23: Darius Milhaud, *Sonata*, 1950. 24: Frederick Jacobi, *Three Quiet Preludes*, 1950. 25: Leo Sowerby, *Whimsical Variations*, 1952. 26: Ellis B. Kohs, *Passacaglia* (organ and piano reduction), 1951. 27: Ulysses Kay, *Two Meditations*, 1951. 28: Maria Castelnuovo-Tedesco, *Fanfare*, 1953. 29: John J. Becker, *Fantasia Tragica*, 1962. 30: Avery Claflin, *Three Pieces*, 1965. 31: Anthony Milner, *Fugue for Advent*, 1965. 32: Russell Smith, *Three Chorale Preludes*, 1965. 33: James H. Case, *Ye Men of Galilee*, 1966. 34: (not published). 35: Quincy Porter, *Toccata, Andante and Finale*, 1966. 36. E. Bacon, *Spirits and Places*. 37: Erkki Salmenhaara, *Prelude, Interlude and Postlude*, 1971. 38: Richard Stewart, *Prelude for Organ and Tape*, 1972. 39: Gerald Near, *Fantasy*, 1972. 40: Robert Moevs, *Prelude: BACH—Es ist genug*, 1972. 41: Myron Roberts, *Nova*, 1973. 42: Leo Sowerby, *Passacaglia*, 1973. 43: Joseph Goodman, *Two Dialogues for Organ and Tape*, 1973. 44: Herbert Bielawa, *Quodlibet SF42569* for organ and tape, 1974. 45: Thomas Janson, *Celestial Autumn*, 1974. 46: Stuart Smith, *Two Makes Three*, for organ and percussion, 1974. 47: James Callahan, *Variations for Organ*, 1974. 48: Paul Sifler, *The Despair and Agony of Dachau*, 1975. 49: Richard Toensing, *Sounds and Changes II*, 1975. 50: Rudy Shackleford, *Canonic Variations: Vom Himmel hoch*, 1975. 51: Wm. James Ross, *The Way from Earth*, 1975. 52: Graham George, *Small Chaconne and Fugue*, 1976.

Contemporary Organ Series, ed. R. Anderson, Chapel Hill, Hinshaw Music. Contains the following separate items. Milton Gill: *Processional*. Adolphus Hailstork: *Suite for Organ*. David Isele: *Prologue and Conjugation; Recitative, Interlogue and Torque; Modentum; Heraldings; Zorgandum* (Organ duet); *Macedon Fanfares*. Gerald Kemner: *First Light and the Quiet Voice; Quotations* for organist, assistant and narrator. Rudolph Kremer: *Sonata*. Elliott Schwartz: *Five Mobiles*, for flute, organ,

harpsichord, and tape; *Cycles and Gongs*, for organ, B♭ trpt, and tape. Rudy Shackelford: *Sonata; Nine Aphorisms*. Randall Snyder: *Florilegium*. Newton Strandberg: *Sanna Sanna Hosanna*. James Tallis: *Sonatina*. Louis White: *Toccata on "London Tune."* Richard Wienhorst: *Reflection and Celebration*.

Early American Compositions for Organ (18th and 19th centuries), ed. and arr. by J. Spong, Nashville, Abingdon, 1968. Contains works by J. Bremner, W. Billings, D. Read, B. Carr, J. Hewitt, R. Atwell, L. Mason, G. Whiting.

A Galaxy of Hymn-Tune Preludes, New York, Galaxy. A collection of works by 20th c. composers: J. Blackburn, R. Vaughn Williams, T.T. Noble, G. Edmundson, Dom G. Brusey, R. Groves, S. Bingham, Ch. Wood, I. Fischer, G. Young, D. Pinkham, G. Edmundson, S.E. Saxton.

Mixture IV, New York, H. Flammer, 1970. Contains short compositions by R. Elmore, R. Purvis, A Wyton, and G. Young.

The Modern Anthology, in 2 parts, ed. by D. McK. Williams, New York, H.W. Gray. Part. I: Works by E.S. Barnes, Bingham, Clokey, Diggle, Edmundson, Friedell, Howells, Langlais, Palmer, Rowley, Sowerby, Thiman, Weitz, Yon. Part 2: Baumgartner, Candlyn, Dickinson, Dupré, Elmore, Howells, P. Hames, Noble, Palmer, Peeters, Sowerby, Titcomb, Willan.

Our American Heritage, 2 vols., ed. & arr. by J. Spong, Buchanan (Michigan), Electro-Voice, Inc. (Agent: Bradley Music Co.), 1967. Vol. I: Works by American composers born in the 18th c. — Selby, Moller, Jackson, Billings, Carr, Mason. Vol. II: Works by American composers born in the 19th century— Paine, Foote, Chadwick, Shelley, Whiting, Parker.

NOTES

[1]The ban on organs applied specifically to the church service. The prejudice against organs in private homes was apparently not so intense.
[2]Ochse. *The History of the Organ in the United States*, p.20.
[3]According to Ellinwood (*The History of American Church Music, p.51*), Valton advertised subscriptions for the publication of

these sonatas, but nothing further is known about these works.

[4]Ochse, *op.cit.*, p.45.

[5]Ellinwood, *op.cit.*, p.76ff.

[6]Machlis, *Introduction to Contemporary Music*, p.584.

[7]Their organ works are listed in earlier chapters.

MUSICAL SOURCES

Ex.1. *A Century of American Organ Music*, p.16.

Ex.2. *19th Century American Organ Music*, p.68.

Ex.3. Parker: *Introduction and Fugue in E Minor*, p.1. Copyright 1974 Augsburg Publishing House. Used by permission.

Ex.4. Ives: *Variations on "America,"* p.6. Copyright 1949, Mercury Music Corp. Used by permission.

Ex.5. Delamarter: *The Fountain*, p.1. Used by permission of Belwin-Mills Publ. Corp., Melville, New York.

Ex.6. Piston: *Chromatic Study on the Name B-A-C-H*, p.1. Used by permission of Belwin-Mills Publ. Corp., Melville, New York.

Ex.7. Sessions: *Chorale No.1*, p.3. Used by permission of Belwin-Mills Publ. Corp., Melville, New York.

Ex. 8. Samuel Barber: *Toccata Festiva*, organ and piano reduction score, p. 22.

Copyright 1961 by G. Schirmer, Inc. Used by permission.

Ex.9. Sowerby: *Symphony*, p.46. Reprinted by permission.

Ex. 10. Virgil Thomson: *Pange Lingua*, p. 14. Copyright 1962 by Virgil Thomson. Used by permission.

Ex.11. Berlinski: *The Burning Bush*, pp.4-5. Used by permission of Belwin-Mills Publ. Corp., Melville, New York.

Ex.12. Hovhaness: *Sonata for Trumpet and* p.1. Copyright 1963 by C.F. Peters Corp., 373 Park Avenue South, New York, New York, 10016. Reprint permission granted by the publisher.

Ex.13. Persichetti: *Sonata for Organ*, p.2. Copyright 1961, Elkan-Vogel, Inc. Used by permission.

Ex.14. Pinkham: *The Other Voices of the Trumpet*, pp.16,17. Used by permission.

Ex.15. Stout: *Three Organ Chorales*, p.4. Copyright 1971 Augsburg Publishing House. Used by permission.

Ex. 16. Lenel: *Four Organ Chorales*, p. 12. Copyright 1951 Concordia Publishing House. Reprinted by permission.

Ex.17. Albright: *Organbook* II, p.27. Copyright 1973, Editions Jean Jobert. Theodore Presser Co., sole representative, U.S., Canada and Mexico.

Ex.18. Shackelford: *Canonic Variations: Vom Himmel hoch*, p.4. Used by permission of Belwin-Mills Publ. Corp., Melville, New York.

Addenda

ORGAN MUSIC BEFORE 1500

Buxheimer Orgelbuch, 2 vols., ed. and transcr. by A. Booth, London, Hinrichsen.

Early German Organ Music, ed. Marr, London, Hinrichsen. Contents: works by Ileborgh, Buchner, Finck, and Isaac.

The First Four Centuries of Music for the Organ, 2 vols., ed. J. Klein, New York, Associated Music Publishers, 1948. This anthology contains many early works, but the editing is misleading.

Historical Anthology of Music, I, ed. Davison-Apel, Cambridge, Harvard Univ. Press, 1949.

Keyboard Music of the 14th and 15th Centuries, ed. Apel (*Corpus of Early Keyboard Music,* I), Dallas, American Institute of Musicology, 1963.

Paumann: *Das Locheimer Liederbuch,* ed. and transcr. by Arnold, Wiesbaden, Breitkopf & Härtel. The same works are transcribed in *Music of the Fourteenth and Fifteenth Centuries,* ed. Apel (*CEKM,* I).

Praeambula, ed. A. Reichling, Altötting, Coppenrath. Contents: 25 preludes of the 15th to 17th centuries from the tablatures of Kotter, Kleber, S. Mareschall, Erbach, the *Buxheimer Orgelbuch,* and other sources.

SPAIN AND PORTUGAL

In the decade that has elapsed since I wrote the first part of this survey, a number of important publications of Iberian music have appeared. Moreover, one sees in Spain, along with a gradually awakening interest in early music, a rising interest in historic instruments.

Bermudo: *Organ Pieces,* Kalmus (through Belwin-Mills).

Blanco, J.: *I Concierto de dos Organos,* ed. Kastner, Mainz, Schott.

Cabanilles: *Organistas españoles,* ed. J. Climent, Madrid, Union Musical Española. Contents: 2 tientos, 2 pasacalles, and a gallardas.

Cabezón: *Collected Works,* 5 vols. (projected), ed. Ch. Jacobs, Brooklyn, Institute of Mediaeval Music, 1967-. The first 3 volumes are available to date. *Obras de musica para tecla, arpa y vihuela* . . . (1578), 3 vols., Barcelona, Inst. Español de Musicología, 1966. In addition, the 4 Cabezón volumes of the *Hispaniae schola musica* set are available in a new reprint by the Johnson Reprint Corporation. *4 Tientos,* ed. Drischner, Tübingen, Schultheiss Verlag. *4 Tientos,* Kalmus (through Belwin-Mills). Selected works by Cabezón are also published in Bks. 30 and 34 of the *Orgue et Liturgie* series (Schola Cantorum).

Conceicao, Roque da: *Livro de Obras de Orgao* (*Portugaliae Musica*, XI), Lisbon, Gulbenkian Foundation, 1967.

Lopez, Miguel Fray: *Lleno para organo* (1719), Madrid, Union Musical Española.

Santa María, T. de: *Arte de Tañer Fantasia* (Selected Works), Kalmus (through Belwin-Mills).

Seixas: The complete edition is now available: *80 Sonatas,* 4 vols., ed. Kastner (*Portugaliae Musica,* X/parts 1-4), Lisbon, Gulbenkian Foundation.

Sesse, Juan: *Seis Fugas para Organo y Clave,* ed. A. Howell, Madrid, Union Musical Española.

Soler: *Seis conciertos para dos organos,* ed. Rubio, Madrid, Union Musical Española. *Sonatas para instrumentos de tecla,* 7 vols., ed. S. Rubio, Madrid, Union Musical Española. Contents: 120 sonatas. *5th Concerto for 2 Keyboard Instruments,* Kalmus (through Belwin-Mills).

Collections

Anthology of Spanish Organists of the 17th Century, Kalmus (through Belwin-Mills).

The *Antologia de Organistas clásico españoles* (1914), ed. Muñoz, has been revised by S. Rubio, Madrid, Union Musical Española. It contains works by T. de Santa María, Pedraza, Clavijo, and Aguilera and is available through Associated Music Publishers.

Antologia de Organistas españoles del siglo XVII, 2 vols., ed. Anglès, Barcelona, Biblioteca Central, 1965. Vol. I: Aguilera de Heredia, Arauxo, Jiménez, Perandreu, Menalt, Bruna, Cabanilles; Vol. II: Heredia, Jiménez, Menalt, Sebastián, Bruna, Cabanilles, Baseya, Bernabé, Xarava, Durón.

Antologia de Organistas do século XVI, ed. Fernandes/Kastner (*Portugaliae Musica,* XIX), Lisbon, Gulbenkian Foundation, 1969. It contains works by Portuguese, Italian, and Spanish composers: Carreira, de Paiva, de Macedo, Segni, da Modena, A. de Cabezón.

Ecole d'orgue de Saragosse du 17ème siècle (*Orgue et Liturgie,* Bk. 74), Paris, Schola Cantorum. Contents: works by A. de Sola and S. Durón.

Organa Hispanica, 6 vols., ed. G. Doderer, Heidelberg, W. Müller Verlag. Vol. I: 6 Spanish and Portuguese batallas of the 17th century; Vol. II: Portuguese sonatas, toccatas, and minuets of the 18th century; Vol. III: Old Iberian versets; Vol. IV: Tientos, fantasias, and works of the 16th century; Vol. V: Tientos de medio registro, fantasias, and other works of the 17th and 18th centuries; Vol. VI: Spanish and Portuguese sonatas of the 18th century.

Organistas de la Real Capilla, ed. Rubio, Madrid, Union Musical Española, 1973. It contains works by the 18th-century composers employed by the Royal Chapel: J. Lidon, F. M. Lopez, J. Oxinaga, J. de Sesse.

ITALY

Amendment to the final paragraphs of the survey of Italian music: In the seven years since this survey was first published, one has seen the restoration of several old instruments in Italy and an increasing awareness of historical organs as national monuments.

Bossi: *Selected Organ Works,* Kalmus (through Belwin-Mills).

Cavazzoni, G.: *Second Livre d'orgue,* in 3 bks., ed. J. Bonfils (*Orgue et Liturgie,* Bks. 34, 38, 41), Paris, Schola Cantorum. Bk. 1: Missa Apostolorum; Bk. 2: Missa Dominicalis and Missa de

Beata Virgine; Bk. 3: Hymns and Gloria and Magnificat versets. *Organ Book,* Kalmus (through Belwin-Mills).

Fantini, Girolamo: *8 Sonatas for Trumpet & Organ* (1678), London, Musica Rara, 1969.

Frescobaldi: *Toccatas, Partitas,* 2 vols., Kalmus (through Belwin-Mills). A new critical edition of Frescobaldi toccatas is in preparation by Etienne Darbellay, to be published by Suvini-Zerboni. Also in preparation is an edition by Kenneth Gilbert.

Gabrieli, A.: *Organ Works,* 5 vols., Kalmus.

Gabrieli, G.: *Canzon Duodecima Toni a 10* (for 4 trumpets, 6 trombones, and 2 organs), London, Musica Rara.

Luchinetti, Giovanni Bernardo: *Concerto a due organi* (Bb), ed. Ewerhart, Vienna, Doblinger.

Merula, T.: *Compositions for Organ or Cembalo,* Kalmus (through Belwin-Mills).

Merulo, C.: *Versetti d'organo,* ed. Dalla Libera, Padua, Zanibon.

Scarlatti, A.: *Toccata primi toni,* ed. T. Klein, Wiesbaden, Breitkopf & Härtel.

Scarlatti, D.: *Two Organ Sonatas,* ed. Goldsborough, London, Oxford Univ. Press.

Trabaci: CORRECTION: There are 2 volumes in the Mischiati edition (*MMI,* I/3-4).

Viviani, Giovanni Bonaventura: *2 Sonatas* (for trumpet and organ) (1678), London, Musica Rara, 1969.

Collections

Altitalienische Orgelmeister: CORRECTION: The editor of this volume is Szigeti; Kaller is the general editor of the series.

Italian Organ Music of the Eighteenth Century, ed. M. Sutter, New York, H. Flammer. Contents: *Sonata Fugata,* Francesco Durante; *Elevazione,* Francesco Feroci; *Sonata No. 6* (Siciliana) and *Sonata No. 8,* Gaetano Valeri; *Pastorale,* Carlo Monza; *All' Elevazione,* Giovanni Battista Martini.

Musiche pistoiesi per organo, 2 vols., ed. Umberto Pineschi, Brescia/Kassel, Paideia/Bärenreiter, 1978. Vol. I: Anonymous composers of the 18th century; Vol. II: Giuseppe Gherardeschi.

SOUTH GERMANY

Note: the Kalmus editions that follow are currently available through Belwin-Mills (Melville, N.Y.).

Erbach: *Selected Compositions,* Kalmus.

Fischer: *Musical Bouquet,* Kalmus.

Froberger: *Toccaten, Fantasien, Ricercari, Canzonen und Capricci,* ed. Walter (*Süddeutsche Orgelmeister des Barock,* VII), Altötting, A. Coppenrath, 1967. *Various Organ Works,* Kalmus. Note also that the 3 volumes of the *DTO* are available separately in a reprint edition published by the Akademische Druck- und Verlagsanstalt (Graz).

Hassler: *Orgelwerke* (*Sämtliche Werke,* XII), Munich, Publication of the Gesellschaft für Bayerische Musikgeschichte. *Ordinarium et Proprium de Apostolis,* ed. Mischiati (*Biblioteca Classica dell' organists,* II), Mainz, Schott. *Ausgewählte Werke,* ed. Kiss, Mainz, Schott. *Variationen: Ich ging einmal spatieren,* ed. Kiss, Mainz, Schott.

Hofhaimer: *Salve Regina,* ed. M. Radulescu, Vienna, Doblinger. Paul

Hofhaimer und Hans Puchner: *Zwei Recordare,* ed. Radulescu, Vienna, Doblinger.

Kerll: *Modulatio Organica,* Kalmus.

Kolb, P. Carlmann: *Certamen Aonium,* ed. G. Klaus, Heidelberg, W. Müller Verlag. The same, ed. Walter (*Süddeutsche Orgelmeister des Barock,* V), Altötting, Coppenrath. The same, Kalmus. *Praeludium tertium,* ed. Siegel, Berlin, Merseburger.

Muffat, Gottlieb: *Apparatus Musico-Organisticus,* Kalmus.

Murschhauser: *Octo-Tonium novum organicum,* Kalmus.

Pachelbel, J.: The Bärenreiter collection of Pachelbel works now has 6 volumes. Vols. V and VI are edited by Stockmeier and contain toccatas, fugues, etc. *Orgelwerke,* 4 vols., ed. Fedtke, Frankfurt, C. F. Peters. Vol. I: 60 chorale fugues and chorales from the *Weimar Tablature Book* (1704); Vol. II: 20 Choralbearbeitungen; Vol. III: 16 Magnificat fugues; Vol. IV: free organ pieces. *Ten Fugues on the Magnificat,* ed. Emery (*Early Organ Music* series), London, Novello. *Hexachordum Apollinis,* ed. Moser/rev. by Fedtke, Kassel, Bärenreiter. Contents: variations on arias and 2 ciaconas. *Organ Works,* 4 vols., Kalmus.

Pachelbel, W. H.: *Werke für Orgel und Klavier,* ed. Moser/Fedtke, Kassel, Bärenreiter.

Poglietti: *Praeludia, Cadenzen und Fugen in den 8 Kirchentonarten,* ed. Walter, Heidelberg, W. Müller Verlag.

Scherer: *Intonations and Toccatas,* Kalmus.

Speth: *Ars Magna consoni et dissoni* (1693), ed. Fedtke, Kassel, Bärenreiter. Contents: 10 toccatas, 8 Magnificats, and 3 partitas.

Collections

Orgelstücke der Orgelschule "Wegweiser" (1689), ed. Walter (*Süddeutsche Orgelmeister des Barock,* VIII), Altötting, A. Coppenrath.

Praeambula, ed. A. Reichling, Altötting, Coppenrath. Contents: 25 preludes of the 15th to 17th centuries from the tablatures of Kotter, Kleber, S. Mareschall, Chr. Erbach, the *Buxheimer Orgelbuch,* and other sources.

Wiener Klavier- und Orgelwerke aus der zweiten Hälfte des 17. Jahrhunderts, ed. Botstiber (*DTO* XIII/2), 1959. Contents: keyboard pieces by Poglietti, F. T. Richter, and G. Reutter the Elder.

NORTH AND MIDDLE GERMANY

Note: the Kalmus editions that follow are currently available through Belwin-Mills (Melville, N.Y.).

Bach, J. C.: *44 Organ Chorales,* Kalmus.

Bach, J. S.: *Complete Organ Works,* 9 vols., Kalmus.

Böhm: *Chorale Works and Miscellaneous,* Kalmus.

Bruhns: *Sämtliche Orgelwerke,* ed. Beckmann, Wiesbaden, Breitkopf & Härtel, 1972. *3 Preludes and Fugues,* Kalmus.

Buxtehude: Note that the Beckmann edition exists both in a musicological edition in 2 vols. and in a practical edition in 2 vols. of 2 parts each (4 books). *Organ Works,* 4 vols., Kalmus. Vols. I/II: free works; Vols. III/IV: Choralbearbeitungen.

Hasse, N.: *Sämtliche Orgelwerke,* ed. Beckmann, Wiesbaden, Breitkopf & Härtel. Contents: the 4 Choralbearbeitungen of the *Pelplin Tablatures.*

Kauffmann: *Six Chorale Preludes*, ed. Emery (*Early Organ Music* series), London, Novello.

Krieger, Joh.: *Preludes and Fugues*, Kalmus.

Kuhnau: *Two Preludes and Fugues and a Toccata*, Kalmus.

Lübeck: *Sämtliche Orgelwerke*, ed. Beckmann, Wiesbaden, Breitkopf & Härtel. *4 Preludes and Fugues*, Kalmus. *Organ Works*, Kalmus.

Praetorius, J.: *Choralbearbeitungen*, ed. Breig, Kassel, Bärenreiter.

Reincken: *Sämtliche Orgelwerke*, ed. Beckmann, Wiesbaden, Breitkopf & Härtel. Contents: 2 choral fantasies, 1 toccata, 1 fugue.

Scheidemann: The Bärenreiter edition is now complete and should read as follows: *Orgelwerke*, 3 vols., ed. Foch/Breig, Kassel, Bärenreiter, 1966-70. Vol. I: *Choralbearbeitungen*, ed. Foch; Vol. II: *Magnificat-Bearbeitungen*, ed. Foch; Vol. III: *Praeambeln, Fugen, Fantasien, Canzonen, und Toccaten*, ed. Breig. *15 Preludes and Fugues*, Kalmus.

Scheidt: *Chorales*, Kalmus.

Schildt: *Choralbearbeitungen*, ed. Breig (*Organum* IV/24), Cologne, Kistner & Siegel.

Siefert: *13 Fantasias à 3*, Kalmus.

Strungk, D.: *Zwei Choralfantasien*, ed. Krumbach (*Die Orgel*, II/12), Lippstadt, Kistner & Siegel.

Strungk, N. A.: *Two Double Fugues*, Kalmus.

Telemann: *12 Easy Chorale Preludes*, Kalmus. *9 variierte Choräle*, Kalmus. *20 Little Fugues*, Kalmus.

Tunder: *Sämtliche Orgelwerke*, ed.

Beckmann, Wiesbaden, Breitkopf & Härtel.

Walther: *Orgelkonzert in A*, ed. Stockmeier, Cologne, Kistner & Siegel. *Concerto per la Chiesa* (Telemann-Walther), ed. Ph. Prince (*Early Organ Music* series), London, Novello. *5 Selected Organ Works*, Kalmus.

Weckmann: *14 Preludes, Fugues and Toccatas*, Kalmus.

Zachow: *Präludium* (C), Berlin, Merseburger Verlag.

Collections

Freie Orgelvorspiele vorbachischer Meister, 2 vols., ed. Seiffert, Leipzig, Kistner & Siegel. Contents: works by Praetorius, Pachelbel, Scheidemann, Tunder, Chr. Flor, D. Meyer, Zachow, Kuhnau, etc.

Lied- und Tanzvariationen der Sweelinck-Schule (for harpsichord or organ), ed. Breig, Mainz, Schott S.

Seasonal Chorale Preludes for Manuals Only, 2 vols., ed. Trevor, London, Oxford Univ. Press. Vol. I: works by German Baroque composers for Advent through Palm Sunday; Vol. II: Easter through Trinity Sunday, plus general use.

The Tablature of Celle, 1601, ed. W. Apel (*Corpus of Early Keyboard Music*, XVII). Early chorale compositions, many by anonymous composers.

Kalmus also has editions of some of the older German anthologies such as Straube's *Old Masters of the Organ.*

GERMANY AND AUSTRIA,
1750-1900

Albrechtsberger: *4 Fugen für Orgel*, ed. Biba, Vienna, Doblinger. *Octo*

Tono ecclesiastici per organo (*Süd-deutsche Orgelmeister des Barock*, XII), Altötting, Coppenrath, 1974. *6 Fugen*, op. 10, Berlin, Lienau. *18 Präludien*, op. 12, 3 vols., Berlin, Lienau. *6 Fugen*, op. 17, Berlin, Lienau. *50 Versetten und 8 Fugen*, 2 parts, Berlin, Lienau. *2 Fugen über österliche Themen* (*Christ ist erstanden; Osterliches Alleluia*), op. 21, ed. Klaus, Augsburg, A. Böhm. *6 Trios*, Kalmus (through Belwin-Mills).

Bach, W. F.: *Organ Works*, Kalmus (through Belwin-Mills). *8 Fugues without Pedal*, Kalmus.

Brahms: *Complete Organ Works*, Kalmus (through Belwin-Mills).

Bruckner: *Zwei Orgelstücke* (*Vorspiel, Nachspiel*), ed. Piechler, Augsburg, A. Böhm. *Vorspiel und Fuge* (c), ed. and completed by F. Phillip, Augsburg, A. Böhm. *Neun Orgelstücke*, ed. Hoppe, Augsburg, A. Böhm. Contents: preludes, postludes, fugues, transcriptions. *Album of Various Pieces*, Kalmus (through Belwin-Mills).

Eberlin: *65 Vor- und Nachspiele, Versetten und Fughetten in den 8 Kirchentonarten*, 2 vols., ed. R. Walter, Vienna, Doblinger. *9 Toccatas*, Kalmus (through Belwin-Mills).

Fischer, M. G.: *18 Ausgewählte Orgelstücke*, 2 vols., ed. Haupt, Berlin, Lienau.

Haydn, F. J.: *Konzert in C für Orgel*, ed. H. Walter, Munich-Duisburg, Henle Verlag, 1969. *Eight Pieces for Musical Clocks*, ed. Ratcliffe, London, Novello.

Haydn, Michael: *Little Organ Pieces*, Kalmus (through Belwin-Mills).

Herzogenberg: *Nun komm der Heiden Heiland*, Berlin, Merseburger.

Hesse: *6 Orgelvorspiele*, op. 32, Berlin, Lienau. *6 Orgelvorspiele*, op. 33,

Berlin, Lienau. *Variationen* (Ab), op. 34, Berlin, Lienau. *Fantasie zu 4 Händen*, op. 35, Berlin, Lienau. *3 Präludien, Trio und Fantasie für den Concertgebrauch*, op. 36, Berlin, Lienau. *3 Präludien, Postludium, Fuge und variierter Choral für den Concertgebrauch*, op. 37, Berlin, Lienau. *2 Fugen selbst Einleitung*, op. 39, Berlin, Lienau. *Variationen über ein eigenes Thema* (A), op. 47, Berlin, Lienau. *Orgelvorspiele*, op. 48, Berlin, Lienau.

Hummel, J. N.: *Complete Organ Works*, ed. Brock, London, Hinrichsen. *Präludium, Zwischenspiel und zwei Fugen für Orgel*, ed. Poos, Berlin, Merseburger.

Kittel: *Three Preludes*, ed. Emery (*Early Organ Music* series), London, Novello.

Krebs: *Acht Choräle für Oboe* (*oder Trompete*) *und Orgel*, Wilhelmshaven, Heinrichshofen's Verlag. CORRECTION: The C. F. Peters collection entitled *Ausgewählte Orgelwerke* was co-edited by Zöllner and Tittel and has 2 volumes.

Lachner, Franz: *Introduction und Fuge* (d), ed. O. Biba, Vienna, Doblinger.

Liszt: *Organ Works*, 2 vols., Kalmus (through Belwin-Mills).

Marpurg: *Capricci e Fughe*, op. 1, Bad Godesberg, Forberg Verlag. *Five Marpurg Fugues*, ed. R. Thompson, Minneapolis, Augsburg.

Mendelssohn: *Orgelsonaten*, op. 65 (*Urtext*), ed. H. Meister/W. Stockmeier, Munich, Henle Verlag, 1976. *Kompositionen für Orgel*, ed. Wm. A. Little, Leipzig, Deutscher Verlag für Musik. This is Vol. IV, part 7, of the new Leipzig edition of the collected works of Mendelssohn. Included are *Prelude* (d); *3 Fugues* (d); *Andante* (D); *Fugues* (g, c); *Nachspiel* (D); *Choralvariationen über "Wie gross ist* des Allmächt'gen Güte." Organ Works (op. 37 and op. 65), Kalmus (through Belwin-Mills).

Merkel: Fugue for Organ Duet, London, Oxford Univ. Press.

Mozart: Orgelwerke, ed. M. Henking, Vienna, Doblinger. K 594, K 608, and 2 church sonatas (K 278, K 329) are available in Kalmus editions (through Belwin-Mills).

Reger: Siegesfeier, op. 145, no. 7, Wiesbaden, Breitkopf & Härtel. Fantasie und Fuge über B-A-C-H, op. 46, ed. Collum, Wiesbaden, Breitkopf & Härtel, 1968. The following works are now available in Kalmus editions (through Belwin-Mills): Choral Fantasy on "Wie schön leucht uns der Morgenstern"; Fantasy and Fugue on the Name of BACH, op. 46; Fantasy on the Choral "Freu Dich sehr, O meine Seele," op. 30; Fantasy on the Choral "Hallelujah! Gott zu loben, bleibe meine Seelenfreud," op. 52/3; Fantasy on "Wachet auf, ruft uns die Stimme," op. 52/2; Introduction and Passacaglia; Six Trios, op. 47; Sonata in F-sharp minor, op. 33; Three Pieces for Organ, op. 7; Variations and Fugue on an Original Theme, op. 73; Organ Pieces, op. 59, 2 vols.; Organ Pieces, op. 65, 2 vols.; 10 Pieces, op. 69; Twelve Pieces, op. 63, 3 vols.; Two Easy Preludes and Fugues, op. 56.

Rembt: 22 vierstimmige Fughetten (selected from the 50 vierstimmige Fughetten), ed. A. Haupt, Berlin, Lienau. Fifty Four-Part Little Fugues, 2 vols., Kalmus (through Belwin-Mills).

Reubke: The 94th Psalm, ed. D. Chorzempa, London, Oxford Univ. Press, 1976. Trio in E-flat, ed. Rollin Smith, New York, H. W. Gray.

Rheinberger: Orgelwerke, I, ed. M. Weyer, Bad Godesberg, Forberg Verlag (to be continued). Characteristic Pieces, op. 156, London, Novello. ORG. & INSTRUMENTS:

Organ Concerto, op. 137, ed. F. Tulan, Gentry (through Theodore Presser). The following works are available in Kalmus editions (through Belwin-Mills): Sonata No. 5, op. 111; Sonata No. 9 (b), op. 142; Sonata No. 10, op. 146; Ten Trios, op. 49; 12 Fughettas, op. 123a; 12 Fughettas, op. 123b.

Schneider, Johann: Drei Präludien und Fugen, Hilversum (Netherlands), Harmonia.

Schubert, F.: Drei Fugen für Orgel (C, G, d), ed. O. Biba, Vienna, Doblinger, 1978. FOUR HANDS: Fuga für Orgel (e), op. posth. 152, ed. O. Biba, Vienna, Doblinger.

Sechter: Drei Fugen, op. 44/2, ed. O. Biba, Vienna, Doblinger.

Thuille, Ludwig: Sonata (a), op. 2, Bad Godesberg, Forberg.

Werner, Gregor Joseph: Pastorella (D) (for organ and strings), ed. Schmid, Kassel, Bärenreiter. Pastorella zur Weihnacht (G) (for organ and strings), ed. Schmid, Kassel, Bärenreiter. Koncertalo darabok cembalora v. orgonara es kamarazenekara (concertante pieces for harpsichord or organ and chamber orchestra), ed. Vecsey (Musica Rinata, no. 5), Budapest, Editio Musica Budapest. Contents: Concerto (Bb), Pastorale (G), Pastorale (D).

Collections

Rondom Johann Sebastian Bach, ed. E. Kooiman, Muiden (Holland), Edition Oresto, 1976. Contents: 6 organ works from Bach pupils and admirers: Preludio (D), J. C. Kittel; Preludio pro Organo plena (a) and Fantasia (g), J. P. Kellner; Herzlich tut mich verlangen, Trio a 2 Claviers e Pedale (C), Trio a 2 Claviers e Pedale (F), J. L. Krebs.

Der vollkommene Organist, 5 vols., Berlin, Lienau. Contents: fugues,

preludes, chorales, fantasies, etc., by
Sechter, Assmayr, Rieder, Kirnberger,
Muffat, and others.

GERMANY AND AUSTRIA
SINCE 1900

Ahrens: *Fünf Leisen* (1969),
Heidelberg, Willy Müller.

David: Vols. 20 and 21 of *Das
Choralwerk* are also available,
Breitkopf & Härtel.

Doppelbauer: *Partita über "O Heiland,
reiss die Himmel auf"* (1973), Vienna,
Doblinger.

Eder: *Partita: Nun danket all und bringet Ehr,* Vienna, Doblinger.

Heiller: *3 kleine Choralvorspiele*
(1975), Vienna, Doblinger. *Jubilatio*
(1976), Vienna, Doblinger. *Meditation
on the Gregorian Easter Sequence,*
Vienna, Doblinger.

Kaminski: *Toccata and Fugue,* Kalmus
(through Belwin-Mills).

Kraft: *Totentanz-Toccata,* available
through Eulenberg.

Krenek: *Orga-Nastro* (for organ and
tape) (1971), Kassel, Bärenreiter.

Kropfreiter: *Exsultet* (1975), Vienna,
Doblinger.

Planyavsky: *Sonata II,* Vienna, Doblinger.

Radulescu, Michael: *5 Pieces,* Vienna,
Doblinger.

Schmidt: *Praeludium und Fuge* (A),
Stockholm, Nordiska. *Der Heiland ist
erstanden,* Stockholm, Nordiska. Doblinger (Vienna) has a new edition of the
4 kleine Praeludien und Fugen, ed. by
A. Forer. Universal has a new edition of
Fuga solemnis. Note that *Variationen*

und Fuge über ein eigenes Thema also
exists in a version for organ alone.

Schönberg: *Sämtliche Werke: Orgel-
Klavierwerke* (II/5), Mainz/Vienna,
Schott/Universal, 1973.

Schroeder: *Septenarium,* Minneapolis,
Augsburg. ORG. & INSTRUMENTS:
Duo da chiesa (for violin and organ),
Btockhoff (through Jos. Boonin).

Schwarz-Schilling: *Sechs kleine
Choralvorspiele mit Intonation,* Berlin,
Merseburger.

Weyrauch: *Partita über "Unüber-
windliche starker Held,"* Wiesbaden,
Breitkopf & Härtel.

FRANCE, 1531-1800

CORRECTION: It has come to my attention that Louis Couperin (c.
1626-1661) has left a fairly sizable body
of organ music in manuscript. As soon
as this music becomes available in a
modern edition, it will fill an important
gap in our knowledge of the development of organ literature between
Titelouze and Nivers.

Attaignant: *Second Organ Book of
1531,* Kalmus (through Belwin-Mills).

Babou: *Thirteen Pieces,* Kalmus
(through Belwin-Mills).

Beauvarlet-Charpentier, Jean-Jacques:
*Douze Noëls variés pour l'orgue avec un
Carillon des Morts,* 2 vols., ed. R. Peek,
St. Louis, Concordia.

Boyvin: *Organ Works,* 2 vols., Kalmus
(through Belwin-Mills).

Corrette: *Magnificat du troisième et
quatrième ton,* ed. Higginbottom (*Early Organ Music,* no. 26), London,
Novello.

Dandrieu, J. F.: *First Organ Book,* Kalmus (through Belwin-Mills).

De Grigny: *Organ Book,* Kalmus (through Belwin-Mills).

Du Mage: *Organ Book,* Kalmus (through Belwin-Mills).

Geoffroy: *Livre d'orgue,* ed. Bonfils (*Le Pupitre,* CIII), Paris, Heugel.

Gigault: *Organ Books,* 3 vols., Kalmus (through Belwin-Mills).

Guilain: *Suites of the 1st to 4th Ton,* Kalmus (through Belwin-Mills).

Lebègue: *Complete Organ Works,* 3 vols., Kalmus (through Belwin-Mills). Vol. I: 1st through 8th mode; Vol. II: Magnificats and various works; Vol. III: Offertoires, Noëls, Magnificats.

Marchand: *Selection of Organ Compositions,* Kalmus (through Belwin-Mills). *Organ Compositions,* Kalmus. Note also that the *L'Oeuvre d'orgue* edited by Bonfils is now complete, 3 vols., Les Editions ouvrières.

Nivers: *Troisième Livre d'orgue,* ed. Dufourcq (*Publications de la Société française de Musicologie* I/14), Paris, Heugel, 1958.

Roberday: *Fugues and Caprices,* Kalmus (through Belwin-Mills).

Titelouze: *Complete Organ Works,* 2 vols., Kalmus (through Belwin-Mills).

Boellmann: *Fantaisie,* Hilversum (Netherlands), Harmonia. *Second Suite,* op. 27, Kalmus (through Belwin-Mills). *Heures mystiques,* 2 vols., Kalmus (through Belwin-Mills).

Dupré: *Variations on "Adeste Fideles"* (a Dupré improvisation reconstructed

by Rollin Smith), New York, H. W. Gray.

Franck: *L'Organiste* is also available in a Kalmus edition (through Belwin-Mills).

Girod: *Suite on the 23rd Psalm,* Kalmus (through Belwin-Mills).

Jolivet: *Mandala,* Paris, Billaudot, 1970. ORG. & INSTRUMENTS: *Arioso Barocco* (for trumpet and organ), Paris, Billaudot, 1970.

Langlais: *Three Voluntaries,* Chicago, H. T. FitzSimons. *Trois Implorations,* Paris, Bornemann, *Cinq Méditations sur l'Apocalypse,* Paris, Bornemann. *Supplication* (1972), Haarlem, Stichting International Orgel Centrum. *Suite Baroque* (1973), Paris, Philippo-Combre. *Plein Jeu à la française* (1974), Paris, Schola Cantorum. *Huits Chants de Bretagne* (1974), Paris, Bornemann. *Trois Esquisses romanes,* Paris, Bornemann. *Trois Esquisses gothiques,* Paris, Bronemann. *Deuxième Symphonie "alla Webern,"* Paris, Combre, 1977.

Litaize: *Low Mass for Every Occasion,* Kalmus (through Belwin-Mills).

Saint-Saëns: *Bénédiction nuptiale,* op. 9, Kalmus (through Belwin-Mills).

Tisné, Antoine: *Luminescences,* Paris, G. Billaudot.

Vierne: *Allegretto,* Kalmus (through Belwin-Mills).

Blow: *Selected Organ Works,* Kalmus (through Belwin-Mills).

Boyce: *Ten Voluntaries for the Organ or Harpsichord* (c. 1785), facsimile edition with editorial preface by J. Caldwell, London, Oxford Univ. Press.

Ten Voluntaries, ed. Fesperman, Boston, E. C. Schirmer.

Bull: *Ten Pieces,* ed. Steel and Cameron, London, Stainer & Bell. Contents: 10 works selected from the *Musica Britannica* edition of Bull works; generally more idiomatic to the harpsichord than to the organ.

Byrd: *Collection of 21 Pieces for the Organ,* Kalmus (through Belwin-Mills).

Clarke, J.: *Selected Works for Keyboard,* ed. Barsham, London, Oxford Univ. Press. ORG. & IN-STRUMENTS: *Suite in D* (for organ and trumpet), ed. R. Block, London, Musica Rara.

Handel: *Fugue in E,* ed. H. Diack Johnstone, London, Novello. *6 Organ Concertos,* op. 4 (arr. for organ alone), Kalmus (through Belwin-Mills). ORG. & INSTRUMENTS: *Konzert Nr. 13* ("Der Kuckuck und die Nachtigall"), ed. Liedecke, Berlin, Merseburger.

James, John: *Two Trumpet Voluntaries,* ed. H. Diack Johnstone, London, Oxford Univ. Press.

Nares, James: *Six Fugues with Introductory Voluntaries for the Organ or Harpsichord,* ed. by R. Langley, London, Oxford Univ. Press.

Purcell: *Works for Harpsichord; Works for Organ,* Urtext edition, New York, Lea Pocket Scores, 1968.

Rogers, B.: *Complete Keyboard Works,* ed. R. Rastall, London, Stainer & Bell.

Stanley: *Concerto in C Major,* ed. Le Huray, London, Oxford Univ. Press.

ENGLAND IN THE 19TH AND 20TH CENTURIES

Bridge: *Three Pieces for Organ,* London, Novello (newly reprinted from the 1905 edition).

Elgar: *Sonata in G* (Urtext), Kalmus (through Belwin-Mills).

Hurford: *Bristol Suite,* London, Novello.

Leighton: *Improvisation in memoriam Maurice de Sausmarez,* London, Novello.

Routh: *Three Teaching Pieces in Canonic Style,* London, Hinrichsen, 1963. *Lumen Christi,* Oceanside (N.Y.), Boosey & Hawkes. *Sonatina,* Oceanside (N.Y.), Boosey & Hawkes, 1975.

Thiman: *44 Hymn Tunes Freely Harmonized for Unison Singing,* London, Novello.

Vaughn Williams: *Prelude and Fugue in C Minor* has been republished by Oxford and now is available for purchase (not only rental).

Williamson: *Fantasy on "O Paradise,"* Carol Stream (Ill.), Agape. *This Is My Father's World,* Carol Stream (Ill.), Agape.

THE LOW COUNTRIES

Badings: *Ricercar,* Amsterdam, Donemus. *Introduction and Variations on "Morning Has Broken,"* Amsterdam, Donemus.

Callaerts: *Cantilène,* op. 23, Brussels, Schott Frères.

Cornet, P.: *Various Organ Works,* Kalmus (through Belwin-Mills).

Jongen: *Petit Prélude,* London, Oxford Univ. Press.

Kee, Cor: *Two Pieces for Organ* (Fantasia on "Wachet auf"; Prelude on "O Sacred Head"), London, Hinrichsen.

Monnikendam: *Prelude "The Bells,"* Amsterdam, Donemus. *Two Themes with Variations,* Amsterdam, Donemus. ORG. & INSTRUMENTS: *Toccata-batalla* (for organ, with 2 trumpets, 2 trombones, ad. lib.), Amsterdam, Donemus.

Peeters: *16 einfache Praeludien für Orgel ohne Pedal,* op. 114, Düsseldorf, Schwann. *Ten Preludes on Old Flemish Carols,* op. 119, New York, C. F. Peters. *10 Studies for Pedal Playing,* Kalmus (through Belwin-Mills).

Berg, G.: *Aatta Koralförspel* (8 hymn introductions), Stockholm, Nordiska Musikförlaget.

Hovland, E.: *Nu la oss takke Gud* (toccata on "Now Thank We All Our God"), Oslo, Norsk Musikforlag.

Lewkovitch: *Koralvariationer,* Copenhagen, Hansen. Contents: 6 partitas on German chorales.

Myklegaard, Aage: *6 Orgelkoraler,* Oslo, Norsk Musikforlag.

Nystedt: *Exultate* (1977), Oslo, Norsk Musikforlag.

Paivianinen: *Koralförspel,* II, Helsinki, Fazer.

Martinu, Bohuslav: *Vigilia,* Mainz, Schott S.

Seeger: *Eight Toccatas and Fugues,* Kalmus (through Belwin-Mills).

Vanhal, J. B.: *Konzert in F* (for organ, 2 violins, string bass), ed. Haselböck, Vienna, Doblinger.

Collections

Nuove Composizioni per Organo now has 4 volumes. Vol. IV: *Per aspera ad astra,* J. Dadak; *2 Chorale Fantasies on Bohemian Hymns,* P. Eben; *L'Introduzione e Fuga su Tema di B-A-C-H,* M. Sokola; *Ricercar sopra B-A-C-H,* O. Simke; *Fantasia Appassionata,* J. Teml.

Organistae Bohemici, ed. Slechta, Prague, Artia. contents: 10 fugues, preludes, and pastorellas by Zach, Vanhal, Brixi, Kuchař, and Kopřiva.

Note: The contents of *Orgelkompositionen alter böhmischer Meister* are: 9 fugues, preludes, and fantasies by Brixi, Vanhal, Kuchař, and Pitsch. The collection is edited by Geist and Kampelsheimer.

Bacewicz, G.: *Esquisse per organo,* Cracow, P.W.M., 1973.

Bauer, J.: *Reminiscenze,* Cracow, P.W.M., 1975.

Bloch, A.: *Jubilate,* Cracow, P.W.M., 1975.

Jablonski, H.: *Suita per organo,* Cracow, P.W.M., 1975.

Jargon, J.: *Triptychon,* Cracow, P.W.M., 1971.

Machl, T.: *Koncert nr. 1* (for organ and orchestra), Cracow, P.W.M. *Koncert na troje organow* (concerto for three organs and symphony orchestra), Cracow, P.W.M., 1972.

Nowowiejsk, F.: *VIII Symfonia,* op. 45, no. 8, Cracow, P.W.M., 1969.

Anthology of Early American Keyboard Music, 1787–1839, parts 1 and 2, ed. J. Bunker Clark, Madison, A-R Editions, 1977. Contains some music appropriate to the organ, although most is pianistic.

Bender: *Twenty Hymn Introductions,* vol. I, St. Louis, Concordia. *Twenty-Four Hymn Introductions,* vol. II, St. Louis, Concordia.

Foote, A.: *Organ Works,* ed. W. Leupold, New York, McAfee.

Fromm, Herbert: *Partita BARUCH HABA,* Boston, E. C. Schirmer. *Suite on Hebraic Motifs* (6 pieces), New York, Transcontinental Music Publications. *Organ Sonata in Four Movements* ("Days of Awe"), New York, Transcontinental. *Fantasy on High Holiday Themes,* New York, Transcontinental.

Gill, Milton: *3 Choral Preludes* ("40 Days and 40 Nights"; "With Broken Heart and Contrite Sigh"; "Drop, Drop Slow Tears"), New York, G. Schirmer, 1976. *Toccata,* New York, H. W. Gray, 1963. *Processional,* Chapel Hill, Hinshaw Music.

Hampton, C.: *Ceremonial Music* (2 pieces), New York, McAfee.

Held: *Six Preludes on Easter Hymns,* St. Louis, Concordia. *Hymn Preludes for the Autumn Festivals* (7 pieces), St. Louis, Concordia.

Johnson, D.: *Twelve Hymn Settings,* 2 vols., Minneapolis, Schmitt. ORG. & INSTRUMENTS: *Easter Music for Organ & Brass,* 2 vols., Minneapolis, Augsburg.

Krapf: *Fantasy on "O Jesus Christ, to Thee May Hymns Be Rising,"* New York, H. W. Gray. *Music for the Service,* Nashville, Abingdon. *Music for a Sunday Morning,* St. Louis, Concordia.

La Montaine, John: *Processional,* New York, H. W. Gray. *Even Song,* New York, H. W. Gray. ORG. & VOICE/INSTRUMENTS: *Wilderness Journey,* op. 41 (for bass-baritone, organ, and orchestra), Hollywood, Fredonia Press.

Manz: *From Heaven Above to Earth I Come,* St. Louis, Concordia.

Near, G.: *Sinfonia Festiva,* New York, H. W. Gray.

Parker, H.: *Quick March: Duo for Two Organists,* Carol Stream (Ill.), Hope.

Roberts, M.: *Blessed Assurance,* Melville (N.Y.), Belwin-Mills.

Rorem: *A Quaker Reader* (suite of 11 movements), Oceanside (N.Y.), Boosey & Hawkes, 1977.

Sifler, Paul J.: *Four Nativity Tableaux,* New York, H. W. Gray. *Music for the Holy Night,* New York, H. W. Gray. *Sinfonia,* New York, H. W. Gray. *The Despair and Agony of Dachau,* New York, H. W. Gray. All other publications are by Fredonia Press, Hollywood. *Fantasia from "In the Days of Herod the King." Autumnal Song. Toccata on "A Mighty Fortress." The Last Supper* (based on a Slovenian Communion hymn). *Prelude on "God of Might." Behold the Man. Sabbath Calm. The Old Mission. Voluntary for Flute Stop. Passacaglia and Fugue in E Minor. Prelude on the Hebrew Hymn "The Lord of All." Prelude on the Hebrew Hymn "Peace Be with You." Prelude on "Break Thou the Bread of Life." Introspection. Two Short Pieces. Contemplations on the Seven Last Words of Christ.* ORG. & HARPSICHORD: *Passacaglia.* ORG. & PIANO: *Autumnal Song.*

Wuensch: *Aria & Fugue* (for oboe and organ), Los Angeles, Western International Music.

Wyton, Alec: *Preludes for Genesis,* Carol Stream (Ill.), Agape.

Bibliography

ABBREVIATIONS

AfMW	*Archiv fur Musikwissenschaft*
AGOQ	*American Guild of Organists Quarterly*
AM	*Acta Musicologica*
CM	*Church Music*
Diap	*The Diapason*
JAMS	*Journal of the American Musicological Society*
MD	*Musica Disciplina*
Mf	*Die Musikforschung*
ML	*Music and Letters*
MQ	*Musical Quarterly*
MuK	*Musik und Kirche*
Mus/AGO	*Music/The AGO & RCCO Magazine*
OIQ	*Organ Institute Quarterly*
OYb	*The Organ Yearbook*
TAO	*The American Organist*
ZfMw	*Zeitschrift fur Musikwissenschaft*

Alain, Marie-Claire. "The Organ Works of Jehan Alain," 3 parts. Trans. by I. Feddern. *Diap,* Jan./Feb./Mar. 1970.

Alker, Hugo. *Literatur für alte Tasteninstrumente: Versuch einer Bibliographie für die Praxis* (*Wiener Abhandlungen zur Musikwissenschaft und Instrumenten Kunde,* vol. 4). Vienna: H. Geyer, 1962.

Amacker, Marianne. "The Chorale Preludes of Leo Sowerby." *Diap,* Aug. 1970.

Anderson, Poul-Gerhard. *Organ Building and Design.* Trans. by J. Curnutt. London: Allen and Unwin, 1969.

Antegnati, Costanzo. *L'Arte Organica* (1608). Modern edition with German trans. by P. Smets, ed. by R. Lunelli. Mainz, Germany: Rheingold, 1958.

Anthony, James R. *French Baroque Music from Beaujoyeulx to Rameau,* 2nd ed. New York: W. W. Norton, 1974.

Apel, Willi. "Die Celler Orgeltabulatur von 1601." *Mf* 19 (1962): 65 ff.

———. "Early German Keyboard Music." *MQ* 23 (1937): 210–37.

———. "Early Spanish Music for Lute and Keyboard Instruments." *MQ* 20/3 (1934): 289–301.

———. *The History of Keyboard Music to 1700.* Trans. and rev. by H. Tischler. Bloomington: Indiana Univ. Press, 1972.

———. *Masters of the Keyboard.* Cambridge, Mass.: Harvard Univ. Press, 1947.

———. "Neapolitan Links between Cabezón and Frescobaldi." *MQ* 24 (1938): 419 ff.

———. "Neu aufgefundene Clavierwerke von Scheidemann, Tunder, Froberger, Reincken und Buxtehude." *AM* 34 (1962): 65 ff.

———. "Spanish Organ Music of the Early 17th Century." *JAMS* 15 (1962): 174–81.

———. "Die Suditalienische Clavierschule des 17. Jahrhunderts." *AM* 34 (1948): 128 ff.

———. "Die Tabulatur des Adam Ile-borgh." *ZfMw* 16 (1933/34): 193 ff.

Arfken, Ernst. "Neue Musik und Orgel-bau." *MuK* 24/6 (1954): 241-47.

Armstrong, Thomas. "The Wesleys, Evangelists and Musicians," *Organ and Choral Aspects and Prospects.* London: Hinrichsen, 1958, pp. 99 ff.

Armstrong, William H. *Organs for America: The Life and Work of David Tannenberg.* Philadelphia: Univ. of Pennsylvania Press, 1967.

Arnold, Corliss. "A Bird's Eye View of Organ Composition since 1960." *Mus/AGO,* May 1975.

———. *Organ Literature: A Comprehensive Survey.* Metuchen, N.J.: Scarecrow Press, 1973.

Azevedo, Carlos de. *Baroque Organ Cases of Portugal.* Amsterdam: F. Knuf, 1971.

Bach, Carl Philipp Emanuel. *Essay on the True Art of Playing Keyboard Instruments* (1753/1762). Trans. by W. J. Mitchell. New York: W. W. Norton, 1949.

Bakken, Howard. "Liszt and the Organ." *Diap,* May 1969.

Banchieri, Adriano. *L'Organo suonarino* (1605). Facsimile reprint, with introduction by G. Cattin in *Bibliotheca Organologica,* vol. 27. Amsterdam: F. Knuf, 1969.

Barnes, William H. *The Contemporary American Organ: Its Evolution, Design and Construction,* 8th ed. Glen Rock, N.J.: J. Fischer, 1964.

Barnes, William H. and Edward B. Gammons. *Two Centuries of American Organ Building: "From Tracker to Tracker."* Glen Rock, N.J.: J. Fischer, 1970.

Bärnwick, Franz. *Die Grosse Orgel im Munster zu Weingarten in Württemberg.* Weingarten, Germany: Konrad Baier, 1922.

Basch, Peter. "Marcel Dupré." *Mus/AGO,* Sept. 1971.

Beckmann, Klaus. "Textkritische Ueberlegungen zu Buxtehudes Orgelwerken." *MuK* 38/3 (1968): 106-13.

Bedbrook, Gerald Stares. *Keyboard Music from the Middle Ages to the Beginnings of the Baroque,* 2nd ed., with introduction by F. Kirby. New York: Da Capo Press, 1973.

Bedos de Celles, Dom François. *L'Art de facteur d'Orgues,* 4 vols. (Paris, 1766-70). Facsimile reprint. Kassel: Bärenreiter, 1934.

Bender, Antoine. *Orgues d'Alsace.* Vol. 1: *Les Orgues Silbermann de Soultz (Haut-Rhin).* Vol. 2: *Les Orgues Silbermann de Marmoutier et Ebersmunster.* Strasbourg: Editions Europea, 1960.

Benestad, Finn, ed. *Norsk Musikk.* Oslo: Studier I Norge, 1968.

Biehle, Johannes. *Die Tagung für Orgelbau in Berlin,* vols. 27-29 (Sept. 1928). Kassel: Bärenreiter, 1929.

Bieske, Werner. "Die Orgelwerke Hugo Distlers." *MuK* 22/5 (1952): 177-81.

Biggs, E. Power. "Josef Rheinberg, The Master from Liechtenstein." *Mus/AGO,* Jan. 1974.

Billeter, Bernhard. *Frank Martin.* Frauenfeld, Switzerland: Verlag Huber, 1970.

Blom, Eric. *Music in England.* West Drayton, Middlesex, England: Penguin Books, 1942.

Blume, Friedrich. *Protestant Church Music: A History.* English trans., expansion, and revision of Blume's *Geschichte der evangelischen Kirchenmusik* (1965). New York: W. W. Norton, 1974.

Bo, Alander. *Die schwedische Musik.* German trans. by I. Gehnich. Uppsala, Sweden: Almquist and Wiksells, 1955.

Bonnal, Joseph Ermend. "Saint-Saëns à Saint-Séverin." *Bulletin Trimestrial des Amis de l'Orgue,* Dec. 1935.

Bornefeld, Helmut. "Hugo Distler und sein Werk." *MuK* 33/4 (1963): 145-55.

———. *Orgelbau und neue Orgelmusik.* Suppl. to *MuK* 22/2 (1952). Kassel: Bärenreiter, 1952.

———. "Orgelmusik heute." *MuK*

31/2 (1961): 55-65.

Bouvet, Charles. *Les Couperins.* Paris: Delagrave, 1919.

Bowles, Edmund A. "A Performance History of the Organ in the Middle Ages." *Diap,* Jan. 1970.

Bradshaw, Murray C. "Pre-Bach Organ Toccatas: Form, Style, and Registration." *Diap,* Mar. 1972.

Breig, Werner. "Der Umfang des choral-gebundenen Orgelwerkes von Sweelinck." *AfMw* 17 (1960): 258 ff.

Brenner, Rosamond Drooker. "An Historical Approach toward the Interpretation of Johann Sebastian Bach's Organ Works." *Diap,* July 1969.

Bricqueville, Eugène de. *Notes historiques et critiques sur l'Orgue.* Paris: Fischbacher, 1899.

Brodde, Otto. "Hans Friedrich Micheelsen zum 60. Geburtstag." *MuK* 32/3 (1962): 100-101.

Brown, Rayner. "Some More German Organ Music." *TAO,* July 1969.

———. "Some New German Organ Music." *TAO,* May 1966.

Bruinsma, Henry A. "The Organ Controversy in the Netherlands Reformation to 1600." *JAMS* 7 (1954): 205-12.

Brunold, Paul. *François Couperin.* Trans. by J. B. Hanson. Monaco: L'Oiseau Lyre, 1949.

———. *Le Grand Orgue de St. Gervais à Paris.* Paris: L'Oiseau Lyre, 1934.

Bukofzer, Manfred. *Music in the Baroque Era.* New York: W. W. Norton, 1947.

Burk, John. *Mozart and His Music.* New York: Random House, 1959.

Burns, Joseph A. "Antonio Valente, Neapolitan Keyboard Primitive." *JAMS* 7 (1959): 133-43.

Bush, Douglas E. "An Introduction to Nicolas de Grigny and His 'Livre d'Orgue.' " *Diap,* July 1974.

Buszin, Walter E. "Johann Pachelbel's Contribution to Pre-Bach Organ Literature," *The Musical Heritage of the Lutheran Church.* St. Louis: Concordia, 1959, pp. 140 ff.

Caldwell, John. *English Keybooard Music before the Nineteenth Century.* New York: Praeger, 1973.

———. "Keyboard Plainsong Settings in England, 1500-1600." *MD* 19 (1965): 129-53.

Camburn, Robert A. "Organ Music in Germany 1400-1600." *Mus/AGO,* Mar. 1970.

Cantagrel, Gilles and Harry Halbreich. *Le Livre d'Or de l'orgue français.* Paris: Calliope, 1976.

Carlson, Effie B. *A Bio-bibliographical Dictionary of Twelve-tone and Serial Composers.* Metuchen, N.J.: Scarecrow Press, 1970.

Cavaillé-Coll, Cécile and Emmanuel. *Aristide Cavaillé-Coll: Ses origines, sa vie, ses oeuvres.* Paris: Fischbacher, 1929.

Cellier, Alexandre. *L'Orgue moderne.* Paris: Delagrave, 1921.

Cellier, Alexandre and Henri Bachelin. *L'Orgue: ses éléments—son histoire—son esthétique.* Paris: Delagrave, 1933.

Chase, Gilbert. *The American Composer Speaks.* Baton Rouge: Louisiana State Univ. Press, 1966.

———. *America's Music from the Pilgrims to the Present,* 2nd ed., rev. New York: McGraw-Hill, 1966.

———. *The Music of Spain,* 2nd ed., rev. New York: Dover, 1959.

Chattingius, Claes M. *Contemporary Swedish Music.* Stockholm: Swedish Institute, 1973.

Cherbuliez, Antoine-Elisée. *Die Schweiz in den deutschen Musikgeschichte.* Frauenfeld, Switzerland: Huber, 1932.

Chybiński, Adolf. "Polnische Musik und Musikkultur des 16. Jahrhunderts. . . ." *Sammelbände der Internationalen Musikgesellschaft* 13 (1912): 463 ff.

Clark, J. Bunker. *Transposition in Seventeenth Century English Organ Accompaniments and the Transposing Organ (Detroit Monographs in Musicology,* no. 4). Detroit: Information Coordinators, 1974.

Clutton, Cecil. "The Present State of

Organ Building in England." *OIQ* 4/4 (1954).

Clutton, Cecil and Austin Niland. *The British Organ.* London: Batsford, 1963.

Cohen, Albert. "The 'Fantaisie' for Instrumental Ensemble in 17th-century France—Its Origin and Significance." *MQ* 48/2 (1962): 234-43.

Cope, David. *New Directions in Music.* Dubuque, Iowa: W. C. Brown, 1971.

Corry, Mary Jane. "Spanish Baroque, the Organ and the Music." *Mus/AGO,* Apr. 1969.

Cotte, Roger. *Compositeurs français émigrés en Suède.* (Publications de l'Institut de musicologie de l'Université de Paris.) Paris: Centre de Documentation Universitaire, 1961.

Cowell, Henry, ed. *American Composers on American Music: A Symposium,* 2nd ed. New York: Frederick Ungar, 1961.

Cudworth, Charles. "Boyce and Arne: The Generation of 1710." *ML* 41/2 (1960): 136-45.

Cudworth, Charles and Franklin B. Zimmerman. "The Trumpet Voluntary." *ML* 41/4 (1960): 342-48.

Curtis, Alan. "L'Opera Cembalo-organistica di Tarquinio Merula." *L'Organo* 1/2 (1960): 141-50.

———. *Sweelinck's Keyboard Music.* Leiden: University Press; London: Oxford Univ. Press, 1969.

Cvetko, Dragotin. *Histoire de la musique slovène.* Trans. by V. Sturm. Ljubljana, Yugoslavia: Edition Založba, 1967.

Dähnert, Ulrich. *Der Orgel- und Instrumentenbauer Zacharias Hildebrandt.* Leipzig: VEB Breitkopf & Härtel, 1960.

———. Die Orgeln Gottfried Silbermanns in Mitteldeutschland. Leipzig: Koehler & Amelang, 1953.

Dalla Libera, Sandro. *L'Organo.* Milan: Ricordi, 1956.

Dalton, James. "The Importance of Frescobaldi in the History of Organ Music." *Musical Opinion* 78 (1955): 559 ff.

———. "The Interpretation of Frescobaldi's Organ Music." *Musical Opinion* 78 (1955): 683 ff.

Damp, George E. "Some Performance Practice Suggestions for the Organ Works of Georg Muffat," 2 parts. *Diap,* Apr./May 1975.

Darbellay, Etienne. "Liberté, varieté et 'affetti cantabili' chez Girolamo Frescobaldi." *Revue de Musicologie* 61 (1975): 197-243.

Dart, Thurston. "Cavazzoni and Cabezón." *ML* 26 (1955): 2-6.

———. "A New Source of Early English Organ Music." *ML* 35 (1954): 201 ff.

David, Hans and Arthur Mendel. *The Bach Reader.* New York: W. W. Norton, 1945.

Davies, Laurence. *César Franck and His Circle.* Boston: Houghton Mifflin, 1970.

Davison, Archibald T. and Willi Apel, eds. *Historical Anthology of Music,* rev. ed., 2 vols. Cambridge, Mass.: Harvard Univ. Press, 1949-50.

Demuth, Norman. *César Franck.* London: Dobson, 1949.

De Wall (Kratzenstein), Marilou. "The Interpretation of French Organ Music of the 17th and 18th Centuries." *Diap,* Apr. 1964.

———. "The Tonal Organization of the 17th Century French Organ," 3 parts. *AGOQ,* Jan./Apr./July 1963.

Dietrich, Fritz. *Geschichte des deutschen Orgelchorals im 17. Jahrhundert (Heidelberger Studien zur Musikwissenschaft,* ed. Besseler, vol. 1). Kassel: Bärenreiter, 1932.

Diruta, Girolamo. *I Transilvano . . .* (1593/1609). Facsimile ed., with introduction by E. J. Soehnlein and M. C. Bradshaw in *Biblioteca Organologica,* vol. 44. Buren, Netherlands: F. Knuf.

Dorian, Frederick. *The History of Music in Performance.* New York: W. W. Norton, 1942.

Douglas, C. Winfred. *Church Music in*

History and Practice. New York: W. W. Norton, 1942.

Douglass, Fenner. *The Language of the Classical French Organ.* New Haven, Conn.: Yale Univ. Press, 1969.

Dufourcq, Norbert. *Esquisse d'une histoire de l'orgue en France du XIIIe au XVIIIe siècle.* Paris: Larousse et Droz, 1935.

————. *Le Grand Orgue et les organistes de Saint-Merry de Paris.* Paris: Floury, 1947.

————. *Les Grands Formes de la musique d'orgue.* Paris: Droz, 1937.

————. *Le Livre de l'Orgue français,* 5 vols. Paris: Picard, 1969–.

————. *La Musique d'orgue française de Jehan Titelouze à Jehan Alain.* Paris: Floury, 1949.

————. *Nicolas Lebègue.* Paris: Picard, 1954.

————. "Organs and Organ Building in France." Trans. by Scharf and Fenstermaker. *Mus/AGO,* Apr. 1969.

————. "Recent Researches into French Organ Building from the 15th to the 17th Century." *Galpin Society Journal* 10 (1957): 66–81.

————. "Terminologia Organistica." *L'Organo* 2/1 (1961): 43–51.

Dupré, Marcel. *Marcel Dupré raconte . . .* Paris: Bornemann, 1972.

Duruflé, Maurice. "Poulenc's Organ Concerto." *Mus/AGO,* July 1974.

Edelhoff, Heinrich. "Dietrich Buxtehude und seine musikalische Unwelt im nordischen Raum." *MuK* 9/2 (1937): 76–87.

Edson, Jean Slater. *Chorale Preludes: An Index to Compositions on Hymn Tunes, Chorales, Plainsong Melodies, Gregorian Tunes and Carols,* 2 vols. plus supple. Metuchen, N.J.: Scarecrow Press, 1970.

Ellerhorst, Winfred. *Handbuch der Orgelkunde.* Einsiedeln, Switzerland: Benziger, 1936.

Ellinwood, Leonard. *The History of American Church Music.* New York: Morehouse-Gorham, 1953.

Erb, Marie-Joseph. "Episodes de la vie d'un musicien d'Alsace," 4 parts. *L'Orgue,* June/Sept./Dec. 1939; Mar. 1940.

Erhardt, Ludwik. *Die moderne Musik in Polen.* Warsaw: Polonia, 1966.

————. *Music in Poland.* Warsaw: Interpress Publishers, 1975.

Erici, Einar. "Eine kurze schwedische Orgelgeschichte," 2 parts. *MuK* 26/3 (1956): 97–104; 26/4 (1956): 176–86.

Erpf, Hermann, *Entwicklungzüge in der Zeitgenössischen Musik.* Karlsruhe, Germany: Braun, 1922.

Fanselau, Rainer. *Die Orgel im Werke Edward Elgars (Göttinger Musikwissenschaftliche Arbeiten,* vol. 5). Göttingen, Germany: A. Funke, 1973.

Fedtke, Traugott. "Der niederländische Orgelbau im 16. Jahrhundert und seine Bedeutung für Sweelincks Instrumentalmusik." *MuK* 26/2 (1956): 60–67.

Fellerer, Karl Gustav. *Orgel und Orgelmusik: Ihre Geschichte.* Augsburg, Germany: Benno Filso Verlag, 1929.

————. *Studien zur Orgelmusik des ausgehenden 18. und frühen 19. Jahrhunderts.* Kassel: Bärenreiter, 1932.

————. "Zur italienische Orgelmusik des 17./18. Jahrhunderts." *Jahrbuch Peters* (1938): 70 ff.

Ferand, Ernest. *Die Improvisation in Beispielen aus neun Jahrhunderten abendländischer Musik (Das Musikwerk,* vol 12). Cologne, Germany: Arno Volk, 1956.

Ferguson, Howard. *Style and Interpretation: An Anthology of Keyboard Music,* 4 vols. New York: Oxford Univ. Press, 1964.

Fesperman, John T. *A Snetzler Chamber Organ of 1761.* Washington, D.C.: Smithsonian Institution Press, 1970.

Finkel, Klaus. *Süddeutscher Orgelbarock.* Wolfenbüttel/Zürich: Möseler, 1976.

Flade, Ernst. *Gottfried Silbermann.* Leipzig: Breitkopf & Hartel, 1953.

Flentrop, Dirk A. and Maarten A. Vente. "The Renaissance Organ of Evora Cathedral, Portugal." *ISO Information,* no. 12, Apr. 1974.

Foch, Gustav. *Arp Schnitger und seine Schule.* Kassel: Bärenreiter, 1974.

Fonteneau, Jean. "French Organs, Will They Survive?" *Mus/AGO,* Dec. 1969.

40 Contemporary Swiss composers. Ed. by the Swiss Composers' League. Amriswil, Switzerland: Bodensee-Verlag, 1956.

Friis, Niels. *Marcussen & Son, 1806-1956.* Aabenraa, Denmark: Det Berlingske Bogtrykkeri, 1956.

_____. "Orgelbau in Dänemark." *MuK* 22/5 (1952): 190-94.

Frotscher, Gotthold. *Deutsche Orgeldispositionen aus fünf Jahrhunderten.* Wolfenbüttel/Berlin: Georg Kallmeyer, 1939.

_____. *Geschichte des Orgelspiels und der Orgelkomposition,* 3rd ed., 2 vols. Berlin: Merseburger, 1966.

_____. *Die Orgel.* Leipzig: J. J. Weber, 1927.

Fruth, Klaus M. *Die deutsche Orgelbewegung.* Ludwigsburg, Germany: Verlag Walcker, 1962.

Gastoué, Amédée. "In memoriam Charles Tournemire." *L'Orgue,* Dec. 1939; Mar. 1940.

Gay, Claude. "Notes pour servir à la registration de la musique d'orgue française des XVIIe et XVIIIe siècles." *L'Organo* 2 (1961): 169-99.

Gay, Harry W. "Tournemire's 'L'Orgue mystique.'" *TAO,* Nov. 1959.

Geiringer, Karl. *The Bach Family.* New York: Oxford Univ. Press, 1954.

_____. *Johann Sebastian Bach, the Culmination of an Era,* rev. ed. New York: Oxford Univ. Press, 1966.

General Catalogue: Dutch Contemporary Music. Amsterdam: Donemus, 1977.

Gibson, Emily Cooper. "A Study of the Major Organ Works of Paul Hindemith." *Diap,* Feb. 1971.

Golos, Jerzy. "An Historical Survey of Organbuilding in Poland until 1900." *Diap,* Apr. 1976.

_____. "Il Manoscritto I/220 della Società di Musica di Varsavia, importante fonte di Musica organistica cinquecentesca." *L'Organo* 2/2 (1961): 129-44.

_____. "Modern Organ Music in Poland." *Polish Music* 3/3 (1968).

_____. "Old Polish Organ Music." *Polish Music* 3/2 (1968).

Goodrich, Wallace. *The Organ in France.* Boston: Boston Music, 1917.

Gotwals, Vernon. "Brahms and the Organ." *Mus/AGO,* Apr. 1970.

Grace, Harvey. *French Organ Music.* New York: H. W. Gray, 1919.

Gravet, Nicole. "L'Orgue et l'art de la registration en France du XVIe au dèbut de XIXe siècle." *L'Orgue* 100 (1961): 202-57.

Grossmann-Vendrey, Susanna. *Felix Mendelssohn Bartholdy und die Musik der Vergangenheit.* Regensburg, Germany: G. Bosse, 1969.

Gudger, William D. "Handel's Organ Concertos." *Diap,* Oct. 1973.

Guenther, Eileen Morris. "Composers of French Noël Variations in the 17th-18th Centuries." *Diap,* Dec. 1973; Jan. 1974.

Guilmant, Alexandre. "La Musique d'orgue, les formes, l'exécution, l'improvisation," *Encyclopédie de la musique,* part 2, vol. 2. Paris: Delagrave, 1926, pp. 1125-80.

Gurlitt, Wilibald, ed. *Bericht über die Freiburger Tagung für deutsche Orgelkunst vom 27. bis 30. Juli 1926.* Augsburg, Germany: Bärenreiter, 1926.

_____. "Die Orgelwerke des Michael Praetorius." *AfMw* 3 (1930): 135 ff.

Haacke, Walter. *Orgeln in aller Welt.* Taunus, Germany: Hans Köster Königstein, 1965.

Haag, Herbert. "Zur französischen

Orgelkunst," 2 parts. *MuK* 29/1 (1959): 28-33; 29/4 (1959): 193-95.

Haller, William. "A Look at Some Recent Organ Works." *Clavier* (Jan. 1974): 32-33.

_____. "Organ Works of the Avant-Garde." *Clavier* (Apr. 1974): 33-36.

Hamann, Heinz Wolfgang. "Abbé Voglers Simplifikations-System im Urteil der Zeitgenossen." *MuK* 23/1 (1953): 28-31.

Hantz, Edwin. "An Introduction to the Organ Music of Wm. Albright." *Diap,* May 1973.

Haraszti, Emile. *La Musique hongroise.* Paris: H. Laurens, 1933.

Hardmeyer, Willy. *Einführung in die schweizerische Orgelbaukunst.* Zürich: Hug, 1947.

Hardouin, Pierre. "François Roberday (1624-1680)." *Revue de musicologie* 45 (1960): 44-62.

_____. *Le Grand-Orgue de St. Gervais de Paris.* Paris: Imprimerie du Campagnonnage, 1949.

Harich-Schneider, Eta. *Die Kunst des Cembalo-spiels.* Kassel: Bärenreiter, 1939.

Harich-Schneider, Eta and Ricard Boadella. "Zum Klavierspiel bei Thomas de Sancta Maria." *Archiv für Musikforschung* 2 (1937): 243-45.

Harley, John. *Music in Purcell's London.* London: Dobson, 1968.

Hartog, Howard, ed. *European Music in the Twentieth Century.* New York: Praeger, 1957.

Haselböck, Hans. *Barocker Orgelschatz in Niederösterreich.* Vienna: Manutiuspresse, 1972.

Haüsler, Josef. *Musik im 20. Jahrhundert.* Bremen, Germany: Schünemann, 1969.

Hedar, Josef. *Dietrich Buxtehudes Orgelwerke.* Stockholm: Nordiska Musikförlaget; Frankfurt: Wilhelmiana Musikverlag, 1951.

Heintze, Hans. "Der Organist Günther Ramin." *MuK* 28/5 (1958): 193-97.

Helfert, Vladimír. *Geschichte der Musik in der Tschechoslo-*

vakischen Republik. Trans. by Steinhard. Prague: Orbis, 1936.

Hell, Henri. *Francis Poulenc.* Trans. by E. Lockspeiser. New York: Grove Press, 1959.

Hellman, Diethard. "Betrachtungen zur Darstellung der Sweelinckschen Werke für Tasteninstrumente." *MuK* 25/6 (1955): 287-92.

Herrenschwand, Franz. "The Organ of Max Reger." *TAO,* Mar. 1961.

Hickmann, Hans. *Das Portativ.* Kassel: Bärenreiter, 1936.

Hill, Arthur George. *The Organ Cases and Organs of the Middle Ages and Renaissance* (1883/91). Rev. ed. by Sumner. Amsterdam: F. Knuf, 1966.

Hillert, Richard. "Sources and Sounds of the New Music." *CM,* no. 72/1 (1972): 1-9.

Hitchcock, H. Wiley. *Music in the U.S.: A Historical Introduction.* Englewood Cliffs, N.J.: Prentice-Hall, 1969.

Hoffmann, Herbert. "Towards an Interpretation of Reger's Organ Music." Trans. by R. Mabry from *MuK* 37 (1967). *Diap,* Aug. 1972.

Högner, Friedrich. "Johann Nepomuk Davids Weg zur evangelischen Kirchenmusik." *MuK* 30/6 (1960): 284-97.

Hoover, Kathleen and John Cage. *Virgil Thomson, His Life and His Music.* New York/London: Thomas Yoseloff, 1959.

Horton, John. *Scandinavian Music: A Short History.* London: Faber, 1963.

Howard, John Tasker. *Our American Music,* 4th ed. New York: Crowell, 1965.

Howell, Almonte C. "Cabezón: An Essay in Structural Analysis." *MQ* (1964): 18-30.

_____. "French Baroque Organ Music and the 8 Church Tones." *JAMS* 11 (1959): 106-18.

_____. "Paired Imitation in 16th-Century Spanish Keyboard Music." *MQ* 53/3 (1967): 377-96.

Hudson, Barton. "Notes on Gregorio Strozzi and His Capricci." *JAMS*

20 (1967): 209-21.

Hudson, Richard. "The Passacaglia and Ciaccona in Italian Keyboard Music of the 17th Century," 2 parts. *Diap*, Nov./Dec. 1969.

Hülphers, Abraham. *Historisk Afhandling om Musik och Instrumenter . . . jemte Kort beskrifning öfwer Orgwerken i Sverige* (1773). Facsimile ed., with an English introduction by T. Lindgren and a note on the organs by P. Williams. Amsterdam: F. Knuf, 1971.

Huray, Peter Le. *Music and the Reformation in England*. London: Jenkins, 1967.

Hutchings, Arthur. "The English Concerto with or for Organ." *MQ* 47 (1961): 195-206.

Indy, Vincent d'. *César Franck*. English trans., with an introduction by R. Newmarch. New York: Dover, 1965.

Isherwood, Robert M. *Music in the Service of the King*. Ithaca: Cornell Univ. Press, 1973.

Jacquot, Jean, ed. *Le Luth et sa musique*. Paris: Editions du Centre national de la Recherche scientifique, 1958.

Jakob, Friedrich. "Introduction to Swiss Organ Building." *ISO Information*, no. 7, Dec. 1971.

Jarociński, Stefan. *Polish Music*. Warsaw: Państwowe Wydawnictwo Naukowe, 1965.

Jeppesen, Knud. "Eine frühe Orgelmesse aus Castell'Arquato." *AfMw* 12 (1955): 187 ff.

————. *Die Italienische Orgelmusik am Anfang des Cinquecento*, rev. ed., 2 vols. Copenhagen: W. Hansen, 1960.

Johns, Donald. "Some Recent Techniques in Contemporary German Liturgical Organ Music." *Diap*, Feb. 1973.

Johnson, Robert Sherlaw. *Messiaen*. Berkeley: Univ. of California Press, 1975.

Kaldy, Julius. *A History of Hungarian Music*, 2nd ed. New York: Haskell House, 1969.

Kastner, Macario Santiago. "Parallels and Discrepancies between English and Spanish Keyboard Music of the 16th and 17th Centuries." *Annuario Musical* 7 (1952): 77-115.

————. "Il Soggiorno italiano di Antonio e Juan de Cabezón." *L'Organo* 1/1 (1960): 49-68.

Kaufmann, Walter. *Die Orgeln des alten Herzogtums Oldenburg*. Oldenburg, Germany: Gerhard Stalling Verlag, 1962.

Keller, Hermann. *The Organ Works of Bach*. Trans. by H. Hewitt. New York: C. F. Peters, 1967.

————. "Die Orgelwerke Max Regers und ihre Bedeutung für die Gegenwart." *MuK* 8/4 (1936): 153-56.

Kessler, Franz. "Merkmale des Distlerschen Orgelstils dargestellt an seinen kleinen Orgelchoralbearbeitungen." *MuK* 34/4 (1964): 171-78.

Kinkeldey, Otto. *Orgel und Klavier in der Musik des 16. Jahrhunderts*. Leipzig: Breitkopf & Härtel, 1910.

Kirby, Frank E. *A Short History of Keyboard Music*. New York: Free Press, 1966.

Kittler, Günther. *Geschichte des protestantischen Orgelchorals von seinen Anfängen bis zu den Lüneburger Orgeltabulaturbüchern*. Ueckermünde, Germany: Wolf Heyer, 1931.

Klinda, Ferdinand. "Die Orgelwerke von Olivier Messiaen." *MuK* 39/1 (1969): 10 ff.

Klotz, Hans. "Bachs Orgeln und seine Orgelmusik." *Mf* 2 (1950): 189-203.

————. "Johann Sebastian Bach und die Orgel." *MuK* 32/2 (1962): 49-55.

————. "The Organ Works of Max Reger: An Interpretation." *OYb* 5 (1974): 66 ff.

————. *Ueber die Orgelkunst der Gotik, der Renaissance und des Barock*, 2nd ed., rev. Kassel: Bärenreiter, 1975.

————. "Um die Bedeutung der

Orgel." *MuK* 36/6 (1966): 257-65.

_____. "Zum Tode von Günter Raphael." *MuK* 30/6 (1960): 289-90.

Knock, Nicolaas Arnoldi. *Dispositien der merkwaardigste Kerk-Orgeln welken in de Provincie Friesland, Groningen en Elders aangetroffen worden* (1788). Facsimile reprint. Amsterdam: F. Knuf, 1972.

Komma, Karl Michael. *Das Böhmische Musikantentum*. Kassel: Joh. Ph. Hinnenthal Verlag, 1960.

Kothe, Bernhard and Theophil Forchhammer. *Führer durch die Orgel-Literatur*. Rev. by Otto Burkert, ed. by B. Weigl. Leipzig: Leuckart, 1931.

Kraemer, Erich. "Vom Orgelbau in Amerika." *MuK* 36/4 (1966): 177-81.

Kraus, Eberhard. *Orgeln und Orgelmusik*. Regensburg, Germany: Pustet, 1972.

Kugler, Michael. *Die Musik für Tasteninstrumente in 15. and 16. Jahrhundert*. Wilhelmshaven: Heinrichshofen's Verlag, 1975.

Lang, Paul Henry. *George Frideric Handel*. New York: W. W. Norton, 1966.

_____. *Music in Western Civilization*. New York: W. W. Norton, 1941.

Lange, Kristian and Arne Östvedt. *Norwegian Music: A Brief Survey*. London: Dobson, 1958.

Laubenstein, Sarah. "Two Early American Organ Builders." *Mus/AGO*, Dec. 1975.

Leirens, Charles. *La musique belge*. Brussells: Ministère des affaires étrangères, 1952.

Liebenow, Walter M. *Rank on Rank —A Bibliography of the History and Construction of Organs*. Minneapolis: Martin Press, 1973.

Lohmann, Heinz. *Handbuch der Orgelliteratur*, vol. 1. Wiesbaden, Germany: Breitkopf & Härtel, 1975.

Long, Page C. "Vierne and His Six Organ Symphonies," 3 parts. *Diap*, June/July/Aug. 1970.

Lord, Robert Sutherland. "Organ Music of Jean Langlais." *TAO*, Jan. 1968.

Lowens, Irving. *Music and Musicians in Early America*. New York: W. W. Norton, 1964.

Lowinsky, Edward E. "English Organ Music of the Renaissance," 2 parts. *MQ* 39 (1953): 373-95; 528-53.

Lukas, Viktor. *Orgelmusikführer*. Stuttgart: Ph. Reclam, 1963.

Lunelli, Renato. *Der Orgelbau in Italien in seinen Meisterwerken vom 14. Jahrhundert bis zur Gegenwart*. German trans. by C. Elis and P. Smets. Mainz, Germany: Rheingold, 1956.

_____. *Studi e Documenti di Storia organaria veneta*. Florence: Olschki, 1973.

Machlis, Joseph. *Introduction to Contemporary Music*. New York: W. W. Norton, 1961.

Mahrenholz, Christhard. "Fünfzehn Jahre Orgelbewegung: Rückblick und Ausblick." *MuK* 10/1 (1938): 8-28.

_____. *Der gegenwärtige Stand der Orgelfrage im Lichte der Orgelgeschichte*. Kassel: Bärenreiter, 1928.

_____. "Johann Sebastian Bach und der Gottesdienst seiner Zeit." *MuK* 20/5 (1950): 145-58.

_____. "Samuel Scheidt und die Orgel." *MuK* 25/1 (1955): 38-50.

Marcase, Donald E. "Adriano Banchieri's 'L'Organo Suonarino,' " 3 parts. *Diap*, July/Aug./Oct. 1973.

Marhefka, Edmund. "Widors Orgelkompositionen." *MuK* 29/5 (1959): 224-29.

Mellers, Wilfrid. *François Couperin and the French Classical Tradition* (1950). Reprint. New York: Dover, 1968.

Merklin, Albert. *Aus Spaniens altem Orgelbau*. Mainz, Germany: Rheingold, 1939.

Messiaen, Olivier. *Technique de mon*

langage musical, 2 vols. Paris: Leduc, 1944.

Metzger, Hans-Arnold. "Max Regers geistliche Chorwerke und sein Orgelschaffen." MuK 36/5 (1966): 213–24.

Metzler, Wolfgang. Romantischer Orgelbau in Deutschland. Ludwigsburg, Germany: Verlag Walcker, 1968.

Meyer, Hermann. Karl Joseph Riepp. Kassel: Bärenreiter, 1930.

Meyers, Hubert. "Der französische Orgeltype." MuK 33/6 (1963): 258–64.

Miller, Hugh M. "16th-Century English Faburden Compositions for Keyboard." MQ 26 (1940): 50 ff.

Moeser, James. "French Baroque Organ Registration." TAO, June 1967.

Moser, Hans Joachim. Dietrich Buxtehude. Berlin: Merseburger, 1957.

———. "Johann Pachelbel." MuK 23/3 (1953): 82–90.

Mulberry, David. "Bach's Favorite Pupil: Johann L. Krebs." Mus/AGO, Feb. 1968.

Nardone, Thomas R., ed. Organ Music in Print. Philadelphia: Musicdata, 1975.

Nef, Walter Robert. "Der St. Gallner Organist Fridolin Sicher und seiner Orgeltabulatur." Schweizerische Jahrbuch für Musikwissenschaft 7 (1938): 12–143.

Nichols, Roger. Messiaen. London: Oxford Univ. Press, 1975.

Noehren, Robert. "The Relation of Organ Design to Organ Playing," 2 parts. Diap, Dec. 1962; Jan. 1963.

———. "Schnitager, Cliquot and Cavaillé-Coll." Diap, Nov./Dec. 1966; Jan./Feb. 1967.

Nolte, Ewald. "The Magnificat Fugues of Johann Pachelbel: Alternation or Intonation." JAMS 9 (1956): 19–24.

Ochse, Orpha. The History of the Organ in the United States.

Bloomington: Indiana Univ. Press, 1975.

Oldham, Guy. "Louis Couperin, a New Source of French Keyboard Music of the Mid-17th c." Recherches (1960): 51 ff.

Opienski, Henryk. La Musique polonaise. Paris: Georges Cres, 1918.

"Orgel," Die Musik in Geschichte und Gegenwart, 14 vols. plus 2 suppl. Kassel: Bärenreiter, 1962, vol. 10, pp. 227–395.

Owen, Barbara. "American Organ Music and Playing, from 1700." Organ Institute Quarterly 10/3 (1963).

Pauly, Hans-Jakob. Die Fuge in den Orgelwerken Dietrich Buxtehudes (Kölner Beiträge zur Musikforschung, vol. 31). Regensburg, Germany: G. Bosse, 1964.

Peeters, Flor. "The Belgian Organ School," Sixth Music Book. London: Hinrichsen, 1950, pp. 270–74.

———. "Charles Tournemire." Diap, Sept. 1964.

———. "The Organ Works of César Franck." Mus/AGO, Aug. 1971.

Peeters, Flor and Maarten A. Vente. The Organ and Its Music in the Netherlands, 1500–1800. Trans. by P. Williams. Antwerp: Mercatorfonds, 1971.

Perrot, Jean. The Organ from Its Invention to the End of the 13th Century. Trans. by N. Deane. New York: Oxford Univ. Press, 1971.

Pfatteicher, Carl F. John Redford, Organist and Almoner of St. Paul's Cathedral in the Time of Henry VIII. Leipzig: Bärenreiter, 1934.

Phelps, Lawrence I. "A Short History of the Organ Revival." CM, no. 67/1 (1967): 13–30.

Piersig, Johannes. "Der Streit um Reger." MuK 24/2 (1954): 49–59.

Pirro, André. L'Art des organistes," Encyclopédie de la musique, 2 parts, 11 vols. Paris: Delagrave,

1926, part 2, vol. 2, pp. 1181-1374.

_____. *Johann Sebastian Bach: The Organist and His Works for the Organ.* Trans. by W. Goodrich. New York: G. Schirmer, 1902.

Plamenac, Dragan. "An Early 15th-Century Italian Source of Keyboard Music." *MD* 13/14 (1959-60).

_____. "Keyboard Music of the 14th-Century in Codex Faenza 117." *JAMS* 4 (1951): 179 ff.

Powell, Kenneth G. "An Analysis of the North German Organ Toccatas." *Diap,* Apr. 1971.

Praetorius, Michael. *Syntagma musicum.* Vol. 2: *De organographia* (1619). Facsimile reprint, ed. by W. Gurlitt. Kassel: Bärenreiter, 1958.

Prince, Philip. "Reger and the Organ." *Diap,* Mar. 1973.

Prunières, Henry. *Histoire nouvelle de la musique,* 2 vols. Paris: Rieder, 1934-36.

Quoika, Rudolf. *Die altösterreichische Orgel der späten Gotik, der Renaissance und des Barock.* Kassel: Bärenreiter, 1953.

_____. *Der Orgelbau in Böhmen und Mähren.* Mainz, Germany: Rheingold, 1966.

_____. *Das Positiv in Geschichte und Gegenwart.* Kassel: Bärenreiter, 1957.

_____. "Uber die Orgellandschaft Johann Gottfried Silbermanns." *MuK* 23/3 (1953): 91-94.

_____. *Vom Blockwerk zur Registerorgel.* Kassel: Bärenreiter, 1960.

Qvamme, Börre. *Norwegian Music and Composers.* London: Narod Press, 1949.

Raugel, Félix. *Les Anciens Buffets d'orgues du département de Seine-et-Marne.* Paris: Fischbacher, 1928.

_____. *Les Grands Orgues des Eglises de Paris.* Paris: Fischbacher, 1927.

_____. *Les Organistes,* 3rd ed. Paris: Laurens, 1961.

Raver, Leonard. "Olivier Messiaen's Méditations sur le Mystère de la Sainte Trinité: A Review of the Music and Its First N.Y. Performance." *Mus/AGO,* Apr. 1974.

Redlich, Hans Ferdinand. "Girolamo Frescobaldi." *Music Review* 14 (1953): 262-74.

Reese, Gustave. *Music in the Renaissance,* rev. ed. New York: W. W. Norton, 1959.

Reeser, Eduard, ed. *Music in Holland.* Amsterdam: Meulenhoff, 1959.

Reuter, Rudolf. *Bibliographie der Orgel.* Kassel: Bärenreiter, 1973.

_____. *Organos españoles.* Madrid: Ministerio de Educación nacional, 1963.

_____. *Die Orgel in der Denkmalpflege Westfalens.* Kassel: Bärenreiter, 1971.

_____. *Orgeln in Westfalen.* Kassel: Bärenreiter, 1965.

Rhodes, Cherry. "Introducing Jean Guillou." *Mus/AGO,* Mar. 1974.

Rice, William Carroll. *A Concise History of Church Music.* New York/Nashville: Abingdon Press, 1964.

Riedel, Friedrich Wilhelm. *Quellenkundliche Beiträge zur Geschichte der Musik für Tasteninstrumente in der 2. Hälfte des 17. Jahrhunderts.* Kassel: Bärenreiter, 1960.

Riemann, Hugo, ed. *Musikgeschichte in Beispielen,* 3rd ed. Leipzig: Breitkopf & Härtel, 1925.

Ritter, August Gottfried. *Zur Geschichte des Orgelspiels,* 2 vols. Leipzig: Max Hesse, 1884.

Robinson, Albert F. "Historic American Organ Builders," 6 parts. *Mus/AGO,* Jan./Feb./Mar./Apr./May/June 1976.

Rokseth, Yvonne. *La Musique d'orgue au XVe siècle et au début du XVIe.* Paris: Droz, 1930.

Routh, Francis. *Contemporary British Music.* London: MacDonald, 1972.

_____. *Early English Organ Music from the Middle Ages to 1837.* London: Barrie & Jenkins, 1973.

Routley, Erik. *Twentieth Century Church Music.* London: Barrie & Jenkins, 1964.

Rowell, Lois, comp. *American Organ Music on Records.* Braintree, Mass.: Organ Literature Foundation, 1976.

Rowntree, John and John Brennan. *The Classical Organ in Britain 1955–74.* Oxford: Positif Press, 1975.

Rudd, Michael. "Stylistic Features and Compositional Activities in Organ Literature since World War II." *Diap,* June 1968.

Rudolz, Rudolf. *Die Registrierkunst des Orgelspiels im ihren Grundlegenden Formen.* Leipzig: Breitkopf & Härtel, 1913.

Rupp, Emile. *Die Entwicklungsgeschichte der Orgelbaukunst.* Einsiedeln, Switzerland: Benziger, 1929.

Sadie, Stanley. *Handel Concertos.* Seattle: Univ. of Washington Press, 1973.

Salzman, Eric. *Twentieth Century Music: An Introduction.* Englewood Cliffs, N.J.: Prentice-Hall, 1967.

Samfundet til Udgivelse af Dansk Musik, 1871–1971: Catalogue. Copenhagen: Dan Fog, 1971.

Samuel, Claude. *Conversations with Olivier Messiaen.* English trans. by F. Aprahamian. London: Stainer & Bell, 1976.

Schäfer, Ernst. *Laudatio organi.* Leipzig: VEB Deutscher Verlag für Musik, 1972.

Scheide, August. *Zur Geschichte des Choralvorspiels.* Hildburghausen, Germany: F. W. Gadow & Sohn, 1923.

Schering, Arnold, ed. *Geschichte der Musik in Beispielen.* Leipzig: Breitkopf & Härtel, 1931.

———. *Die Niederländische Orgelmesse in Zeitalter des Josquin.* Leipzig: Breitkopf & Härtel, 1912.

Schilling, Hans Ludwig. "Hindemiths Orgelsonaten." *MuK* 33/5 (1963): 202–9.

Schlick, Arnold. *Spiegel der Orgelmacher und Organisten* (1511). Modern German edition, ed. by E. Flade. Mainz, Germany: P. Smets, 1932.

———. *Tabulaturen etlicher Lobgesang und Lidlein auff die Orgel und Lauten zu spielen* (1512). Ed. by G. Harms. Hamburg: Ugrino, 1957.

Schmidt, Eberhard. "Zum 65. Geburtstag von Eberhard Wensel." *MuK* 31/2 (1961): 49–50.

Schmidt-Bayreuth, Hans. "Untersuchungen zum Orgelchoral Ernst Pepping." *MuK* 24/3 (1954): 101–8.

Schoenstedt. Arno. *Alte Westfälische Orgeln.* Gütersloh, Germany: Rufer Verlag, 1953.

Scholes, Percy, ed. *Dr. Burney's Musical Tours in Europe,* 2 vols. London: Oxford Univ. Press, 1959.

Schrade, Leo. "The Organ in the Mass of the 15th Century," 2 parts. *MQ* 28 (1942): 329–36, 467–87.

Schuh, Willi. *Schweizer Musikbuch.* Zürich: Atlantis, 1939.

Schuh, Willi and Edgar Refardt, eds. *Schweizer Musikerlexikon.* Zürich: Atlantis, 1939.

Schuneman, Robert. "Brahms and the Organ: Some Reflections on Modern Editions and Performance." *Mus/AGO,* Sept. 1972.

———. "Organ Chorales of Georg Böhm." *Diap,* Mar. 1970.

Schwarz, Peter. *Studien zur Orgelmusik Franz Liszt.* Munich: Katzbichler, 1973.

Schweinsberg, Karl Heinrich. "Johannes Driessler." *MuK* 20/1 (1950): 12–17.

Der Schweizerische Tonkünstlerverein 1900–1950. Zürich: Atlantis, 1950.

Searle, Humphrey and Robert Layton. *Twentieth Century Composers.* Vol. 3: *Britain, Scandinavia and The Netherlands.* New York: Holt, Rinehart and Winston, 1973.

Seiffert, Max. "J. P. Sweelinck und seine direkten deutschen Schüler,"

Vierteljahrsschrift für Musikwissenschaft 7 (1891): 145 ff.

Senn, Kurt Wolfgang. "Uber die musikalischen Beziehungen zwischen Johann Gottfried Walther und Johann Sebastian Bach." *MuK* 34/1 (1964): 8-18.

Serauky, Walter. *Georg Friedrich Händel: Sein Leben, Sein Werk*, 3 vols. Kassel: Bårenreiter, 1956.

Servières, Georges. *Documents inédits sur les organistes françaises.* Paris: Schola Cantorum, 1923.

Sessions, Roger. *Reflections on the Music Life in the United States.* New York: Merlin Press, 1956.

Shackelford, Rudy, "Vincent Persichetti's Hymn and Chorale Prelude, 'Drop, Drop Slow Tears'—An Analysis." *Diap*, Sept. 1973.

———. "Vincent Persichetti's 'Shimah B'koli' (Psalm 130) for Organ—An Analysis." *Diap*, Sept. 1975.

———. "Vincent Persichetti's Sonata for Organ and Sonatine—An Analysis," 2 parts. *Diap*, May/June 1974.

Shannon, John R. "North-German Organ Music." *Mus/AGO*, Sept. 1969.

———. "A Short Survey of the Free Organ Forms in Italy, 1450-1650." *AGOQ* 6/3 (July 1961).

Shay, Edmund. "French Baroque Registration." *Diap*, Nov. 1969.

Siebert, F. Mark. "Performance Problems in Fifteenth-Century Organ Music." *OIQ* 10/2 (1963): 5-12.

Siegele, Ulrich. "Die Disposition der Gabler-Orgel zu Ochsenhausen." *MuK* 26/1 (1956): 8-18.

Silbiger, Alexander. *Italian Manuscript Sources of Seventeenth-Century Keyboard Music.* Ph.D. diss., Brandeis University, 1976.

Simpson, Robert. *Carl Nielsen: Symphonist, 1865–1931.* Biographical appendix by Tobern Meyer. London: J. M. Dent, 1952.

Slim, H. Colin. "Keyboard Music at Castell'Arquato by an Early Madrigalist." *JAMS* 15 (1962): 35-47.

Smets, Paul. *Handbuch des Orgelspiels*, vol. 1, part 1. Mainz, Germany: Rheingold, 1938.

———. *Neuzeitlicher Orgelbau.* Mainz, Germany: Rheingold, 1933.

———. *Die Orgelbauer-Familie Silbermann in Strassburg.* Mainz, Germany: Rheingold, n.d.

Smith, Rollin. "American Organ Composers: Arthur Foote." *Mus/AGO*, May 1976.

———. "American Organ Composers: Dudley Buck." *Mus/AGO*, Mar. 1976.

———. "American Organ Composers: George Whitefield Chadwick." *Mus/AGO*, Apr. 1976.

———. "American Organ Composers: Horatio Parker." *Mus/AGO*, June 1976.

———. "American Organ Composers: John Knowles Paine." *Mus/AGO*, Feb. 1976.

———. "Camille Saint-Saëns." *Mus/AGO*, Dec. 1971.

———. "Dupré in the Twenties." *Diap*, June 1971.

———. "Elgar's Organ Sonata." *Mus/AGO*, Nov. 1973.

Southern, Eileen. *The Buxheim Organ Book (Musicological Studies*, vol. 6). Brooklyn: Institute of Medieval Music, 1962.

Speer, Klaus. "The Organ Verso in Iberian Music up to 1700." *JAMS* 11 (1958): 189-99.

Spelman, Leslie. "20th Century Netherland Organ Music." *Mus/AGO*, Sept. 1970.

Spies, Hermann. *Abbé Vogler und die von ihm 1805 simplifiziert Orgel von St. Peter in Salzburg (Orgelmonographien*, vol. 5). Mainz, Germany: Verlag Paul Smets, 1932.

Spitta, Philipp. *Johann Sebastian Bach: His Work and Influence on the Music of Germany*, 3 vols. English trans. by C. Bell and J. A. Fuller-Maitland. London, 1889. Reprint, New York: Dover, 1951.

Squire, Russel N. *Church Music.* St. Louis: Bethany Press, 1962.

Stěpánek, Vladimír and Bohumil Karásek. *Zur Geschichte der Tschechischen und Slowaksichen Musik.* Part 1: *Tschechische Musik.* Prague: Orbis, 1964.

Stevens, Denis. *The Mulliner Book: A Commentary.* London: Stainer and Bell, 1952.

———. "Thomas Preston's Organ Mass." *ML* 41/1 (1960): 46–52.

———. "A Unique Tudor Organ Mass." *MD* 6 (1952): 167 ff.

Stevenson, Robert Murrell. *Protestant Church Music in America.* New York: W. W. Norton, 1966.

Stevlingson, Norma. "Performance Styles of French Organ Music in the 17th and 18th Centuries." *Mus/AGO*, Feb./Mar. 1969.

Stout, Alan. "A Conversation between B. Hambraeus and A. Stout." *CM* 72/1 (1972): 40–42.

Sumner, William Leslie. *The Organ,* 4th ed. New York: St. Martin's, 1973.

———. *The Organs of Bach.* London: Hinrichsen, 1954.

Sutherland, Gordon. "The Ricercari of Jacques Buus." *MQ* 31 (1945): 448–63.

Sutkowski, Adam. "L'Intavolatura di Pelplin." *L'Organo* 2 (1961): 53ff.

Swedish Music—Past and Present. A special edition of *Musikrevy.* Stockholm: Swedish Society of Composers, Authors and Publishers (STIM), n.d.

Tagliavini, Luigi F. "Mezzo secolo di storia organaria." *L'Organo* 1/1 (1960): 70–83.

———. "The Old Italian Organ and Its Music." Transcript of a lecture given at the Midwinter A.G.O. Conclave (1965). *Diap,* Feb. 1966.

———. "Il Ripieno." *L'Organo* 1/2 (1960): 197–210.

Tarr, Edward H. "Original Italian Baroque Compositions for Trumpet and Organ." *Diap,* Apr. 1970.

Terry, Charles Sanford. *The Music of Bach: An Introduction* (1933). Reprint. New York: Dover, 1963.

Tessier, André. "Les Messes d'orgue de Couperin." *Revue musicale* 6/1 (1925): 37–48.

Tradition and Progress in Swedish Music. A special edition of *Musikrevy.* Stockholm: Swedish Society of Composers, Authors and Publishers (STIM), n.d.

Tusler, Robert L. *The Organ Music of Sweelinck,* 2 vols. (*Utrechtse Bijdragen tot de Musikwetenshap,* no. 1). Bilthoven, Netherlands: A. B. Creygthton, 1958.

———. "Style Differences in the Organ and Clavicembalo Works of Sweelinck." *Tydschrift voor Musikwetenshap* 17 (1959): 149–66.

———. *The Style of Bach's Chorale-Preludes.* New York: Da Capo Press, 1968.

Tuthill, Barnet C. "Leo Sowerby." *MQ* 24 (1938): 249–64.

Vente, Maarten A. *Die Brabanter Orgel.* Amsterdam: H. J. Paris, 1958.

———. "Mitteilungen über iberische Registrierkunst der Orgelkompositionen des Juan Cabanilles." *Annuario Musical* 17 (1962).

Vogelsänger, Siegfried. "Passacaglia und Chaconne in der Orgelmusik." *MuK* 37/1 (1967):14–24.

Wagner, Peter. *Geschichte der Messe.* Vol 1: *Bis 1600. Leipzig:* Breitkopf & Härtel, 1913.

Walcha, Helmut. "Kurt Hessenberg zum 50. Geburtstag." *MuK* 28/5 (1958): 197–200.

Wallner, Bo. *La Musique en Suède.* Trans. by O. Pleijel. Stockholm: Swedish Institute, 1951.

Walter, Rudolf. "Max Reger und die Orgel um 1900." *MuK* 43/6 (1973): 282–89.

Watters, Clarence. "Marcel Dupré." *Diap,* May 1966.

Weyer, Martin. *Die deutsche Orgelsonate von Mendelssohn bis Reger.* Regensburg, Germany: G. Bosse, 1969.

White, John Reeves. "The Tablature of Johannes of Lublin." *MD* 17 (1963): 137-62.

Widor, Charles-Marie. *L'Orgue moderne: La Décadence dans la facture contemporaine.* Paris: Durand, 1928.

Williams, Peter F. *Bach Organ Music.* Seattle: Univ. of Washington Press, 1972.

_____. *The European Organ, 1450-1850.* London: Batsford, 1966.

_____. "J. S. Bach and English Organ Music." *ML* 44/2 (Apr. 1963): 140-51.

_____. "Sweelinck and the Dutch School." *Musical Times,* no. 1522, vol. 110 (Dec. 1969): 1286-88.

Woersching, Joseph. *Der Orgelbauer Karl Riepp,* 4 parts. Mainz, Germany: Rheingold, n.d.

Wolff, Christoph. "Conrad Paumanns Fundamentum organisandi und seine verschiedenen Fassungen." *AfMw* 25 (1968): 196 ff.

Wouters, Jos. "Dutch Music in the Twentieth Century." *MQ,* 51 (1965): 97-110.

Wyton, Alec. "An Interview with R. Felciano." *Mus/AGO,* Nov. 1970.

_____. "Méditations sur le Mystère de la Sainte Trinité." *Mus/AGO,* May 1972.

Yoell, John H. *The Nordic Sound.* Boston: Crescendo, 1974.

NOTE: *Music/The AGO & RCCO Magazine,* is now *The American Organist.*

Name Index

[The page numbers for musical examples are in italics.]

Subject Index